Local Government in India

Local Government in India

Pardeep Sachdeva

Associate Acquisitions Editor: Qudsiya Ahmed
Associate Production Editor: Amrita Naskar
Composition: Mukesh Technologies Pvt. Ltd

ISBN 978-81-317-6044-4

First Impression, 2011
Third Impression, 2022
Fourth Impression

Published by Pearson India Education Services Pvt. Ltd, CIN: U72200TN2005PTC057128.

Head Office: 15th Floor, Tower-B, World Trade Tower, Plot No. 1, Block-C, Sector 16, Noida 201 301, U.P., India.
Registered Office: 7th Floor, SDB2, ODC 7, 8 & 9, Survey No. 01 ELCOT IT/ ITES SEZ, Sholinganallur, Chennai 600119, Tamil Nadu, India.
Phone: 044-66540100,
Website: in.pearson.com, Email: companysecretary.india@pearson.com

Printed in India at Shree Maitrey Printech Pvt. Ltd., Noida

Contents

Preface

The significance of urban local governments, not only as a system of local self-government and administration but as a totality of political processes is being slowly realized. After independence and with the inauguration of the constitution embodying the principles of democracy and the welfare state, municipal governments are expected to assume an increasing role in the political and administrative setup of our country. Moreover it has also been widely realized that urban governments have to be definitely recognized as an organ for promoting grassroots democracy and providing not only civic services for the welfare of the local people but also for carrying out the task of urban development and planning. But unfortunately the urban governments are faced with numerous problems of multi-dimensional nature and complexities due to the rapid pace of urbanization, population growth and industrialization. The urban population of the country is projected to exceed 36 crores out of the total population of 100 crores and the number of million-plus cities to rise from 12 to 40 by 2001. The urban bodies are incapable of meeting the existing challenges and it would be next to impossible for them to manage the emerging problems as per apprehensions of various commissions and committees including those of National Commission on Urbanization.

Municipal governments in our country have failed miserably to achieve the twin objectives of serving as nurseries or training grounds of democracy and as agencies for providing adequate civic amenities. Their supersession have been rampant, the general level of their efficiency has been deplorably low, the standard of civic amenities has been disgusting, factionalism and groupism have been vicious, corruption has been endemic, a healthy civic sense has not evolved, the right type of civic leadership has not developed, and morale has been, by and large, at a very low ebb. This frustrating state of affairs has been the result of the nineteenth century framework of municipal administration, laws and bylaws, rules and regulations, procedures and practices, substandard personnel, poor finances, stringent state control and, above all, uncalled for interference by political parties in making partisan decisions and implementing them on party basis. The establishment of numerous specific purpose agencies in the name of specialization or efficiency has further eroded the powers of municipal governments without any commensurate gains in terms of municipal effectiveness or delivery of services.

Of late, awareness of restructuring, revamping and rejuvenating urban local governments has dawned upon the concerned authorities and they have started to realize that vital and far-reaching reforms need to be made in urban governments to serve the people in the best possible way, chief among the contemplated reforms being the provision of constitutional basis to the third tier of government, ensuring regular elections to them by an independent election commission, appointment of a statutory municipal finance commission for allocation of resources, audit of municipal finance by the comptroller and auditor general of India, genuine transfer of powers to the people through decentralization, etc. The Nagarpalika Bill 1991 incorporates all these reforms. Hopefully, the urban governments will emerge stronger with the passage of this Bill and the implementation of its various provisions in letter and spirit.

Realizing the significance of urban local governments in our polity, its study has been included as a part of the curricula of undergraduate and postgraduate departments of Political Science and Public Administration in our country. But no single book is available covering all the various aspects of the discipline of urban local governments with the latest facts and figures, policies and programmes of urban development, and the mechanism of their administration. This volume is intended to fill in that gap.

It is hoped that the book shall be of great interest and use to the politicians, policy makers, planners and administrators concerned with urban development, government and administration in general and the students preparing for university and competitive examinations in particular.

Pardeep Sachdeva

1

Meaning, Scope and Significance of Urban Local Government

Local government is an integral part of the three-tier system of government in our country—the other two tiers being the union (central) government and the state governments. Local government is at the bottom of a pyramid of governmental institutions with the national government at the top and the intermediate government, i.e. the state government occupying the middle range. Local government operates both in urban and rural areas and is therefore designated as urban local government and rural local government, respectively. The former manifests itself in urban local government institutions such as municipal corporations, municipal committees, nagar panchayats and the latter in rural local institutions comprising zila parishads, panchayat samities, gram panchayat and gram sabhas.

Local government has been defined in numerous ways. It has been defined in the Encyclopaedia Britannica as 'an authority to determine and execute measures within a restricted area inside and smaller than the whole state. The variant local self-government is important for its emphasis on the freedom to decide and act.'[1]

According to P. Stones, 'Local Government is that part of the government of a country which deals with those matters which concern the people in a particular locality.'[2] He points out further that it acts as the communities' housewife, in that it makes our surroundings fit to live in, keeps the streets clean, educates our children, builds our houses, and does all those other similar jobs which enable us to lead a civilized life. V. Vankata Rao points out that '[l]ocal government is that part of the government which deals mainly with local affairs, administered by authorities subordinate to the State Government but elected independently of the state authority by the qualified residents.'[3] According to L. Golding, 'Local Government is the management of their own affairs by the people of a locality.'[4]

In the words of John J. Clarke, 'Local government appears to be that part of the government of a nation or state which deals mainly with such matters as concern the inhabitants of particular district or place.'[5] G. Montagu Harris defines local government as government by the people themselves through freely elected representatives.[6] A more appropriate definition of local government has been given by K. Venkatarangaiya. According to him, 'Local Government is the administration of a locality—a village, a city or any other area smaller than the state—by a body representing the local inhabitants, possessing a fairly large amount of autonomy, raising at least a part of its revenue through local taxation and spending its income on services which are regarded as local and, therefore, distinct from State and Central services.'[7] According to

B.K. Gokhale, 'Local self government is the government of a specified locality by the local people through the representatives elected by them.'[8] Professor W.A. Robson opines that local government may be said to involve the conception of a territorial, non-sovereign community possessing the legal right and the necessary organisation to regulate its own affairs. This in turn presupposes the existence of local authority with power to act independently of external control as well as the participation of the local community in the administration of its own affairs.[9]

The study of various definitions of local government given here reveals that local government is a combination of various aspects and there is no single definition which includes all of them. These aspects are: (*a*) a local body, (*b*) local inhabitants electing and ultimately controlling that body, (*c*) autonomy of that body in the sense of freedom from the control of higher authorities within atleast a limited sphere, (*d*) recognition of the distinction between local and non-local services, and (*e*) local taxation. In other words, a local government institution has many attributes. Apart from possessing a fixed territory and a population, it possesses a governmental organisation which is responsible and responsive to the needs and wishes of the local community. However, it is not sovereign but is subordinate to the superior authorities of the country. Its powers and jurisdiction are limited and it functions within the limits laid down in the law of the state government. Within such jurisdiction, it has complete autonomy. G.M. Harris, defining the term 'local self government', describes it as:

> [A] government by local bodies, freely elected, while subject to the supremacy of the national government; is endowed, in some respect, power, discretion and responsibility, which it can exercise without control over its decisions by the higher authority. The extent of power, discretion and responsibility which the local bodies possess is a matter of degree, which varies considerably in the various countries.[10]

An analysis of the aforementioned definitions of local government reflects that there are two aspects of local government: (*a*) the relation of the local bodies to the Central/state governments; (*b*) their relation to the community, which should be determined by the following principles:

1. It is desirable to aim at the smallest possible unit that can perform a particular task efficiently so as to bring local government as nearer as possible to the people.
2. If a unit is so large that members of council cannot regularly attend its meetings, local government tends to lose its representative character.
3. Wherever possible the unit should be based on natural local loyalties, though this principle will often have to be sacrificed to efficiency or alternatively we will have to abandon the idea of progress.

Thus, the essential characteristics of a local government are: (*a*) its statutory status; (*b*) its power to raise finance by taxation in the area under its jurisdiction; (*c*) participation of local community in decision making in specified subjects and their administration; (*d*) the freedom to act independently of central control; and (*e*) its general purpose, in contrast to a single-purpose character.[11]

Characteristics of Local Government

The discussion regarding meaning and concept of local government makes it clear that there are certain characteristics on which the system of local government is based. Some of its important characteristics are as follows:

1. Local Area: A local government unit, as far as its jurisdiction is concerned, has a well defined area which is fixed by the concerned state government. This area can be termed as a city, a town or a village. The territorial limits of a local body unit are fixed by the state government subject to changes from time to time through legislation.

2. Local Authority: The administration of a particular locality is run by an authority or body of persons who are elected directly by the people residing in that particular area. That authority which includes the elected representatives of the people is responsible for management of local affairs in that area.

3. Civil Amenities for Local Inhabitants: The primary objective of local government is to provide certain civic amenities to the people at their door-steps. The provision of these civic amenities ensures the healthy living of the local community. These services are specifically meant for those inhabitants who are living in that restricted area for which the local government unit has been created. It has been rightly pointed out that all those amenities which make living better physically, economically, socially and culturally should be assigned to the local inhabitants.

4. Local Finance: In order to perform its functions effectively, it is necessary that every local government unit is provided with adequate finances. The services provided to the local inhabitants are largely financed out of funds raised locally. The local inhabitants are required to pay taxes imposed by the concerned local authority. The central and state governments also render them financial aid through a system of grants-in-aid and permission to raise loans to enable them to perform the tasks assigned to them.

5. Local Autonomy: Local autonomy means the freedom of the local government to decide and act in the sphere of activities and functions allotted to them by the statutes under which they are created. Among other things, it implies the legal right of the inhabitants of a local area to choose their representatives to govern the locality concerned, according to the laws framed by the local council, and to adopt the budget. It is, however, to be understood that the authorities which have been given the responsibility to run the local government are neither sovereign nor self created entities and they will have to depend upon the higher levels of government for their creation, rank, powers and functions.

6. Local Participation: The success or failure of developmental plans at the local level depends upon the active participation of local people for whom these plans are made. It is the local government which provides an opportunity to the local people to participate in administration. If the goals of development have to be achieved, people's participation is a prerequisite for it.

7. Local Leadership: The people who come under the purview of local government, especially those living in rural areas, are generally illiterate, inexperienced, non-professional, and unaware about the functioning of local bodies. Strong leadership, therefore, needs to be provided to those people. This leadership is provided to the people from the local area in the shape of elected representatives and elected office-bearers of the elected councils in regard to the policies and programmes of the government.

8. Local Accountability: Local government units which are created to provide civic amenities to the people are accountable to the local people. The residents of a local area keep a watch on local authorities to ensure effective performance of their functions. If a local body becomes inefficient and is not in a position to provide satisfactory services to the people, it faces severe criticism by local residents.

9. Local Development: Local government is concerned with the overall development of the people living within its area. Every activity of local government is therefore aimed at development.

Distinction Between Local Government and Local Self-government

Local government and local self-government are interchangeably used. The distinction between them is a legacy of alien rule. The term 'local self-government' has been used in those countries which were under colonial rule. For instance, in our country, the term originated when the country was ruled by the British and we did not have any self-government at the central and provincial levels. After the British government decided to associate us in administering local affairs, it meant a slice of self-government for the people. Hence the term 'local self-government' was meaningful at that time. But now the word 'self' has become redundant as the country enjoys self rule at all levels. The term 'self-government' may also appear embarrassing as well, because it has a ring of virtue around itself which it is unnecessary to claim but, on occasions, difficult to justify.[12] Moreover self-government, which reflects the government by the people of a local area through their elected representatives, sometimes is conspicuous by its absence as election to local bodies does not take place for years after they have been created or superseded for indefinite periods. (Though now it is obligatory for the state governments to hold election to the local government bodies regularly and to the superseded local bodies within six months as provided in the Constitution [74th Amendment] Act, 1992). That is why the term 'local government' and not the term 'local self-government' is used in Entry 5 of List II of the Seventh Schedule of our Constitution.[13] Despite this distinction, both the terms continue to be in vogue in our country. The terms signify a government, representative of local inhabitants, more or less autonomous in character instituted under state legislation, in a village, a district, a city or in urban areas to administer services as distinguished from state and central services.[14]

Nature and Scope of Urban Local Government

Municipal government and administration is no longer a simple affair. It has become quite complicated and complex with the phenomenal increase in the process of urbanization and consequent spurt in the emergence of urban problems and the increase in their functions. In the post-independence period it was envisaged that in the new set-up local bodies as the instrument of national policy would be used more and more, and there would be a steady increase in their functions.[15] In the first Five Year Plan, the Planning Commission's thinking was that the general direction of policy should be to encourage self-governing bodies and to assist them in assuming responsibilities for as large a portion of the administrative and social functions as possible.[16] Accordingly, the local governments are called upon not only to provide for civic services and facilities like water supply, sewerage, transport, health and sanitation, recreation, etc. but also to carry out the programmes of national development. Their responsibilities have consequently increased manifold to provide better conditions of living, ameliorate the lot of the urban poor, and ensure an adequate infrastructure and suitable administrative and managerial structure to cope with the urban problems of an unprecedented nature and magnitude. The scope of local governments has thus become very wide and includes numerous areas in its sphere of study. The following areas can be easily discerned as constituting the subject-matter of its study:

Urbanization and Urban Problems

The process of urbanization in India is going on at an accelerated pace due to industrialisation, migration from rural areas, and the natural increase in population due to population explosion with the result that the urban population which constituted 50 million at the time of independence had reached 350 million by the end of the last century. The growth of urbanization on such an unprecedented scale has confronted urban governments with gigantic urban problems such as unplanned and haphazard growth of towns and cities, unbearable strain on urban governments for provision of civic amenities, traffic congestion, growth of slums, shortage of houses, urban poverty, pollution, lack of employment opportunities, etc.

Structure of Urban Governments

The local affairs of cities and towns are to be administered by local institutions of various forms such as nagar panchayats, municipal committees, municipal corporations and cantonment boards, each urban area to be assigned the form of local government it deserves by virtue of the criteria laid down in terms of its population, territorial dimensions, and revenue resources, depending on the size of their population and the financial viability as provided in the Constitution (74th Amendment) Act, 1992.

Municipal Legislation

Local government, being a state subject, is created by the concerned state legislature. It enacts appropriate laws determining its status and providing for the constitution of the elected councils, co-option and nomination of members, procedure of election, term of the council, election and removal of office-bearers, their powers and functions, finances, state control, etc. The various Acts are also amended from time to time in the light of the changing needs of the urban governments.

Municipal Personnel Management

The urban governments with their enlarged responsibilities and complicated financial, technical and administrative problems require efficient and well qualified personnel to man various positions. They can be attracted to municipal services only when they are selected on merit and are given salaries, avenues of promotion, and other conditions of service comparable to those available to their counterparts in other government departments. The provincialisation of municipal services in various states has, no doubt, improved matters to a great extent, but it would be desirable to merge the state cadres of municipal services in corresponding state cadres. This would not only give a psychological boost to the personnel in local bodies, but the homogeneity between the sources of the state government and the local government will also raise the level of local performance.

Municipal Finance Administration

Municipal governments, in order to be viable, require finances commensurate with their responsibilities and obligations, but unfortunately they suffer from acute paucity of funds. The urban governments have not shown much aptitude for efficient financial management and control; there is wastage, leakages of revenues, and extensive under-assessment; several sources of income have not been tapped; and they have not been able to impose new taxes or increase the existing ones. The refusal by the central and state governments to share the revenue that the urban governments are entitled to, the rigid stipulation for raising loans, and the inadequacy of grants by the Central/state governments are other factors responsible for poor finance of the urban local bodies. In order to put urban governments on a sound footing, budgetary processes have to be streamlined by training budget officers and introducing a good system of continuous internal and external audit, for which the central and state governments are expected to provide necessary help and guidance to the urban local bodies. The state finance commissions provided in the Constitution (74th Amendment) Act, 1992, will ensure the financial viability of the urban local bodies on their recommendation being accepted by the state governments.

State Control over Urban Governments

The state governments exercise supervision and control over urban governments to ensure a minimum standard of services and proper performance of their functions through legislative, administrative, and financial control. The urban governments are subject to judicial control also for their acts of omission and commission. But instead of providing guidance, advice, and support to the urban governments in the discharge of their functions in an effective and efficient manner, the state governments' control over them is of a negative, regulatory, and restrictive nature, the worst kind of which is supersession, which metes out punishment not only to the elected councillors but also to the whole lot of citizens by depriving them of the elected institution of local government. Urban centres contribute immensely to national prosperity. The central and state governments should, therefore, act as their friends and benefactors and not as their powerful rivals or disinterested spectators.

Special Purpose Agencies

The state governments, on the pretext of inadequacies of financial resources, lack of technical expertise, and inefficiency in the performance of the obligatory functions by urban governments, create certain special unipurpose or multipurpose agencies to perform functions which legitimately belong to the domain of urban governments. These agencies include improvement trusts, water supply and sewerage boards, housing boards, pollution control boards, etc. The study of these urban institutions regarding their constitution, functions, powers, finances, and their relationship with the urban governments and their performance forms an important segment of the scope of urban local governments.

Urban (Town) Planning

The phenomenon of urban growth has resulted in unplanned, haphazard, and ugly urban settlements. Planning is therefore necessary to combat the menace of urbanization and its resultant problems. An important function of planning, in purely physical terms, is the judicious use of land—a scarce commodity in most urban areas—and its rational and timely reservation for future use. Roads have to be widened; new ones built; sites are required for schools, hospitals, parks and playgrounds, housing, industry, shopping, community facilities, and a number of other uses. Land planning is thus a very essential need. The state governments, therefore, have to legislate on planning and to ensure its implementation, which is ultimately the responsibility of the urban governments. The state governments have accordingly set up departments of town and country planning for this purpose.

Ministry of Urban Development and Its Attached and Subordinate Offices

The Central Ministry of Urban Development, set up in 1985 and now known as the Ministry of Urban Affairs and Employment, has the responsibility of broad formulation and monitoring of programmes in the areas of urban development, housing, urban poverty alleviation, and urban water supply. These are essentially state subjects but the Government of India plays a coordinating and monitoring role, and also supports these programmes through central sector schemes, institutional finance and expertise.

The attached offices of the Ministry of Urban Affairs and Employment are the Central Public Works Department, Directorate of Printing, Directorate of Estates, and National Building Organization. Its subordinate offices comprise the Land and Controller Development Office, Town and Country Planning Organization, Controller of Stationery, and Controller Publication. Its public sector undertakings are the Housing and Urban Development Corporation (HUDCO), National Buildings Construction Corporation Ltd, and Hindustan Prefab Ltd, and its statutory and autonomous bodies are the Delhi Development Authority (DDA), Delhi Urban Art Commission, National Institute of Urban Affairs, and National Capital Region Planning Board.

The Constitution and functions of all these institutions would form a part of the study of those interested in urban or local governments.

Reports of Commissions and Committees

The Government of India has been constituting commissions and committees from time to time for studying various urban issues, making recommendations for their solutions, and passing a number of resolutions with respect to municipal governments. The most prominent among them in the pre-independence period have been: the Royal Army Sanitation Commission (1863), Lord Mayor's Resolution on Provincial

Finance (1870), Lord Ripon's Resolution on Local Self Government (1882), the Royal Commission on Decentralization (1909), the Government of India Resolution (1918), the Taxation Enquiry Commission on Local Taxation and Local Government (1925), and the Indian Statutory Commission on Local Self Government (1929). Important committees in the post-independence period were: the Local Finance Enquiry Committee (1950), the Taxation Enquiry Committee (1953), the Committee on Augmentation of Financial Resource of Urban Local Bodies (1963), the Rural–Urban Relationship Committee (1963), the Administrative Reorganization Committee (1966–70), and the latest National Commission on Urbanization (1988). Similarly the state governments have also been appointing committees to look into their urban affairs. The study of these reports would constitute an integrated part of the scope of urban local governments.

Seminars and Conferences

The Central Council of Local Self-government has been organizing a number of conferences and seminars, most notable of which are the annual conferences of state ministers, of local self government and town and country planning, and of mayors and corporation members. The erstwhile Ministry of Urban Development convened conferences of Municipal Executive Officers and Nagarpalika sammelans on the eve of the formulation of Nagarpalika Bill in 1989. Similarly, the state governments also hold conferences of presidents and councillors of municipal bodies and of their executive authorities. The urban regional centres and various universities, in their departments of public administration, hold seminars on various themes of urbanization and administration of urban areas. A study of the proceedings of these seminars is of considerable advantage to the students of urban government.

Municipal Reforms

The Central government and state governments, in their concern to improve urban governments, have been considering the recommendations made by various commissions and committees in their respective reports and have been taking appropriate action in accepting and implementing them by enacting required legislation with a view to incorporate the necessary changes for the improvement of the constitution and functioning of urban local bodies. Among the numerous such attempts, made as a sequence of the reports of the Commissions and Committees referred to above, the latest one is the introduction of Nagarpalika Bill (1989) in the Parliament, which included provisions of great significance for restructuring and revamping urban local governments. The Bill was since rejected by Rajya Sabha, and had again been presented in 1991 and was passed as the Constitution (74th Amendment) Act, 1992. It will usher in an era of substantial reforms in urban local government.

Municipal Bureaucracy

The state bureaucracy is endowed with vast power in the administration of urban local bodies. Deputy commissioners, despite the creation of the Directorate of Local Bodies and the offices of the Regional Deputy Directors, still play a predominant role in the management of urban affairs. The administrator appointed to administer a superseded local body functions both as the deliberative and executive authority. The municipal bureaucracy, especially the municipal commissioner in municipal corporations, is a key figure in administration and enjoys greater authority in comparison to the elected mayor who represents the elected body of the city. A study of the relationship between the deliberative and executive wings of the city governments is of great interest in the study of urban local governments.

Associations and Unions of Municipal Employees

Municipal employees organize themselves in unions at the local, state, and national levels for the furtherance of their interests and hold protest meetings and demonstrations to put forth their demands in a forceful way and to get these accepted by the concerned municipal and state authorities by resorting to strikes, causing unavoidable inconveniences to the public. Many a time, the agitational approach has proved to be successful in getting their demands accepted—the latest ones being the grant of pensionary benefits and gratuity to them.

The presidents of municipal committees and mayors of municipal corporations also constitute their associations for the promotion of their interests.

Role of Political Parties

Despite the fact that local issues should not be decided on partisan basis, political parties participate in urban governments by putting up their candidates in elections, and party symbols are allotted to them by the election authorities, for elections to municipal corporations and municipal committees in some states and the winning political parties elect their own mayors and chairman of municipal corporations/committees. In certain states, the municipal Acts do not provide for any role to be played by political parties in elections as such, but they do influence the functioning of municipal governments in several ways. The questions of constitution of municipal bodies, their tenure, and their supersessions are determined by the party in power in the state government, and their internal functioning is determined by the decisions taken by the municipal councillors on partisan basis. The victory of a particular party at the local level boosts the morale of its members at the higher level of government. The triumph of Congress (I) in various municipal corporations in Maharashtra in the local elections in February 1992 proves this thesis.

Research and Evaluation

Research and evaluation of urban policies, strategies, and programme is of vital importance in the study of urban governments. The central and state governments make provisions for these activities. Various universities conduct research on different problems of urbanization and management of urban areas. Their findings can be utilized in the formulation of urban policies such as National Urbanization Policy, National Housing Policy, etc. The evaluation of the programmes introduced for improvement of urban areas and the living conditions of their residents enables the concerned governments to make necessary modifications and alterations in them to make them more effective.

Comparative Urban Local Government

Comparative study makes it possible to examine the extent to which solutions adopted abroad may be taken advantage of at home. Accordingly students of urban local governments in our country study foreign systems of local government to see if we can derive benefit for our own country from the experiences abroad. In this context, the local government system of UK (maximum autonomy to local governments), USA (decentralization), and France (which was once over-centralized and is since in the process of decentralization) are of significant importance to the study of urban local government in our country.

Evidently, the universe of urban local government is very vast; its scope is very wide and comprehensive, encompassing every conceivable issue concerning urbanization, urban growth, urban development and redevelopment, urban infrastructure, provision of urban basic services, urban planning, and urban management. The nature and scope of the study of urban governments is bound to increase with the unabated pace of urbanization, the growing complexities of urban problems, and the advancement of science and technology.

Significance of Local Government

A democratic form of government must be sustained by a system of vigorous local self governing institutions. Local government institutions provide an opportunity to the people to participate freely and actively in the government which they formulate for their respective areas. These are necessary to encourage and foster initiative, independence, and enterprise on the part of the people. Our first prime minister, Jawaharlal Nehru, while inaugurating the first Local Self-Government Ministers' Conference in 1948, had said that 'Local Self Government is and must be the basis of any true system of democracy. We have got rather into the habit of thinking democracy at the top and not so much below. Democracy at the top may not be a success unless you build on its foundation from below'.[17] 'The local assemblies of citizens', says De Tocqueville, 'add to the strength of free nations.' 'Town meetings are to liberty what primary schools are to science; they bring it within the people's reach, they teach men how to use and how to enjoy it. A nation may establish a free government, but without municipal institutions it cannot have the spirit of liberty.'[18] Lord Bryce regards local government as the best school of democracy and the best guarantee of its success. W.A. Robson opines, 'Democracy on the national scale can function in a healthy manner only if it is supported and nourished by democratic local government.'[19] Emphasizing the importance of local self government, Professor Laski says, 'Local Self-government offers the best opportunity to the people to bring local knowledge, interest and enthusiasm to bear on the solution of their problems.'[20]

The importance of local government has also been expressed by T. Appa Rao. According to him,

> The local government fulfils all the domestic needs of civilized community. It also creates among the citizens personal interest in their common affairs and throws the field open for their constructive and creative activities. It also serves as an expression of political consciousness and as a means of political education and renders the citizens fit for their civic duties and responsibilities, by enabling them to participate in public affairs. It also generates in people an aesthetic sense that makes them beautify and adorn the land they inhabit. It provides the best opportunity to men and women to bring their local knowledge and enthusiasm to bear on the solution of their own peculiar problems.[21]

The significance of local government may be discussed in details as follows :

Instrument of Political and Popular Education

Lord Ripon's Resolution of 1882 emphasized the need of political and popular education through local government. 'It is not primarily with a view to improvement in administration that this measure is put forward and supported. It is chiefly designed as an instrument of political and popular education.'[22] Highlighting the importance of local government as an educational institution Prof. Laski says, '[T]he institution of local government is educative in perhaps a higher degree at least contingently, than any other part of government. And it must be remembered that there is no other way of bringing the mass of citizens into intimate contact with persons responsible for decisions.'[23] Local government is a system which ensures effective participation of citizens in administration and makes them realize their responsibilities towards society.

School of Democracy

The success of national democracy largely depends upon the success of democracy at the grassroots level. The proposition that self-governing localities are the citadels and schools of democracy has been stressed by an advisory committee of the Commission on Inter-governmental Relations (USA):

> Local Governments are to total government what basic tissues are to human body. Without them, government would have no vitality. The countries, cities, towns, villages, and boroughs serve as training schools for the leaders of government, and in the affairs of local government are tried those who aspire to state and national offices.[24]

Symbolizing democracy by local government, G.D.H. Cole points out: 'Democracy is nothing unless it means, in the last resort, letting the people have their own way, not only in the mass, by means of an aggregate vote in a nation-wide scale, but also in their lesser groups and societies of which the greater societies are made up, and through which it is made articulate in such a way that the less clamorous voices can be heard.'[25] Jawaharlal Nehru, underlying the importance of local self government in free democratic India, had remarked, 'Local Self Government is and must be the basis of any true system of democracy.'[26] W.A. Robson had also endorsed the above observation by opining, 'Democracy on the national scale can function in a healthy manner only if it is supported and nourished by democratic local government.'[27]

Training Ground for Emerging Leaders

Local government is also an invaluable training ground for emerging leaders who, after acquiring experience in the art of politics and government at the local level, rise as such to the state and national level. In our country local governments have produced many leaders of national eminence and stature like Ferozeshah Mehta, Motilal Nehru, Jawaharlal Nehru, Subhash Chander Bose, Vallabh Bhai Patel, and Lala Lajpat Rai, who were shining examples of healthy local politics and restored to these local institutions the authority and dignity they deserved.[28] Lord Bryce has remarked,

> It is enough to observe that the countries in which democratic government has most attracted the interest of the people and drawn from their ranks have been Switzerland and the United States, especially those northern and western states in which rural local government has been most developed. These examples justify the maxim that the best school of democracy and the best guarantee for its success is the practice of local self-government.[29]

Solution of Local Problems in Effective Manner

All the problems are not supposed to be solved by the central and state governments. In fact, there are some problems which occur at the local level and need to be solved locally in accordance with local needs, the atmosphere, the environment, and wishes of the people. To be acquainted with all these things, the government shall have to step down to the local level in order to solve local problems in an effective manner. According to H.J. Laski, 'We cannot realize the full benefits of democratic government, unless we begin by the admission that all problems are not central problems, and that the results of problems in their incidence require decision at the place, and by the persons, where and by whom the incidence is most deeply felt.'[30]

Provision of Civic Amenities

Local bodies perform multifarious functions to provide various civic amenities to the people. Though the functions performed by these bodies, such as garbage collection, cleaning of streets, drainage, water supply, fire service, and health service, appear to be minor, routine and unimportant chores, they are, in fact, of considerable importance for a healthy and comfortable civic life. We tend to miss their significance except in the event of a breakdown that results in the entire dislocation of social and economic life of the community. According to J.H. Warren, 'If these services were suddenly to cease, we would relapse into chaos.'[31]

Economical Management of Local Services

The performance of not only local government, but also that of any government at any level, largely depends upon the availability of finances at its disposal. Most of the functions of local governments are financed by locally raised funds in the shape of taxes levied by them. Local governments make the people conscious about financial management. People try to manage their own affairs most economically, because they know that it is their money that is spent on local services. The central and state governments are not in a position to provide adequate finances to the local bodies to enable them to discharge their obligations. Therefore, it becomes necessary for the local people to be more vigilant and conscious to make services more economical, and to avoid wastage.

Reduction in the Burden of Central Government

A large number of functions are performed by local government that otherwise would have been performed by the Central/state government. Thus, local government not only provides certain essential services to the people, but also reduces the burden of Central/state government as well. If the central/state government is overloaded with work, it becomes incompetent, incapable, and inefficient to perform its duties. Therefore, local government is necessary for the development of initiative and interest of local masses in government and responsibility. Local government is an invaluable socio-political laboratory for trying and testing on a small scale various new proposals for government organization and socio-economic policies. It is a preserver of local colour in the national life.[32]

Efficient and Effective Management of Local Affairs

Local government, being concerned generally with the welfare of the people, deals mainly with those functions which contribute to the socio-economic development of the country. Being more conversant and concerned with the local problems as compared to the government in the capital, it can manage the local affairs more efficiently and effectively.

Channel of Communication Between the State Government and the Community

Local government serves as a channel of communication between the state government and the community. The demands made by the local community are on the one hand transmitted to the state government, the creator of local government, and on the other hand, people living in far-flung areas come to know about the government policies and programmes through local bodies. Thus, local government ensures close relationship between the people and the higher level of governments through this device of communication.

Check Against Bureaucracy

The control of bureaucracy over the community increases in the absence of a strong local government system. A centralized system of administration, even though democratic, results in control of the community by the bureaucracy. The rigid behaviour of bureaucrats largely affects the people's initiative and their confidence in the government. The transmission of powers from bureaucrats to the democratically formed local government has positively checked the influence of bureaucracy. A. Venkatarao has rightly remarked, 'One of the virtues of local government is the easy intimacy and ready access to local government officials.'

Mitigation of the Evils of Party System

Political parties have always influenced the democracy not only at the state and national levels, but at the local level as well, because it is not possible for democracy to function without the political parties. Local government in urban areas in England has been operating on party lines. But we in India advocate the avoidance of participation of political parties in local bodies as they bring into the management of local affairs the evils usually attributed to them such as factionalism, groupism, favouritism, and nepotism. The role of political parties as such is, therefore, not encouraged in local governments, and thus they are expected to remain immune from the evils of the party system.

The significance of urban local governments has all the more increased after independence. They are expected not only to provide for the basic civic amenities for the safety and convenience of the citizens, but also mobilize local support and public cooperation for the implementation of various programmes of welfare. It has been increasingly realized that urban governments have to be definitely recognized as an organ for promoting grassroots democracy and providing not only services for the welfare of the local people but also for carrying out the task of urban development and planning.[33] According to the Rural–Urban

Relationship Committee, 'the social and economic changes ensuing from the developmental efforts and the problems created in the process of urbanization impose new responsibilities upon urban local governments. An important aspect of economic planning is the accelerated pace of industrialization. Urban centres attract industries and the process of industrialization and economic development leads to a rapid increase in the urban population. This has resulted in serious shortfalls in housing, public utilities and community facilities. Consequently, the urban environments have deteriorated, giving rise to shanty towns and slums, heavy population concentration, uncontrolled land use, inadequate urban services such as water supply, sewerage, and transport, and deficient educational, recreational, and public utilities. Adequate planned and controlled community facilities are to be provided if haphazard urbanization is to be avoided.'[34]

Conclusion

Local government means the administration of the affairs of a locality in urban and rural areas by the people through their elected representatives. It may be described as government by popularly elected bodies charged with the administrative and executive duties in matters concerning the inhabitants of a particular district or place and vested with powers to make bylaws for their guidance. The urban local government operates in towns and cities through municipal corporations, municipal committees, cantonment boards, town and notified area committees. The chief characteristics of an urban local government institution are:

1. Its jurisdiction is limited to a specific area and its functions relate to the provision of civic amenities to the population living within its jurisdiction;
2. It functions within the provisions of the statute which has created it;
3. It has the power to raise finance by taxations in the areas under its jurisdiction; and
4. It is subordinate to the state government which exercises control and supervision over it and can supersede or dissolve it.

The scope of urban local governments extends to the study of the phenomenon of urbanization and its problems, urban planning, structure of urban governments and their classification, municipal legislation, personnel management, financial administration, state–local relations, special purpose agencies, organization and functions of the Union Ministry of Urban Affairs and Employment and its subordinate and attached offices, as also that of the state departments of the urban local government, reports of various commissions and committees appointed from time to time by the Central and state governments to study the various aspects of the working of urban local governments and the recommendations made by them, municipal bureaucracy, role of political parties, research and evaluation, and comparative urban local governments. The sphere of the activities of urban local governments is increasing considerably with the assignment of developmental, environmental and welfare responsibilities with the scientific and technological advancements in the present times and the innovations that are called for in their structures, and modes and mechanism of functioning to meet the aspirations of the people in this democratic age and to ensure their efficient and effective performance to their satisfaction.

The significance of urban local government lies in the numerous benefits that it bestows upon the inhabitants of the area it operates in. It functions as a school for democracy wherein citizens are imparted political and popular education regarding issues of local and national importance. It develops qualities of initiative, tolerance and compromise, so essential for the working of a democracy. It not only relieves congestion at the centre but it also checks the increasing powers of bureaucracy. It stands positively for distribution and diffusion of powers leading to administrative deconcentration and political decentralization. It opens an outlet for the articulation of lesser groups in a large society. Being close to the original base, it finds solutions for local problems. It provides facilities for minimum basic needs. It serves as a reservoir of talents for local and national leadership.

The significance of urban local governments in India has considerably increased in the post-independence era with the inauguration of the constitution embodying the principles of democracy and a welfare state, and emphasizing upon the governments in urban areas to promote social and economic development.

NOTES AND REFERENCES

1. *Encyclopaedia Britannica*, Volume 14, pp. 261–62. London.
2. P. Stones, *Local Government for Students* (London: McDonald and Evons Ltd., 1963), p. 1.
3. V. Venkata Das, *A Hundred Years of Local Self-Government in Assam* (Calcutta: Beni Parkash, Mander, 1965), p. 1.
4. L. Golding, *Local Government* (London, 1955), p. 19.
5. John, J. Clarke, *Local Government of the United Kingdom* (London: 1948), p. 1.
6. G.M. Harris, *Comparative Local Government* (London: 1948), p. 9.
7. Venkatarangiya and Pattabhiram (ed.), *Local Government in India: Selected Readings* (Bombay: Allied Publishers, 1969), p. 1.
8. B.K. Gokhale, *The Constitution of India* (Bombay: Sheth and Company, 1972), pp. 1307–8.
9. W.A. Robson, *Encyclopaedia of Social Sciences*, Volume 9 (New York: The Macmillan Company), p. 574.
10. Harris, *Comparative Local Government*, p. 5.
11. S.R. Maheshwari, *Local Government in India* (Agra: Lakshmi Narain Aggarwal, 1984), p. 5.
12. Ibid., p. 3.
13. The Entry 5 of List II (State List) of the Seventh Schedule reads: 'Local Government, that is to say, the constitution and powers of municipal corporations, Improvement Trusts, District Boards, Mining Settlement authorities and other local authorities for the purpose of local self government or village administration.'
14. G.S. Bandhu, 'Local Self Government in India', *Quarterly Journal of Local Self Government Institution*, Bombay, April–June, 1967, p. 382.
15. 'Report of the Punjab Local Government (Urban) Enquiry Committee', 1957, p. 98.
16. First Five Year Plan, Planning Commission, Government of India, 1951, p. 141.
17. Jawaharlal Nehru's address to the Conference of Provincial Local Self Government Ministers (1948).
18. Alexis de Tocqueville, 'Democracy in America', in Phillips Bradley (ed.), *The Henry Reeve Test* (New York: Alfred A. Knopf, 1953), p. 61.
19. Robson, *Encyclopaedia of Social Sciences.*
20. Harold Laski, *A Grammar of Politics* (London: George Allen and Unwin, 1961), p. 412.
21. T. Appa Rao, 'Municipality: Its Significance', *Civic Affairs*, 1973, p. 11.
22. Lord Ripon's Resolution of September 1881.
23. Laski, *A Grammar.*
24. Quoted by Anwar Hussain Syed, *The Political Theory of the American Local Government* (New York: Random House, 1969), p. 93.
25. G.D.H. Cole, *Local and Regional Government* (London: Cassell and Co. Ltd., 1974), p. 64.
26. Jawaharlal Nehru's address (1948).
27. Robson, *Encyclopaedia of Social Sciences.*
28. P.R. Dubhashi, Foreword, in S.L. Kaushik, *Leadership in Urban Governments in India* (Allahabad: Kitab Mahal, 1986).
29. Bryce James, *Modern Democracies* (New York: Macmillan, 1921), p. 133.
30. J.H. Warren, *The Local Government Service* (London: 1952).
31. Ranney Austin, *Governing of Men* (New York: 1958), p. 484.
32. Third Five Year Plan, Planning Commission, Government of India, 1969, p. 5.
33. 'Report of the Rural-Urban Relationship Committee', Volume 1, New Delhi, Government of India, 1966, para 303.

Urbanization: Indian Scenario

Urbanization is defined as a process of the movement of the population towards urban areas—towns and cities. The process may proceed either through an increase in the number of cities or through a rise in the size of the population in each city. Urbanization thus refers to the growth of cities, and to the total population living in urban settlements. In other words, it implies an increase in the urban population at a rate higher than that of the increase in the total/rural population. Urbanization may be distinguished from urban growth. The latter term refers to an increase in the percentage of urban population to the total population.

Urbanization is characterized by movement of people from rural communities concerned chiefly or solely with agriculture (rural communities) to other communities where activities are primarily centred on management, trade, manufacture or allied interests (urban communities).[1] In short, urbanization is a multifaceted phenomenon—a process which reveals itself through temporal, spatial, and sectoral changes in the demographic, socio-economic, technological and environmental aspects of life in a given society. These changes manifest themselves in the increasing concentration of population in human settlements larger than villages, in the increasing involvement of the people in the secondary and the tertiary production functions and in the progressive adoption of certain social traits which are atypical of traditional rural societies.[2]

Urbanization: A Global Phenomenon

Urbanization is a world-wide phenomenon. It has been going on at a very accelerated pace in recent years. According to the estimates and projections of the United Nations Population Division, the urban population in the world had risen from 1,361 million in 1970 to 2,286 million in 1990 and is likely to be about 5 billion in 2025. In terms of urban population in the total world population, it implies an increase from 36.9 per cent in 1970 to 43.6 per cent in 1990 and 62.5 per cent in 2025. By the turn of the century, over 50 per cent of the world population will be urban as against 29 per cent in 1950, 39 per cent in 1975, and 43 per cent in 1985. In other words, the urban population of the world which doubled between 1850 and 1975 will further double between 1975 and 2000. Massive urbanization is engulfing the Third World. Within the span of the last two decades, towns and cities all over Asia, Africa and Latin America have doubled and tripled in size. The developing countries are urbanizing not only more rapidly than the industrial nations are now, but also more rapidly than the industrial nations did in the heyday of their urban growth. UN forecasts that by the end of this century 41 per cent of the population in the developing countries will be living in towns, and of these about 80 per cent will be in Latin America, the most urbanized region. In keeping with the global trend, there has been an accelerated growth of urbanization in India. In 1951, the urban population was 62.28 million. Thirty years later (1981), it had gone up by two-and-a-half times to 160 million, and was estimated authoritatively in 1988 to have reached 200 million. This is expected to touch about 350 million by the end of the century.[3]

Definition of Urban Area

In the context of India, the census reports of 1961 to date have defined those places as urban areas which have a local authority such as municipality, cantonment board, notified area committees, and all other places which satisfy the requirements of a minimum population of 5000 with a density of population of at least 400 persons per square km, and at least 75 per cent of the male working population engaged in non-agricultural pursuits.[4] Apart from the above criterion, the state government can declare a place as an urban area if it has a pronounced urban characteristic and amenities like newly founded industrial areas, large housing settlements or places of tourist importance usually have.

Urban Agglomeration

Another concept of *urban agglomeration* is used in the census. Very often large railway colonies, university campuses, port areas, military camps, etc. come up outside, but adjoining, the statutory limits of the city or town. Such areas may not qualify to be treated as urban, but as an extension of the town these areas deserve to be treated as urban. Such towns, together with their outgrowths, have been considered as one unit and are called urban agglomerations. An urban agglomeration may thus be defined as an actual urban spread in a specific location irrespective of the limits of institutional boundaries. To quote the Census Report, 2001,

> An urban agglomeration is made up of the main town together with the adjoining areas of urban growth and is treated as one urban spread. The population covered by such spreads is categorized as urban. Each such agglomeration may be made up of more than one statutory town adjoining one another such as a municipality and the adjoining cantonment etc., and also other urban growths such as a railway colony, university campus etc. Such outgrowths which did not qualify to be treated as individual towns in their own right and have pronounced urban characteristics are shown as constituents of the agglomeration.

The total number of urban agglomerations, as reported in 1971 census, was 69 and many more have since been identified in the 2001 census; for example, Pimpri–Chinchwad in Pune urban agglomeration, Avadi and Ambattur in Madras urban agglomeration and Ambala comprising Ambala Cantt (CB) and Ambala Sadar (MC) with a population of 100,000 and above, in Haryana.

The concept of urban agglomeration has numerous useful implications. The urban spread around a municipality beyond its statutory jurisdiction is marked by haphazard growth and unregulated population, as the municipal building by-laws are not applicable in the peri-municipal zone. It creates problems for municipal services planning, and the residents immediately outside the municipal boundary live in an administrative vacuum; they would be enjoying municipal services without paying for them. By marking the area of an urban agglomeration coterminous with a municipality, the above mentioned difficulties can be removed, and planning and civic reorganization can be facilitated.[5]

Salient Features of Urbanization in India

The salient features of the urbanization process in India may be described as follows:

1. Tremendous Increase in Urban Population: India has witnessed tremendous increase in its urban population since independence. The total population of the country had doubled from 350 million in 1947 to 800 millions in 1988, and it stood at 84–94 million on 1 March 1991. From 1947 to 1988, the urban population had increased four-fold from 50 million to 200 million. According to the 2001 census, India's urban population has increased to 33 crores in 2001, and it is estimated that it will touch 59.1 crores in 2020 and 65.8 crores in 2025 when the total population of India is expected to be 122.9 crores.

2. Uneven Distribution of Urban Population in Various States/UTs: Urban population is unevenly distributed in different states and union territories in the country. At the end of the spectrum, we have Arunachal Pradesh and Himachal Pradesh with 6.6 per cent and 7.6 per cent urban population, respectively. At the other end are Maharashtra and Tamil Nadu with 35 per cent and 33 per cent urban population, respectively. In between, we have states with proportion of urban population ranging from 11 to 32 per cent. The union territory of Chandigarh is 93.6 per cent urban while Dadra and Nagar Haveli Union Territory is only 6.7 per cent urban.[6]

3. Rise in Urban India and Decline in Rural Growth to Continue: The annual exponential growth rate in urban India as a whole is 3.4 per cent and 0.7 per cent for rural India. In economically backward states and high urban states the urban and rural growth rates are estimated to be as follows (see Table 2.1):

In Punjab and Haryana the rural and urban growth rates are estimated to be 0.3 and 0.4 (rural) and 3.2 and 4.3 (urban), respectively.

4. Even Balance Between Natural Increase in the Population of Urban Centres and Growth Through Migration: There are three components of urban growth in our country namely, (*a*) natural increase in population in urban areas, *i.e.* increase in urban population as a result of natural growth through births in urban areas; (*b*) net increase through migration to urban areas, and (*c*) the impact of reclassification of rural areas as urban. According to estimates made by the National Institute of Urban Affairs in 1988, during the decade 1971–81, natural increase accounted for a little over 41 per cent of the total urban growth, immigration for a little over 40 per cent, and reclassification for about 19 per cent.[7] It is thus evident that there is almost even balance between the natural increase in the population of the urban centres and growth through migration, each accounting for approximately 40 per cent of the increase with a less than 20 per cent accounting from reclassification. It is to be noted that while the natural increase of large cities tends to remain within these cities, the migration stream tends to be from villages to towns and towns to large cities; the present trend of migration is likely to bring about a massive increase in the size of existing large cities.

5. Rise in the Number of Urban Areas: The country is becoming urbanized at an alarming rate. Consequently the number of urban areas is increasing. According to the Census Report of 1971, urban India comprised 1,921 towns, including 69 urban agglomerations. In 1989, there were 3,301 urban settlements. Their number is to increase inevitably with the anticipated increase in urban population.

Table 2.1

	Economically Backward States	
	Urban growth rate	*Rural growth rate*
Uttar Pradesh	5.1	0.5
Orissa	4.7	0.4
Rajasthan	4.4	1.1
Bihar	4.4	1.4
Madhya Pradesh	3.9	1.4
Andhra Pradesh	2.9	0.5
	High Urban States	
	Urban growth rate	*Rural growth rate*
Karnataka	3.5	0.2
Maharashtra	2.6	0.6
West Bengal	2.3	0.8
Gujarat	2.3	0.6
Tamil Nadu	1.8	0.6

6. Classification of Urban Areas: The Indian Census customarily classifies urban areas into six population size groups as follows:

Class	Range of Population
I	100,000 and above
II	50,000 to 99,991
III	20,000 to 49,999
IV	10,000 to 19,999
V	5,000 to 9,999
VI	below 5000

(According to Census practice, Class I cities denote towns with population of one lakh and above). This classification, which was introduced over hundred years ago, now, seems to be obsolete in view of the expanding urban base and the rate of urban growth. The National Commission on Urbanization has therefore recommended a new criterion for classification of cities and towns as follows:

Class Cities	Range of Population
C 1	1 lakh to 5 lakh
C 2	5 lakh to 10 lakhs
C 3	10 lakhs to 20 lakhs
C 4	20 lakhs to 50 lakhs
C 5	50 lakhs to 100 lakh
C 6	100 lakh and above

Towns	
T 1	20,000 to 50,000
T 2	50,000 to 100,000

The Commission is also of the view that there is not much point in considering towns with population below 20,000 as urban except in special cases like new factory towns, hill towns, etc.

Of the 218 Class I cities in India (excluding Assam) there are 12 with a population of one million (ten lakhs) and more, 30 with a population in the range of 500,000 to 999,999, 91 in the range of 250,000 to 499,999 and 135 in the range of 100,000 to 249,999.[8] The increase in urban population has resulted not only in increase in the number of urban areas but also in their upgrade from a city of low grade to a city of higher class.

This phenomenon is evident in almost all the states which can be substantiated by delineating, for example, the demographic context of the state of Haryana as a representative of the other states of India. According to the 1991 census, Haryana occupies the 12th position among the states on the basis of the percentage of its urban population to the total population. But it ranks 15th according to the size of its total population. The urban population of the state had multiplied by about seven times, while its total population had increased by only 3.5 times during the past nine decades. In the 1971–81 decade, there was an increase of about 12 lakh in the urban population of the state and an equal number was added in 1981–91. The proportion of the urban population to the total population had doubled in 90 years. In other words, it rose from 12.42 per cent in 1901 to 24.79 per cent in 1991.

The urban population percentage is the highest in Faridabad district (48.66), which contains 17.64 per cent of the total urban population of the state, while Mahendergarh district is the least urbanized with only 12.70 per cent of its population living in the urban areas. It claims only 2.09 per cent of the state's urban population. Besides, Faridabad district heads the list of all districts in the state with an urban growth rate of 74.64 per cent during 1981–91, while Mahendragarh district with an urban growth rate of 27.99 per cent is at the bottom.

Although the number of towns has increased steadily in Haryana since 1901 and the number of town dwellers has also increased, 75.21 per cent of the Haryana's population is still rural.

There are 12 class I towns in Haryana of which 11 have a population of 100,000 and above and qualify to be treated as cities. These are Faridabad Complex, Rohtak, Panipat, Hisar, Karnal, Yamuna Nagar, Sonepat, Bhiwani, Gurgaon, Ambala and Sirsa. Sirsa and Gurgaon are the latest addition to the list of cities.

In addition to this, there is one urban agglomeration—Ambala—which has a population of 100,000 and above. The UA comprises Ambala Cantt (CB) and Ambala Sadar (MC). The twelve class I towns and UA account for 58.54 per cent of the state's urban population.

The proportion of the state's urban population in Class II towns is 15.11 per cent. Class III towns claim 11.95 per cent and Class IV towns 10.43 per cent of the state's urban population. There are 20 Class V towns claiming only 3.74 per cent of the urban population.[9]

7. Concentration of Large Percentage of Population in Metropolitan Cities: Urbanization in India is characterized by the concentration of large percentage of urban population in Class I and metropolitan cities. In 1981, the 218 Class I cities accounted for more than 60 per cent of the total urban population of the country. In absolute numbers, out of 20 crores of urban population, Class I cities contained about 12 crore people and the metropolitan cities of Delhi, Calcutta (Kolkata), Bombay (Mumbai) and Madras (Chennai) alone had about five crores and sixty-five lakh people living in them. These cities are under the greatest strain because their infrastructure is overloaded to the point of breakdown.

8. Development of New Townships on the Periphery of Big Cities: All cities with a population of 20 lakh and more are reaching a size which renders them difficult to manage. They are characterized by excessive densities in core areas, non-availability of land, overloaded infrastructure no longer amenable to improvement, lack of housing, and a transportation system which, for want of land space, can no longer be augmented. This leads to movement of population towards the periphery as is discernible by the outcropping of Calcutta (Kolkata), Madras (Chennai) and Bombay (Mumbai) and the new townships being developed in the periphery of Delhi by the adjoining state governments.

Factors Contributing to Urbanization

The causes responsible for accelerated pace in the rise of the process of urbanization, and factors contributing to the increase in the number of urban areas and the magnitude of urban growth can be discerned as

1. Migration from rural to urban areas,
2. Natural increase in population in urban areas, and
3. Classification of earlier rural settlements as urban.

These causes or factors may be discussed in detail as follows:

Migration from Rural to Urban Areas

The following factors contribute to migration from rural to urban areas:

Push and Pull Factors: Urbanization is mainly attributed to migration of people from rural to urban areas due to 'push' and 'pull' factors. The 'push' factors push or force the village people to move to towns or cities. These factors include population pressure on agricultural land, unemployment and under-employment (between sowing and harvesting seasons); a life of drudgery in villages, little source of income and lack of adequate employment opportunities, orthodoxy in ideas and thinking, enchaining of individual freedom to traditional social codes, and superstitions and conventional approach to life stifling a person physically and intellectually.

The 'pull' factors lure or attract village folk to towns and cities. These comprise money; good economic prospects and better standards of living; well developed network of civic amenities and facilities in every sphere making life smoother and comfortable as compared to the villages; more independence and freedom; more independent outlook and progressive ideas; better educational, cultural, medical and social life facilities; and prospects of a prosperous and glorious future. For, in most cities, there is a cornucopia of opportunity awaiting village folk. Some come to a town or a city looking for a life free from the shackles of orthodoxy and ignorance, a place of aware and enlightened people. A handful come to be a part of the 'jet-set' modern society.[10] In short, the lure of the city, like El Dorado, is irresistible and beckons the rural people from their native villages to alien cities.

Migration Due to Agricultural Prosperity: It is not only the rural poverty which induces urbanization, but the agricultural prosperity brought about by green revolution in some states also induces urbanization. In Punjab, for example, the urban growth rate increased from 25.3 per cent during 1961–71 to 44.5 per cent during 1971–81, while in Haryana, the comparable figures were 35.6 per cent and 56.4 per cent.

Migration from Urban to Urban (Small Towns to Cities): Urban to urban migration also plays an important role in process of urbanization. There is no doubt that by virtue of higher education and skill—even in small urban areas compared to rural areas—the potential migrant from the small town to the big cities has an edge ever his counterpart from the rural areas in finding employment in the city except when the demand is for unskilled labour or labour of a specialized type like contract labour. According to 1981 census, of the 3 crores 40 lakhs migrants, 1 crore 70 lakhs were rural–urban migrants and a little over 1 crores 30 lakhs were urban–urban migrants.

Industrialization: Urbanization is the inevitable consequence of industrialization. Industrialization and urbanization are inseparable. Just as agriculture fosters the village, industry encourages the growth of cities.[11] In fact, urbanization is accomplished through a shift from agrarian to industrial economy. Britain was transformed into an urbanized society in a span of one hundred years (1801–1900) due to industrialization. The intensive urbanization in most of the advanced countries began during the past 100 years; in the developing countries, including India, it got underway more recently primarily due to industrialization and the resultant economic growth. Industrialization, by the very nature, demands a huge force of labour, which gets concentrated in the areas where industries are set up or expanded.

Industrial development contributes to the growth of new towns as well, to provide housing, civic amenities and other services to the people engaged in the industrial concern, and to counter the increasing concentration in large cities. Many new towns were set up to meet such requirements in the industrial centres; for example, single industry (steel) townships like Rourkela and Bhilai; townships having an industrial complex such as Durgapur, Nangal, Chittranjan, Ranchi, etc.; small townships like Heavy Electrical Township near Bhopal; the township of Indian Telephone Industries and Hindustan Aeronautics Ltd. near Bangalore; Indian Ordinance Factory near Dehradun; company towns at Sindri and Modinagar; and Hindustan Machine Tools at Pinjore.

Expansion of Means of Transport: The development of transport infrastructure has also accelerated the pace of urbanization. The development of railways throughout the length and breadth of the country, the construction of roads and bridges, and the consequent expansion of transport linked together different parts of the country and facilitated an easy movement of goods and people, giving an impetus to the growth of cities.

Natural Increase in Population

Urban growth is also substantially affected by a natural increase in population. During the 1971–81 decade, a natural increase accounted for a little over 41 per cent of the total urban growth, with the higher percentage in the more urbanized states—60 per cent in Tamil Nadu, 46 per cent in Maharashtra and 44 per cent in West Bengal. It would thus be wrong to assume that it is migration that is sustaining urbanization, the share of natural increase is momentous.

Reclassification of Urban Areas

The impact of reclassification of rural areas as urban areas, has also led to a rise in the number of urban areas. Some states like Uttar Pradesh have adopted a liberal policy of classifying erstwhile rural settlements as towns while states like Tamil Nadu have made almost no addition to the list of towns during 1971–81. In India as a whole, in the 1981 census list of towns, as many as 881 new towns were added to the 1971 list as a result of reclassification of villages into urban settlements.[12]

In addition to the factors mentioned above contributing to urbanization process, the urban growth can be attributed to the following causes as well:

1. **Population Explosion:** The population in India is increasing on an unprecedented scale. It had increased from 350 million in 1947 to 843.9 million in 1991, which further increased to 1000.27 million as per the 2001 census. The overall rate of population growth itself generates urbanization, as is evident in the increase of urban population from 50 million in 1947 to 280.5 million in 2001.

2. **Partition of the Country and Resultant Migration:** The unfortunate division of the country into India and Pakistan at the time of independence led to the exodus of migrants from West Punjab

and East Bengal to various towns and cities of India, where they preferred to settle primarily for safety of lives and security of property. The influx of refugees thus resulted in the increase of urban population. A large number of new townships had also to be developed to rehabilitate the displaced people. New capitals were also developed on planned basis such as Chandigarh (Punjab and Haryana), Bhubaneshwar (Orissa) and Gandhinagar (Gujarat) which now accommodate millions of urbanites.

3. Militants' activities: The activities of terrorists and militants have also been responsible for migration of rural people to urban centres and the residents of small towns to bigger cities for reasons of security and safety, which the urban areas are expected to provide in greater measure in comparison to the rural areas. The migration of people who had actually suffered at the hands of the terrorists, or were scared by threats of being on their hit lists was evident in substantial degree in their movement from villages to towns and from towns to cities, from Punjab and Jammu and Kashmir to other parts of the country, and similarly of the Sikh community of other states to Punjab for fear of reprisals for atrocities committed by the militants in Punjab.

Other Factors Promoting Urbanization

The process of urbanization and the growth of urban centres was stimulated by several other factors such as tradition, patronage of rulers of ancient and medieval periods, and the colonial trade and administrative policy of the British. India has a long tradition of urban living and it has been a land of cities since the time of the Indus valley civilization; Mohanjodaro and Harappa were amongst some of the oldest planned cities. Cities like Ayodhya, Kashi, Pataliputra, Nalanda, Takshila, Mathura, Ujjain, Prayag, Nasik, etc. belonged to the ancient historical period, and the cities like Delhi, Agra, Lucknow, and Hyderabad bear the imprint of Muslim influence.

During the British rule, Calcutta, Bombay and Madras, apart from being port cities and commercial centres, served as the seats of political power. The development of colonial trade stimulated the growth of a number of towns and cities, especially the port cities. Military deployment for the security and expansion of British territories in the country necessitated the establishment of cantonments and the setting up of administrative centres in district and tehsil headquarters which promoted urban growth, and so did the establishment of educational, technical, and medical institutions. The role of religion was also of great significance in the establishment of urban centres of pilgrimage and their subsequent growth into cities of millions. The post-independence period has witnessed the creation of new towns for the rehabilitation of refuges, rendered houseless by partition of the country, communal frenzy, and militants' activities.

The process of urbanization continues unabated; it is difficult to reverse it, despite the fact that it has generated gigantic problems of a multi-dimensional nature. Yet efforts have to be made to counter the problems of unprecedented magnitude and to arrest the tide of migration of people to urban areas.

Problems and Challenges of Urbanization

Urbanization poses several problems of a multi-dimensional nature, such as slums, insanitation, environmental pollution, and scarcity of housing, water, electricity, transport and medical aid. The speed with which the urban population is growing, overflowing the boundaries, and forming sprawling agglomeration of buildings has created difficulties, and the tasks of city governments have become formidable.[13] With the increasing pace of urbanization, demands made on municipal bodies have vastly increased which those institutions, presently constituted as they are, are grossly inadequately structured and equipped to meet. They are a hangover of the early nineteenth century and are, therefore, not in a position to meet the demands of the cities standing on the threshold of the twenty-first century. Some of the major problems and challenges posed by urbanization in India are as follows:

1. Shortage of Housing: The most visible and dehumanizing manifestation of urbanization in a developing country is the large number of squatters and shanty dwellers found in all the major cities. The reason for this state of affair is the housing crisis. The reality of the urban housing scene in India is that more than two lakh urban households are without any shelter and as many as 45 per cent are living in just single-room houses—nearly five persons to a room—in a state of extreme over-crowding. In 1981, nearly 37 per cent were without electricity and about 66 per cent were without latrines. The Seventh Five Year Plan document states:

> In fulfilling the basic needs of the population, housing ranks next only to food and clothing in importance. A certain minimum standard of housing is essential for healthy and civilized existence. The development of housing therefore, must enjoy high priority in a poor society such as ours where housing amenities are far below the minimum standards that have been internationally accepted. Housing activity serves to fulfil many of the fundamental objectives of the plan providing shelter, raising the quality of life, particularly of the poorer sections of the population, creating conditions which are conducive to the achievement of crucial objectives in terms of health, sanitation and education, creating substantial additional employment and dispersed economic activity, etc.

The urban housing stock, which was 14.1 million in 1961, had increased to 18.5 million in 1971 and to 28 million in 1981. Policy statements in successive Plan documents have continued to emphasize the importance of the housing sector, but in reality, investments in housing as a percentage of total investments have declined.

In 1981, out of a total urban population of nearly 160 million, 32 to 40 million were estimated to be in slums alone.

The failure to provide adequate, proper, and affordable housing manifests itself in many forms: overcrowding, congestion, high prices, formation of slums and squatter settlements, and a sharp decline in the quality of the overall living environment. Rapid population growth, inadequate investment, and widespread poverty are some of the principal causes of the housing crisis.

The key to success in increasing supply, both quantitatively and qualitatively, i.e. in sheltering the millions and providing need-based, appropriate houses, lies in ensuring success to housing inputs—land, building material, finance, and services: the state facilitating land supply; all city dwellers being served equally in the matter of provision of basic environmental and social services, and strengthening the resource base of the local bodies to ensure this; creating properly designed, structured, and staffed housing finance agencies which may effectively reach out to and service the poor; making arrangements that would accelerate production of low-cost building materials; and above all creating an effective industrial housing policy providing minimum required accommodation to every employee as a pre-condition.

2. Strain on Civic Amenities: Under Article 47 of the Constitution, it is the duty of the state to improve the standard of living of the people, in particular, to improve public health standards. Water, sewerage, and drainage are three crucial elements for life, without which there can be neither health nor comfort.

A major feature of an urban scene is the misery and serious health hazards caused by lack of water supply and sanitation. Almost all urban centres, even those which once had reasonably adequate water supply, are now suffering from crippling shortages. It is a national disgrace that in 1988, there were prolonged periods when Hyderabad and Madras received piped water supply for only about 20 minutes a day with many localities going without water for many days. Delhi, too, had to face severe problems in the summer of 1988.

3. Haphazard Growth of Transportation: All major cities are plagued with traffic congestion. The obvious factors responsible are the concentration of too many people and activities in too small a place, and the inefficient relationship of work places and residences. In the past two decades, the situation has further deteriorated significantly. In the absence of an integrated policy and coordinated approach, intra-city transportation has grown in a haphazard manner, without any long term perspective, causing congestion and severe crisis in the cities. An urban transportation system can be developed optimally, only when transport and land use planning are examined together.

4. Growth of Slums: People who migrate from villages to urban areas in search of employment or for other reasons cannot afford to pay the high prices of pucca shelters, or are not in a position to buy land at the higher prices charged near their work places. They cannot afford to buy means of transport to reach their destinations. Therefore, they settle on marginal lands near their work places, which are considered unfit for habitation by the non-poor classes. These places are river banks, railway lands, unconstructed residential plots in private colonies, etc. They construct their living places with cheap scrap and material like gunny bags, tarpaulin, tin sheets, wooden planks, mud, etc. These places are always without civic amenities. As a result, public sanitation and personal hygiene break down.

The growth of slums is on the increase. In Calcutta, about 35 per cent of the population lives in slums; in Madras, about 38 per cent of population lived in slums in 1971; in Hyderabad, the slum population jumped from one lakh in 1962 to a staggering five lakhs by 1981; and in Delhi, squatters are estimated to have grown from 12,741 in 1951 to 1.3 lakhs by 1975–76. The rise in slum population continues unabated.

5. Urban Poverty: The most demanding of the urban challenges is the challenge posed by urban poverty; the worst pollution of all manifests in the urban slums which dominate the townscape; and the mass of beggars, petty hawkers, and casual workers struggling to eke out a living. The task of adequately feeding, educating, housing and employing a large and rapidly growing number of under-nourished, semi-literate, semi-skilled, under-employed, and impoverished city dwellers—living on pavements, in poorly serviced crawls, in unhygienic slums, in illegal squatters, colonies and in other forms of degraded and inadequate settlements, and struggling to make a living from low paying and unstable occupations—is the challenge facing urban planners. The phenomenon of urban poverty has altered the landscape, the social fabric and the overall character of Indian cities. In the coming years this can be expected to worsen, as the Indian cities will have one-third of their population living below the poverty line.

6. Scarcity of Urban Land: The most disastrous feature of urbanization in India has been that urban land has become extremely scarce and expensive, beyond the reach of the poor. The shortage of land has forced both sellers and buyers into disrespect for the law. Black money has proliferated, corruption has become rife, and moral values have been eroded. The colonizers are making huge profits by fleecing those who are in dire need of shelters. Inevitably the poor have been affected most. With legal, institutionalized, and simplified access of urban land at affordable prices denied to them, they have had to take to the only option available—illegal occupation of land resulting in squatter colonies, deprived of basic municipal services and thus presenting the most brutish abuses of human dignity.

7. Pollution: The gravest challenge to urbanization is that of pollution of water, air, noise, and solid waste. The Environment (Protection) Act, 1986 defines environmental pollutants as any solid, liquid or gaseous substance present in such concentration as may or tend to be injurious to the environment. Industrial effluents, municipal sewage and agro-chemicals are the major pollutants of water. According to WHO estimates, as much as 80 per cent of the world's diseases are traceable to water pollution. Long exposure to polluted air caused by industries and vehicles is responsible for a variety of diseases including lung cancer, pneumonia, bronchitis, asthma, and even the common cold. Noise pollution causes blood vessels to contract leading to high-blood pressure and may affect the brain. Pollution also causes serious damage to animals, birds, aquatic life, crops, and vegetation. Solid waste consisting mainly of municipal refuge and garbage is hazardous as it harbours disease carrying organisms and vectors, attracts stray dogs, and pollutes the surface and ground water. During the last two decades, as a result of industrial development, more and more wastes are being generated. This is more hazardous than municipal waste as it is ignitable, corrosive, reactive, or toxic and can pollute the ground water used for farming.

8. Lack of Employment Opportunities: Migrants to the urban areas are hopeful of employment as the towns and cities are expected to provide numerous job opportunities. But they get frustrated when their hopes are belied, as it is not easy to procure an employment commensurate with their qualifications and skills. Graduates and postgraduates working as peons and rickshaw-pullers are a common sight. Although the lower class migrants are mostly absorbed in building or construction work and in the labour force of the factories, the semi-literates form an unstable, excitable mass who are eventually used by anti-social hoodlums for sinister and sadistic designs and diabolical actions of arson and looting during agitations.

9. Increasing Social Development Problems: Urbanization, according to Kingsley Davis, represents a revolutionary change in the whole pattern of social life.[14] To quote a UN report, 'The explosive nature of urban growth and the dire poverty in which it typically takes place, poses special problems for social development. Illiterate, unskilled and socially bewildered rural migrants fill squatter shack towns and find little work, a bare subsistence and barren opportunities for self-employment. They are nearly a complete burden on the treacherously thin layer of public services. Illegitimacy, disease and crime symbolize demoralizing social enzymes at work.'[15] Besides, many immigrants remain semi-urbanized, as they maintain strong ties with their native culture. The immigrants with the same culture and background usually have a strong tendency to congregate together for various social reasons. With a variety of jobs in urban areas, various castes and communities cannot retain their traditional occupations. The migrants may thus influence the social character of the cities and generate social problems and shortage of social amenities.

10. Ruralization of Urban Areas: Another problem of urbanization is the transfer of the phenomenon of ruralization to urban centres, especially those traits of rural living which give the towns and cities their ugly looks and cause unhygienic conditions, enormously straining the municipal administration and civic services. The rural migrants, unable to get employment in urban areas, continue with their traditional rural occupations, such as animal husbandry and livestock. This results in spreading of cowdung all over the streets; urban centres being crowded with buffaloes, cows, goats, poultry birds, pigs, and stray cattle; and the green belts and parks turning into grazing grounds and cattle sheds.[16]

11. Encroachment on Agricultural Lands: The process of urbanization has also assumed a new dimension of encroachment on agricultural lands at an unprecedented rate. For example, urbanization in Haryana has swallowed up over five lakh acres of fertile rival land in the past 23 years since its inception in 1966. The proximity of Faridabad and Gurgaon to Delhi has accelerated the pace of urbanization in the villages. The areas between Delhi and Faridabad, Delhi and Gurgaon, Delhi and Bahadurgarh, and Delhi and Sonepat are all merging into large urban agglomeration and the agricultural land between Delhi and these towns of Haryana has thus been lost forever.

12. Other Problems of Urbanization: The urban centres suffer from numerous other evils of city life. The rural migrants feel bewildered when they experience that the city people are selfish, self-centred, and do not bother about what is happening to others; one is totally lost amidst the din and monotony of the rat race, and no one has the time to pause and look around. Most of the city folk are losing touch with the Indian culture and are becoming more and more Westernized. Moral values thrive in rural areas even today. Elders are respected, guests welcome, love and affection for fellow beings are still found in plenty. In towns and cities there is moral decay. Selfishness and devil-may-care attitudes have made the city life boring. The migrants are often alone, resentful, and vulnerable to drug-addiction, the contaminating influence of city life.

Major Policy Pronouncements in Relation to Urbanization, Urban Planning and Development

In order to meet the challenges posed by the accelerated process of urbanization and the problems created by it, as reflected in the fast deteriorating conditions of essential civic services in urban India as discussed earlier, it was only in the Third Five Year Plan that the national planners had addressed to the detailed study of urbanization and its menacing impact on urban areas. The public policy issues in relation to urbanization, urban planning, and development as delineated in the various five year Plans are as follows:

The Third Five Year Plan (1961–66)

The Third Plan looked at urbanization as an important aspect of the process of economic and social development. It had observed that there were many problems associated with urbanization such as rural–urban migration; levels of living in urban and rural areas; relative costs of providing economic and social services in towns of varying sizes; housing for different consumer groups; provision of facilities like water supply, sanitation, transport, and power; pattern of economic development; location and dispersal of industries; civic administration; and fixed policies of land use planning. It had attributed high costs of urban development to rising costs of providing housing, water supply, drainage, transport, and other services. Unemployment, overcrowding, growth of slums, and rise in the number of persons without shelter tended to worsen the urban situation further. To quote the Third Plan:

> The problems to be faced were formidable in size and complexity, and solutions for them could be found only if their nature was fully appreciated not only by the State Governments, but also by municipal administrations and by the public generally and if an increasing amount of community effort and citizenship participation could be called forth within each urban area.

In laying down the development policy, the Plan had accordingly suggested that: (*a*) as far as possible, new industries should be established away from large and congested cities; (*b*) the concept of region should be adopted in the planning of large industries; (*c*) the rural and urban components of development should be blended properly in community development projects or other areas within the district; and (*d*) diversification of occupational pattern should be attempted in each rural area in order to reduce the dependence on agriculture. It had proposed the following to achieve these objectives:

1. Control of urban land values through public acquisition of land and appropriate fiscal policies.
2. Physical planning of the use of land and the preparation of master plans.
3. Defining tolerable minimum standards for housing and other services to be provided for towns according to their requirements and also prescribing maximum standards to the extent necessary.
4. Strengthening of municipal administration for undertaking new development responsibilities.

The Fourth Five Year Plan (1969–74)

The Fourth Plan observed that for the lack of financial and organisational resources, not much headway could be made with implementation of the development plans which the Third Five Year Plan had prepared for a large number of urban cities. It expressed concern about the alarming growth of population in the metropolitan centres and other larger cities. For the metropolitan giants like Calcutta and Bombay, it suggested the policy to prevent future growth of population as well as to decongest them by a phased dispersal of population, and for other cities, to stabilize population at a desirable optimum figure and planning new towns in the region for absorbing the spill-over population, and to explore the development potentials of small towns in a region in this context.

The Fourth Plan laid special emphasis on the following important problems:

1. In the rapidly growing cities, it was necessary to create larger planning regions, while the jurisdictions of corporations or municipalities should coincide with the boundaries of appropriate planning areas.
2. Planning had to be supported by full legal structure for formulation and implementation. The importance of planning law had thus to be realized.
3. The administrative structure of the local implementation of development plans.
4. Specific functional schemes on water supply, roads, etc. had to be cast within the frame of a long term plan, and in the long run, plans of development of cities and towns must be self-financing.
5. Due to rapid increase in urban land values, land in urban areas had become a potent source of unearned income. Rising land prices, on the other hand, stood in the way of low income housing. So, a radical urban land policy had to be evolved to facilitate speedy and planned urban development.
6. To solve the housing problem in urban areas was an uphill task. Through proper planning and land policy an adequate supply of housing had to be attempted.
7. So far as urban slums are concerned, the immediate attempt would be to ameliorate the living conditions of slums.

Thus, the Fourth Plan suggested a much more cautious policy, taking due cognizance of the constraint of resources of all kinds.

The Fifth Plan (1975–80)

The Fifth Plan had noted that despite growing awareness in the states of the problems of urban development, they had not been able to make much headway in taking comprehensive action for the adoption and implementation of master plans, due primarily to financial and organizational bottlenecks at the local level. The Fifth Plan had identified the broad objectives of: (*a*) augmenting civic services in urban centres in order to make them fit for a reasonable level of living; (*b*) trying to deal with the problems of metropolitan cities on a more comprehensive and regional basis; (*c*) developing the smaller towns and new urban centres to ease the pressure of urbanization on the larger metropolitan centres; and (*d*) conceiving and pushing through projects of national importance, such as those relating to metropolitan areas or inter-state projects.

The Plan had underlined the need for a multifaceted strategy to tackle the complex problems of urbanization. For a more desirable and balanced spatial distribution of economic activity, it had emphasized on the adoption of appropriate measures to attract industries to new urban centres and to create certain disincentives to prevent the city-ward movement of population.

The Sixth Five Year Plan (1980–85)

The Sixth Five Year Plan had emphasized on an Integrated Development of Small and Medium Towns (IDSMT) for which the central sector was to provide Rs 96 crores with the concerned state governments making matching contributions. The plan also provided for the cluster of villages approach for provision of roads in the case of hilly, tribal, desert and coastal areas where the population was sparse and settlements were located far apart from one another. It had a definite approach to poverty issues—provision of additional consumption benefits and better and more equitable distribution of health, education, sanitation, housing, and drinking water, and slum upgrading and environmental improvement programmes. Housing programme for economically weaker sections formed another integral part of the Plan.

The Seventh Five Year Plan (1985–90)

The Plan provided for the continuation of the scheme of IDSMT and revised the eligibility criteria to include towns with a population up to three lakh. It also laid greater stress on sites and services, slum improvement, urban community development projects (UCD), Integrated Child Development Service (ICDS), and schemes of house and shelter upgradation. It made the first conscious effort to solve the problems of urban poverty in a coordinative manner by developing a package of programmes such as Nehru Rozgar Yojna, urban basic services for the poor, environmental improvement of urban slums, low cost sanitation, night shelter scheme for footpath dwellers, etc. It placed considerable emphasis on improvement in the living conditions of dwellers, a major thrust towards employment generation and creation of productive jobs, housing for economically weaker sections and low income groups with HUDCO support, expansion of nutrition programmes, public distribution system, national housing planning with the assistance from National Housing Bank, etc.

National Urbanization Policy Resolution, 1975

The Town and Country Planning Organization of the Government of India had prepared the National Urbanization Policy Resolution in 1975. Its main feature was the conscious recognition of the fact that rural development and urban development are complimentary to each other and both have to be pursued together to promote healthy human settlement patterns throughout the country. The main objectives of the policy were identified as follows:

1. Evolving a spatial pattern of economic development and location of a hierarchy of human settlement consistent with the exploitation of natural and human resources of the region, and ensuring functional linkages *inter se*.
2. Securing the optimum distribution of population between rural and urban settlements within each region and also among the towns of various sizes.
3. Securing the distribution of economic activities in small and medium-size towns and in new growth centres in order to achieve maximum economic growth for the future.
4. Controlling and, where necessary, arresting the further growth of metropolitan cities by dispersal of economic activities, legislative measures and establishment of new counter magnets in the region.
5. Providing a minimum level of services for improving the quality of life in rural and urban areas and reducing gradually the differences between rural and urban living.

The Policy Resolution spelt out that at the bottom of hierarchy, towns having a population between 5,000 and 9,999 would be agro-service centres wherefrom necessary inputs for agricultural production would be supplied. In the next size class, towns with population ranging between 10,000 and 50,000 would have agricultural processing industries with appropriate market yards. Necessary infrastructure for the development of large-scale industries would be available in towns having population between 50,000 and 250,000. These towns if properly planned and developed could act as intermediate dams checking the migration of population to large and metropolitan cities.

Within this broad framework, the different urban centres have been sought to be classified into: metropolitan cities with a population of one million and above; Class I cities with a population of 100,000 to one million; medium size towns with a population of 50,000 to 100,000; and small towns with a population of 5,000 to 50,000.

With a view to guiding future urban growth along desirable lines, the Resolution had suggested action programmes in respect of the above types of urban centres. In the first category, the fast expanding metropolitan cities had to be subjected to proper planning and development to guard against unregulated urban growth in future. These cities had been expanding mainly due to the existence of a strong economic infrastructure which attracted new industries. Despite many policy pronouncements discouraging further growth of industries in the metropolitan cities, in fact new industries continued to be attracted toward these centres, hence, a policy of decongestion of these cities and decentralization of industries needed to be followed up by a proper industrial location policy that would provide incentives to new industrial units to move away from the metropolitan cities. Also such a policy would have certain disincentives for industries to come up in the already congested metropolitan centres.

Another method would be to extend the planning frame to a wide region surrounding the metropolis and to set up new towns to receive population over-spills from the metropolitan cities. The intermediate cities which offered the second best opportunity for the development of large and medium industries, if developed within proper plan frames and endowed with necessary urban infrastructure, could also act as counter magnets to the metropolitan cities. As agriculture would continue to undergo a process of modernization, various farm and non-farm needs of the rural population could be met from the medium towns where agro-industries and small-scale industries could be located, providing in the process opportunities for employment to job-seekers. The small towns at the bottom of the hierarchy would grow as rural service centres catering to the needs of their surrounding areas. The Policy Resolution has also suggested the regulation of urban land and improvement of living conditions of the urban poor. As regards urban land, the suggestion was to ensure equitable distribution of this scarce resource.

Implementation of Urbanization Policy Directives: Measures Taken to Meet the Challenges of Urbanization

The urbanization policy directives as announced in the successive Five Year Plans and the National Urban Policy Resolution have been laudable but unfortunately they have not been fully implemented with the result that the process of urbanization continues at an alarming rate; it presents a frightening spectre in the form of unplanned urban growth resulting in development of slums, deterioration in civic amenities to a breaking point, and rendering cities and towns unliveable. Despite repeated policy pronouncements recommending location of big industries from the larger metropolitan cities, major new industries continue to be set up in or around the metropolitan cities, the urban land policy has not been seriously pursued, and so on. Yet there is no denying the fact that urbanization and its various problems has been receiving the attention of central, state, and local governments since the Third Five Year Plan period. There have been some notable achievements in the field of urbanization, urban planning and development, as is evident from the following credit points:

1. The Town and Country Planning Organization was set up by Government of India in 1962 as the apex technical advisory body on matters relating to urban and regional planning strategies, research, monitoring, and evaluation of central government schemes and development policies. It also provides consultative services of project assistance to different state organizations. The state governments/union territories have their own departments of town and country planning to advise regarding urban planning and development.

2. Master plans have been prepared for all major towns and cities to promote orderly growth of urban areas and to check unregulated urbanization.

3. The concept of regional planning is being promoted especially in large metropolitan areas to reduce their burden of unmanageable population by arranging for the habitation of over-spill population in the new towns being set up in the region.

4. Efforts are being made to improve the infrastructural facilities in the urban areas, such as water supply and sewerage, transportation, etc. under the centrally sponsored schemes for Integrated Development of Small and Medium Town (IDSMT) with a view to reduce the migration of population from rural areas to major urban areas, to generate employment by creating resource generating ventures in small and medium towns, and also to provide sufficient infrastructure facilities in these towns so that their hinterland is served better. The World Bank is also assisting various states in urban development programmes.

5. The awareness about creating a healthy urban environment is growing day by day and pollution problems—water pollution and air pollution in particular—are receiving due attention at the various levels of the government and community as is substantiated by the enactment of Water (Prevention and Control of Pollution) Act, 1974 and the Air (Prevention and Control of Pollution) Act, 1981 passed by the Central government providing for the constitution of the central board for the prevention and control of water and air pollution and the setting up of similar boards by the state governments, and enforcement of these Acts by taking punitive action for the violation of the provisions of the Acts.

6. The problem of urban slums is being tackled vigorously. The initial idea of slum clearance has been replaced by the concept of slums improvement, and efforts are being made to give the slum dwellers a better deal through the scheme of Environmental Development of Urban Slums for the slum population between 51 to 56 millions in 1990. The scheme was made an integral part of the Minimum Needs Programme (MNP) in 1976. The scheme aims at ameliorating their living conditions through provisions of drinking water, drainages, community baths, community latrines, widening and paving of existing lanes, street lighting, and other community facilities. The total outlay on this scheme during the Seventh Five Year Plan was Rs 269.95 crores based on a per capita expenditure of Rs 300 per slum dweller for a target of nine million slum dwellers, which has since been achieved.

7. To meet the housing needs in the urban areas, the Housing and Urban Development Corporation (HUDCO) was set up in April 1970 at the national level to provide capital funds for housing and allied urban development operations. HUDCO is a major instrument of national housing policy and has been entrusted with the priority programmes of low cost sanitation, night shelters for footpath dwellers, shelter upgradation under Nehru Rozgar Yojna, etc. It is a multi-dimensional and multi-functional organization addressing the entire gamut of shelters' issues in the country. Similarly housing boards have been set up in almost all the states to increase the supply of housing in the urban areas. National Housing Policy has been announced. National Housing Bank has been set up to facilitate availability of housing finance.[17]

8. Administrative organization for urban development is being revamped by funnelling more funds for municipal governments, improving their personnel structure and training the municipal employees through Regional Centres for Urban and Environmental Studies at Bombay, Lucknow and Hyderabad in addition to the Centre for Urban Studies, IIPA, New Delhi.

9. Urban development authorities have been set up in the states to devote exclusive attention to urban development such as building of new roads; construction of trunk sewers, water reservoirs, houses, etc.; acquisition, development and disposal of urban lands; planning and construction of new colonies, and similar other capital development functions. The achievements of these urban development authorities, such as Delhi Development Authority, are commendable in tackling some of the urban problems in a satisfactory manner.

10. Our policy makers have not been unaware of the problems of urban poverty. The Seventh Five Year Plan had taken explicit note of the growing incidence of poverty in urban areas and placed considerable

emphasis on improvement in the living conditions of slum dwellers, employment generation and improving the access of the urban poor to basic amenities such as education, health care, sanitation, and safe drinking water. The governments had accordingly introduced schemes and programmes like slum improvement and the sites and services schemes, nutrition supplement programmes, Integrated Child Development Scheme (ICDS), Urban Basic Services (UBS) and urban community development (UCD) projects, etc. for the amelioration of the urban poor.

11. The most notable development in the context of urbanization in India has been the setting up of Ministry of Urban Development in 1985 as the nodal ministry to oversee in totality the process of urbanization and government reaction to the process, to evolve urban policy, and to try and ensure that suitable plan priorities are assigned to urban development together with adequate funds. Since urban planning, development, and management is a state subject, the states have an elaborate governmental and organizational structure comprising state departments of town and country planning, environment, urban development, local government (urban), public health engineering, etc. which either individually or in different combination of departments manage urban affairs.

12. Ministry of Urban Development had appointed the National Commission on Urbanization under the chairmanship of Charles Cores to look into the issues of urbanization. The Commission submitted its report in August 1988, in which it has made significant recommendations in respect of various facets of urbanization and the management of urban governments with a view to effectively tackle the problems caused by urbanization and ensure better administration of urban local bodies. The government has since considered favourably some of these recommendations and included them in the Nagarpalika Bill of 1989.

13. Government of India, in the Ministry of Urban Development, had introduced Nagarpalika Bill 1989 (65th Constitution Amendment Bill) in August 1989 to revamp and revitalize urban local bodies. The Bill had failed in the Rajya Sabha. The government again introduced it as the Constitution (74th Amendment) Bill in September 1991. The Bill aimed at reconstituting, reclassifying, democratizing, and strengthening urban governments by giving them more powers, greater finances on the recommendations of state finance commissions, elections managed by the state election commissions, and by granting them constitutional status. The Bill had been hailed as historic and revolutionary. It was passed as the Constitution (74th Amendment) Act, 1992. It will usher in a new era for urban local governments and ensure their better administration in grappling with the enormous problems of urbanization.

14. *National Capital Region Plan*—In order to check migration to Delhi and mitigate the problems arising out of continued migration, National Capital Region Planning Board was set up in March 1985 to propose a plan for the National Capital Region (NCR). The Plan is the only statutory plan of its own kind in the country, providing planned development of an inter-state region, which has been prepared with the active involvement of not only the participating state governments of Haryana, Rajasthan, and Uttar Pradesh and the Union Territory of Delhi Administration but also includes proposals which have been prepared in consultation with the concerned Central ministries. The NCR Plan, 2001, has laid primary stress on development of infrastructure, both at the regional and local levels and large-scale employment generation in the identified priority towns to prevent continued migration. In the implementation of the NCR Plan, as many as 50 projects comprising residential, industrial, commercial, institutional infrastructures, and work-cum-shelter programmes for informal sector activities were taken up, mainly in Meerut, Hapur, Bulandshahar-Khurja in Uttar Pradesh; Gurgaon and Panipat in Haryana; and Alwar and Bhiwadi in Rajasthan. The allocation of resources during the Seventh Plan had been meagre and, therefore, the investment in the projects could not provide significant impact in checking migration to Delhi.

The Union Government is planning to create a national capital region (NCA) around Chandigarh, on the Delhi pattern, covering an area up to a radius of 20 km from the periphery of Chandigarh, including two satellite towns of Mohali (Punjab) and Panchkula (Haryana), for development and to create an authority under a statute to be enacted by the Parliament for the implementation of the proposal. The formation of the NCR aims at integrated development of Chandigarh and its suburban areas. This will help in substantially reducing population pressure on Chandigarh, saving the ecology of the city and preserving green belts in different sectors of the union territory. Punjab Government is also setting up a new town, Anandgarh, to meet these objectives. It has also proposed to develop some 'counter magnet centres' in the suburban areas of the union territory with adequate transport arrangements. This would help middle and lower middle class people to own houses at cheaper prices.[19]

15. *Generation of more employment in non-agricultural sector*—In order to stem migration from rural to urban areas the government should generate more employment in the non-agricultural sectors, and it should speed up the implementation of growth centres to improve non-farm employment opportunities.

The FICCI is also of the view that in order to improve non-farm employment opportunities, the operational scope of the district industries centres (DICs) should be widened to encourage the development of village and small-scale industries in rural areas, and they should be better geared to set up short gestation and low cost establishments; the government should give a boost to the agricultural waste based industries. According to FICCI's reckoning, as much as 322 million tonnes of agricultural waste including crop residues such as paddy, jawar, wheat, and gram straws are available which could be utilized for substitution of industrial chemicals, generation of non-renewable energy and inorganic fertilisers.[20]

16. *Training scheme for rural youth and rural poor women*—With a view to ameliorating the rural people, the government has launched a massive scheme to train rural youth to make them capable of earning their livelihood. The scheme, launched under the training of rural youth for self-employment (TRYSEM), is applicable to the rural youth in the age group of 18 to 35 years; 50 per cent of those undergoing training under the scheme should belong to the scheduled castes/scheduled tribes communities and a minimum of 40 per cent should be women.

Reasons for the Failure to Check Urbanization

Despite the remedial measures taken to halt the process of urbanization, it continues unabated. The causes responsible for the failure of reversing urbanization and solving urban problems can be identified as follows:

Population Explosion

India's population is set to explode. Population growth at the rate of 2 to 3 per cent has inevitably led us to an unmanageable 100 crores by the turn of the century. Twenty-five million urbanites in 1947 will have a zooming jump to 350 million in 2001, the parallel to which may be hard to find in the annals of history and civilization. Demographers predict that the total land and water resources in the country will not be able to produce enough food for a population of 'dreaded level'. All this would bring a train of miseries—starvation deaths, diseases, unrest, violence, law and order disturbances, etc. Our population control programmes must succeed, otherwise even the best of urbanization strategies will fail.

Absence of National Urbanization Policy

A comprehensive national urbanization policy has not been evolved so far, although piecemeal methods to come to grips with the gigantic problem of urbanization have been adopted by the central and state governments. The connecting theme in all these efforts has been a planned intervention in the process of urbanization. A comprehensive national urbanization policy is, therefore, required to be formulated and implemented to arrest migration to urban areas and render our towns and cities liveable.

Lack of Political Will

Population is not being controlled due to lack of political will notwithstanding the massive financial inputs for family planning. Similarly the planners tend to ascribe the failure to combat urbanization to the lack of will on the part of the governments, as in a democracy it is difficult to reconcile conflicting interests which influence implementation of decisions. The urbanization policies and urban development plans, however well intentioned these may be, cannot, therefore be implemented.

Pressure of Interest Groups

Urban planning, in its manifestations of master plans for various cities and redevelopment programmes, fail due to conflict of interests and influence of interest groups. The zonal plans, in spite of the care taken by the planners in identifying different areas of redevelopment, err in assuming that the people would be willing to shift; they discount or ignore the political influence that the business and the industry could wield as organized interest groups.

Town Planning Authorities Lack Statutory Backing

The Town and Country Planning Organization, Government of India, and the departments of town and country planning in the states prepare plans for urban development including master plans which, with their rigid land-use, zoning, and development control, have proved extremely poor instruments for regulating the dynamic process of urban growth. The core problems of urban planning are not only spatial but functional as well. A master plan fails to be truly comprehensive if its comprehensiveness is restricted to land-use allocations only. Moreover, master plans are violated with impunity by the vested interests. The town and country planning authorities function as advisory bodies only and they lack any statutory backing to get their development plans implemented.

Low Priority to Urban Development in the National Planning Process

After nearly five decades of planned economic development, urban development continues to remain isolated from the national planning process. In the five year plans so far, urban development has been treated as an item of social expenditure with the result that it accounts for a very small fraction of the total plan budget. There are competing demands for plan funds. The investments on urban development have low priority, as these are generally considered as consumption-oriented. Rural lobby is much more powerful and is naturally able to get more funds from the plan budget, as much as 50 per cent for rural development in the current plan.

Limited Role of Central Government

The country being federal, the central government can at best give policy leadership in urbanization and urban development, and the actual implementation would depend on the state governments, under whose jurisdiction urban local government and urban development fall. Moreover, the plan funds that are directly expendable by the centre on urban development are too meagre to goad the states to fall in line with the central policy guidelines.

Financial Scarcity of the States

The states being in acute financial stress are unable to divert funds for urban development. Metropolitan cities like Calcutta, Mumbai, and Chennai require thousands of crores of rupees for their redevelopment and supply of basic civic services, which they can ill afford but for the Centre coming to their rescue. The gigantic problems of urban development ultimately have to be shouldered by the state governments. Yet there is general reluctance to face these problems. The state plans usually pay lip service to urban development since agriculture and other items have much more pressing claims. In general, the cities and towns are exhorted to pursue urban development tasks by raising more resources from their own domestic sources of revenue, without depending much on state financial assistance.

Antiquated Organization of Urban Bodies

The municipal bodies are antiquated organizations dating back to the nineteenth century. The modernization of their administrative structure and operation is long overdue. In most municipal organizations, the political processes have failed to match the needs of growing urban problems. Nor has the quality and quantity of managerial personnel corresponded to the ever increasing administrative responsibilities. The Constitution (74th Amendment) Act, 1992, is expected to remove the existing deficiencies in the structure and organization of municipal bodies, and to revitalize and strengthen them to meet the challenges posed by urbanization.

Role of Politics

Politics has played a great role in determining the urban policies and in securing their implementation. Politics is viewed as an activity intended to make one set of interests prevail over the other, and as an attempt by various forces to maintain and establish supremacy over urban environment. It is because of the game of politics that the various political parties at the helm of affairs in the state and local governments indulge in, that the urban bodies are superseded and the urban legislation aimed at the orderly development of urban areas is flouted by vested interests.

Need for National Urbanization Policy

Despite the care taken by the urban development policies since planned development in our country began, the problems being faced by urban India are colossal even now. The growth of cities and towns is not uniform. The infrastructural facilities are totally inadequate and in some cities are in a critical stage. The availability of urban land and housing especially for the poor is scarce. About 25 per cent of the urban population lives in slums and squatter settlements. Immigrants continue to flow into the urban areas and will continue to do so in the future. Hence, it is necessary to take a look into the long-term perspective of channelizing urbanization, to lay down a national urbanization policy and to take effective measures for its implementation so that a healthy and orderly urban development takes place in the years to come. This was the view expressed by experts on urbanization in 1975, but it holds good even today.

Essentials of National Urbanization Policy

Urbanization may be defined as a process by which a population becomes concentrated in cities. The process may proceed either through an increase in the number of cities or through a rise in the size of the population in every city. Urbanization in India is taking place due to the process of industrialization by various measures in different parts of the country. In fact, urbanization is accomplished through a shift from agrarian to industrial economy. The migration is from village to cities, as well as from cities to cities and from one state to another. The migration from rural areas to urban or semi-urban areas is largely due to the fact that the migrant population is in search of better or alternative job opportunities. Since only lucrative employment can promise a better material well-being, it seems impossible to stop people from migrating from villages to cities. This facility cannot be denied to anyone because it is the birthright of an individual to look for suitable opportunities to ameliorate his condition. And since it seems nearly impossible to make any plans for absorbing the migrant population in urban areas in a well-ordered way, slums will continue to exist as shadows of urbanization.

A comprehensive national urbanization policy will have to cover all types of towns and cities. But because of the federal political structure of the country, as also the lack of a common national language, it seems well nigh impossible to frame any national policy of urbanization that can be implemented in different parts of the country without provincial resistance. Moreover, Indians, by and large, are a very informal people and, therefore, resent any kind of formal control or organization. Anyhow, a national urbanization policy should have the following essentials:

1. About 80 per cent of the population of India lives in the villages and is, by and large, engaged in agricultural and allied activities. Considering that the population of the country will be one billion by the turn of the century, we will have to cater to a population of approximately 25 million people, who will be migrating from the rural hinterland to various urban areas. At present, about 55 per cent of our population is engaged in agricultural activity. So, we will have to plan our urban centres to absorb this enormous exodus of population from the rural areas. Agriculture has not so far been fully developed and utilized in our country. There is a great potential in this activity which must be exploited. For example, Punjab, which is approximately equal to the area of a large district of Madhya Pradesh, can yield so much of agricultural produce as to be called the granary of India. Thus, the vast tracts of land which are there in the country can be put to greater use for agriculture.

2. A national policy of urbanization should be based on a three-tier approach comprising (*a*) preventive measures, (*b*) remedial measures, and (*c*) conceptual measures.

(*a*) *Preventive measures*: A strong agrarian base, to be developed to its full potential, should be created by diversifying agricultural activity. This will also entail the location and planning of collection and distribution centres at appropriate places throughout the country. Adequate measures, including legislation, will have to be taken to check political exploitation of established urban areas by contiguous states. For example, Panchkula (Haryana) and S.A.S. Nagar (Punjab) are parasites on Chandigarh because these towns exploit all that is good in the 'City Beautiful', without having to spend anything themselves. These towns have been flourishing on the urban infrastructure of Chandigarh such as educational, health, and commercial facilities. The same is true of Delhi, with NOIDA (Uttar Pradesh) and Faridabad and Gurgaon (Haryana) straining the Capital's infrastructure and resources to the hilt.

(*b*) *Remedial measures*: To relieve some of the existing cities from congestion, satellite towns should be built by decentralizing industry and commerce. For making preventive as well as remedial measures effective, a national plan based on detailed studies of regional requirements should be drawn up.

(*c*) *Conceptual measures*: New urban centres should be built from the centre outward, using high technology in the heart of the town, followed by indigenous technology, to be surrounded by a ring of farmland. Use of solar, water, and wind energy should be popularized to create a pollution-free environment which is ideal for the pursuit of multifarious urban activities. The emphasis should be on the creation of energy-efficient human settlements, involving minimal travel within the 'neopolis'. Architecture of the 'new city' will similarly be designed with energy as the basic constraint.

3. Adequate infrastructure will have to be planned on a regional basis and suitably located in various parts of the country. Appropriate strategies will have to be worked out to ensure smooth implementation of the national urbanization policy. Unless the centre plays an active and helpful role in the process of implementation, not much can be expected of any national plan and programme. It is, therefore, imperative that some of the key-centres for providing implementational infrastructure on a regional basis should function under the care of the central government itself.

4. No national urbanization policy can ever work in India unless it takes into account regional constraints, the most important of which will be geography and the chief occupation of the people of different states; for instance, in Punjab, where the economy is based on agriculture, the concentration of population in isolated urban centres will be antithetical. Urbanization based on ribbon development may be more appropriate here. Geographically, what works best in plains may not be workable on a hilly terrain. The topography of the hills precludes any large-scale development that may be done as a matter of course in the plains. Similarly, due to its elongated geographical shape as well as sea-front location combined with fishery, coconut cultivation and coir industry, the state of Kerala requires a linear development. Besides, it has the unique virtue of having obscure urban rural boundaries.

5. The national urbanization policy should be subjected to a periodic review, say, every 10 years, so that it is continually updated in view of the new scientific and technological advancements.

6. Good urbanization is an enormous money-making proposition. Beyond a limited initial investment, it does not require large resources as it can generate its own. However, an inherent malaise which will have to be checked is the people's ambition to make quick bucks by treating land as a commercial proposition (real estate). The customary 'in kind' transaction in agrarian economy changing over to 'in cash' business gives an individual a heightened sense of immediacy and personal worth—which he would like to exploit to the maximum.

7. Schools of architecture and planning can play a vital role in creating professional awareness of the need for good urbanization policies at the national level and their implementation in the pursuit of making India a nation with a rich tradition of culture recreated in modern terms.

8. As a major strategy to achieve positive results, the decision-making as well as implementing agencies will have to be made by autonomous organizations with minimal political and bureaucratic interference.

9. As the bulk of the population to be affected by such policies will be rural, it will be in the fitness of things to associate more and more experts, such as architects, planners, urban designers, environmentalists, economists, sociologists, demographers, etc., to get a first-hand experience and background of Indian rural life and culture.

10. Proper studies should also be conducted to identify what is characteristically 'Indian' in our rural art and vernacular architecture.

11. A chain of data banks should be set up throughout the country for monitoring the urbanization programmes and providing feedback for policy reviews.

12. What is worth preserving must be preserved not so much as a 'museum' material as in the form of a living tradition by incorporating it in the planning and design fabric of all new urban centres.

In a nutshell, an urbanization policy in India may work much better if we decide to ruralize our cities rather than urbanize our villages. This may be absolutely necessary, not in a chauvinistic sense but as a rationale, for, after all, India can remain India only when we preserve and continue those time-honoured traditions which are characteristically 'Indian'. Otherwise, in our misguided ambition to urbanize on a national scale, we may lose our Indian identity because industrialization, which is a major tool of accomplishing urbanization, has a tendency to impersonalize everything, including human relations, cultural traditions, and lifestyles.[21]

Conclusion

Urbanization in India, as elsewhere in the world, is taking place at an accelerated pace. The urban population in India, which was 25 million in 1947, is projected to reach 350 million in 2001. This unprecedented growth in urbanization is attributed to migration of the people from rural to urban areas, natural increase in population, and the reclassification of rural into urban areas. Factors contributing to migration from rural to urban areas are the push and pull factors; the former forcing or pushing the rural people to towns and cities due to explosion in population, the pressure on agricultural land, and the lack of employment avenues, and the latter attracting or luring the rural people to urban areas due to better job opportunities, availability of civic amenities, and comfortable standards of living. The other factors stimulating urbanization are: industrialization, economic growth, expansion of the means of transport, increase in trade and commerce, establishment of new towns in the industrial zone, partition of the country, and militants' activities.

The phenomenal rise in urbanization has posed serious challenges and grave problems for the urban governments in the form of shortage of housing, strain on civic amenities, haphazard growth of towns, growth of slums, urban poverty, scarcity of urban land, menace of pollution, lack of employment opportunities, social maladjustments, ruralization of urban areas, encroachment on agricultural lands, various ills of city life, erosion of moral values, etc.

The government has been making major policy pronouncements in relation to urbanization, urban planning, and development in Five Year Plans with a view to combat urbanization and taking necessary steps to ensure that large size cities, especially the 'one million' cities, should not be allowed to expand any further and as far as possible new industries and other economic activities which accentuate urban growth should be located away from these centres. New urban centres in proximity to the metropolitan cities should be developed as counter-magnets so that the migrant population can go into these counter-magnet locations and, thereby, reduce the pressure on the metropolitan cities. New urban nuclie should be planned in resource-rich areas with a view to generate employment in these areas. The medium size towns should be provided with adequate services and amenities, and properly laid out industrial estates and industrial areas should be set up so that they could attract new growth into them. The locations of these various growth centres and focal points are to be chosen within the scope of integrated regional or area development plans.

Efforts have also been made to urbanize rural areas by providing them with electricity supply, roads, water supply, hospitals and dispensaries, educational institutions, means of communication, etc., and thus improving the village life to bring the rural people closer to their urban counterparts. But despite all this, the urbanization trend is irrevocable; it is rather difficult to halt it. Yet, if better and more job opportunities were created and better amenities provided, perhaps the rate of rural migration would fall considerably. The population explosion needs to be controlled effectively. Other issues such as the formulation of a comprehensive national urbanization policy and its implementation; planned urban areas; enforcement of legislation relating to planned urban development; implementation of schemes, especially master plans for various cities prepared by the town and country planning authorities; execution of national capital region plans; restructuring of the urban governments to cope with their ever increasing problems; establishment of urban development authorities in place of multiple urban institutions like improvement trusts, water supply and sewerage boards, etc.; provision of adequate finances to the state governments by the central government and by the state governments to the local governments, commensurate with at least their obligatory functions; dispersal of government offices and industries from metropolitan cities and capitals to other cities; alleviation of urban poverty; renovation of slum areas; research in urban governments; evaluation of urban development programmes, etc., if addressed seriously with a strong political will, the process of urbanization can be controlled considerably and the urban areas can be made worth living.

NOTES AND REFERENCES

1. Projections made by the Expert Committee, Registrar General, Census, Government of India.
2. 'Report of the National Commission on Urbanisation', Volume 2 (New Delhi: Ministry of Urban Development, Government of India, 1988), pp. 55, 88.
3. Thomas Adam, *Encyclopaedia of Social Sciences*, Volume 3, p. 982.
4. John T. Howard, *Encyclopaedia Britannica*, Volume 5, p. 815.
5. 'Report of the Health Survey and Development Committee', Volume 1 (Delhi: Manager of Publications, 1940), p. 133.
6. 'Report of the National Commission on Urbanisation', Volume 2, pp. 165–66.
7. Aditya Parkash, 'Chandigarh's Future', *The Tribune*, 29 February 1992.
8. B.R. Kargal, 'Report of Town and Village Planning in India', in 'Report of the Health Survey and Development Committee', p. 83.
9. *Ibid.*
10. 'Report of the Health Survey and Development Committee', p. 86.
11. *Ibid.*
12. K.V. Sundram, *Urban and Regional Planning in India* (New Delhi: Vikas Publishing House, 1977), pp. 269–79.
13. 'Report of the Rural–Urban Relationship Committee', Volume 1 (New Delhi: Ministry of Health and Family Welfare, 1966), p. 46.
14. S.R. Maheshwari, *Local Government in India* (Meerut: Lakshmi Narain Aggarwal, 1984), p. 235.
15. Five Year Plans, Planning Commission, Government of India, New Delhi (1951–1990).
16. R.L. Khanna, *Municipal Government and Administration in India* (Chandigarh: Mohindra Capital Publishers, 1967), p. 3.
17. 'Report of the Study Team on Machinery of Government of India and its Procedure of Work', Part I (Delhi: Manager of Publication, 1967), p. 33.
18. 'Annual Report of the Ministry of the Urban Development', Government of India (1990–91), pp. 42–43.
19. 'Annual Report of the Town and Country Planning Department', Government of Punjab (1988–89).
20. Mohit Bhattacharya, 'Urbanisation and Urban Problems in India: Some Policy issues', *Nagarlok* 7 (4), October–December, 1975: 13.
21. P.N. Sharma, 'Integrating Urban and Rural Development', *Nagarlok* 7 (4). October–December, 1975: 55–58.
22. 'Report of the National Commission on Urbanisation', p. 65.

Evolution of Urban Local Government in India

The evolution of municipal government in India from the prehistoric times to the present day presents a chequered but a fascinating history. It has emerged through many stages and phases which can be broadly divided in chronological order and time sequence into the following:

1. From the prehistoric times to the advent of the British rule.
2. From the commencement of the British rule to its termination in 1947.
3. Post-independence period, from 1947 to the present day.

Phase-I (Ancient and Medieval Period)

Municipal government is deeply rooted in Indian history. The excavations in Mohenjodaro and Harappa of Indus Valley Civilization (3000 BC) speak volumes of the organized urban life in ancient times and reveal that they were amongst some of the oldest planned cities of the world.[1] They were laid out with wide streets, market places, public offices, community baths and drainage and sewerage system. They thus testify to the existence of a vigilant and effective municipal government. The people of the Indus civilization had the proud distinction of giving to the world its earliest cities, its first urban civilization, its first town planning, its first drainage system, and its earliest example of city government.

Reference to a highly organized system of urban local government can also be found in the Vedas, in the epics of *Ramayana* and *Mahabharata*, in the Upanishads and in Kautilya's *Arthshastra*.

The *Mahabharata* mentions that every town was administered by an officer assisted by a team of his subordinates.[2] Kautilya envisaged a regular plan of town administration which was specially designed to deal with the typical urban problems.[3] In his scheme of things the mayor of the city was called *nagaraka* who used to perform various functions in connection with day-to-day administration of the city. Like the Kautilyan *nagaraka,* there used to be a chief executive officer in the city administration in the post-Mauryan times also. One of the important duties of civic administration seems to have been a prompt arrangement of the city's sanitation which included maintenance of the drainage system and cleanliness of the roads. In those times, the village was the basic unit of local government and there was no clear dividing line between a village (*gram*) and a town (*nagar*). *Gramini* villages developed into large towns and city culture reached its high water mark in the Mauryan and the Gupta empires in their famous cities of Patliputra, Ujjain, and Takshila. Town administration was on a firm footing during the Gupta period. During this period the towns were generally administered by a council called the *Parishad*, and there was a provision of having elected administrative officers who used to play a crucial role in the city administration.[4] Megasthenes has given a graphic account of municipal administration of Chandra Gupta's Patliputra. 'The administrative council of the city', says Havell, 'as modelled upon that of village communities and it may be assumed that like the latter it was an elected body though certain matters were reserved for the control of imperial officials.'[5] Democracy was thus no exotic growth in India and centuries before the advent of Mughal or British rule, the stress was on self-governing institutions and a corporate life.[6]

Many of the cities like Delhi, Agra, Lucknow, Hyderabad, etc. bear the imprint of Muslim influence. The Sultanate of Delhi was despotic with a highly centralized bureaucracy. The civil administration of the city was vested in a Muhtasib. He had multifarious functions including looking after public utilities such as water supply and wells, provision of amenities for travellers, maintenance of public buildings, demolition of houses likely to collapse, supervising the markets, inspection of weights, and measures and prevention of adulteration of food, which in modern times are regarded as municipal functions. During the Mughal times municipal administration was vested in the 'Kotwal'.[7] In his classic *Aaini Akbari*, Abul Fazal has described his functions in minute details. He was the city governor, combining in him official powers and duties of the chief of the city police, magistrate and prefect of the municipal administration. In this period, structure of the society was predominantly feudal and, therefore, the vast powers and various functions of the state were centred in an individual or institution. The very nature and style of the Mughal Emperors were loath to any kind of democratic administration in the local areas. Democratic administration was denied not only to a city but the village was also stripped of its administrative functions. It was reduced to an executive committee of the village community on purely social affairs.[8] The local people were not associated with the management of civic affairs and the urban government functioned as direct dependence of and rigorously controlled by the central administration. It can thus be concluded that in medieval and Mughal India, there was no municipal institutions enjoying powers of self-government and the municipal self-government traditions of ancient India had simply withered away under the military despotism of the Sultanate of Delhi and the Mughal Empire.

Phase-II (British Period)

The development of municipal government since the advent of British rule in India can be divided into the following periods on the basis of the introduction and acceleration of democratization process and transfer or grant of powers and functions to urban local governments :

1. 1687 to 1881
2. 1882 to 1919
3. 1920 to 1937
4. 1937 to 1947

First Period (1687–1881)

The origin of municipal administration in India dates back to 1687 when a municipal corporation was set up at Madras under a charter granted by James II, the then British monarch with a view to transfer the financial burden of local administration to the local city council. In writing to the Madras Council on 28th September, 1687, the Directors, with the consent of the Crown, had observed, 'The people would more willingly and liberally disburse five shillings towards the public good being taxed by themselves, than six pence imposed by our despotic powers.'[9] A Royal Charter of 1720 established a mayor's court in each of the three presidency towns of Madras, Bombay, and Calcutta. These courts were more judicial than administrative bodies. A statutory basis of the urban local government was not provided until 1793 when the Governor-General in Council was empowered to appoint justices of peace for the presidency towns from among converted civilians and the British subjects, who were vested with the authority to impose taxes on houses and lands to provide for the sanitation of the towns. In 1842, the Bengal Act was passed to set up town committees for sanitary purposes but the Act failed to operate as it was based on voluntary principle, and the taxation enforceable under it was of a direct nature. In 1850, an Act was passed for the whole country permitting the formation on the application of the inhabitants, of local committees to make better provisions for public health and convenience. Though the Act still maintained the voluntary principle, it was more practicable as it made provision for the levy of indirect taxes to which the people were accustomed.

In 1863, the government's attention was drawn by the Royal Army Sanitation Commission to the appalling, unhealthy, and fast deteriorating sanitary conditions of towns all over the country. Consequential to this note of warning, the Government of India passed several municipal acts for various provinces authorizing governors to order the formation of a municipality in any urban area of the province. He could nominate any number of persons—a minimum of five—as its members, either *ex-officio* or otherwise, or direct the appointment by elections. The municipal committees were empowered to administer municipal funds but were obliged to expend the proceeds of taxes in the first instance for the maintenance of the police, and the surplus, if any, could be utilized for the sanitary improvements of the town.

The next step forward was taken in 1870 by the publication of Lord Mayor's Resolution in 1870 which in providing for a measure of decentralization from the centre to the provinces emphasized the idea of increased association of Indians in the administration and indicated the extension of municipal self government as the most promising field for its attainment. The resolution encouraged the general application of the principle of election with the avowed object of developing self government. The resolution declared,

> '[L]ocal interest, supervision and care are necessary to success in the management of funds devoted to education, medical relief and public works. The operation of this resolution in its full meaning and integrity will afford opportunities for the development of self government, for strengthening municipal institutions and for the association of natives and Europeans to a greater extent than before in the administration of local affairs. The central grants to the provinces were much less than the actual expenditure. They were, therefore, required to meet the balance by local taxation.[10]

In pursuance of this policy, municipal acts were passed which not only enlarged the municipal powers and extended the election system but also marked the beginning of the system of local finance. But in practice, the principle of election was introduced wholly or partially in a few places only and the members continued to be nominated in most of the municipal committees. The population of a municipality thus did not, in any sense, govern itself, except that some of its leading men, nominated by the government, were placed on the municipal body. The government of a municipality was, in fact, an oligarchy dependent on a superior power which might control its action to almost any conceivable extent. The control and supervision of the government over the municipalities was complete and they did no more than register the order of the Deputy Commissioner of the district.

The development of municipal government during this period confirms that it was introduced primarily to serve the British interests rather than promote self governing bodies in the country; that local government institutions were dominated by the British and most of the Indian population remained deprived of participation in their functioning; and that the dominant motive behind the institution of local government in India was to give relief to the imperial finances.

Second Period (1882–1909)

Lord Ripon's Resolution (1882)

The next stage of development of municipal government in India was Lord Ripon's famous resolution, of 18 May 1882.[11] The historic resolution is regarded as a landmark in the development of local government and is hailed as its Magna Charta. It became the foundation of local government and earned the title of 'Father of Local Self Government in India' for its founder. It explicitly aimed at satisfying adequately the national urge for self-government, and envisaged local bodies as an instrument of political and public education, and to this end, it advocated: (*a*) the establishment of a network of local self-government institutions, (*b*) the reduction of the official element to not more than a third of the total membership, (*c*) exercise of control from without and not from within, (*d*) a large measure of financial decentralization, and (*e*) the adoption of election as a means of constituting local bodies.

Lord Ripon's recommendations were accepted by various provincial governments and to give effect to the reforms envisaged therein, municipal acts were passed for the introduction of elective principle at the discretion of provincial governments to limit the number of official members to one-third of the total and to give municipal committees the power to elect their presidents subject to government approval.

The reforms enunciated by Lord Ripon for rejuvenation of local self government had initially met considerable success as is substantiated by the figures of elected members and presidents of municipal bodies. But subsequently these were hampered by a conservative paternalistic administration wedded to the cult of efficiency. As pointed out by Prof. Hugh Tinker, the number of municipal Chairman had been reduced, all presiding over petty municipalities. The actual implementation of Lord Ripon's reforms was thus half hearted and achieved little success. This could be attributed to several factors such as (*a*) the adoption of obstructive tactics of the bureaucracy, (*b*) the hostile attitude of Lord Curzon, the successor of Lord Ripon, who considered the reforms to be too radical to be implemented and preferred administrative efficiency to political education, (*c*) the Deputy Commissioner dominated these institutions as he enjoyed vast powers of supervision and control, and (*d*) elections had also proved unpopular as these were not based on adult franchise. The electorate comprised of only 2 per cent of the total urban population.

The educative principle was thus subordinated to immediate results.[12] The will of the Deputy Commissioner operated in all spheres of activity in the districts.[13] 'A rigid system of supervision was created which ran from the smallest municipality to the Secretary of State.'[14] Besides, the people did not have civic consciousness and their religious and caste basis was stronger which resulted in the emergence of communal electorate. Originally communal representation was intended to give representation to the Muslims in local bodies on account of their educational and economic backwardness,[15] but had subsequently to be conceded as a means of representation to the various religious communities.

Royal Commission on Decentralization (1907)

A significant development since Ripon's resolution came up in 1907, when the rising discontent among the Indian masses led to the appointment of the Royal Commission on Decentralization to enquire into the financial and administrative relations of the Government of India, and the provincial governments and the authorities subordinate to them.

The Commission examined the entire subject of local self government and attributed its failure to: (*a*) excessive official control, (*b*) narrow franchise, (*c*) meagre resources, (*d*) lack of education and training, (*e*) shortage of capable and committed persons, and (*f*) inadequate control of local bodies over services.

In order to increase devolution of power and gradual democratization of the local bodies, the Commission had recommended: (*a*) the chairman should be elected non-officially, (*b*) majority of the members should be elected non-officially, (*c*) municipalities should be given more powers of taxation and control over their budgets, and (*d*) large municipalities should be endowed with greater power and required to appoint qualified health officers along with the executive officers.

The Government of India, in its resolution of 28 April 1915, suggested the gradual implementation of these recommendations which were largely a replica of Lord Ripon's proposals of 1883. But a programme that was prominent in 1883 was hopelessly outdated in 1915.[16]

Punjab was the first province to incorporate the recommendations of the Royal Commission in its Municipal Act of 1911. The other provinces had thereafter passed similar Acts.

The acts provided for the reduction of official control over municipal bodies; the provincial governments could introduce the elective system in any municipality and permit the election of non-official chairman. But in practice, no material changes in the structure and style of functioning of the municipal institutions could be possible as the object of the acts was to retain the provisions of the previous acts as far as possible. No real progress had been therefore registered in municipal administration. The elective system remained at a rudimentary stage. Curiously enough, the number of elected non-official presidents had declined in 1918 as compared to their number in 1908. The Government of India Act, 1909, had introduced communal electorates for Muslims for legislative councils. In 1910, the Muslim League had demanded separate electorates in local bodies as well. Consequently some municipalities had been constituted on the basis of communal electorates. The introduction of communal electorates in municipal government had become a great impediment in its healthy development. The Montague–Chelmsford Report had rightly regarded the system of communal electorates as a very serious hindrance to the self-governing principles.[17] The Simon Commission had observed that communal dimension had impaired the efficiency of local bodies and it was clearly the greatest obstacle to the development of a sense of common citizenship which was the necessary basis for healthy civic life.[18]

It may be concluded from the above facts that during this period the roots of democracy started having their grip on the Indian mind and some progress was registered in widening the elected element in the constitution of urban local bodies, enlargement of functions and increase in powers, financial responsibility and financial resources. But as remarked by Simon Commission, no substantial progress was made in political and popular education in the art of self government; that local self government continued to be, as in the past, one of the functions of the District Officer and it was his will and not the will of the people that operated in the sphere of municipal administration; that the embryo of communal representation took birth in the local bodies which ultimately attained a mature shape in the political life terminating in the partition of the country.

Third Period (1927–37)

Government of India Resolution, 1918

The national movement for independence was gaining momentum, causing great concern to the government in Britain and India. With the outbreak of the First World War (1914–18), the British Government felt it necessary to solicit support and cooperation from the people of India. It, therefore, came out with the historic declaration of 20 August 1917 to seek increasing association of Indians in every branch of the administration and the gradual development of self-governing institutions with a view to the progressive realization of responsible government in India. The Montague–Chelmsford Report (1918), to make local self government both fully representative and responsible, had suggested, 'There should be as far as possible, complete popular control on local bodies and the largest possible independence for them of outside control.'[19] Accordingly, the Government of India, in its resolution dated 16 May 1918, had recommended to the provinces that municipal boards were to contain a majority of elected members, franchise was to be lowered, and official chairmen were to be replaced by non-official ones. At this time franchise was enjoyed by only 6 per cent of town's people and two-thirds of municipal boards were presided over by officials, and the board's executive was to be strengthened for abdication of official leadership. The boards were also to be free to raise local taxes within statutory limits, they could not, however, spend beyond the budgetary balance fixed for individual local bodies. They were free to allot any portion of their revenue to the subjects of their choice. Senior appointments in local government services were subject to government approval. Outside control was reduced to suspension or supersession of grossly incompetent boards and the grant of certain powers to the divisional commissioner or the district magistrate to act in emergency, should a local authority fail to take the necessary action.[20] The Resolution also laid down that minorities should be represented through nomination rather than by separate electorates. The Punjab Government endorsed this policy but found it impossible to implement it in practice without allotting separate seats to different communities. Accordingly, communal representation was introduced in twenty-eight more towns.

Government of India Act, 1919

The Government of India Act, 1919, introduced the diarchical system of government. The local self government department, being a transferred subject, came under the charge of a popular minister responsible to the provincial legislature. The Act laid down a schedule of taxes which could be levied only by or for the local bodies. This enlarged not merely the effective sphere of taxation, but also enabled the local bodies to feel relatively independent. There was an increased activity on the part of the provincial legislatures in the domain of local self government. Municipal acts in various provinces were amended which further increased the powers and independence of the municipal councils, lowered the franchise and reduced the nominated element, and encouraged the election of non-official presidents and vice-presidents. In Punjab, for example, only five municipalities remained wholly nominated. The elective element ranged between 75 per cent and 85 per cent barring eight municipalities where it was less than 75 per cent. In view of the meagre representation of Muslims, as compared with their population in the local bodies, the communal electorate was extended to a larger number of municipalities.

These measures undoubtedly gave democratic touch to the municipal structure but the administrative process and efficiency deteriorated. Some municipalities were superseded on the charges of corruption and inefficiency. The Punjab Government memorandum to the Simon Commission had attributed the increasing deterioration in municipal administration, *inter alia* to the relaxation of official control from within. It was felt that the expert advice, guidance, and assistance of the district government were denied at a time when these were needed most. Government and their officials were left with disciplinary powers exercisable only when local bodies were in utter chaos. Where spurs and reins were needed the government was given the pole-axe.[21] The Simon Commission had accordingly recommended sufficient control over these institutions as in their view the transfer of power from official hands had resulted in considerable fall in the level of efficiency.[22] In order to restore administrative efficiency and to reassert government control, the provincial governments were asked to make provisions for municipal executive officers. Accordingly the Punjab Municipal (Executive Officers) Act, 1931 was passed. The Act empowered the government to appoint an executive officer in a municipality which had failed to discharge its obligations properly. The Punjab Municipal Amendment Act, 1933, provided for the establishment of a local self government board or an inspector of the local bodies for exercising greater control on municipal committees. As a result of the use of the power conferred on the government by these acts, more municipalities were superseded by the mid 1930s.

A study of the development of municipal institutions during this period shows that the democratic principles enunciated in the Montague–Chelmsford Report and recommended in the Government of India Resolution were duly implemented, and thereby the municipal government had come to be constituted on democratic lines. Eminent persons like Jawaharlal Nehru, Sardar Vallabhbhai Patel, and Parshotam Dass Tandon had entered the municipal councils and gained insight into the functioning of these democratic institutions. But simultaneously with a measure of democratization, there had occurred a decline in efficiency in administration of local affairs. The working of municipal bodies during the period of diarchy presents neither a picture of unrelieved failure nor of unqualified success. 'In every province, while a few local bodies have discharged their responsibilities with undoubted success and others have been equally conspicuous failure, the bulk lies between these extremes.'[23] Many of the failings of the municipal bodies were due to the hybrid framework within which they had to function. It was neither democratic nor autocratic. Lack of administrative experience in elective members coupled with woeful want of expert guidance and trained managerial personnel also contributed to these failures.

Fourth Period (1937–47)

The inauguration of provincial autonomy under the Government of India Act, 1935 gave further impetus to the development of municipal government in India. The Act abolished the system of diarchy and introduced popular governments in the provinces. Local government was classified as a provincial subject. But no taxes were earmarked for local bodies under the Act. Taxes which could be imposed by the provincial governments were included in the provincial list (7th Schedule to the Act) without any indication as to the taxes reserved for local bodies. This change had proved rather unfavourable for local authorities as state governments had in certain areas utilized what were previously recognized to be purely local taxes for their own purposes.[24] Almost all provinces enacted legislation which aimed at further democratization of local bodies and improvement of administrative machinery. Municipal institutions were proposed to be revitalized with the installation of popular ministries in the provinces but no headway could be made due to the outbreak of Second World War in 1939. Popular ministries in all the Congress dominated provinces resigned. Though the popular ministries had continued in other provinces, their entire energy was diverted primarily to defence activities. As a matter of fact, it was no time to concentrate on the local government institutions. The municipal bodies instead of providing civic amenities were performing functions relating to practices in black-outs, raising voluntary organizations for defence, increasing first aid, etc. under the guidance and direct supervision of the district administration.[25] It was a definite setback to the development of municipal government. Thus no significant efforts could be made to bring about reforms in municipal government during the period of provincial autonomy. The British left in 1947 without firmly establishing a self-reliant, virile, healthy, and efficient system of municipal government.

Post-Independence Period (1947 to the Present Day)

India got independence on 15 August 1947. Its new constitution, declaring it a sovereign democratic republic, which came into force on 26 January 1950, directs the state *vide* its Article 40 to organize panchayats and to empower them adequately so that they become viable units of self government,[26] but it does not contain counterpart provision for urban settlements. Thus while the constitution casts a mandate on the state to ensure the working of village panchayats, there is no specific corresponding mandate regarding urban local bodies. The only reference to urban self government is to be found in two entries: Entry 5 of List II of the Seventh Schedule (the State List) and Entry 20 of the List III (Concurrent list). Entry 5 reads: 'Local Government, that is to say, the constitution and powers of municipal corporations, Improvements Trusts, District Boards, mining settlement authorities and other local authorities for the purpose of local self-government or village administration.' Entry 20 of the concurrent list reads: 'Economic and Social Planning and Urban Planning would fall within the ambit of both Entry 5 of State List and Entry 20 of the Concurrent list.' The Constitution thus places local government including urban local government within the legislative competence of the states, and the role of the central government will necessarily have to be advisory and catalytic rather than one of dominance.

It was expected that in the new setup emerging after independence local bodies would be used more and more as instruments of national policy and there would be steady increase in their functions.[27] But in the absence of constitutional recognition of urban local bodies and clear statutory delineation of their powers, functions and resources, they have remained neglected. It has been rightly observed

> [T]hat in the post-independence period, problems of urban local government did not receive from the state and the Union authorities or the Planning Commission as much attention as rural government did. Consequently, only a few changes, several of them of minor character, were made in their structure and functioning. Several of the defects found in them before 1947 have continued and some in heightened form till today.[28]

In the words of an eminent academician, even after independence the situation is no better and remains the same. However, feeble attempts have been made from time to time in tinkering with urban local self government and giving it a face lift but the response from those who are in power has generally been lukewarm and occasionally hostile.'[29]

It was strange that the urban local government was not mentioned in the constitution, not even in the Directive Principles of State Policy, and nor did the Planning Commission make any policy statement about it. The first time it made a brief mention of it was in the Third Five Year Plan when it observed: 'The general direction of the policy should be to encourage self-governing bodies and to assist them in assuming responsibilities for as large a portion of the administrative and social services as possible.'[30]

As a matter of fact, the Planning Commission has been expressing its helplessness at being a silent spectator of the ineffective role of municipal governments in urban development and the utter lack of any innovation in this regard. In the First Five Year Plan, it had made a frank criticism of the state governments and local authorities in the following words:

> [W]e have already seen how haphazard growth and ribbon development have been caused by inadequate legal powers to control use of land and construction of buildings, though it must be admitted that neither the state governments nor legal authorities have shown a full appreciation of the situation or utilised such powers as they already have to arrest the unhealthy growth.[31]

The Second Five Year Plan admits the failure of the present system of municipal administration to cope with the problems of urban planning. It observes:

> [I]t is sufficient to remark here that for urban development to proceed on desirable lines competent municipal administration with adequate powers, resources and administrative and technical staffs are essential, urban development and redevelopment throws increasing responsibilities on municipal administration which few of them are at present able to discharge.[32]

The Third Five Year Plan reiterates the weaknesses of the present municipal system. It says:

> [A]t the local level, municipal administration alone can undertake satisfactorily the task of providing the services needed for development in urban areas, expansion of housing and improvement of living conditions. Most municipal administrations are not strong enough to carry out these functions.[33]

The Fourth Five Year Plan refers to recommendations made by the Rural–Urban Relationship Committee and the Local Self Government Ministers' Council on Augmentation of Financial Resources and hopes that the state governments will take all the measures necessary to augment resources at the local level.[34] The Planning Commission continues to portray the dismal urban local government scenario in the subsequent plans. It also makes the following remarks in the Seventh Five Year Plan:

> The Urban conglomerations by their very nature, need a minimum of basic services for their healthy existence. However, the state of urban areas in this respect is far from satisfactory. In fact, in general the picture is extremely bad. Many of the municipal bodies have undeveloped and/or eroded tax systems and suffer from lack of capital funds for development. The services, if provided, have deteriorated over the years and there seems no sign of reversal. Over-crowded and under-serviced, an increasing proportion and area of urban conglomeration are being turned into slums.[35]

It continues to state that many of the municipal bodies are moribund or have been superseded and are being administered badly.[36] National Commission on Urbanization has also observed that urban India is in a mess.[37]

Anyhow, we cannot blame the Central or state governments for neglecting the urban local government altogether. They have been contributing their bit in strengthening the system for improving the civic services though much more was possible and feasible. The steps taken by both the central and state governments in this regard may be discussed as follows:

Committees and Commissions Appointed by the Central Government

The central government has been appointing various committees/commissions to enquire into the working of urban local governments and to make suggestions for their improvement. The important amongst them are:

1. The *Local Finance Enquiry Committee* (1949–51), had pleaded for a separate and distinct tax zone available for utilization by local governments alone without any encroachment by the state or central government.[38]

2. The *Taxation Enquiry Commission* (1953–54) had observed that the growth of municipal revenue was inadequate in relation to the growth of expenditure on important civic services, and had recommended the segregation of certain taxes for exclusive utilization by or for local government.[39]

3. The *Committee on the Training of Municipal Employees* (1963) had laid emphasis on the need for imparting training to municipal personnel and recommended the setting up of training institutes at the central level and also in the states. It had entrusted, among other things, the central institute with the responsibility to prescribe the standards of training and research and itself serve as a model in this respcet.[40] The central government, in accepting the recommendations of the Committee, had set up the Centre for Training and Research in Municipal Administration at the Indian Institute of Public Administration, New Delhi. Immediately and shortly thereafter, it set up the Regional Centre for Training and Research in Municipal Administration at Lucknow University, Lucknow, and at Osmania University, Hyderabad; Indian Institute of Social Welfare and Business Management, Calcutta; and the All India Institute of Local Self-government, Bombay.

4. The *Rural–Urban Relationship Committee* (1963–66), in its three-volume report, made a comprehensive enquiry into the urban government set-up, urban development and planning machinery, the structure of urban local bodies, municipal personnel, finances of urban local bodies, public participation in urban community development, relation between the state government and local administration, and above all, into the rural–urban relationship, and recommended the evolution of a system of local government which is capable of responding to the process of interaction and interdependence between the town and its adjoining villages.[41]

5. The *Committee of Ministers on Augmentation of Financial Resources of Urban Local Bodies* (1963), set up by the Central Council of Local Self Government, lamented the reluctance of local bodies to step up taxation even in the field earmarked for it and exhorted them to evince courage and enthusiasm in the levy and

collection of taxes put at their command, to take up remunerative activities which would create perennial non-tax revenue, and to set up statutory urban development boards to undertake town development.[42]

6. The *Committee on Service Conditions of Municipal Employees* (1965–68), also set up by the Central Council of Local Self-Government, recommended the constitution of state-wide cadres of municipal employees to ensure that the personnel available for municipal employment would have the desired competence and prestige enjoying appropriate conditions of service.[43]

The urban local government has also been a subject of enquiry by the Administrative Reforms Commission. A chapter in the Report of the Study Team on District Administration, set up by the Administrative Reforms Commission (1967), is devoted to urban local bodies. The team is in agreement with the recommendations made by the Rural–Urban Relationship Committee (1966) and differs in only one or two minor points. Similarly the task forces set up by the Planning Commission in 1983 have suggested the strengthening of municipalities by improving their tax-base, ensuring timely elections, providing better personnel, improving training programmes, etc., and to merge the urban development authorities into the municipal system.

Committees Appointed by the State Governments

The state governments have also been appointing committees and commissions to look into one or the other aspect of urban local governments but mainly into their finances, system of grants-in-aid and personnel system. Some of the committees/commissions constituted by them are as follows:

1. *Assam*: The Finances of Municipal Committee (1969).
2. *Delhi*: The Delhi Municipal Organization Enquiry Committee (1948); the Commission on Finances of the Municipal Corporation of Delhi; and New Delhi Municipal Committee (1968).
3. *Gujarat*: The Municipal Rationalization Committee (1961) and the Grants-in-aid Code Committee for Municipalities (1964).
4. *Haryana*: Resource Committee (Local Bodies), 1988 and Municipal Grants Commission (1969).
5. *Kerala*: The Municipal Grants Enquiry Committee (1965).
6. *Madhya Pradesh*: The Urban and Local Self Government Committee (1959); the Committee of Enquiry on the Emoluments and Conditions of Service of the corporation and Municipal Employees (1965).
7. *Maharashtra*: The committee for the unification of acts relating to municipalities in Maharashtra State (1963).
8. *Orissa*: The Orissa Local Body (Urban) Administration Enquiry Committee (1963).
9. *Punjab*: the Local Government (Urban) Enquiry Committee (1957); Reorganization of District Administration (1969); The Punjab Municipal Employees Pay Committee (1969).
10. *Tamil Nadu*: White Paper on the Reforms of Local Administration in Madras State (1950).

Besides these committees set up by individual states to study specifically the problems of urban local governments in their respective jurisdictions, some committees appointed by the states on administrative reforms have also included urban local governments in their areas of study. The Punjab Administrative Reforms Commission (1964–66), for instance, made a series of recommendations for reform in local government as well. Similarly the committees/commissions of enquiry have been instituted to look into the functioning of individual local bodies, such as the Corporation of Calcutta Investigation Commission (1950) and the commission to enquire into the affairs of Patna Municipal Corporation, (1969); the committee to look into the working of Improvement Trust, Ludhiana (1988) and the Punjab Water Supply and Sewerage Board in Punjab (1989); the committee to look into the matter of abolition of Chief Executive Officers in Haryana (1989); and so on.

The Central Council of Local Self Government

The central government in the Ministry of Health had, for the first time, convened a conference of the state local self government ministers in August 1948 under the chairmanship of the central minister of health when a resolution was passed that to ensure coordination, a conference of local self government ministers should be held once a year. The Central Council of Local Self-Government, though convened in 1948, was constituted by an order of the president in 1954. It consisted then of the central minister of health (but now the minister of urban development) as its chairman and the ministers of local self government in the states. It can invite experts and technical advisers to its meetings but they have no right to vote. Originally it addressed itself to the problems of both the rural and urban local government but since 1958 it deals with urban local government only.

Its main functions are to consider and recommend broad lines of policy in matters relating to local government in all its aspects; to make proposals for legislation on matters relating to local government; to draw up a common programme of action, to make recommendations to the central government regarding the allocation of financial assistance to local bodies and to review the work accomplished in different areas with such central assistance.

It passes resolutions at its annual meetings and also reviews implementation of earlier resolutions. It is a purely advisory body. It sets up committees also to look into problems of urban local governments, as it did set up the committee of ministers on Augmentation of Financial Resources of urban local bodies in 1963 and the Committee on Service Conditions of Municipal Employees in 1965.

Seminars and Conferences

The central government has been convening conferences of state ministers of local self government, All India Council of Mayors, municipal commissioners of municipal corporations, state ministers of town and country planning, and housing ministers, periodically in Delhi or some other convenient place in the country and sponsoring a number of seminars of regional and all India level on various topics of urban government. The Indian Institute of Public Administration, for example, held a seminar on Improving City Government in 1958 and Cabinet System in Municipal Government in 1969. A brief mention of the various conferences regularly convened by the Ministry of Urban Department is made here:

The Conferences of All India Council of Mayors: All India Council of Mayors is a forum of the mayors of municipal corporations in the country. It has been meeting annually since 1959 under the chairmanship of the minister of health, when urban development was a part of the ministry of health, and under the union minister for urban development since 1985, when a separate ministry of urban development was created. The Council discusses subjects of common interest to the mayors such as delegation of additional powers to mayors, amendments of corporation acts in order to enable effective control over the executive wing, grant of emergency powers to mayors, introduction of mayor-in-council system to make the mayor political executive, grant of constitutional status to local bodies, etc. The All India Council of Mayors has set up an executive committee which meets in between the sessions of the Council and opines on various aspects of the problems of municipal corporations.

The Municipal Commissioners' Conference: It was convened for the first time in 1965 at the initiative of the municipal commissioner of Delhi Municipal Corporation to discuss the common problems of the municipal corporations. It was subsequently merged into All India Council of Mayors in 1961, which was designated as Conference of Municipal Corporations instead of Conference of Mayors. Similar organizations of presidents of municipal committees and executive officers of municipal committees also exist at the state level. The former discuss and take joint decisions about the implementation of decisions taken by the state government as did the conference of municipal presidents in Haryana not to implement the hike in civic taxes announced by the state government in 1988, and demanded the abolition of the posts of chief executive officers. The latter also discuss civic problems but concentrate more on the improvement of their service conditions.

Conferences of State Ministers of Local Self Government/Ministers of Town and Country Planning/Housing Ministers: The Ministry of Urban Development also convenes conferences of state ministers of local self government, ministers of town and country planning and housing ministers from time to time to enable them to exchange their views on civic problems, matters relating to regional and urban planning, suggest legislative, administrative and financial measures to solve the problems confronting the states in these fields and to report on the decisions previously taken, and to formulate new policies on the subjects under discussion.

Ministry of Urban Development: The greatest landmark in the evolution of urban local government in the post-independence period is the setting up of Ministry of Urban Development in 1985. To begin with, urban local government was the responsibility of the Ministry of Health as local government had its beginning in an urge to improve sanitary conditions as recommended by the Royal Army Sanitation Commission (1863). The Ministry of Health looked after both rural and urban government until 1958 when the former was separated from it and put under the charge of Ministry of Community Development. In January 1966, a part of local government, namely, urban development was made the responsibility of the Ministry of Works and Housing which was later renamed as the Ministry of Works, Housing and Urban Development. In 1967, the subject of urban development was transferred to the Ministry of Health, which was designated as Ministry of Health, Family Planning, Works, Housing, and Urban Development. In February 1973, the subject of urban development was transferred to the Ministry of Works and Housing.

It was in 1985 that on realizing the magnitude and complexity of urban problems resulting from urbanization taking place at an alarming rate in the country that Government of India decided to set up a separate Ministry of Urban Development and entrusted it with the responsibilities of broad policy formulation and monitoring programmes in the areas of housing, urban development, urban poverty alleviation, urban water supply and urban transport, in addition to construction and maintenance of central government buildings and management of central government land and property. The ministry has under its administrative control the Central Public Works Department, Directorate of Estates, and National Building Organization as attached offices; Controller of Stationery, Controller of Publications, Land and Development Office, and Town and Country Planning Organization as subordinate offices; Delhi Development Authority, Delhi Urban Arts Commission, National Capital Regional Planning Board, and National Institute of Urban Affairs as autonomous and statutory bodies; and National Building Construction Corporation Ltd., Housing and Urban Development Corporation Ltd. (HUDCO), and Hindustan Prefab Ltd. as public sector undertakings.

The state governments have also set up departments/directorates of urban local government in conjunction with other departments of allied nature or as separate departments, on the recommendations of the Committee on Augmentation of Financial Resources of Urban Local Bodies (1963), the Central Council of Local Self Government (1965), the Rural–Urban Relationship Committee (1966), and the Study Team on District Administration of the Administration Reform Commission (1967), to reduce the congestion of work at the secretarial level, to fulfil the need for a field organization on the pattern of the directorates of other departments, and to serve as a bridge between the municipalities and the state level institutions.

National Commission on Urbanization: Another landmark in the evolution of urban local government was the setting up of National Commission on Urbanization in 1985 by Government of India to make a comprehensive analysis of the rapidly growing phenomenon of urbanization and of the problems caused by it for the urban governments, and to suggest measures to combat it. The Commission was set up after a lapse of twenty years after the submission of the reports of the Rural–Urban Relationship Committee (1966) which had also examined the urban government setting comprehensively. The National Commission on Urbanization had examined the various urban problems in depth especially those of dimensions of urbanization, urban future, urban pattern, spatial planning, urban poverty, finance, urban management, housing, conservation, transport, water and sanitation, energy, people's participation, information system, and legal framework, and made recommendations for their solution in its seven volume report submitted in 1988.[44] The government had since accepted most of these recommendations and incorporated them in the Constitution (63rd Amendment) Bill, 1989, which was later enacted as the Constitution (74th Amendment) Act, 1992.

The central government has been conscious of the deficiencies in the organization and functions of urban local government and the factors responsible for their dismal performance and deterioration in the post-independence period, such as (*a*) the drafting of top national leaders in the Parliament and the central government and to some extent in the state legislatures and state governments, resulting in the domination of local bodies by inept politicians and consequent increase in political nepotism and corruption; (*b*) the increase in functions of municipal bodies due to the increasing pace of urbanization has not been matched by a corresponding increase in their finances resulting in their inability to cope with their increased responsibilities and the deterioration in the quality and quantity of services; (*c*) local bodies continue to be governed by the early nineteenth century framework of municipal administration, laws and by-laws, rules and regulations, practices and procedures—the cities today have to plan for the twenty-first century while the institutions which are supposed to implement these plans are a hangover of the nineteenth century; (*d*) the Five Year Plans have hopelessly admitted the severe limitations of municipal administration while doing very little about introducing radical changes in such administration; (*e*) the Finance Commission which is appointed every five years under the constitution of India is not required to look into the problem of local finance; (*f*) the states do not generally consider urban problems as of any particular consequence and usually the Ministry of Local Self Government is one of the unimportant ministries; (*g*) the state governments superseded municipalities and corporations on political grounds though some other excuse was given; (*h*) the corporations and municipalities are, by and large, centres of inefficiency, corruption, and political nepotism. Most of them are bankrupt and cannot in any way tackle the big problems in the field of housing, transport, environmental pollution, etc. In short, the municipal bodies are not geared to urban planning as understood today but perform municipal functions as understood in the nineteenth century. They have neither the financial viability nor the legal backing to confront urban problems except in the limited sphere of zoning, land use planning, etc.[45]

The government had introduced the Constitution (63rd Amendment) Nagarpalika Bill, in August, 1989, with a view to give power to the people and to strengthen, revamp, and rejuvenate urban local governments. Its main provisions were the constitution of nagar panchayat for areas in transition from rural to urban areas, ward committees in nagarpalikas and zonal committees in mahanagarpalikas, reservation for Scheduled Cases/Scheduled Tribes and women, state finance commission to recommend the principles to ensure soundness of local bodies finances, conduct of elections by the State Election Commission, audit of accounts by the Comptroller and Auditor General of India, and above all, the grant of constitutional status to local bodies.

The Constitution (74th Amendment) Bill, 1991: The Nagarpalika Bill introduced in 1989 was hailed as historic and momentous. It was passed by the Lok Sabha, but it was defeated in the Rajya Sabha by a narrow margin of three votes. The Congress (I) Government again in power, introduced the bill in the form of Constitution (73rd Amendment) Bill on 16th September, 1991. The Bill was passed as the Constitution (74th Amendment) Act, 1992. It would prove to be the greatest landmark in removing the deficiencies that the urban local governments have been suffering from for the last one hundred years and in strengthening them to ensure their efficient and effective organization and functioning in the best interests of the residents of urban areas in the country.

CONCLUSION

To conclude, it may be observed that the evolution of urban local governments in the post-independence period has been characterized by inertia on the part of central and state governments as is evidenced by the sporadic and piecemeal efforts made by them in realizing and recognizing the significance of city governments and taking half-hearted measures in improving their organization and functioning. It was only during the 1980s that the central government took momentous decisions in setting up the Ministry of Urban Development, appointment of National Commission on Urbanization, and introducing Nagarpalika Bill in 1989 and 1991 to rejuvenate urban self government institutions in the country. The momentum to streamline, strengthen, and revamp urban local governments needs to be not only maintained but also accelerated to meet the challenges of urbanization, which is taking place at an alarming rate. The urban population, which was 160 million in 1981 and 200 million in 1990, swelled to 280.5 million population in 2001. To meet the existing and the emerging urban problems in the wake of unabated urbanization and industrialization, the central and state governments have to be concerned about the state of urban local governments and to take appropriate measures to equip them adequately to perform their functions effectively in making their cities liveable. It can be hoped that the faithful execution of the various provisions of the Constitution (74th Amendment) Act, 1992, will revolutionize and revitalize for functioning of the urban local bodies.

REFERENCES

1. R.L. Khanna, *Municipal Government and Administration in India* (Chandigarh: Mahindra Capital Publishers, 1967), p. 3.
2. Vijay Kumar Thakur, *Urbanisation in Ancient India* (New Delhi: Abhinav Publications, 1981), p. 243.
3. *Ibid.*, p. 230.
4. *Ibid.*, p. 247.
5. E.B. Havell, *The History of Aryan Rule in India* (London: 1918), pp. 77–78.
6. Mores Frank, *Jawaharlal Nehru, A Biography* (New York: 1956), p. 407.
7. 'Kotwal' was a generalist administrator performing both police and Civic functions.
8. Amar Nath, 'The Development of Local Self Government in Punjab', Punjab Government Record Office, 1929, p. 6.
9. Hugh Tinker, *The Foundations of Local Self Governments in India, Pakistan and Burma* (London: The Athlone Press, 1954), p. 25.
10. Government of India Resolution No. 3434 dated 19 December 1870.
11. Government of India Resolution No. 171749–75, dated 18 May 1882.
12. Montague–Chelmsford. Reforms, 1918, paragraph. 3.
13. Simon Commission Report, 1930, p. 301.
14. Hugh Tinker, *The Foundations,* p. 59.
15. Proceedings of the Legislative Council of the Governor-General of India, 1883, p. 13.
16. Hugh Tinker, *The Foundations,* p. 98.
17. Montague–Chelmsford Report, 1918, p. 123.

18. Simon Commission Report, Vol. I, p. 314.
19. Montague–Chelmsford Report, p. 123.
20. Simon Commission Report, paragraphs 5, 10, 13 and 16.
21. *Ibid.,* p. 343.
22. *Ibid.,* Vol. II. p. 308.
23. Jawaharlal Nehru, *An Autobiography* (London: 1936), p. 144.
24. Report of the Local Finance Enquiry Commission, 1951.
25. D.R. Sachdeva, *Local Government Services in India* (Jalandhar: Raj Publishers, 1974), pp. 27–28.
26. Article 40 reads: '[O]rganisation of village Panchayat, the State shall take steps to organise village panchayats and endow them with such powers and authority as may be necessary to enable them to function as unit of self government.'
27. Report of Punjab Local Government (Urban) Enquiry Committee, 1957, p. 98.
28. M. Venkatarangaiya and M. Pattabhiram (eds.), *Local Government in India Select Readings* (New Delhi: Allied Publishers, 1969), p. 38.
29. M. Kistaiah, 'Sarkaria Commission and Local Self Government', Paper presented at the Tenth Annual conference of the Indian Public Administration Association, Waltair, 29 November–1 December, 1985.
30. Government of India, Planning Commission, Third Five Year Plan, 1961–66, p. 693.
31. The First Five Year Plan, 1951–56, p. 603.
32. The Second Five Year Plan, 1956–61, p. 569.
33. The Third Five Year Plan, 1961–66, p. 693.
34. The Fourth Five Year Plan, 1969–74, p. 401.
35. The Seventh Five Year Plan, 1986–91, paragraph 12.27.
36. *Ibid.,* p. 12.27.
37. Report of National Commission on Urbanization, 1988, p. 149.
38. 'Report of the Local Finance Enquiry Committee' (Delhi: Manager of Publications, 1951), p. 61.
39. 'Report of the Taxation Enquiry Commission', Volume 3 (New Delhi: Ministry of Finance, Government of India, 1953–54), p. 347.
40. 'Report of the Committee on the Training of Municipal Employees' (New Delhi: Ministry of Health, 1963), p. 7.
41. 'Report of the Rural–Urban Relationship Committee', Volume 1 (New Delhi: Ministry of Health and Family Welfare, 1966), p. 45.
42. 'Report of the Committee of Ministers on Augmentation of Financial Resources of Urban Local Governments' (New Delhi: Manager of Publications, 1965), pp. 29–30.
43. 'Report of Committee on the Service Conditions of Municipal Employees' (New Delhi: Ministry of Health and Family Planning and Urban Development, 1968), p. 32.
44. 'Report of National Commission on Urbanisation', Government of India, Ministry of Urban Development, 1988, Vol. I.
45. A Survey of Research in Public Administration, Allied Publishers New Delhi, 1973 Vol. I. pp. 220–221.

4

National Commission on Urbanization

In 1986, the Government of India appointed National Commission on Urbanization comprising Shri C.M. Correa as its Chairman, Shri M.N. Buch as Vice-Chairman and Sarv-Shri P.M. Ashish Bose, Nilay Chaudhary, B.G. Fernandes, Cyrees Guzder, V.K. Pathak, Amit Jyoti Sen, Kirtee Shah as members and Shri Naresh Narad as Member Secretary. It was entrusted with the task of making a comprehensive and in-depth study of the various facets of the process of urbanization, and the issues arising therefrom, especially concerning urban planning and development, structure, organization, powers, functions, and the status of the existing urban local government institutions, including the mechanism of their management in respect of their personnel, finances and state control, the role of special purpose urban institutions, and the allied matters. It was also to suggest strategies for policy formulations and their implementation with a view to meet the challenges posed by the phenomenon of increased urbanization on an unprecedented scale by making amendments in the constitution, enacting necessary legislations, adequately providing the necessary infrastructure, and bringing about other reforms to streamline the apparatus and mechanism to ensure planned development of urban settlements and the provision of necessary facilities to make the lives of citizens healthier and richer.

The commission performed this stupendous task with the help of various working groups, study teams, research institutes, institutions engaged in urban studies such as National Institute of Urban Affairs (New Delhi), the Institute of Economic Growth and the National Institute of Human Settlements (Bhopal), and officers/officials of the Union Ministry of Urban Development, state governments and union territories administrations. The commission also interacted with a large number of eminent specialists, sought the views of citizens and public organizations on various issues, and obtained valuable insights into the problems of urbanization at the grass roots through field visits.

The commission submitted its interim report in January 1987 and the final report in August 1988, a total of seven volumes. Volume I outlines the issues and strategies and concludes with recommendations in respect of various facets of urbanization and matters connected therewith. Volume II, in six parts, deals with (*a*) dimensions of urbanization and urban future; (*b*) urban pattern and spatial planning; (*c*) urban poverty, land as a resource, finance, and urban management; (*d*) planning the city, urban form, housing, and conservation; (*e*) transport, water and sanitation, and energy; (*f*) peoples' participation, information system, and legal framework. Volume III contains a memorandum; Volume IV contains working groups reports; Volume V research study reports; Volume VI lists bibiliography; and Volume VII consists of annexures. The findings, observations, and recommendations of the commission in respect of vital issues of urbanization in brief are as follows:

Main Recommendations of the Commission

1. Dimension of Urbanization: The commission had identified urban centres which could generate economic momentum and require priority in development. They include National Priority Cities (NPCs), State Priority Cities (SPCs), Spatial Priority Urbanization Regions (SPURs), and the small towns which serve the rural hinterland. The commission stated that from the eighth Plan onwards fullest support must be given to the development of the identified growth centres; the process of urbanization can and must be used to improve agricultural performance and create localized employment opportunities; and population control messures must be made really effective in both urban and rural areas in order to stabilize the urban situation.

2. Proper Land Use: Since the most disastrous feature of Indian urbanization has been the failure to anticipate the rising demand for urbanized land—a key resource of urban planning—the supply of such land should be given the top most priority; a Settlement Survey of India should be established at the national level and a directorate of urban land in each state. At the city level there should be an Urban Land Manager under the control of the District Collector, the urban land tenure system must be changed to ensure security of tenure; future land requirements, especially for housing the poor, should be anticipated and provided for; squatting on public land may be regularized where possible, but land required for public and social purposes must be protected and selective relocation of squatters from ecologically sensitive land must be undertaken; the state must intervene to provide equitable access to land; to bring increasing quantities of land to the market, the Urban Land (Ceiling and Regulation) Act, 1976, should be drastically amended, and supplemented by taxation measures that would discourage landowners from keeping their land vacant and encourage proper utilization; various forms of land assembly, through land exchange scheme, layout approval, and other similar measures should be encouraged; the Land Acquisition Act should be amended to eliminate delay and ensure timely payment to the affected citizens; and all laws which inhibit or restrict the recycling of land should be suitably modified.

3. Water and Sanitation: A holistic rather than a compartmentalized view of water resource management should be taken. Water, being an absolutely critical for human survival, must be treated as such and accorded suitably high priority in the planning process. The immediate objective should be the provision, on an equitable basis, of at least 70 litres of water per capita per day in urban areas for domestic requirements. To ensure better maintenance of existing water systems, an additional Rs 1000 crore per annum must be provided to local bodies. Waste water recycling and its use for non-domestic purposes should be encouraged. To ensure water conservation, a differential tariff on water use should be applied, with a sharp increase in the rate charged for consumption in excess of 100 litres per capita per day. Legislation should be introduced to control water drawn even from private sources in order to maintain the water table; this may include nationalization of all water sources. The collection of solid waste and its use in compositing and as an energy source should be made more efficient; where possible the service should be transferred to private hands, and laws relating to control of pollution must be strictly enforced.

4. Energy: Energy demands of urban areas should be anticipated and advance action should be taken to meet them and optimize energy use; energy supply planning and pricing should be used to influence activity location; land-use planning should be used as a means of reducing the energy need of the transport sector; development control rules and building bye-laws should be modified to ensure the construction of energy efficient buildings; an integrated pricing and supply policy covering all fuels should be evolved to achieve equity and efficiency; and a database on energy use in urban areas should be built.

5. Transport: To ensure increase in city efficiency, land use and transportation planning should be integrated; the bias towards personalized forms of transport must be corrected and mass transportation encouraged.

By allowing a wide variety of multipurpose vehicles to operate, including luxury buses, the use of road space by private case must be reduced. Short-term affordable solutions rather than capital-intensive, long-term plans should be resorted to; this implies optimizing the use of currently available transportation modes. Cycling and pedestrian facilities should be improved, and management of transportation at city level should be unified under a single authority.

6. Urban Poverty: The amelioration of urban poverty should be accorded the same priority as is given to rural poverty; four lakh urban youths should be selected from poor households every year and trained in skills for which there is a demand; self-employment of the urban poor should be encouraged by appropriate credit-support programmes; production and market support should be given to the self-employed urban poor; city planning should be geared to providing shelter and sites for employment generation programmes; local bodies should be supported in their efforts to create special employment facilities, including work-sheds for tiny manufacturers; the shelter programme should be used to provide employment to the urban poor; wage employment for the urban poor should be provided through a programme for creation of such urban assets as water supply, drainage systems, and land development; the public distribution system should be strengthened to meet consumption requirements; community development should be the strategy for the improvement of the living conditions of the poor; and an urban community agency should be set up at national level.

7. Housing: Housing policy should aim at increasing the supply of serviced land and low-cost shelters, improving and upgrading slums, and conserving the existing housing stock. The state must facilitate housing and ensure access to basic inputs; it should not become a real-estate developer. The sites and services programme should be extended to cover the entire cross-section of society. Besides providing housing, the programme should be used to generate employment. Apart from providing access to land, the housing programme must also provide for finance, infrastructure development, and community facilities; inner-city upgradation and housing repair must be encouraged; public agencies in the housing sector should be restructured for fulfilment of their new role as facilitators rather than providers of housing. Rent acts should be modified to limit tenancy protection to the poor and to the existing tenancies, and to provide for annual revision of rents to reflect increases in the cost of living, the increases varying between residential and non-residential premises, and houses above and below 80 square metres.

8. Urban Form: Low-rise, high-density development should be the predominant built-form in urban India; municipal regulations regarding minimum plot sizes, buildable plot area, etc., should be amended, building envelopes should be designed and building codes should be modified so that the desired built-form is achieved; controlled streetscapes should be achieved through mandatory building lines and developing appropriate building envelopes; public squares, parks, promenades and other nodal points of urban centres should be rahabilitated by restricting vehicle entry and ensuring controlled development; civic landmarks should be treated as urban events that lend identity to a city neighbourhood and enhance civic pride; and land allocation must be consistently monitored and readjusted to ensure equitable city growth.

9. Conservation: Conservation should go beyond preservation of monuments and encompass the whole built heritage; rules and regulations should be amended to encourage conservation of the living environment; city planning must encourage conservation of old city areas and not just development of new areas; and direct fiscal and other incentives should be offered as an encouragement to individuals to conserve places and sites.

10. Spatial Planning: There is a need to supplement economic development planning by inter-sectoral coordination through the spatial planning process. Spatial planning at the state and district levels should concentrate on national priority cities, state priority cities and spatial priority urbanization regions with a view to bringing about integrated development. Therefore, multi-level spatial planning at the national, state, and district levels is recommended. At the city level, to make planning more comprehensive, the local government should adopt the three-fold development planning process—viz. Master Directive Plan for the entire city, and Execution Plan and Action Area Plans—as programmes, taking into consideration major sectors of development such as employment, housing, transport, and the essential urban infrastructure. The execution plan should replace the present zonal development plan and should correspond in the periodization of national and state Five Year Plans, thus forming a capital investment plan as a budgetary tool and also as an instrument of coordination and implementation of public and private sector projects. The action area plans should be used as a means of detailed planning.

11. Finance: The priority accorded to urbanization in the Five Year Plan should be raised from the current share of about 4 per cent of the total to at least 8 per cent. Half of this should be from the central sector; to ensure devolution of funds from the state governments to local bodies, there should be a constitutional provision for setting up quin-quennial State Finance Commissions; the tax base of local bodies must be strengthened; and four major banking institutions—a metropolitan cities development bank, a national housing bank, an urban infrastructure development bank, and an urban small business development bank—should be set up.

12. Management: The Planning Commission should have a full-time member in charge of urbanization; the Urban Development Ministry should be nodal and should have divisions dealing with urbanization and urban poverty alleviation; at the national level, there should be a National Urbanization Council, with a counterpart State Urbanization Council in each state. The councils will formulate urbanization policies. To encourage citizens' participation, there should be an Indian Council for Citizens' Action, with counterparts at state and city level. The municipal administration should be restructured so that cities with a population of more than five lakhs have a two-tier administration consisting of the city corporation and local councils; the division of functions between the elected, deliberative wing and the executive wing of local bodies should be codified. The responsibility and accountability of each functionary must be made specific and the management of city services professionalized. The supersession of local bodies should be the exception rather than the rule, and the holding of elections for reconstituting a superseded local body within the specified period should be made mandatory, and the municipal electoral process should be brought under the umbrella of the state chief electoral officer.

13. Information System: Various data sources at the national level should be modified to provide spatially disaggregated data. Access to data at the source should be made easier. Two new data systems pertaining to land and the environment should be organized. The information system should be designed to facilitate decision-making; the information system at the local level should use data generated through the normal administrative processes; to facilitate urban planning, location-specific information systems should be devised; remote sensing should be used to monitor changes in regional land-use and expansion of urban areas; and pilot projects for developing integrated urban information systems should be launched in selected major cities.

Appraisal

The National Commission on Urbanization is the first ever commission to have made a comprehensive and in-depth study of all conceivable aspects of urbanization: urban development; urban planning; the structure, powers and functions of urban local bodies; their finances; state supervision and control over them; the urban slum; urban poverty alleviation; etc. It is also the first ever commission to have given due consideration to the opinion of the various state governments, institutions engaged in and concerned with urban local government in one way or the other, while making recommendations for the solutions of the challenges and problems posed by the accelerating process of urbanization and their consequential impact on the various facets of urban management.

Another outstanding characteristic of the commission is its uniqueness in the sense that its terms of reference were all-embracing as against those of the earlier commissions/committees appointed by the central government, which were limited to exclusively one aspect of the urban governments; for example, the Royal Army Sanitation Commission (1863), Taxation Enquiry Commission on Local Taxation (1925), Local Finance Enquiry Committee (1950), Committee on Augmentation of Financial Recourses of Urban Local Bodies (1963), Rural Urban Relationship Committee (1963), and Nur-ud-din Committee on the Training of Municipal Employees (1963). The report of the National Commission on Urbanization was consequently bound to be voluminous—it consisted of seven volumes encompassing practically all the issues concerning urban development.

The observations made by the commission on various areas and fields of the subject, and recommendations made thereon, assume the highest degree of credibility and significance, made as they are by experts and specialists in their respective fields as members of the commission and of the numerous study and research teams and working groups. The Government of India has hailed the recommendations of the commission as appreciable, positive, constructive, and practicable, and accordingly has incorporated most of these in the Constitution (74th Amendment) Act, 1992, which is claimed to be the most historic in revamping and rejuvenating the urban local governments by according them constitutional status and strengthening them as a genuine democratic institution by guaranteeing regular elections, decentralization, devolution of powers, and financial viability.

The government has also implemented the recommendations of the commission in the formulation of urban policy, urban poverty alleviation, finance, housing, etc., and restructuring of the local governments. The other findings, observations, and recommendations of the commission, though commendable, are yet to be finally adopted, as these entail substantial alterations in the existing organizations. For instance, its suggestions regarding the revamping of the Ministry of Urban Development in relieving its extraneous work—creating an additional division of housing, health engineering, etc., setting up of national/state urbanization councils, and inclusion of a full-time member of urbanization in the Planning Commission, and so on.

All in all, the National Commission on Urbanization's contribution to the realm of urban development and its allied topics has been most valuable and can be rightly termed as 'encyclopaedic' in its treatment of problems of every kind faced by urban local governments in the fields of urban development and its management. The Report of the National Commission on Urbanization, unlike many reports of other commissions, has not been allowed to gather dust; its numerous recommendations were accepted and implementing to enable urban local governments to develop and grow as healthy institutions.

The Constitution (74th Amendment) Act, 1992

Our urban local governments, it is rightly alleged, have failed to achieve their twin objectives of working as primary units of democratic government and field agencies for the development and maintenance of civic services. They have also failed to meet the aspirations of the people. Their general level of administrative efficiency has been deplorably low, the standards of civic amenities have been disgusting, factionalism and groupism have been vicious, corruption has become endemic, a healthy civic sense has not evolved, right type of civic leadership has not developed, and morale has been, by and large, very low.

Further, the structure and composition of our urban local bodies has been faulty, their powers are limited and circumscribed, their elections are not held on time or regularly, their supersessions on partisan basis have been frequent, the superseded bodies are not restored for indefinite periods, the state supervision and control of government over them is excessive, their finances are scarce and incommensurate with the functions assigned to them, and above all, they are not granted the autonomy which the local democratic institutions should enjoy through active participation in the formation and execution of plans for the development of local areas.

The Government of India and the state governments have been appointing commissions and committees from time to time to examine the problems of urban local governments and to make recommendations for their effective functioning. The various governments have not been giving due consideration to their findings, much less accepting and implementing their recommendations. Prime Minister Rajiv Gandhi, with a view to give power to the people at the grass roots level and to strengthen local bodies, had introduced in the Lok Sabha the Constitution (64th Amendment) Bill on 15th May, 1989 to revitalize Panchayati Raj institutions and Constitution (65th Amendment) Bill on 7th August, 1989 to strengthen urban municipal bodies. Though the bill relating to the Panchayati Raj was numbered as the Constitution (64th Amendment) Bill and the bill relating to urban local bodies as the Constitution (65th Amendment) Bill, they were renumbered as Constitution (62nd and 63rd Amendment) Bills, respectively, as the earlier amendment bills had not been passed. The bill was based on the consensus emerging from threadbare discussions at the conferences of the municipal officers, the conventions of elected representatives of municipal bodies (Nagarpalika Sammelans) held in different parts of the country, and the conference of chief ministers (boycotted by those of the non-Congress [I] states). The Bill envisaged *inter alia* devolution by the State Legislatures of powers and responsibilities upon the nagarpalikas for preparation of plans for economic development and social justice and for implementing development schemes.

Salient Features of the Bill

The bill, among other things, provided for:

1. Three categories of nagarpalikas: Nagar Panchayats for transitional areas, that is areas in transition from rural to urban, with a population between 10,000 and 20,000; municipal councils for urban areas with a population between 20,000 and three lakhs; municipal corporations with a population exceeding three lakhs.
2. Wards committees in nagarpalikas with a population of 100,000, and zonal committees in territorial areas of municipal corporations as an intermediate level between the ward committees and the municipal corporations.
3. Direct elections of nagarpalikas and ward committees, and constitution of zonal committees by the chairpersons of the wards committees comprised within the territorial areas of the zonal committees; representation of chairpersons for ward committees in municipal councils and of chairpersons of, zonal committees in municipal corporations.
4. Reservations in nagarpalikas and wards committees for the scheduled castes and the scheduled tribes in proportion of their population, and 30 per cent reservation for women.
5. A fixed tenure of five years for nagarpalikas including the nagar panchayats and ward committees, and in the event of their dissolution the holding of elections within six months.
6. A committee at the district level for harmonizing and consolidating the plans of panchayats and nagarpalikas in the district and preparing a draft development plan for the district as a whole, and its elections from among the members of the panchayats and nagarpalikas in the district in proportion to the ratio of the population covered by them.
7. Sound finances by securing authorization from state legislatures for grants-in-aids from the consolidated fund of the state as also assignment to or appropriation by nagarpalikas of the revenue of designated taxes, duties, tolls and fees.
8. A finance commission to review the finances of the nagarpalikas, and recommend principles on the basis of which their soundness could be secured.
9. Superintendence, direction and control of elections to the nagarpalikas, including nagar panchayats and other elected committees by the Election Commission.
10. The Comptroller and Auditor General of India to cause the accounts of the nagarpalikas, ward committees, and zonal committees to be audited in such manner as he may deem fit.
11. Factors that would disqualify a person from membership;
12. The governor's decision on the question of disqualification, which he would take after obtaining the opinion of the Election Commission, to be treated as final;
13. Barring of the jurisdiction of the courts in matters relating to elections.

The bill had been hailed as historic, revolutionary, and momentous. The government had assured that it would try to remove all the difficulties that it might encounter in its implementation. The Bill was passed by the Lok Sabha but it failed to get the support of two-thirds majority in Rajya Sabha—it was defeated by a narrow margin of three votes only—and therefore could not become a statute.

The Congress (I) government was replaced by the National Front government as a sequence of general elections held in November, 1989. The new government, under the stewardship of Shri V.P. Singh, was committed to strengthen the local governments, both urban and rural, and to bring a new legislation in the near future to recast, restructure, revamp, and revitalize them in a much improved form. This was to be done by incorporating the provisions of the defeated legislation with a view to remove the deficiencies inherent in the structure, organization, and functioning of urban local governments, and to ensure their rehabilitation as instruments of genuine democracy at the grassroots level and agencies for provision of basic civic amenities, development, and welfare of the people living in the towns and cities. But the National Front government could not honour its commitment to the people by introducing the promised legislation for due to its preoccupation with other complex problems demanding its immediate and urgent attention, and the eclipse of its rule within a short span of eleven months. The Janta Dal government under the prime ministership of Shri Chander Shekher would survive only four months.

A Critique of the Bill: Its Strengths and Weaknesses

There can be no divergence of opinion on the dismal performance of our municipal governments due to their outdated nineteenth-century structure and outmoded administrative organization. They suffered from mounting pressure on their slender resources to provide basic civic amenities to tremendously increasing number of urbanites in the wake of industrialization and influx of migrants from rural areas; of the reduction of their powers and erosion of their functions by the creation of several specific-purpose agencies; excessive state control reflected especially in the spate of supersessions and their continuation for indefinite periods, resulting in the denial of the fundamental right of the electorate to elect their local representative to manage the affairs of their cities/towns; the apathy of citizens; absence of sound leadership; undue interference by politicians; and above all the denial of constitutional status to local bodies.

Issues Confronting Urban Local Governments

The issues therefore requiring in-depth study, discussions, deliberations, and decisions were the need for the constitutional recognition of local bodies and the need for clear statutory delineation of the powers, functions, and resources of urban bodies:

1. What should the criteria for the constitution of different types of local authorities be—population, non-rural character of population, density of population, income or combination of all these?—Should there be a reclassification of municipal bodies?
2. What should be the nature of the relationship between the urban area and its hinterland, the rural area, and at what stage does a rural area become urban?
3. What kind of machinery can be set up at the local level to harmonize the process of growth and development of the urban and rural areas?
4. For change to the democratic and transformation to be cognizant of ground realities, as Panchayati Raj is as much an urban need as a rural requirement. In the Panchayati Raj system, the basic unit of the local self-government was the village panchayat. Could a mohalla panchayat be the equivalent of a village panchayat in an urban environment, in other words, should the lowest tier of self-government be a small elected unit for each locality (mohalla, colony, or basti)? The question was whether this measure would facilitate democratic decentralization, more effective participation, and a more responsive administration.
5. What measures are necessary to ensure that municipal bodies are not frequently superseded? What are the special circumstances under which supersessions can be done and for how long?
6. Who should conduct the elections to municipal bodies, the Election Commission or the state government, and who should bear the expenses?

7. Should there be a reservation of seats in municipal or corporation council, for scheduled castes and scheduled tribes, and women, and if yes, in what proportion?
8. What should be the functions of municipal bodies?
9. What can be done to strengthen their financial base?
10. What should be the relationship between municipal bodies and Panchayati Raj institutions?

Procedure Adopted for Discussions

In order to generate a full and frank discussion on the problems of nagarpalikas, a conference of officials of municipal bodies was held at New Delhi from 5 to 8 June 1988, followed by a conference named 'Nagarpalika Sammelan' of elected representatives of municipal bodies from the southern region at Bangalore from 12 to 14 June; from eastern region at Bhubaneshwar from 18 to 20 June; and of northern and western regions at New Delhi from 24 to 26 June. The local self-government ministers from the states had deliberated on the subject on 30 June and in the chief secretaries' conference on 27 June in New Delhi. A chief ministers' meeting was held on 7 July. Earlier the Parliamentary Committee attached to the Ministry of Urban Development had made their own suggestions on the subject on 29 June. The suggestions emerging from the deliberations of the above mentioned forums formed the basis of the Nagarpalika Bill. The government had appointed the Charles Correa Commission (National Commission on Urbanization) to deal with urban problems. The Commission had submitted its report in August 1988. The government had incorporated many of its suggestions as well in the Nagarpalika Bill.

The bill aimed at rectifying the defects, deficiencies, and inadequacies in the structure and organization of urban local governments and at revitalizing and strengthening them. The government had introduced the Nagarpalika Bill as the Constitution (65th Amendment) Bill in the Parliament, which was highly commended on account of its strong points. These were

(*a*) The setting up of three types of nagarpalikas—the nagar panchayats for transitional areas, municipal councils, and municipal corporations for urban areas. The nagar panchayats are meant for areas in transition from rural to urban with a population between 10,000 and 20,000, the municipal council for urban areas with a population between 20,000 and three lakhs, and municipal corporations for urban areas with a population exceeding three lakhs.

(*b*) Setting up ward committees and zonal committees to enable the local bodies become the training ground for democratic institutions in the country.

(*c*) Apart from giving power to the people, placing responsibility on them at various levels so that a new leadership emerges.

(*d*) Empowering the state election commission to hold the elections in order to see that periodical elections of local bodies are free and fair.

(*e*) Reserving thirty percent of the seats for women and for the scheduled castes and scheduled tribes in proportion to their population in the areas concerned.

(*f*) Appointing a state finance commission to look into the needs of local bodies, and empowering the Comptroller and Auditor General to audit the accounts to provide a safety valve to the people against the misuse of funds.

(*g*) Banning the jurisdiction of the courts in matters relating to the elections to urban local bodies.

(*h*) Above all, granting the urban local bodies constitutional status by amending the constitution.

These provisions would strengthen democracy right from the grassroots level and enable the people to shape their own destinies.

Criticism of the Bill

The provisions of the bill are by and large exceptional, as they fulfil the long-standing need of the urban local bodies to revamp and thus enable them to serve as efficient instruments—exercising the inherent democratic right of the people to govern themselves, and providing civic amenities to them. But the Bill has been criticized for its following weak points:

1. Political Parties and People Not Consulted: A government that wants to take power to the people must go about its task in a democratic way by consulting political parties and the people first and bureaucrats next. But Rajiv Gandhi had done just the opposite; he consulted the municipal bureaucrats first. In his defence he had said, 'We are determined to give power to the people. But in determining the mode and modalities of doing so, we wish to begin with the municipal officers who by virtue of their experience and expertise are best suited to set the ball rolling.' He had further observed that in its interaction with the district bureaucracy, the Government found the civic services having a pervading conviction that responsive district administration is not possible without representative district administration; the IAS and provincial services officers were unanimous in the view that bureaucratic administration, however well-intentioned, was no substitute for democratic administration. It is with their wholehearted backing that we have introduced the Panchayati Raj Bill. The government believed that the municipal bureaucracy hold a similar view about the municipal administration. But critics have said that it is sheer arrogance to believe that the party in power at the centre alone knows what is good for the country and the Prime Minister alone knows what is good for the party. They suggest that the Inter-state Council to be set up by the President under Article 263 of the Constitution could be the best mechanism to discuss with the states such vital problems as Panchayati Raj and Nagarpalika, and in a true federal spirit come to broadly agreed conclusions. But that council did not exist at that time. Therefore, the question of consulting it did not arise. (The Inter-state council was, however, set up in 1990 by the Chander Shekhar government).

2. Boycotting of Chief Ministers' Conference by the Chief Ministers of Non-Congress Governments: The chief ministers of non-Congress (I) states had boycotted the Chief Ministers' Conference called by the centre to have a threadbare discussion on the proposed constitutional amendment for providing more powers to urban local bodies. It was alleged that the chief ministers concerned could not be faulted for their decision because the Prime Minister had already made up his mind to amend the constitution (on the strength of his brute majority in the Lok Sabha). Under the circumstances, the Chief Ministers Conference could be nothing but mere eyewash to give his ideas the trappings of a national consensus. They felt that it was a potentially dangerous idea aimed at undermining the federal structure of the constitution by breaking it into districts and nagarpalikas owing direct allegiance to the Centre.

3. Timing of the Introduction of the Bill and Suspects on Sponsors' Motives: The critics further aver that Nagarpalika Bill suffers not so much in its context but in its timing and in the sponsor's motives. The sincerity of any government waxing eloquent or the need to take power to the people at the fag end of its five-year term is open to question. Even if it is granted that in the game of political one-upmanship parties always reserve their best programmes for the end, there does remain the question about the time. The massive funds promised for the urban people under Nehru Rozgar Yojna and the pledge to devolve funds to urban local bodies directly from the Centre point to a grand political design. The proposed massive transfer of funds from the government to the people is being termed and trumpeted about as the ruling party's infinite generosity bestowed on the people. For the voters at large, the pre-election bonanza is welcome but it cannot escape the stigma of a populist gimmick.

4. States Not Consulted in Passing on Their Jurisdiction to Nagarpalikas: Self-government is a state subject under the constitution but the states have not been consulted about the bill. It is not for the centre to legislate on it or even to suggest a uniform pattern. The jurisdiction of the state is being passed on to the nagarpalikas without the states being taken into confidence. It is alleged that the meeting of a hundred officials cannot be a substitute for constitutional consultation with the states.

5. Involvement of Centre–state Relations in the Bill and Therefore Challengeable in Courts of Law: Notwithstanding the claim of the government that the bill did not involve Centre–state relations, these are definitely involved. In the Twelfth Schedule attached to the bill, public health is Item 6 of the state list, and so are sanitation, sewerage, and sewage disposal, as well as hospitals and public health clinics. Veterinary services is Item 15 of the state list, and burials and burial grounds is Item 16. In fact, out of 37 items mentioned in the Twelfth Schedule, the majority are from the state list, and only a few are from the concurrent list. These items in the state or concurrent lists would be affected in the new scheme of things. Whether this also affects the basic structure of the Constitution is a highly complex constitutional question, and will no doubt be challenged in the courts, if they do become a part of the Constitution.

6. No Clear-cut Relationship Between the Tiers of Governments: The bill creates a third tier of administration but does not very clearly establish the correlation between the centre, states, and the nagarpalikas. As far as the Centre–state relations are concerned, experts are of the opinion that the constitution is tilted in favour of the centre. Where does the third tier of administration get in? Can or ought there be a direct relationship between the centre and the nagarpalikas? Moreover, the attempt to put the tiny local bodies in the large constitutional framework is fraught with major difficulties. After all, most of the development schemes and non-plan urban activities in the areas under local self-government will have to be done by the state administration.

7. Place of MLAs, MPs and Bureaucrats Not Defined: It is essential for the success of the bill that the role and place of members of the State Legislatures and Parliament as also that of bureaucrats should be clearly delineated in the administrative process of nagarpalikas. There is hardly any mention in the bill of the manner in which MLAs and MPs are to be accommodated in view of the influence they command in the cities and towns, and also in regard to the position of the bureaucrats who do not know who their bosses would be in the new scheme of things.

8. Election Commission Not Adequately Equipped to Conduct Elections: It is common knowledge that the Election Commission, which enjoys the ultimate authority of fixing the duties for conducting all elections, has no means of supervising polls on its own. It has to depend on both the Centre and the state governments. The bill does not mention the safeguards that the government proposes to ensure that the imposition of grassroots democracy will be followed up with faithful implementation, though the government assures that the Election Commission shall be strengthened to cope with the additional responsibility of conducting elections to urban local bodies.

9. Discretionary Powers of the Governor: The bill gives wide powers to the governor. For instance he has the power to declare by public notification an area with a population of between 10,000 and 20,000 as a transitional area. He is also given the power to declare the existing town committees and notified areas committees with a population of less than 10,000 as nagar panchayats.

10. Different Treatment for Scheduled Areas: The scheduled areas are treated differently in the bill. The bill provides, 'Notwithstanding anything in the Constitution, the Governor of a State may in his discretion and subject to such exceptions and modifications as he may specify, by public notification, extend Chapter II to IV to the Scheduled Areas referred to in clause 1 or the tribal areas referred to in clause C of Article 244, comprising within that state.'

It has been clarified by the Government that the term 'governor' actually means the government. This is a correct interpretation and in keeping with the rest of the constitution. It is true that the governors have some discretionary powers but these are specifically mentioned in the constitution. Even in the Nagarpalika Bill, the governor has to use his own discretion in respect of some matters connected with the scheduled areas.

The criticism offered by the critics of the bill, when analysed objectively and dispassionately, would confirm that there was no dispute whatsoever about the contents of the bill, which had been applauded and appreciated by one and all, and the criticism centres round the undemocratic manner of eliciting the opinion of the public, political parties, and the states. The crux of the whole issue, that the states had been bypassed and their jurisdiction had been invaded by the Centre and the basic structure of the constitution had been changed, could be decided by the Supreme Court. The government planned to get constitutional sanction for ensuring democracy in urban local bodies and to endow them with the responsibilities and finances required to ensure that 'urban India flourishes and leads the country forward to progress and prosperity'.

The Constitution (73rd Amendment) Bill, 1991, pertaining to urban local bodies introduced in the Lok Sabha on 16 September 1991, was passed as the Constitution (74th Amendment) Act, 1992 in the winter session of 1992, and it received the assent of the President on 29 April 1993. The Act seeks to provide a common framework for the structure and mandate of urban local bodies to enable them to function as effective democratic units of local self-government.

Government of India had specified 1 June 1993 as the date from which the 74th Amendment Act came into force. The Act provided a period of one year from the date of its commencement, within which the municipal laws that were then in force in the states/union territories, were required to be changed, amended, or modified in order to bring them in conformity with the provisions of the Constitution (74th Amendment) Act, 1992.

The various states/union territories have since enacted new legislations as required by the Government of India within the stipulated period. It is hoped that their implementation in letter and spirit would usher in a new era for the urban local governments, endowed as they would be with the genuine democratic structure (power to the people), devolution of powers (decentralization), active participation in the formulation of the plans for the development of their respective areas and their implementation, adequate resources assured to them by way of augmenting their revenues by enhancement of their powers of taxation, share in the state revenues, generous grants-in-aid, reservation of seats for scheduled castes in proportion to their population and 33 per cent quota for women, and finally to accord due respect and prestige to the elected representatives by the bureaucracy.

The Act has been in force for a short period only. It will take some time to realize the objectives enshrined in the various provisions of the Act. But what has been actually observed so far seems to fall short of the expectations raised by the Act, as it is taking unnecessarily long to convince the people about the seriousness on the part of the politicians to let the urban local governments evolve as institutions of self-government. Lack of political will and the obstructive attitude of the bureaucracy are considered to be the greatest hurdles in the devolution of powers to the local bodies.

TEXT OF THE CONSTITUTION (74TH AMENDMENT) ACT, 1992

An Act

Further to amend the Constitution of India

Be it enacted by Parliament in the Forty-third Year of the Republic of India as follows:

1. **Short Title and Commencement**—(1) This Act may be called the Constitution (74th Amendment) Act, 1992.

   (2) It shall come into force on such date as the Central Government may, be notification in the Official Gazette, appoint.

2. **Insertion of New Part IX-A**—After Part IX of the Constitution, the following Part shall be inserted, namely:

Part IX-A

The Municipalities

243-P. Definitions

In this Part, unless the context otherwise requires—

(*a*) 'Committee' means a Committee constituted under Article 243-S;

(*b*) 'district' means a district of a State;

(*c*) 'Metropolitan area' means an area having a population of ten lakhs or more comprised in one or more districts and consisting of two or more Municipalities or Panchayats or other contiguous areas, specified by the Governor by public notification to be a Metropolitan area for the purposes of this Part;

(*d*) 'Municipal area' means the territorial area of a Municipality as is notified by the Governor;

(*e*) 'Municipality' means an institution of self-government constituted under Article 243-Q;

(*f*) 'Panchayat' means a Panchayat constituted under Article 243-B;

(*g*) 'Population' means the population as ascertained at the last preceding census of which the relevant figures have been published.

243-Q. Constitution of Municipalities

(1) There shall be constituted in every State—

(*a*) a Nagar Panchayat (by whatever name called) for a transitional area, that is to say, an area in transition from a rural area to an urban area;

(*b*) a Municipal Council for a smaller urban area; and

(*c*) a Municipal Corporation for a larger urban area in accordance with the provisions of this Part:

Provided that a Municipality under this clause may not be constituted in such urban area or part thereof as the Governor may, having regard to the size of the area and the municipal services being provided or proposed to be provided by an industrial establishment in that area and such other factors as he may deem fit by public notification, specify to be an industrial township.

(2) In this Article, 'a transitional area', 'a smaller urban area' or 'a larger urban area' means such area as the Governor may, having regard to the population of the area, the density of the population therein,

the revenue generated for local administration, the percentage of employment in non-agricultural activities, the economic importance or such other factors as he may deem fit, specify by public notification for the purposes of this Part.

243-R. Composition of Municipalities

(1) Save as provided in clause (2), all the seats in a Municipality shall be filled by persons chosen by direct election from the territorial constituencies in the Municipal area and for this purpose each Municipal area shall be divided into territorial constituencies to be known as wards.

(2) The Legislature of a State may, by law, provide—

(*a*) for the representation in a Municipality of—

(*i*) persons having special knowledge or experience in Municipal administration;

(*ii*) the members of the House of the People and the members of the Legislative Assembly of the State representing constituencies which comprise wholly or partly the Municipal area;

(*iii*) the members of the Council of States and the members of the Legislative Council of the State registered as electors within the Municipal area;

(*iv*) the Chairpersons of the Committees constituted under clause (5) of Article 243-S:

Provided that the persons referred to in paragraph (*i*) shall not have the right to vote in the meetings of the Municipality;

(*b*) the manner of election of the Chairperson of a Municipality.

243-S. Constitution and Composition of Wards Committees, etc.

(1) There shall be constituted Wards Committees, consisting of one or more wards, within the territorial area of a Municipality having a population of three lakhs or more.

(2) The Legislature of a State may, by law, make provision with respect to—

(*a*) the composition and the territorial area of a Wards Committee;

(*b*) the manner in which the seats in a Wards Committee shall be filled.

(3) A member of a Municipality representing a ward within the territorial area of the Wards Committee shall be a member of that Committee.

(4) Where a Wards Committee consists of—

(*a*) one ward, the member representing that ward in the Municipality; or

(*b*) two or more wards, one of the members representing such wards in the Municipality elected by the Members of the Wards Committee.

shall be the Chairperson of that Committee.

(5) Nothing in this Article shall be deemed to prevent the Legislature of a State from making any provision for the constitution of committees in addition to the Wards Committees.

243-T. Reservation of Seats

(1) Seats shall be reserved for the Scheduled Castes and the Scheduled Tribes in every Municipality and the number of seats so reserved shall bear, as nearly as may be, the same proportion to the total number of seats to be filled by direct election in that Municipality as the population of the Scheduled Castes in the Municipal area or of the Scheduled Tribes in the Municipal area bears to the total population of that area and such seats may be allotted by rotation to different constituencies in a Municipality.

(2) Not less than one-third of the total number of seats reserved under clause (1) shall be reserved for women belonging to the Scheduled Castes or, as the case may be, the Scheduled Tribes.
(3) Not less than one-third (including the number of seats reserved for women belonging to the Scheduled Castes and the Scheduled Tribes) of the total number of seats to be filled by direct election in every Municipality shall be reserved for women and such seats may be allotted by rotation to different constituencies in a Municipality.
(4) The office of Chairpersons in the Municipalities shall be reserved for the Scheduled Castes, the Scheduled Tribes and women in such manner as the Legislature of a State may, by law, provide.
(5) The reservation of seats under clauses (1) and (2) and the reservation of office of Chairpersons (other than the reservation for women) under clause (4) shall cease to have effect on the expiration of the period specified in Article 334.
(6) Nothing in this Part shall prevent the Legislature of a State from making any provision for reservation of seats in any Municipality or office of Chairpersons in the Municipalities in favour of backward class of citizens.

243-U. Duration of Municipalities, etc.

(1) Every Municipality, unless sooner dissolved under any law for the time being in force, shall continue for five years from the date appointed for its first meeting and no longer:
Provided that a Municipality shall be given a reasonable opportunity of being heard before its dissolution.
(2) No amendment of any law for the time being in force shall have the effect of causing dissolution of a Municipality at any level, which is functioning immediately before such amendment, till the expiration of its duration specified in clause (1).
(3) An election to constitute a Municipality shall be completed,—

(*a*) before the expiry of its duration specified in clause (1);
(*b*) before the expiration of a period of six months from the date of its dissolution:

Provided that where the remainder of the period for which the dissolved Municipality would have continued is less than six months, it shall not be necessary to hold any election under this clause for constituting the Municipality for such period.

(4) A Municipality constituted upon the dissolution of Municipality before the expiration of its duration shall continue only for the remainder of the period for which the dissolved Municipality would have continued under clause (1) had it not been so dissolved.

243-V. Disqualification for Membership

(1) A person shall be disqualified for being chosen as, and for being, a member of a Municipality—

(*a*) if he is so disqualified by or under any law for the time being in force for the purposes of elections to the Legislature of the State concerned:
Provided that no person shall be disqualified on the ground that he is less than twenty-five years of age, if he has attained the age of twenty-one years;
(*b*) if he is so disqualified by or under any law made by the Legislature of the State.

(2) If any question arises as to whether a member of a Municipality has become subject to any of the disqualifications mentioned in clause (1), the question shall be referred for the decision of such authority and in such manner as the Legislature of a State may, by law, provide.

243-W. Powers, Authority and Responsibilities of Municipalities, etc.

Subject to the provisions of this Constitution, the Legislature of State may, by law, endow—

(*a*) the Municipalities with such powers and authority as may be necessary to enable them to function as institutions of self-government and such law may contain provision for the devolution of powers and responsibilities upon Municipalities, subject to such conditions as may be specified therein, with respect to—

(*i*) the preparation of plans for economic development and social justice;
(*ii*) the performance of functions and the implementation of schemes as may be entrusted to them including those in relation to the matter listed in the Twelfth Schedule;

(*b*) the Committees with such powers and authority as may be necessary to enable them to carry out the responsibilities conferred upon them including those in relation to the matters listed in the Twelfth Schedule.

243-X. Power to Impose Taxes by, and Funds of, the Municipalities

The Legislature of a State may, by law—

(*a*) authorize a Municipality to levy, collect and appropriate such taxes, duties, tolls and fees in accordance with such procedure and subject to such limits;
(*b*) assign to a Municipality such taxes, duties, tolls and fees levied and collected by the State Government for such purposes and subject to such conditions and limits;
(*c*) provide for making such grants-in-aid to the Municipalities from the Consolidated Fund of the State; and
(*d*) provide for constitution of such Funds for crediting all moneys received, respectively, by or on behalf of the Municipalities and also for the withdrawal of such moneys therefrom.

as may be specified in the law.

243-Y. Finance Commission

(1) The Finance Commission constituted under Article 243-I shall also review the financial position of the Municipalities and make recommendations to the Governor as to—

(*a*) the principles which should govern—

(*i*) the distribution between the State and the Municipalities of the net proceeds of the taxes, duties, tolls and fees leviable by the State, which may be divided between them under this Part, and the allocation between the Municipalities at all levels of the respective shares of such proceeds;
(*ii*) the determination of the taxes, duties, tolls and fees which may be assigned to or appropriated by, the Municipalities;
(*iii*) the grants-in-aid to the Municipalities from the Consolidated Fund of the State;

(*b*) the measures needed to improve the financial position of the Municipalities;
(*c*) any other matter referred to the Finance Commission by the Governor in the interests of sound finance of the Municipalities.

(2) The Governor shall cause every recommendation made by the Commission under this Article together with an explanatory memorandum as to the action taken thereon to be laid before the Legislature of the State.

243-Z. Audit of Accounts of Municipalities

The Legislature of a State may, by law, make provisions with respect to the maintenance of accounts by the Municipalities and the audit of such accounts.

243-ZA. Elections to the Municipalities

(1) The superintendence, direction and control of the preparation of electoral rolls for, and the conduct of, all elections to the Municipalities shall be vested in the State Election Commission referred to in Article 243-K.

(2) Subject to the provisions of this Constitution, the Legislature of a State may, by law, make provision with respect to all matters relating to or in connection with, elections to the Municipalities.

243-ZB. Application to Union Territories

The provisions of this Part shall apply to the Union territories and shall, in their application to a Union territory, have effect as if the references to the Governor of a State were references to the Administrator of the Union territory appointed under Article 239 and references to the Legislature or the Legislative Assembly of a State were references in relation to a Union territory having a Legislative Assembly, to that Legislative Assembly:

Provided that the President may, by public notification, direct that the provisions of this Part shall apply to any Union territory or part thereof subject to such exceptions and modifications as he may specify in the notification.

243-ZC. Part Not to Apply to Certain Areas

(1) Nothing in this Part shall apply to the scheduled areas referred to in clause (1), and the tribal areas referred to in clause (2), of Article 244.

(2) Nothing in this Part shall be construed to affect the functions and powers of the Darjeeling Gorkha Hill Council constituted under any law for the time being in force for the hill areas of the district of Darjeeling in the State of West Bengal.

(3) Notwithstanding anything in this Constitution, Parliament may, by law, extend the provisions of this Part to the scheduled areas and the tribal areas referred to in clause (1) subject to such exceptions and modifications as may be specified in such law, and no such law shall be deemed to be an amendment of this Constitution for the purposes of Article 368.

243-ZD. Committee for District Planning

(1) There shall be constituted in every State at the district level a District Planning Committee to consolidate the plans prepared by the Panchayats and the Municipalities in the district and to prepare a draft development plan for the district as a whole.

(2) The Legislature of a State may, by law, make provision with respect to—

(*a*) the composition of the District Planning Committees;

(*b*) the manner in which the seats in such Committees shall be filled:

Provided that not less than four-fifths of the total number of members of such Committee shall be elected by, and from amongst, the elected members of the Panchayat at the district level and of the Municipalities in the district in proportion to the ratio between the population of the rural areas and of the urban areas in the district;

(*c*) the functions relating to district planning which may be assigned to such Committees;

(*d*) the manner in which the Chairpersons of such Committees shall be chosen.

(3) Every District Planning Committee shall, in preparing the draft development plan,—

(*a*) have regard to—

(*i*) matters of common interest between the. Panchayats and the Municipalities including spatial planning, sharing of water and other physical and natural resources, the integrated development of infrastructure and environmental conservation;

(*ii*) the extent and type of available resources whether financial or otherwise;

(*b*) consult such institutions and organizations as the Governor may, by order, specify.

(4) The Chairperson of every District Planning Committee shall forward the development plan, as recommended by such Committee, to the Government of the State.

243-ZE. Committee for Metropolitan Planning

(1) There shall be constituted in every Metropolitan area a Metropolitan Planning Committee to prepare a draft development plan for the Metropolitan area as a whole.

(2) The Legislature of a State may, by law, make provision with respect to—

(*a*) the composition of the Metropolitan Planning Committees;

(*b*) the manner in which the seats in such Committees shall be filled:

Provided that not less than two-thirds of the members of such Committee shall be elected by, and from amongst, the elected members of the Municipalities and Chairpersons of the Panchayats in the Metropolitan area in proportion to the ratio between the population of the Municipalities and of the Panchayats in that area;

(*c*) the representation in such Committees of the Government of India and the Government of the State and of such organizations and institutions as may be deemed necessary for carrying out of functions assigned to such Committees;

(*d*) the functions relating to planning and coordination for the Metropolitan area which may be assigned to such Committees;

(*e*) the manner in which the Chairpersons of such Committees shall be chosen.

(3) Every Metropolitan Planning Committee shall, in preparing the draft development plan,—

(*a*) have regard to—

(*i*) the plans prepared by the Municipalities and the Panchayats, in the Metropolitan area;

(*ii*) matters of common interest between the Municipalities and the Panchayats, including coordinated spatial planning of the area, sharing of water and other physical and natural resources, the integrated development of infrastructure and environmental conservation;

(*iii*) the overall objectives and priorities set by the Government of India and the Government of the State;

(*iv*) the extent and nature of investments likely to be made in Metropolitan area by agencies of the Government of India and of the Government of the State and other available resources whether financial or otherwise;

(*b*) consult such institutions and organizations as the Governor may, by order, specify.

(4) The Chairperson of every Metropolitan Planning Committee shall forward the development plan, as recommended by such Committee, to the Government of the State.

243-ZF. Continuance of Existing Laws and Municipalities

Notwithstanding anything in this Part, any provision of any law relating to Municipalities in force in a State immediately before the commencement of the Constitution (74th Amendment) Act, 1992, which is inconsistent with the provisions of this Part, shall continue to be in force until amended or repealed by a competent Legislature or other competent authority or until the expiration of one year from such commencement, whichever is earlier:

Provided that all the Municipalities existing immediately before such commencement shall continue till the expiration of their duration, unless sooner dissolved by a resolution passed to that effect by the Legislative Assembly of that State or, in the case of a State having a Legislative Council, by each House of the Legislature of that State.

243-ZG. Bar to Interference by Courts in Electoral Matters

Notwithstanding anything in this Constitution,—

(*a*) the validity of any law relating to the delimitation of constituencies or the allotment of seats to such constituencies, made or purporting to be made under Article 243-ZA shall not be called in question in any court;

(*b*) no election to any Municipality shall be called in question except by an electron petition presented to such authority and in such manner as is provided for by or under any law made by the Legislature of a State.'

Amendment of Article 280

In clause (3) of Article 280 of the Constitution, sub-clause (*c*) shall be lettered as sub-clause (*d*) and before sub-clause (*d*) as so relettered, the following sub-clause shall be inserted, namely:

'(*c*) the measures needed to augment the Consolidated Fund of a State to supplement the resources of the Municipalities in the State on the basis of the recommendations made by the Finance Commission of the State.'

Addition of Twelfth Schedule

After the Eleventh Schedule to the Constitution, the following Schedule shall be added, namely—

Twelfth Schedule

(Article 243-W)

1. Urban planning including town planning.
2. Regulation of land-use and construction of buildings.
3. Planning for economic and social development.
4. Roads and bridges.
5. Water supply for domestic, industrial and commercial purposes.
6. Public health, sanitation, conservancy and solid waste management.
7. Fire services.
8. Urban forestry, protection of the environment and promotion of ecological aspects.
9. Safeguarding the interests of weaker sections of society including the handicapped and mentally retarded.
10. Slum improvement and upgradation.
11. Urban poverty alleviation.
12. Provision of urban amenities and facilities such as parks, gardens, playgrounds.

13. Promotion of cultural, educational and aesthetic aspects.
14. Burials and burial grounds; cremations, cremation grounds and electric crematoriums.
15. Cattle pounds; prevention of cruelty to animals.
16. Vital statistics including registration of births and deaths.
17. Public amenities including street lighting, parking lots, bus stops and public conveniences.
18. Regulation of slaughter houses and tanneries.

Extract of Article 243-I and 243-K from Clause 2 of the Constitution (73rd Amendment) Act, 1992 Which Are Referred to in the Constitution (74th Amendment) Act, 1992

243-I. Constitution of Finance Commission to Review Financial Position

(1) The Governor of a State shall, as soon as may be within one year from the commencement of the Constitution (73rd Amendment) Act, 1992, and thereafter at the expiration of every fifth year, constitute a Finance Commission to review the financial position of the Panchayats and to make recommendations to the Governor as to—

(*a*) the principles which should govern—

(*i*) the distribution between the State and the Panchayats of the net proceeds of the taxes, duties, tolls and fees leviable by the State, which may be divided between them under this Part and the allocation between the Panchayats at all levels of their respective shares of such proceeds;

(*ii*) the determination of taxes, duties, tolls and fees which may be assigned to, or appropriated by, the Panchayats;

(*iii*) the grants-in-aid to the Panchayats from the Consolidated Fund of the State;

(*b*) the measures needed to improve the financial position of the Panchayats;

(*c*) any other matter referred to the Finance Commission by the Governor in the interests of sound finance of the Panchayats.

(2) The Legislature of a State may, by law, provide for the composition of the Commission, the qualifications which shall be requisite for appointment as members thereof and the manner in which they shall be selected.

(3) The Commission shall determine their procedure and shall have such powers in the performance of their functions as the Legislature of the State may, by law, confer on them.

(4) The Governor shall cause every recommendation made by the Commission under this article together with an explanatory memorandum as to the action taken thereon to be laid before the Legislature of the State.

243-K. Elections to the Panchayats

(1) The superintendence, direction and control of the preparation of electoral rolls for, and the conduct of, all elections to the Panchayats shall be vested in a State Election Commission consisting of a State Election Commissioner to be appointed by the Governor.

(2) Subject to the provisions of any law made by the Legislature of a State, the conditions of service and tenure of office of the State Election Commissioner shall be such as the Governor may by rule determine:

Provided that the State Election Commissioner shall not be removed from his office except in like manner and on the like grounds as Judge of a High Court and the conditions of service of the State Election Commissioner shall not be varied to his disadvantage after his appointment.

(3) The Governor of a State shall, when so requested by the State Election Commission, make available to the State Election Commission such staff as may be necessary for the discharge of the functions conferred on the State Election Commission by clause (1).

(4) Subject to the provisions of this Constitution, the Legislature of a State may, by law, make provision with respect to all matters relating to, or in connection with elections to the Panchayats.

6

Municipal Councils

India has a three-level system of government: the Union, the states and local government. Earlier, the Constitution of India prescribed the legislative, administrative, and financial powers of the Union and the states only. It did not specify anything so far as local government was concerned. Local government was exclusively a state subject,[1] and the structure and powers of urban local bodies were defined by the municipal laws enacted by the concerned state. The local government thus did not enjoy any constitutional status of its own but had statutory status under the state laws. The Constitution (74th Amendment) Act, 1992, grants constitutional status to local bodies (urban) and provides for their structure, powers and functions.

The urban areas comprise different types of municipal bodies constituted with reference to character, size, and importance of different towns and cities.[2] The structure and operation of municipal institutions are also largely influenced by the modes of community living and philosophical formulations, besides the interactions between the political and socio-economic systems. Municipal corporations, municipal committees, notified area committees, town area committees, and cantonment boards were the usual types of municipal bodies, and while the first four types were created under state municipal laws, the cantonment boards owed their origin to the central act called the Cantonments Act, 1924. In most of the states, all these types of urban local bodies existed except in the town area committees, which had since been abolished and converted into Class-III municipal committees. Town area committees were semi-municipal committees constituted for small towns by a separate act of the state legislature. Their members were elected or nominated by the state government and were assigned a limited number of functions such as street lighting, drainage, and conservancy.

The state government may by notification propose any area except a military cantonment area to be a municipality, as well as define its territorial limits and make alterations in them. A municipality is a body politic and corporate constituted by the incorporation of the inhabitants of a city or town. Its chief attribute is independent succession and continuity of identity, notwithstanding increase or decrease in its membership.

The criteria for the setting up of a municipality in a town or city differed from state to state and even within the same state. The factors weighing with the state governments in this regard were generally the size; the occupation, composition, income and density of its population; political considerations, and commercial and economic potentialities. Bihar and Gujarat, for example, stipulated a population of 5,000, three-fourths of the adult male population pursuing professions other than agriculture, and a density of 1,000 persons per square mile; Uttar Pradesh prescribed a population of 8,000 to 10,000 and annual income of Rs 25,000. However, the Balwant Rai Mehta Committee had observed that all municipalities having a population of less than 10,000 may be included in the rural areas. The municipal acts of various governments themselves laid down the criterion for setting up a municipality in terms of its population and income. But the finances or the ability and willingness of the residents of the town or city concerned to provide for civic amenities must be a guiding factor for determining the grant of municipal status to a town or a city.

Classification of Municipal Committees

In almost all the states, municipalities are classified on the basis of their population, income and other relevant factors, as it is detrimental to the interest of different municipalities if they are all to be governed by the same provisions of the Municipal Act. Powers that might be granted to large towns cannot be extended to municipalities that are a mere collection of villages.[3] It is but natural that a high-income generating town would expect a higher powers, status, and level of civic services than a low-income generating one. The Rural–Urban Relationship Committee had also pointed out that categorization of municipal bodies into suitable grades is inescapable, if any homogeneity in administrative services, civic facilities, tax resources, grants, and the like with each grade is to be introduced.[4]

Accordingly, the various municipalities are classified into first, second, and third classes.

Size of the Municipal Council

The size of a municipal council is determined by the state government. It should neither be too large or too small. It is true that the larger the council, the greater the scope for participation and for adequate representation of the public, but there is also the danger of ineffectiveness. The smaller the council, the greater the scope for the councillor to participate effectively, but it cannot provide wide representation and it carries the risk of the councillors to be involved in personal relationships.[5] In France, a municipal council consists of 10 to 36 members in such a way that the proportion of councillors to population is higher in the smaller communes than in large ones.[6] In this way, the smallest communes have enough members to ensure full discussion and participation of almost all interests and the largest communes are not over-crowded with councillors. This is a very sound proportion and could be adopted with distinct advantage. On balance, a council with 10 to 30 members would represent a golden mean though the number may be slightly larger in higher cities subject to a ceiling of 50. In short, the size should neither be too unwieldy nor too small; it should be representative as well as responsive to the needs of the city. The Rural–Urban Relationship Committee had suggested the size of the municipal council on the basis of population as follows (see Table 6.1):

Table 6.1 *Table showing size of municipal council in relation to population*

Population	*Number of councillors*
20,000–50,000	15–25
50,000–100,000	25–35
100,000–500,000	35–45

The committee had further recommended that a city with a population of more than five lakh should be converted into a corporation. Generally, the minimum number of councillors is fixed at five and it increases progressively with the corresponding increase in population of the concerned town or city. With the increase of population by 5,000, the number of councillors is increased by one. This process of addition of one member continues upto one lakh of population. Thereafter with every increase of 10,000 population, one member is added, and when the population exceeds two lakh then after every 20,000 increase in population, one member is added. Similarly, if the population exceeds three lakh, one member is added after 25,000 increase in population.[7]

The Municipal Council, President, and the Executive Officer constitute the main components of municipal government structure and organization.

STATE ELECTION COMMISSION

The Constitution (74th Amendment) Act, 1992, provides that each state or union territory will have to constitute a state election commission,[8] for the superintendence, direction, and control of the preparation of the electoral rolls for, and the conduct of, all elections to the panchayats and municipalities in the state and to provide for all matters relating to or ancillary or in connection with the election to the panchayats and municipalities in terms of the provisions of Parts IX and IX-A of the Constitution of India. The said commission will be headed by a state election commissioner appointed by the governor of the state concerned. A person to be appointed as state election commissioner should be an officer of the state government not below the age of 55 years and of the rank of financial commissioner or the principal secretary to the state government, having service as such for a minimum period of two years, or should be a serving or retired judge of the High Court. But an officer who has attained age of superannuation shall not be appointed as election commissioner and, on ceasing to hold the office of election commissioner, shall be eligible for any other appointment under the state government.

The governor of the state may determine the rules governing the conditions of service and tenure of office of the state election commissioner. The state election commissioner cannot be removed from office except in a manner similar to and on grounds similar to those by which a judge of the High Court can be removed from his office. The conditions of service of the state election commissioner cannot be varied to his disadvantage after his appointment. The governor of a state would make available to the state election commissioner such staff as may be requested by him and which he may consider necessary for the discharge of the functions conferred on the state election commission.

Administrative Machinery for the Conduct of Elections

The state government may appoint one or more deputy election commissioners and a secretary to the election commissioner. There shall be for each district a district election officer who shall be such officer of the government as the election commissioner may on consultation with the state government designate or nominate. He shall supervise the preparation, revision, and correction of the electoral rolls in the district, and perform such other functions as may be entrusted to him by the election commissioner.

The election commissioner shall also in consultation with the state government designate or nominate a returning officer for every constituency. It shall be his duty to do all such acts and things as may be necessary for effectively conducting an election.

The district election officer shall with the previous approval of the election commissioner provide a sufficient number of polling stations for every constituency within his jurisdiction, and appoint presiding officer for each polling station and such polling officers as he thinks necessary.

As soon as the notification calling upon a constituency to elect a member or members is issued, the election commission shall appoint the last date for making nomination, the date for scrutiny of nominations, the last date for the withdrawal of candidates, and the date or dates on which a poll, if necessary, shall be taken.

A contesting candidate may appoint his election agent and he or his election agent may appoint his polling agent at each polling station and a counting agent at the time of the counting of votes.

The votes shall be counted by or under the supervision and guidance of the returning officer and when the counting of the votes has been completed, he shall declare the result of the election and shall report it to the election commissioner.

The state government, in consultation with the election commission, appoint an election tribunal for each district, or part thereof at the district or sub-divisional headquarters, to try election petition which may be presented by any candidate or by an elector. At the conclusion of the trial of an election petition, the election tribunal may dismiss it and declare the election of all or any of the returned candidates to be void, and the petitioner or any other candidate to have been duly elected. The election tribunal shall intimate the decision to the election commission as soon as possible. He shall cause the order to be published in the official gazette. An appeal against the order of the election tribunal can be preferred in the High Court which shall decide it and intimate the decision to the election commissioner.

It may be mentioned that the civil court shall have no jurisdiction to question the legality of any action taken or of any decision given by the returning officer or by any other person appointed in connection with the election.

Nagar Panchayats and Municipal Councils

The Constitution (74th Amendment) Act, 1992 aimed at reconstructing, revamping, and revitalizing urban local governments. The Government of India had notified 1 June 1993 from which the act came into force. The act provided for a period of one year from the date of its commencement within which municipal laws, which were in force at that time in the states and the union territories, were required to be changed, amended, or modified in order to bring them in conformity with the provisions of the Constitution (74th Amendment) Act, 1992. Various states and union territories have accordingly enacted legislation for the government of the urban local bodies in their respective jurisdictions. The Punjab Government, for example, has enacted the Punjab Municipal Bill, 1998 to replace the Punjab Municipal Act, 1911, the Punjab Municipal (Executive Officers) Act, 1931, and the Punjab Municipal Corporation Act, 1976 by a comprehensive new act to comply with the provisions of the 74th Amendment Act, 1992.

The objectives of the new Punjab Municipal Act, 1998, as also those of the acts passed by several other states and union territories, are:

1. To adhere to the basic framework laid down in the Constitution (74th Amendment) Act, 1992, which would ensure that the municipalities in the state, that is to say, the municipal corporations for the larger urban areas, the municipal councils for smaller urban areas, and the nagar panchayats for transitional areas are in a position to function effectively as vibrant units of self-government.
2. To provide for greater participation of the people in the administration of urban local bodies with a view to ensuring democratic decentralization and to ensure financial self-sufficiency of the three levels of municipalities in the state and to improve financial management thereof.
3. To provide for adequate devolution of powers and functions to the municipalities.

In our country, various forms of urban local bodies have been existing before the commencement of the Constitution (74th Amendment) Act, 1992. These were municipal corporations, municipal committees, town area committees, and notified area committees. But now these have been restricted to three types only, namely nagar panchayats, municipal councils, and municipal corporations.[9] The first two are discussed in this chapter and the third in the following chapter.

Nagar Panchayats

A nagar panchayat (by whatever name called) is constituted for a transitional area, that is to say, an area in transition from a rural area to an urban area. The population of such an area is five thousands or more but is less than fifteen thousands and the revenue generated from tax and other sources exceeds such amount per capita per annum as may be specified by the government from time to time.

Every nagar panchayat is a body corporate and has a perpetual succession and a common seal with power to acquire, hold, or dispose of properties and may sue and be sued.

A nagar panchayat shall consist of such number of elected members, not less than nine and more than fifteen, as the government, may determine by rules: the members of the legislative assembly representing in constituencies comprising the transitional area or any part thereof, and two members nominated by the government from amongst the persons having special knowledge or experience in municipal administration. The nominated members shall not have the right to vote in the meeting of the nagar panchayats.

The government may, in consultation with the nagar panchayat, include within a transitional area any area adjacent thereto, exclude from a transitional area any area comprised therein, and specify a transitional area to be a smaller urban area in which case members of the nagar panchayat shall be deemed to be the members of the municipal council, where the municipal council shall be of class-C status.

The government shall divide a traditional area into a number of territorial constituencies to be known as wards and each ward shall elect only one member.

The term of a nagar panchayat shall be of five years unless sooner dissolved on the charges of being incompetent to perform, showing gross neglect in the performance of its duties, persistently making default in the performance of its duties, exceeding or abusing its power or its financial position, and thus its credit being seriously threatened in the opinion of the government.

When a nagar panchayat has been dissolved, its members shall vacate their offices forthwith and the elections to the new nagar panchayat shall be held within six months. An administrator to be appointed by the government shall administer the affairs of the nagar Panchayat during the period it remains dissolved.

Reservation of Seats

Out of the total number of seats in the nagar panchayat to be filled by direct election, seats for Scheduled Castes and Scheduled Tribes shall be reserved in the same proportion of the total number of seats to be filled by direct election in the nagar panchayat, as the population of Scheduled Castes, Scheduled Tribes bears to the total population of that area, and such seats shall be allotted by rotation to different wards in the area; one-third of total number of reserved seats for Scheduled Castes and Scheduled Tribes shall be reserved for women belonging to the Scheduled Castes. Further, one-third of the total seats to be filled by direct election shall be reserved for women (including the number of seats reserved for women belonging to the Scheduled castes and the Scheduled Tribes). It is optional for the government to reserve seats for the backward classes also.

A nagar panchayat shall elect from among its members, one President and one vice-president in a meeting to be convened and presided over by the deputy commissioner or an officer not below the rank of an extra assistant commissioner, authorised by the deputy commissioner. The president may be removed by the nagar panchayat by adopting a motion expressing lack of confidence on him. But no such motion shall be moved within two years from the date of assumption of office by him. The government may also remove the president any time on the ground of abuse of power or persistent failure to perform his duties.

Powers and Functions of Nagar Panchayat

It shall be the duty of nagar panchayat to consider all periodical statements of the receipts and disbursements and all progress reports and pass such resolution thereon as it may think fit. It may, at any time, require the executive officer to produce any records, correspondence, plan or other documents, and to furnish any return, plan, estimate, accounts, or statistics relating to the administration of nagar panchayat.

Every nagar panchayat shall perform obligatory functions of water supply, drainage, scavenging of streets, street lighting, prevention of diseases, etc. and discretionary functions of providing primary education, organisation and management of fairs, bathing places, and planning for social and economic development subject to financial resources at its disposal.

Executive Officer

Each nagar panchayat shall have one executive officer appointed by the state government who shall be a member of the Punjab Service of Executive Officer. He may be asked to act as an executive officer of another nagar panchayat also. His allowances and salary and such facilities as residential accommodation and conveyance shall be paid out of the municipal fund of the nagar panchayat which shall also make contribution towards his pension and provident fund.

The powers and functions of the executive officer are:

1. carrying on the day to day administration of the nagar panchayat,
2. exercising the powers and perform the functions conferred or imposed upon him by law, and
3. assign the duties, and supervise and control the acts and proceedings of the officers and employees of the nagar panchayat.

All officers and employees of the nagar panchayat shall be subordinate to him.

Municipal Council

A municipal council is constituted for a small urban area, the population of which is fifteen thousands or more but is less than three lakh, and the revenue generated from tax and other sources exceeds such amount per capita per annum as may be specified by the government from time to time. The government shall also classify the municipal councils as –Class A (population of one lakh or more), Class B (population fifty thousands or more but less than one lakh), and Class C (population fifteen thousands but less than fifty thousands). A municipal council, however, may not be constituted for area or part thereof, as the government may, having regard to the size of the area and the municipal services being provided by an industrial establishment in that area and other factors, as the government may think it.

Composition of the Municipal Council

A municipal council shall have, in the case of Class A, not less than twenty and more than fifty elected members; in the case of Class B, not less than fifteen and more than thirty; and in case of Class C, not less than ten and more than fifteen. The members of the legislative assembly (MLAs) of the state representing constituencies comprising the smaller urban area or any part thereof, are *ex-officio* members, and not more than three members are nominated by the government from among the persons having special knowledge or experience in municipal administration. The nominated members, however, shall not have the right to vote in the meetings of the municipal council.

Election of Councillors

Members are elected through adult franchise based on secret ballot, the voting age used to be twenty-one years till 1988 when it was reduced to eighteen years under the Constitution (62nd Amendment) Bill, presented in the Parliament by B. Shankranand, Minister for Law and Justice on December 13, 1988 and passed unanimously by the Lok Sabha on December 17, 1988, and by Rajya Sabha on December 21, 1988. The reason given in the statement and objectives of the bill was that the youth of today are literate, enlightened, and politically conscious, and the lowering of voting age would provide to the unrepresented youth an opportunity to give vent to their feelings and help them become a part of the political process.

Elections are held in accordance with municipal election rules. The whole municipal area is divided into as many wards as there may be the number of councillors to be elected. While demarcating the territorial limits of these wards, care is taken that the number of electors in each ward is almost equal. This is done to keep the elector–councillor ratio on a rational basis. The delimitation work is undertaken periodically by the director of local government.

A candidate seeking election must be a resident of the city concerned and at least twenty-five years of age. He should possess a sound mind and must not be an insolvent. He should not be on the pay roles of the municipality and none of his close relations should be on contract for any municipal work.

Electoral rolls of the legislative assembly in relation to municipal area are generally taken as the voters lists, but the state government may direct the preparation of fresh rolls for each ward.

The candidates contesting the elections are allotted symbols subject to their availability on the approved list, according to their preferences, which cannot exceed three. Symbols of the recognized political parties are allotted only to the candidates sponsored or adopted by them. Thereafter starts electioneering by the candidates and their supporters. The candidates, who are put up by the political parties, issue their manifestoes, whereas others bring out pamphlets and posters containing their concern for certain issues and problems of the local residents. Public meetings, corner, and road side meetings, etc. are held by the candidates and their supporters. Loudspeakers, fixed on rickshaws, three wheelers, and other automobiles are frequently used to announce the programmes of the concerned candidates. Door-to-door canvassing is also the usual feature of the campaign. The voters exercise their right to vote on the election-day at the allotted polling stations.

After the time for casting of votes is over, the presiding officer collects the ballot boxes duly sealed by the polling officers and signed by the candidates or their polling agents. The counting of votes is done at a place decided by the district election officer in the presence of candidates or their election agents. The presiding officer gives a reasonable opportunity to the candidates or their election agents to check those ballots that are likely to be declared as invalid and settles the objections, if any. Applications for recounting can be entertained and considered by the presiding officer before the declaration of the results. After the completion of the counting of votes, the district election officer or the presiding officer declares a candidate securing the largest number of valid votes, as elected; and if there is a tie, the matter is decided by drawing of lots.

The deputy commissioner has to call the meeting of the elected members within fourteen days of the notification to administer oath of office to them and to hold the election of president and vice-president.

Reservation of Seats for Scheduled Castes, Scheduled Tribes, and Women

The Amendment Act, 1992 also provides for reservation of seats for scheduled castes and scheduled tribes in every municipality.[10] The proportion of seats to be reserved for them shall be the same as the proportion of their population in the municipal area to the total population of the area. Not less than one-third of the total number of seats reserved for SC and ST shall be reserved for women belonging to the SC and ST. Further, not less than one-third—including the number of seats reserved for women belonging to SC and ST—of the total member of seats to be filled by direct election in every municipality, shall be reserved for women, and such seats may be allotted by rotation to different constituencies in a municipality.

Secondly, the state legislatures shall have to make provision by law for the reservation of chairpersons in municipalities for SC, ST, and woman.

There shall be no bar on the state legislatures in making provision for reservation of seats in any municipality or office of the chairperson in the municipalities in favour of backward classes of the citizens.

Ward Committees

The Constitution (74th Amendment) Act, 1992 provides for the constitution of ward committees consisting of one or more wards within the territorial area of a municipality, having a population of three lakh or more.[11] The legislature of a state may, by law, make provisions with respect to the composition and the territorial area of a ward committee, and the manner in which the seats in the ward committee shall be filled. But a member of a municipality representing a ward within the territorial area of the ward committee shall be a member of the ward committee. And if a ward committee consists of one ward, the member representing that ward in the municipality or two or more wards, one of the members representing such wards in the municipality elected by the members of the ward committee shall be the chairman of the committee. The ward committees shall ensure immediate contacts between the electorate and the elected members, and increased participation of the people in the affairs of the urban bodies.

Standing Committee

A municipal council shall constitute a standing committee which shall consist of the president, senior vice-president and the vice-president, and four other members in the case of Class A council and two members in the case of Class B councils to be elected by the members of the municipal council from amongst elected members—for a period of two and a half years. All the matters coming before the standing committee shall be determined by a majority of votes of the members present, and in the case of equality of votes, the chairman shall have a right of a second or a casting vote. The standing committee has the power to ask the executive officer to produce any record, correspondence, plan, and other documents in his possession or under his control, or which is recorded or filed in his office or in the office of any officer of the municipal council, and furnish any return, plan, estimate, statement, accounts, or statistics relating to the administration of the municipal council.

Duration of Municipalities

Every municipality, unless disallowed earlier, shall continue for a period of five years from the date appointed for its first meeting after its constitution, and no longer.

Dissolution of the Municipality

If, in the opinion of the government, a municipality is not competent to perform or has shown gross neglect in the performance of the duties imposed on it, or if it persistently makes default in the performance of such duties or in complying with lawful directions and orders issued by the government or any authority, empowered under any law, or exceeds or abuses its power, or if the financial position and the credit of the municipality is seriously threatened, the government may, by an order published in the official gazette with reasons, therefore dissolve the municipality. But a municipality shall be given a reasonable opportunity of being heard before its dissolution.

The consequences of the dissolution shall be that all members of the municipality shall vacate their offices forthwith; all properties vested in the municipality during the period of dissolution rest with the government. Elections shall be held before the expiry of a period of six months from the date of dissolution.[12]

Co-option or Nomination of Members

Co-option is one of the methods used for giving representation to minority community and special interests. It is based on the British system of elderman who the councillors elect for his rich municipal experience, expertise in municipal administration, and spirit of public service. This system is preferable to the system of nominations as the onus of nomination falls not on the government but on the council itself. But it is regrettable that in our country members are co-opted not on the basis of their merit but on party affiliations. This is not a healthy practice. The members should be co-opted irrespective of party allegiance and on the basis of proportional representation to enable every party to co-opt members in proportion of its strength in the council.

Associate Members

The state governments also make a provision for associating the MLAs, representing the whole or part of the area covered by the municipal committee, with the municipal council. An associate member has the right to take part in the deliberations of the municipal council but he has not the right to vote. There is divergence of opinion on the issue of associating legislators with the municipal council. Its advocates argue that the legislators can create healthy impact on the standard of debates and on the functionaries of the municipal institutions and that their association enhances the prestige of local bodies and makes for direct ventilation of local problems in the state legislatures. But the opponents are of the opinion that local problems should be solved exclusively by the local leaders and that the presence of legislators would bring into play a number of extraneous forces, most disruptive of which would be politics. Anyhow, the practice of associating the legislators with the council continues to be in vogue.

Removal or Disqualification of Municipal Councillors

The methods of removal of members vary from state to state. For instance, in Bihar, the municipal act provides for the recall of elected members if three-fourth of the voters of the concerned ward represent to the state government on his removal, but no such members can be removed unless he has held office for one year. Provision of removal of members exists in Punjab and Haryana also. The government may, by notification, remove any member: (*a*) if he refuses to act, or becomes in the opinion of the government incapable of acting, or has been declared a bankrupt or an insolvent, or has been convicted of any such offence or subjected by a criminal court to any such order as implies in the opinion of the government a defect of character which unfits him to be a member; (*b*) if he has been declared to be disqualified for employment in or has been dismissed from the public service; (*c*) if he has, without reasonable cause, absented himself for more than three consecutive months from the meetings of the committee; (*d*) if his continuance in office is dangerous to the public peace or order; (*e*) if he has flagrantly abused his position as a member of the committee or has through negligence or misconduct been responsible for the loss or misappropriation of any money or property of the committee. It is usually under this provision of the act that the party in power in the respective states has usually taken action against its rivals and opponents in the municipal government.

Meetings of the Council

Municipal council meets for the transaction of business at least once in a month which is usually presided over by the president or, in his absence, by the vice-president and, in the absence of both, by a member chosen by the council for this purpose. A meeting can also be called, either special or ordinary, by the president or in his absence by the vice-president on his own, or on a requisition specifying the purpose of the meeting, made in writing by at least one-fifth of the total membership. The quorum necessary for a special meeting is one half, but not less than three, of the council members actually serving at that time. The quorum for an ordinary meeting can be decided by the municipality in accordance with its bylaws but, in any case, it cannot be less than three. Normally, all the decisions are taken by a majority of votes of the members present and by voting. In case of a tie, the chairman can exercise a second or casting vote. The minutes of proceedings of each meeting are recorded in the 'proceedings book' of the municipality and are signed by the chairman and a copy of every resolution is forwarded within three days to the deputy commissioner. The recorded proceedings are normally open to the citizens for inspection without charge.

Committee System

The municipal council, over-burdened with increasing load of work and suffering from paucity of time, is not in a position to examine every issue coming before it threadbare. It, therefore, elects sub-committees comprising councillors from amongst itself to study a problem in depth and make recommendations for its solution. In the words of R.M. Jackson, 'The Committee system is the most distinctive mark of British local government; a committee may examine a matter, thrash it out in detailed discussion and so be able to make to the council a recommendation that is based on a more careful and prolonged examination than could be made in a council meeting; a committee may also carry out a number of the functions of the council, acting under powers delegated to it and thus act as an agent of the council.'

The sub-committees may be of two types: (*a*) statutory committees, required to be created by municipal act; and (*b*) non-statutory committees, created by the council under its bylaws. The ward committees, as mentioned in the foregoing, have statutory status. A ward committee is to manage the affairs of a ward or wards as the case may be on behalf of the municipality. Municipal committees constitute standing sub-committees under its bylaws, such as building, octroi, vehicle, conservancy, finance and works sub-committees, and *ad hoc* sub-committees like the lease sub-committee. Each sub-committee consists of five members including its chairman and is elected annually from amongst the members of the council on the basis of majority votes whereby the candidates of majority party are sure to be elected.

Municipal councils also appoint special sub-committees for certain specific purposes and follow the same procedure for their election as it adopts for the constitution of standing sub-committees. Some of such special sub-committees are constituted, for example, to celebrate Independence and Republic Days, to eradicate corruption in municipal committee, to enquire into the report of the executive officer regarding disciplinary action against an employee, to give reception to VIP's, to extend municipal limits, to merge the adjoining areas in it and to convert itself into a bigger municipality as a result of the amalgamation of twin cities, and so on.

The opposition parties have been consistently raising the issue that the election to the sub-committees should be on the principle of proportional representation but the party in power has been rejecting it on the plea that the sub-committees in that case would be just a replica of the party position in the council. In a petition filed by some members of Ambala City municipal committee in the Punjab and Haryana High Court, Chandigarh, the adoption of single majority vote for the election of sub-committees as against single transferable vote as provided in Rule 18 of bylaws of Haryana Municipal Act had been challenged. The petitioners had also contended that the government, with a view to favouring municipal president, had adopted a procedure not provided by law. The court had stayed the election of the sub-committees. The state governments, therefore, should ensure the adoption of proportional representation system to give due representation to all the political parties on the sub-committees.

The composition of sub-committee also reveals that one councillor serves on a number of sub-committees. He cannot, therefore, be expected to contribute anything worth the name to their deliberations. It would, therefore, be advisable that the membership of a councillor should be restricted to two or three sub-committees at the most. That would ensure their better functioning and also minimize the monopolistic attitude of party bosses and heart-burning among the councillors.

It is also observed that the recommendations made by the sub-committees are often rejected, altered, or modified by the council in a number of cases. For example, a sub-committee in a municipal committee had investigated charges against a superintendent and found him guilty, but the council had decided with the casting vote of the president that no action should be taken; a sub-committee had recommended generous grant of licences to scooter rickshaws, but the council had turned it down; a sub-committee was constituted to report on the extension or reversion of deputationists, but before it could make any recommendations, the council wrote to the department concerned for the extension of the term of deputationists. Similarly, the decision of a special sub-committee to renew the terms of certain plots on lease was not accepted by the council, and so on. Since the recommendations of the sub-committees are not binding on the council, their role could be termed as insignificant. The Rural–Urban Relationship Committee (1966) had underlined the need for streamlining the committee system to make their best possible use. But satisfactory progress in this regard has not been achieved mainly due to lack of coordination, difficulty in drawing a clear line of demarcation between the powers of the council and those of the committees, tendency to interfere in the day-to-day working of officials, apathy of members with regard to municipal affairs, and tendency to monopolize membership of committees in a few hands. These defects need to be rectified to ensure smooth and useful working of the committee system in municipal bodies.

Municipal President

A municipal council elects its president from amongst its members within one month of its constitution. He is thus elected indirectly and not directly by the city people themselves. The systems of direct and indirect election of president have their relative merits and demerits. The case against direct election is summed up by the Punjab Local Government (Urban) Enquiry Committee as follows:[13]

1. The president elected by the direct vote has no link with the council and it is not imaginable how he can work without carrying a majority with him.
2. Direct election would not be conducive to smooth and harmonious working of the municipal government; it is likely to create deadlocks between the president and the members.

On the other hand indirect election secures to the president independence from often irksome dependence on the votes of councillors and makes him directly responsible to the citizens.

The direct election of the president was tried in Uttar Pradesh and Madhya Pradesh in 1948, but did not lead to harmony in relationship between the councillors and the president and was, therefore, replaced by the old system of indirect election.[14]

Mere election by the council does not entitle the president to assume powers and responsibilities of his office; his election has to be approved by the government and duly notified. There have been a few cases of delaying the notification of the elected president by the state government for extraneous consideration. To quote one such instance, an independent candidate in Patiala municipal committee, who was returned with Congress support, had joined Jan Sangh after the election as he had brighter chances of being elected as the president as a Jan Sangh candidate. He had secured equal votes with his rival Congress candidate but since the lot was drawn in his favour he was declared elected. But the government delayed his notification till he had to reconcile himself to join the Congress again.

The state government has also the power to appoint a president on a special request made by the committee, or if it fails to elect one within the stipulated period. Nomination or appointment of the president by the state government does not seem conducive to the dignity of this office as it can be misconstrued and exploited by the party in power at the state level, for harassing a person elected by a different party having a majority in the council. Again, approval or confirmation of the election of the president by the state government is contrary to the basic principle of responsible municipal democracy and should, therefore, be abandoned. The Haryana government has discontinued the practice of such an approval and the Punjab government should follow suit.

The president is elected for a period of five years or for the residue of his term as a member, whichever is less. He can be removed by the state government, even before the expiry of his term, on grounds of abuse of power, habitual failure to perform his duties, or in pursuance of resolution passed by two-thirds of the members of the council asking for his removal.

The power of the state government to remove the president is not in consonance with the ideas of democracy, and it smacks of colonial orientation. The government, therefore, needs to be divested of this power. Removal of the president on a vote of no-confidence is a democratic right of undoubted value, for it enables the committee to get rid of a president who has forfeited the confidence of the council. But motions of no-confidence are often moved on false, frivolous, and vexatious ground to grind the factional or partisan axe. The frequency of no-confidence motion has been alarming in Rajasthan and in some other states, and from their study it has been revealed that these have been used as a pressure tactics to harass the president and to derive certain benefits from him; that these have been sponsored due to intra-group, inter-group, and personal rivalries, and that it is easier for the opposition parties to join hands in a negative venture of moving no-confidence than to have a united front for the positive task of sharing power.[15] In order to prevent the misuse of power by the councillors, of moving a vote of no-confidence on frivolous and flimsy grounds, the president should be vested with the power to recommend the dissolution of the council, as the rigours of contesting election again and the possibility of defeat will deter the members from moving a vote of no-confidence against him on grounds too flimsy to be sustained before the people, whom they will have to face during the elections.[16]

The council also elects one or two vice-presidents, one senior and the other junior, from amongst its members. A vice-president is removable in the same manner as the president, except that his removal is not subject to the government approval.

The presidents of municipalities in various states draw monthly salary in addition to conveyance or travelling allowance. Punjab probably is the first state to pay salary to its urban civic chiefs in recognition of the fact that municipal administration is a complex job requiring whole-time attention and occupation which persons working on honourary basis cannot afford, at the cost of their personal and private business or other assignments.

Presidents and vice-presidents of municipal committees often complain that the sword of Democles constantly hangs on their heads. Dr M.P. Sharma has rightly observed:

> [T]he frequent and often suspicious use of power of no-confidence in the committees has reduced the position of the president unstable. Since there is no effective organisation within the local bodies to provide for the president a constant majority support, he often feels a prey to the wanton attacks of the various groups against him, possessed as he is of a fairly larger power or patronage he has many occasions of creating enemies. His situation, in short, bears a close resembianee to that of French Ministry under the Third Republic.[17]

Position of the President

President occupies a pivotal position in municipal administration and enjoys considerable authority and power in both the deliberative and executive organs of the municipality. He convenes and presides over the meetings of the council and ensures that these are conducted with proper decorum and decency. He decides points of order and gives his ruling on all controversial matters. He is empowered to take disciplinary action against the offending councillors and suspend or adjourn any meeting in case of pandemonium.

He not only guides the deliberations of the council but also executes its decisions and directives as its chief executive, and as such supervises the work of the officers of the municipality. He has access to all municipal records and may ask for any information relating to municipal administration. He is to keep in touch with the day-to-day administration as he is supposed to convey to the council the working of the administrative machine. No matter of financial commitment is placed before the council without his approval. He can authorize any expenditure to meet an emergency threatening imminent danger to public life and property, but such an action has to get the approval of the council in its next meeting. He enjoys special extraordinary powers, under which he can order the immediate execution or suspension of any work. These powers cannot be challenged in any court of law. He is also powered to make appointments to class-IV posts and some other menial jobs.

He is the chief spokesman of the council and represents it at official functions and the correspondence with the government is channelized through him. Being the civic chief and the first citizen of the city, he represents it in all ceremonial occasions and functions.

The powers of the president, as depicted above, confer on him an enviable and exalted position but in practice he cannot make best use of his powers, as in their exercise, he is to depend on majority support of the councilors, of which he cannot be sure due to the vagaries of municipal politics. This state of affairs had led the Punjab Local Government (Urban) Enquiry Committee to remark:

> Constant endeavour of groups seeking enlistment of support of members in dislodging the people in authority and the dual position of the president who has to supervise the day to day administration and has also to carry the majority with him, make the municipal administration more susceptible to extraneous influence, and this in turn sows the seeds of discord and constant party bickerings.[18]

The remedy lies in separation of the deliberative and executive functions and vesting the former in the municipal council and the president and the latter in the executive officer. In this scheme of things, the president would be the first citizen of the city, ceremonial head of the municipality, and the presiding officer of the municipal council. This position would be consistent with the republican spirit and democratic system of government.[19]

The Executive Officer

The need for having a separate executive in the interest of the efficiency of municipal administration had prompted the state governments to provide for appointment of executive officers. The Punjab government had passed the Punjab Municipal (Executive Officers) Act, 1931, under which every municipal committee to which the act was extended was required to appoint an executive officer. The act laid down that the executive officer might be appointed by the municipality with five-eighth majority within a period of three months of its notification, subject to the approval of the government, for a renewable period of five years. He could be removed by the state government at any time and by the resolution of the municipal committee passed by a five-eighth majority in a special meeting called for the purpose. The appointments of executive officers were made by the state government entirely on political considerations and the extension in their terms also depended on the whims of the government, the municipal council having no say whatsoever in these matters. Sometimes, the presidents had maneuvered to get the orders passed by the government in their favour to act as executive officers.

The position of the executive officers under this arrangement had not been easy. A supine subservience to the wishes of the members made their office ineffective while an uncompromising independence led to such friction as would bring the municipal machinery almost at a standstill. There had been complaints of friction between the executive officer and the elected council with the result that municipal administration had suffered. Many a time, the decision taken by the executive officer had been reversed, altered, or modified by the sub-committees or the council itself.

The practice of appointment and removal of executive officer by the municipal council had not proved successful because of the tensions, lack of cordiality, compromise, and distrust inherent in the system. The Taxation Enquiry Committee (1953) had, therefore, recommended that the municipalities should have executive officers in whom the executive powers and administrative responsibilities shall vest by statutory provision, and they should be selected and appointed by the government or by an independent statutory board. These recommendations were endorsed by the Conference of Local Self Government Ministers (1954), the Punjab Local Government (Urban) Enquiry Committee (1957), and the Rural–Urban Relationship Committee (1966). Accordingly, the Punjab government had established the Punjab Service of Executive Officers in 1976. Thereafter, executive officers to all municipalities in the state are appointed by the state government on the recommendation of the State Public Service Commission or a specially constituted selection committee, and they can be transferred from one municipality to the other by the state government.

Now all the executive powers of the municipality are with the executive officer. He is the principal executive authority and, as such, all the municipal staff is subordinate to him. He is responsible for exercising general control and supervision over the municipal office. He can request the state government for the transfer of municipal engineer and other officers with the approval of the council. Other clerical employees can be transferred by him from one branch of the municipality to another. All communications addressed to the state government or its officers are to be signed by him. He is obliged to present before the council all important correspondence exchanged between the municipality and the state government.

Being the principal officer of the municipality, he is responsible for the preparation of the municipal budget and its presentation to the municipal council. He can enter into contracts on behalf of the municipality but, while doing so, he shall be bound by any resolutions of the council fixing terms, rates, or maximum prices in a particular case or any class of cases. He is charged with the responsibility of collection of taxes, fees, and fines and removal of encroachments of municipal property. He is to keep an eye on expenditure and take measures for recovering the municipal dues and arrears, get the accounts audited, and meet the audit objections.

Powers of the Council

Municipal council is the governing body of municipality. It is collectively responsible for municipal administration and for the exercise of all the legislative powers authorized by law. As the local legislature it gives expression and effect to the will of the civic community through its meetings and resolutions. Besides, it makes bylaws governing place and time of council meetings, the manner of giving notices, the conduct of meetings, preservation of order and decorum in them, and the powers which the chairman may exercise for the purpose of using his rulings. It also frames bylaws governing the constitution, powers, and functions of sub-committees. It has the power to pass a no-confidence motion against the president and send it to the government for approval. It passes the budget and formulates resolutions for the effective and efficient implementation of various items included in the budget.

The council exercises control over the administrative staff and as such supervises and investigates into the functioning of the various departments of the municipality. It can, with the prior approval of the government, impose and collect a variety of taxes, licence fees, etc. and raise loans, and undertake remunerative enterprises. It has thus an effective voice in laying down the policy, deciding the level of taxation, and budget formulation.

The council also enjoys some punitive powers as it can take action against those who are guilty of causing public nuisance by selling adulterated and unwholesome food-stuffs and other consumable articles, or are guilty of plying unlicensed vehicles. It can also forbid the use of buildings declared unfit for human habitation.

The councilors are expected to keep themselves in touch with the citizens and enquire about their grievances against municipal bureaucracy and bring the same to the notice of the appropriate administrative head and/or raise the matter in the council. Besides, in the performance of their role as local leaders, they have to encourage public participation in municipal affairs and enlist the cooperation of the people, as enlightened and active cooperation and participation in the affairs by the people would go a long way in generating consciousness and civic pride for building up a sound and responsible municipal administration.

Powers, Authority and Responsibilities of Municipalities

The state legislatures may, by law, endow the municipalities with such powers and authority as may be necessary to enable them to function as institution of self-government, and such law may contain provision for the devolution of powers and responsibilities upon municipalities in respect of preparation of plans for economic development and social justice and for implementation of schemes as may be entrusted to them including those in relation to the matters listed in the Twelfth Schedule of the Constitution, viz.,

1. Urban planning including town planning;
2. Regulation of land use and construction of buildings;
3. Planning for economic and social development;
4. Roads and bridges;
5. Water supply for domestic, industrial, and commercial purposes;
6. Public health, sanitation conservancy, and solid waste management;
7. Fire services;
8. Urban forestry, protection of the environment, and promotion of ecological aspects;
9. Safeguarding the interests of weaker sections of society, including the handicapped and mentally retarded;
10. Slum improvement and upgradation;
11. Urban poverty alleviation;
12. Provision of urban amenities and facilities such as parks, gardens, and playgrounds;
13. Promotion of cultural, educational, and aesthetic aspects;
14. Burials and burial grounds, cremations, cremation grounds, and electric crematoriums;
15. Cattle ponds, prevention of cruelty to animals;
16. Vital statistics including registration of births and deaths;
17. Public amenities including street lighting, parking, bus stops, and public conveniences;
18. Regulation of slaughter houses and tanneries.[20]

A perusal of these functions assigned to the municipalities shows that the municipalities shall not only confine themselves to mere provision of civic amenities, but also play a crucial role in the preparation of plans for local development and in the implementation of development projects and programmes, including those specially designed for urban poverty alleviation.

Committee for District Planning

In order to prepare a draft development plan for the district as a whole, the Amendment Act provides for the constitution of a committee for district planning in every state at the district level. The committee shall consolidate the plans prepared by the panchayats and the municipalities in the district.

Composition

The state legislature may, by law, make provision with respect to the composition of the district planning committees and the manner in which the seats in such committees shall be filled. The law shall provide that not less than four-fifths of the total number of members of the committee shall be elected by and from amongst the elected members of the panchayats at the district level and of the municipalities in the district, in proportion to the ratio between the population of the rural areas and of the urban areas in the district.

Functions

The law shall also specify the functions relating to the district planning which may be assigned to the committees, and the manner in which the chairpersons of the committees shall be chosen. Every district planning committee shall, in preparing the draft development plan, have regard to the matters of common interest between the panchayats and the municipalities—spatial planning, sharing of water and other physical and natural resources, the integrated development of infrastructure and environmental conservation, the extent and type of available resources whether financial or otherwise—and consult such institutions and organizations as the governor may, by order, specify.

The chairperson of every district planning committee shall forward the development plan as recommended by such committees to the governor of the state.

Municipal Finance

In order to raise revenue for discharging its duties and performing its functions, the legislature of a state shall specify by law (*a*) the taxes, duties, and fees which could be levied and collected by the municipalities such as tax on lands and buildings, a scavenging tax, an octroi, a tax on advertisements (other than advertisements published in newspapers), a fire tax, and a toll on roads and bridges; (*b*) taxes, duties, and fees which could be levied and collected by the state government and wholly or partially assigned to the municipalities, such as excise duty on liquor in lieu of octroi, motor vehicle tax, entertainment tax, stamp duty, electricity duty, etc.; (*c*) grant-in-aid by the government and loans.

The Constitution (74th Amendment) Act, 1992 has made it obligatory for the state governments to constitute state finance commission within one year from the commencement of the act and thereafter at the expiry of every five years. The commission shall make recommendations to the government regarding (*i*) distribution between the state government and municipalities of the net proceeds of taxes, duties, tolls, and fees to be assigned or appropriated by the state; (*ii*) allocation of share of such proceeds between the municipalities at all levels in the state; (*iii*) determination of taxes, duties, tolls, and fees to be assigned or appropriated by the municipalities; (*iv*) grants-in-aid to municipalities from the consolidated fund of the state; (*v*) measures needed to improve the financial position of the municipalities.

The governor may refer any other matter to the commission as he may deem fit in the interest of sound financial arrangement of the municipalities.

All our state and union territories governments had constituted the state finance commissions which have since submitted their reports. It is mandatory for the governor to lay before the state legislature every recommendation made by the commission together with the explanatory memorandum on the action to be taken on such recommendations. It can be hoped that the finances of the municipalities shall substantially improve on the acceptance of the recommendations by the state governments.

Moreover, it has also been made mandatory that the central finance commission shall, *inter alia*, make specific recommendations with regard to the measure that are needed to augment the resources of a state with a view to supplement the resources of the municipalities in the state on the basis of the recommendations made by the state finance commission. The arrangement will certainly provide adequate financial resources to the municipalities to discharge their obligations imposed upon them by unprecedented rise in urban populations and their ever increasing demands.

Appraisal of the Performance of Municipal Committees

It is regrettable that the performance of municipal committees has been disappointing in carrying out their functions. They have not been able to provide basic civic amenities to their population generally and especially in the suburbs which comprise of unauthorized and unplanned colonies accommodating 50 per cent of their population. Piped water supply and sewerage facilities have covered only a minority of population, roads are in deplorable conditions, encroachments are galore, unsafe buildings continue to constitute a constant threat to the life of the inhabitants, stray cattle menace is on the increase, traffic hazards have not abated, insanitation and unhygienic conditions in the form of heaps of garbage are a nuisance even in posh localities, slums have emerged in almost all parts of the cities. This state of affairs has resulted in earning many a city, once known as the cleanest cities, the ignominy of decaying cities and even the dirtiest and the most polluted cities.

The failure of municipal bodies in discharging their functions in a satisfactory manner can be attributed to their incapacity to manage the problems arising out of the alarming increase in their population, the inadequacy of finances which have never been commensurate with their obligations, the prevalence of corruption on a large scale, political interference, apathy of the government, bottlenecks created by the bureaucracy, and so on.

The cities can be restored their pristine glory and made liveable if the state governments make a judicious selection of functions to be assigned to them and do not impose upon them such functions as transport which have proved a great liability for every city, and make adequate provisions for finance, the lack of which has rendered many municipal bodies unable to take up any development work in their respective areas. It has been rightly observed that devolution of powers and functions necessarily involves devolution of finances also. The state governments, therefore, should observe this principle if they want the urban bodies to discharge their functions effectively.

Erosion of Functions of Municipal Committees

Municipal committees in our country undertake only such functions which have been specifically assigned to them by respective state legislative enactments. In this respect, we follow the British method of 'specific grant' which means that no local authority may do anything which it is not definitely entitled to do by virtue of a statute. In other words, their functions are limited by the state government. This restrictive approach to municipal functions no longer holds good in the changed political context and needs of the country.

The Punjab Local Government (Urban) Enquiry Committee had accordingly expressed the hope that in the new set-up local bodies as instruments of national policy would be used more and more and there would be steady enlargement of their functions. In the First Five Year Plan, the Planning Commission's thinking was that the general direction of policy should be to encourage self-governing bodies and to assist them in assuming responsibility for as large a portion of the administrative and social services as possible.[21]

But, on the contrary, there has been an increasing tendency on the part of the state governments to take over more and more local functions either directly or by creating special purpose agencies. The Local Finance Enquiry Committee had deplored the tendency to transfer functions from local bodies to the state governments in the fields of elementary education, public health, and communications and expressed the opinion that wholesale transfer of functions from the local bodies to the state governments are a retrograde step and should be avoided. Whatever be the criteria for demarcation of functions between the state governments and local bodies, the desperate financial position of the latter should not be made a ground for reducing them to practical impotence. The transfer of functions is not only a retrograde step but also anachronistic. It could have some justification in the pre-independence era when the central government worked to spread its tentacles in every sector of life but not in the post-independence era when we are free from all alien pressures.[22] The Rural–Urban Relationship Committee was also of the view that the remedy for the inefficiency and non-performance of their duties does not lie in depriving the municipal bodies of their functions but in improving and strengthening their organizational and administrative set-up, allocating to them adequate resources and giving them expert and technical help in the discharge of their functions.[23] The argument of incapability or inefficiency of municipal governments has proved to be a handy argument for the state government in favour of demunicipalization of the management of certain local services.[24] Thus, the rise of competitive bureaucratic urban local institutions and state takeover of municipal functions have led not only to erosion of municipal functions but has also created an atmosphere of distrust in regard to urban local government.[25]

NOTES AND REFERENCES

1. Entry 5 of the State list in the Seventh Schedule of the Constitution of India.
2. 'Report of the Committee on Budgetary Reform in Municipal Administration' (New Delhi: Government of India, 1974), p. 10.
3. B.R. Kargal, *op. cit.,* p. 50.
4. 'Report of the Rural–Urban Relationship Committee', para 4.12.
5. A.P. Padhi, 'Municipal Government in Orissa', in A. Avasthi (ed.), *Municipal Administration in India* (Agra: Lakshminarain Aggarwal Press, 1972), p. 261.
6. Chapman Brian, *Introduction to French Local Government* (London: Allen and Unwin Co. 1953), p. 38.
7. 'Report of the Punjab Local Government (Urban) Enquiry Committee', 1957, pp. 26–27.
8. The Constitution of India Article 243-ZA.
9. *Ibid*, Article 243-Q.
10. *Ibid*, Article 243-T.
11. *Ibid*, Article 243-S.
12. *Ibid*, Article 243-U.
13. Report of the Punjab Local Government (Urban) Enquiry Committee.
14. S.R. Maheshwari, *Local Government in India* (Agra: Lakshminarain Aggarwal, 1984), p. 191.
15. D.S. Chaudhary, 'Municipal Administration in Rajasthan', in A. Avasthi (ed.), *Municipal Administration in India,* p. 329.
16. Vishnoo Bhagwan, *Municipal Government and Politics in Haryana* (New Delhi: S. Chand & Co., 1974), p. 70.
17. M.P. Sharma, *Local Self Government in India* (Allahabad: Kitab Mahal, 1967), p. 12.

18. Report of the Punjab Local Government (Urban) Enquiry Committee, p. 8.
19. Proceedings of the Seminar on 'Improving City Government', Indian Institute of Public Administration, New Delhi, 1978, p. 21.
20. Report of the Punjab Local Government (Urban) Enquiry Committee, 1967, p. 98.
21. Government of India, Planning Commission, First Five Year Plan, p. 141.
22. Report of the Local Finance Enquiry Committee, 1950, p. 51.
23. Report of the Rural-Urban Relationship Committee, 1966 p. 16.
24. Ashok Makhopadhyaya, *Municipal Government and Urban Development: A Study of the Reforms in West Bengal* (New Delhi: Indian Institute of Public Administration), p. 6.
25. Anil Bhatt, 'Municipal Government in Gujarat: Structure, Process and Style', in Abijit Datta (ed.), *Municipal and Urban India* (New Delhi: Indian Institute of Public Administration, 1980), p. 35

7

Municipal Corporations

Municipal corporations constitute the highest or the top-most form of urban local government. They are created for big cities by the enactments of the state legislatures or of the parliament in case of union territories. They are described in the *Encyclopaedia of Social Sciences* as purely political institutions created by the legislative power without the necessary consent of the people. As organs or agencies of the state, they are endowed with government powers, but their rights, privileges and powers are conferred upon them as trustees of the public welfare and are subject to the legislative powers of the state within the limits of the constitution, within the sphere assured to them by their charters. However, they are independent corporation entities. The scope of their functions is often broader than that of the state government and affects the life of the citizens far more directly than that of the federal governments.[1] In the words of W.B. Munro, 'A municipal corporation is a subordinate political body established by the authority of law, its existence evidenced, by general or special character, with a corporate name, with defined limits and population and with delegated powers of local government.' It is created by law and depends for its existence as well as its powers upon the state or nation. According to *American Encyclopaedia*, 'A Municipal Corporation is a legal institution formed by the sovereign power creating a popular community of prescribed area into a body politic and corporate with a corporate name and continuous succession and for the purpose and with authority of subordinate self-government for improvement and administration of the affairs of the area'. In more concrete terms, a municipal corporation is a body politic, created by the incorporation of the people of a prescribed locality and invested with subordinate powers of legislation, for the purpose of assisting in the civil government of the state and regulating and administering its local and internal affairs.[2]

Main Features of a Municipal Corporation

An analysis of the definitions of municipal corporations given above brings out the following main features of a municipal corporation:

Municipal corporations are set up in big cities. The largeness of a city is to be determined by the state government concerned in terms of its population, area, or revenues. That is why there is no fixed criterion to be followed in the establishment of a municipal corporation.

A municipal corporation possesses a statutory status. It is created by an act passed by the state legislature concerned, and by the Parliament in case of union territory. Some states create a corporation under a specific act passed exclusively for that city as was done in the case of the Bombay Municipal Corporation Act, 1888; the Madras City Corporation Act, 1951; The Delhi Municipal Corporation Act, 1957; and Calcutta Municipal Corporation Act, 1951, since replaced by Act, 1981. In other states, a general or omnibus act is passed for the creation of municipal corporations. For example, the municipal corporations in Kanpur, Agra, Varanasi, Allahabad, and Lucknow (KAVAL) cities in UP have been set up under the UP Mahanagarpalika Adhiniyam, 1959; municipal corporations in Gwalior, Indore, Rajpur, and Jabalpur (GIR) under the Madhya Pradesh Municipal Corporation Act, 1956; and municipal corporations in Jalandhar, Amritsar, and Ludhiana (JAL) and Patiala in Punjab under the Punjab Municipal Corporation Act, 1976.

A municipal corporation enjoys a non-sovereign status. Since it is created by the state government, it has no inherent powers of its own and enjoys only such powers as are allocated to it. In other words, its powers are derivative and not original. As such, it is subject to the control of the state government, which exercises the powers of determining its area, the size of its council, its term of office, powers and responsibilities, and financial resources, and can also dissolve it in case of consistent default in the performance of its duties.

A municipal corporation is based on the democratic principle of management of local affairs by the representatives of the people of the city concerned, who are to be elected periodically on the basis of universal adult franchise with reservation of seats for scheduled castes and scheduled tribes in proportion to their population (and lately for women also), and in some cases with provision for representation of special interests like industry, commerce, etc., and through the device of cooption by the councils of elders from amongst persons having experience and expertise in the management of urban affairs.

A municipal corporation is marked by statutorily separation of deliberative and executive wings. The corporation (council) and the standing committee constitute the deliberative wing and the municipal commissioner and comprises the executive wing. The council, consisting of elected representatives and a few nominated members, is responsible for the exercise of legislative powers, and its presiding officer, the mayor, is simply a ceremonial head and does not possess any executive or administrative authority. The standing committee functions as an auxiliary of the corporation; all the matters to be passed by the council pass through it after it has considered the proposals and recommendations made by the municipal commissioner. The municipal commissioner is the chief executive authority responsible for the execution and implementation of the decisions taken by the council.

This model constitutes a cardinal feature of the Bombay Municipal Corporation Act, 1888, and has since then been followed by all the municipal corporations with the exception of the Calcutta Municipal Corporation, which opted for the mayor-in-council model in 1980. This century-old model is credited with the advantages of freedom from political interferences, objectivity, and expeditious implementation of decisions. But it is criticized for lack of a political executive, for appointment of a salaried chief executive by the state government as an encroachment upon democratic principles, a source of conflict between the deliberative and executive wings and negligible control of the representative bodies on the bureaucracy. The Calcutta model of mayor-in-council provides for three authorities—the corporation, the mayor-in-council, and the mayor. The executive power of the corporation is exercised by the mayor-in-council, and the municipal commissioner functions under the supervision and control of the mayor. The mayor-in-council is a small body consisting of the mayor and six to 10 members collectively responsible to the corporation. Under the new dispensation, in addition to his role as the first citizen of Calcutta, it is the mayor and not the municipal commissioner who also fills up the executive leadership role.

DIFFERENCES BETWEEN A MUNICIPAL CORPORATION AND A MUNICIPAL COMMITTEE

A municipal corporation differs from a municipal committee in the sense that a corporation is the highest form of municipal government. The basic unit of urban administration is the municipality. Broadly speaking, towns have municipalities headed by a president and cities have municipal corporations headed by a mayor. For this purpose, however, there is no distinct definition of a town and a city, and the norms applied to determine what constitutes each differ from state to state. A council is assisted in its work by a permanent executive, headed in the case of a municipality by a chief executive officer and a commissioner in the case of a municipal corporation. While a CEO is the subordinate of the municipality he serves, a commissioner is one of the three constituents of the corporation to which he is seconded, the other two wings being the mayor and council, and the standing committee. In Calcutta this position is somewhat different because it has a mayor-in-council and a commissioner, though a legal entity, under which the municipal services work, is still subordinate to the corporation, somewhat on the model of CEO.[3] A municipal corporation is set up under a special statute passed by the state legislature. It enjoys more powers in financial and administrative matters as compared to those enjoyed by a municipal committee. It is set up in a large city having some minimum population and income. But the significant difference between a municipal corporation and a municipal committee is that the former enjoys powers of dealing directly with the state government whereas the latter has been tied to the apron-strings of the district collector and divisional commissioner.[4] In other words, a corporation is more autonomous than a municipal committee. Moreover, in a corporation there is complete separation of the deliberative organ from the executive wing, which ensures better administrative efficiency and, therefore, better talent is attracted to both the wings. In short, the idea of a corporation carries with it a certain amount of prestige and civic pride and raises the hopes and aspirations of the citizens which the councillors and the administrators endeavour to fulfil.[5]

CRITERIA FOR THE CREATION OF A MUNICIPAL CORPORATION

A perusal of the various municipal corporation acts of different states in India reveals that no scientific basis, guidelines or criteria have been laid down or followed for determining the eligibility of a city for the grant of corporation status. Consequently decisions for upgrading any municipality to corporation are taken arbitrarily by the state government concerned, often under the pressures and pulls exerted by political and vested interests. It should, therefore, not be surprising to observe that whereas small cities like Chandarnagar, Rajpur and Ujjain with populations of 75,238, 174,518, and 203,278, respectively, had corporations, bigger cities like Jaipur and Srinagar, with a population of 617,208 and 403,414 respectively, were being governed by municipal committees.

The Rural–Urban Relationship Committee (1966) had recommended the setting up of municipal corporation in cities having a minimum population of five lakh and a minimum annual income of rupees one crore.[6] The Constitution (74th Amendment) Act, 1992, lays down the criterion of three lakh or more population for the creation of a municipal corporation.[7]

The following requirements are desired to be met by a municipal committee for its elevation to the status of a corporation:

1. A city should have a sufficiently large population to be governed by the corporation when its multi-dimensional problems caused by increasing population cannot be solved by a municipal committee.

2. A city must also possess quite a large territorial jurisdiction in order to be eligible for a corporation status because, in smaller areas, the highest form of government may be under-used. In India 69 per cent of corporations have areas exceeding 70 sq km, which may be taken as an average for a corporation to be set up.
3. A city must have a certain optimum level of income to be able to maintain an appropriate level of civic services befitting a corporation and to employ suitable and properly qualified personnel.
4. Due weightage needs to be given to the industrial and commercial importance of city before it is promoted to a corporation.
5. A large majority of people should be literate, politically very conscious and aspiring for municipal corporation status for their city.

Before independence there were only three municipal corporations in the country—in the presidency towns of Calcutta, Bombay, and Madras—but their number had increased to 66 by 1983[8] and to 73 in 1990. The number of corporations is going to increase substantially with the provision of a population of three lakh for the constitution of a corporation in the Constitution (74th Amendment) Act, 1992. It is up to the state government concerned to decide in setting up a corporation in a city that, in its view, deserves this status by virtue of its population, area, revenue, and economic importance. But as a matter of fact, the decision to establish a corporation in a city is taken more or less on political considerations and the endeavours of the enlightened sections of the population of the city concerned. The state governments confer the corporation status on a city not by passing a special legislation but in exercise of the powers enjoyed by them under the general or omnibus law already existing on the subject. There is a tendency on the part of some state governments to create corporations for more and more of their cities, unmindful of the fact whether such cities are economically able to perform the functions which are entrusted to them on acquiring the status of a corporation. That is why we find that some corporations have woefully failed in the performance of their duties with respect to the development of the cities or provision of even the essential services for their inhabitants.

Some states have not set up corporations in their capitals, not to talk of other big cities, perhaps on realizing, and rightly so, that they do not have the adequate infrastructure or the resources to meet the requirements of services expected to be undertaken by a corporation: Rajasthan has no corporation, not even for its capital, Jaipur; Haryana has only one corporation in Faridabad, though Janata Dal government had announced in 1990 that it would set up corporations in the twin cities of Jagadhari—Yamuna Nagar, Ambala, Karnal, Bhiwani, and Hissar. It is desirable that at least the biggest city or the capital of a state should have a corporation in view of the pride that it affords to its citizens and better services that it is designed to provide to them. However, Chandigarh, which is capital of Punjab and Haryana and is also a union territory, has a municipal corporation.

Structure Pattern of Municipal Corporations: The Municipal Authorities

Municipal corporations in India are generally structured on the pattern of Bombay Municipal Corporation, which was provided in Bombay Municipal Corporation Act, 1888. Its chief feature is the separation of deliberative and executive functions, wherein the deliberative wing comprises the corporation and the standing committee, and the executive wing consists of the municipal commissioner. Accordingly, almost every municipal corporation provides for three coordinate authorities—the corporation, the standing committee, and the municipal commissioner. The 'corporation' or the corporation council, comprising directly elected representatives of the people, is one of the municipal authorities, but 'municipal corporation' refers to the entire body corporate inclusive of all the three authorities, viz., the corporation, the standing committee and the commissioner. All the three authorities and their constitution, powers and functions, status, and position are discussed in the following section.

The Corporation Council

The councillors are elected on the basis of adult franchise through secret ballot. The city is divided into as many wards as may be the number of councillors to be elected. The franchise age used to be 21 years but it has been reduced to 18 as a result of the Constitution (62nd Amendment) made in 1988. A person is qualified to be chosen as a councillor if his name has been included in the electoral rolls for the ward.

Removal of Councillors

The government can remove a councillor if he has become physically or mentally incapacitated, intentionally abuses his position, is responsible for the loss or misappropriation of any money or property of the corporation, absents himself from the meetings of the council for three successive times without permission of the corporation, or is unable to attend the meetings during 12 successive months for any cause whatsoever whether approved by the corporation or not. This may be done without being communicated the reasons for his proposed removal or an opportunity for tendering an explanation.

These provisions reflect arbitrariness and authoritarianism on the part of the government and are likely to be misused by any ambitious minister for political ends. The power of removal should, therefore, rest with the council as has been provided in Bombay Municipal Corporation Act.

Reservation for Scheduled Castes, Scheduled Tribes, and Women

There shall also be reservation of seats for the Scheduled Castes and the Scheduled Tribes, and the number of seats so reserved shall bear the same proportion to the total number of seats to be filled by direct elections, because the population of the Scheduled Castes and Scheduled Tribes in the municipal area bears to the total population of the area, and such seats may be allotted by rotation to different constituencies in the corporation. Not less than one-third of the total number of reserved seats shall be further reserved for women belonging to SC/ST. Further, not less than one-third (including the number of seats reserved for women belonging to SC/ST) of the total number of seats, to be filled by direct election, shall be reserved for women and may be allotted by rotation to different constituencies in the corporation. The state legislature may also reserve seats in favour of backward classes.[9]

In addition to the elected members, the state legislature may, by law, provide that persons having special knowledge or experience in municipal administration, members of the House of People and the members of the legislative assembly of the state representing constituency which comprise wholly or partly the municipal areas, and the members of the council of states and the members of the legislative council of the state registered as voters within the municipal area, shall also be the members of the council but they shall not have the right to vote.[10]

Duration of the Corporation

The term of a corporation, unless sooner dissolved, shall continue for five years. Election to the corporation shall be completed before the expiry of its term and before the expiry of six months from the date of dissolution and if the remainder of the period from where the dissolved municipal corporation would have continued is less than six months, it shall not be necessary to hold the election, and a reconstituted corporation after dissolution shall continue for the remainder of the period for which the dissolved corporation would have continued.

Ward Committees

The Constitution (74th Amendment) Act, 1992, provides for wards committees which shall be constituted for one or more wards within the territorial area of a corporation. Where a ward committee consists of one ward, the member shall be the chairman of the committee and where a wards committee consists of two or more wards, one of the councillors representing such wards in the corporation shall be elected by the members of the wards committee as the chairperson. The chairperson shall be elected for one year and shall be eligible for re-election. The duration of the wards committee shall be coterminous with the duration of the corporation. The corporation shall nominate one of its officers as the secretary of the wards committee.

A ward committee, subject to the general direction of the standing committee, supervises within the territorial limit of the wards the functions of the corporation relating to the provision of water supply, pipes and sewerage, drainage connections to premises, removal of accumulated water on streets or public places due to rain or otherwise, collection and removal of solid waste, provision for health immunization, services for civic services in slum and for lighting, repair of roads, maintenance of parks and drains, and such other functions as may be prescribed.[11]

Standing Committee

A municipal corporation shall have a standing committee constituted by it, consisting of the mayor, the senior deputy mayor, and other councillors elected by the councillors of the corporation from amongst members. The mayor shall be the chairperson of the standing committee. The commissioner shall be its *ex-officio* member and shall have the right to vote. The executive officer of the corporation shall be its secretary. The term of the standing committee shall be three and a half years and the election of a new standing committee shall be held before the expiry of the term of the existing standing committee.

The Powers, Functions and Duties of the Standing Committee

The standing committee may require the commissioner to produce any record, correspondence, plan or other documents which is in his possession or under his control or which is recorded or filed in his office or in the office of any officer of the corporation and to furnish any return, estimate statement, accounts, or statistics relating to the administration of the corporation.

Subject Committees

A municipal corporation may also constitute subject committee to deal with (*i*) water supply, sewerage and drainage, and solid waste management; (*ii*) other civil services, including streets and street lighting; and (*iii*) slum improvement, town planning and land use, and control and improvement of environment.

Each subject committee shall consist of not less than three and more than five. The mayor, the senior deputy mayor, deputy mayor, and the members of the standing committee shall not be the member of any subject committee. Its term shall be one year. Its recommendations shall be submitted to the standing committee for its consideration.

Finances of Municipal Corporation

The 1992 Amendment Act provides that a state legislature may, by law (*a*) authorize a municipal corporation to levy, collect, and appropriate such taxes, duties, tolls, and fees in accordance with such procedure and such limits; (*b*) assign to a municipal corporation such taxes, duties, tolls, and fees levied and collected by the state government for such purposes, and subject to such conditions and limits; (*c*) provide for making such grants-in-aid to the municipal corporations from the consolidated fund of the state; and (*d*) for constitution of such funds for crediting all moneys realized separately by or on behalf of the municipal corporation and also for the withdrawal of such moneys therefrom, as may be specified in the law.

The Act of 1992 also enjoins upon the state governments to constitute a state finance commission to review the financial position of the municipal bodies, and to recommend to the governor, as to the distribution between the state and the municipal bodies the net proceeds of the taxes, duties, fees, and tolls levied by the state which may be divided between the municipalities at all levels of their respective shares of such proceeds; the determination of the taxes, duties, tolls, and fees which may be assigned to and appropriated by the municipalities; the grants-in-aid to the municipalities from the consolidated fund of the state; and the measures needed to improve the financial position of the municipalities.

Functions of Municipal Corporation

A list of eighteen functions to be performed by municipal corporation has been given in the 12th Schedule of the constitution. These are: urban planning including town planning; roads and bridges; water supply for domestic, industrial, and commercial purposes; public health, sanitation conservancy, and solid waste management; fire services, urban forestry, protection of the environmental and promotion of ecological aspects; safeguarding the interests of the weaker sections of the society including the handicapped and mentally challenged; slum improvement and upgradation; urban poverty alleviation; provision of urban amenities and facilities such as parks, gardens, playgrounds, and promotion of cultural, educational, and aesthetic aspects; burials and burial grounds, cremations, cremation grounds and electric crematoria; cattle pounds; prevention of cruelty to animals; vital statistics including registration of births and deaths; public amenities including street lighting, parking lots, bus stops, and public conveniences; and regulation of slaughter houses and tanneries.

Dissolution of Municipal Corporation

In the past, municipal bodies could be superseded by the state governments and they were not reconstituted for an indefinite period. This was anti-democratic and denied the local people the administration of their affairs. The Constitution (74th Amendment) Act, 1992, provides for dissolution of a municipal corporation, if in the opinion of the government, it is not competent to perform or has shown great neglect to the performance of the duties imposed upon it; persistently makes defaults in the performance of such duties or complying with the lawful directions and orders issued by the government or any authority empowered by it; and exceeds or abuses its power or the financial position and the credit of the corporation is seriously threatened. The corporation shall, however, be given a reasonable opportunity of being heard before dissolution. Upon the dissolution of the corporation, all its members shall vacate their offices forthwith. Election to the dissolved municipal corporation shall be completed before the expiry of a period of six months from the date of its dissolution. But if the remainder of the period for which the dissolved corporation would have continued is less than six months, it shall not be necessary to hold any election for constituting the corporation for such period; and a corporation constituted upon the dissolution before the expiration of its duration shall continue only for the remainder of the period for which the dissolved corporation would have continued. The state government may appoint an administrator if, on account of any order of court, elections to the municipality cannot be completed before the expiry of six months from the date of its dissolution.

Obligations and Privileges of the Councillors

The councillors have some obligations and privileges. They have to take an oath of allegiance to the Constitution of India and for the faithful discharge of their duties. They have the privilege of access to all records of the corporation unless the executive authority in public interest withholds such access. They can ask the mayor to conduct special meetings for valid purpose. They can ask questions, move and second resolutions, proposals and amendments, speak on all questions of policy and on all subjects placed before the council and bring to the attention of the executive authority any wastage, leakage of revenue, any act of negligence or failure in the discharge of duties by a municipal employee, and suggest improvements to secure betterment in the working of the city government.

Committees for Metropolitan Planning

Metropolitan areas comprise the area of the municipality, corporation, and the areas of a number of other local bodies—both rural and urban—surrounding the main city corporation. These metropolitan agglomerations need planning for the orderly development of urbanizing fringe areas in association with the plan of the main city. Hence the need for a committee for metropolitan planning.

The Amendment Act accordingly provides for such a committee for preparing a draft development plan for the metropolitan areas as a whole.

Composition of the Committee

The legislature of a state, may, by law, make provision for the composition of the metropolitan planning committee and the manner in which the seats to such committees shall be filled. The law stipulates that not less than two-thirds of the members of such committee shall be elected by and from the elected members of the municipalities and chairpersons of the panchayats in the metropolitan area in proportion to the ratio between the population of the municipalities and of the panchayats in that area. The representation in such committees of the Government of India and the government of the state and institutions which may be deemed necessary for carrying out the functions assigned to such committees, the functions relating to planning and coordination for the metropolitan area which may be assigned to such committees, and the manner in which the chairpersons of such committees shall be chosen.[12]

Functions of the Committee

Every metropolitan planning committee shall, in preparing the draft development plan, have regard to the plans prepared by the municipal committees and the panchayats in the metropolitan areas. Matters of common interest between the municipalities and the panchayats are: coordinating spatial planning of the areas, sharing of water and other physical and natural resources, the integrated development of infrastructure and environmental conservation, the overall objectives and priorities set by the Government of India and the government of the state, the state and nature of investment likely to be made in the metropolitan area by agencies of the Government of India and the state, and other available resources whether financial or otherwise, to consult such institutions and organizations as the governor may, by order, specify.

The chairperson of every metropolitan planning committee shall forward the development plan as recommended by the committee to the government of the state.

MAYOR

All municipal corporation acts of various states provide for the office of mayor and deputy mayor. The Punjab Municipal Corporation Act, 1999 provides for the office of senior deputy mayor also. The mayor, senior deputy mayor and deputy mayor are elected by the councillors from among themselves.

The mayor is generally elected for a one year renewable term. But in Punjab he and the senior deputy mayor and the deputy mayor are elected for a two-and–a-half year term. In UP, the deputy mayor is elected for full five year term of the council against the mayor's tenure of one year only. This arrangement is to ensure the dignity of the office of the mayor by keeping him above controversy with a one year term not subject to vote of confidence, whereas the deputy mayor was to provide continuity of leadership for the term of the council. Again the deputy mayor is the *ex-officio* chairman of the statutory committees. This makes him more powerful than the mayor. But the deputy mayor can be removed by a vote of no-confidence passed by more than half of the total members, but only after he has held the office for twelve months. In Punjab, the position of mayor/deputy mayor has been rendered all the more insecure, as no-confidence motion can be introduced against them by simple majority which would, of course, have to be passed by two-thirds of the members of the corporation. The short-term of the mayor, and the introduction of no-confidence motion against him by simple majority of the councillors not only weakens his position as chief of the city government but also hinders the smooth working of the city government, headed as it is by a weak mayor.

Powers and Functions of the Mayor

Mayors in India do not exercise powers or perform functions of a uniform pattern. They derive these from the respective corporation acts under which the corporations have been established. Their powers and functions, therefore, differ from state to state. But broadly these can be mentioned as follows:

The most important statutory function of the mayor is to preside over the meetings of the council and guide its deliberations, to maintain decorum, and exclude any objectionable portion from the record of the proceedings of the council. He is also empowered to expel and even suspend members for gross misconduct or disorderly misbehaviour. In case of a tie, he exercises his casting vote. He may call special meetings of the council when considered necessary and shall have to call a meeting when asked by a specified number of councillors.

Because of separation of deliberative and executive functions, the municipal commissioner is the executive authority of the corporation and the mayor exercises general supervision over the administration of the corporation. He has access to all records of the corporation. He can issue directions to the commissioner asking him to report on any matter, as is the case in Delhi Corporation. He can supervise and inspect the work of the corporation. In some corporations all the correspondence between the corporation and the state government has to pass through him. Some statutes specifically empower him to direct execution or stoppage of any work or any act in emergent situations and authorize any expenditure in this regard. His orders, however, have to be placed before the council for approval at the next meeting.

In some corporations, the mayor is authorized to constitute committees. He is *ex-officio* member of every standing committee in the Chennai and Bangalore corporations. He is, thus, in a position of knowing all that is going in the corporation and to coordinate its work.

He has certain specified executive powers, especially of making appointments in consultation with State Public Service Commission, as in UP for certain posts. In Calcutta Corporation, he can hear the appeal in all establishment cases where an employee has been punished for certain specific offences.

In certain corporations he exercises financial powers also. In UP, his concurrence is necessary when the municipal commissioner has to incur expenditure between Rs 10,000 to 20,000 at a time. There, he has also the power to refer any matter including the budget estimates or taxation proposals, even if these have been approved by the council, to the Directorate of Local Bodies for his final decision.

He, being the first citizen of the city, has to perform a large number of social duties and most of his official time is, therefore, consumed by functions of social and public nature, such as receiving distinguished visitors, visiting institutions as the chief guest, laying foundation stones, performing opening ceremonies, attending public meetings, and participating in national celebrations.

A perusal of the above-mentioned powers and functions of the mayor confirms that he is the ceremonial or figure head of the city government and, bereft as he is of executive powers, his position is very weak in the administrative structure of the corporation.

Strengthening the Mayor's Position

Undoubtedly the office of the mayor is the most dignified and is eagerly sought after. He is the civic head of municipal corporation, first citizen of the city representing its dignity and personality. As such, it is a prize post and keenly contested by different political parties. The election of a mayor, therefore, attracts a lot of political manipulation and manoeuvring. But, in reality, he is only a figure head and he has the role and the influence in the affairs of the corporation which may come to him as its member, presiding officer, and civic head. He is the leader of the majority party. He has full rights of participation in the proceedings of the council. As a presiding officer, he is not passive and non-partisan. Beyond this, he may exercise the influence in the corporation's administration depending not on legal and formal provisions but on his own personality, tact, will, and time. It is rightly observed, 'People approach him with several of their problems and grievances, and it is a sorry plight to see that he cannot do more than nodding his head expressing his sympathies. At the most he would invite the attention of the concerned authorities to the grievances. It is true that sometimes in his anxiety to solve a problem, he resorts to extra legal methods and by virtue of his political weight, he might succeed.'[13] This reflects the weak position of the mayor, which is attributed to his indirect election, short tenure, and the scheme of separation of deliberative and executive functions.

The indirect election of the mayor, combined with his one year tenure, makes him more a figure head than an active functionary.[14] Since he is elected by the councillors, not directly by the people, he cannot be said to have obtained a mandate from the people, and therefore, cannot speak and assert in the name of the people. A demand has therefore been made for the direct election of the mayor among others by the All India Council of Mayors. But the system of direct election of mayor suffers from two main problems. First, a directly elected mayor would have to be clothed with adequate powers for it will be anachronistic to keep a popularly elected mayor a mere figure head. This may bring him into conflict with the council. Second, the direct election contains seeds of disharmony between the mayor and the council as the mayor so elected may not be acceptable to the councillors which may lead to friction and discord between the two.

As regards the one year term, it is obviously too short to enable a mayor to acquire insight into the problems of municipal administration and help planning on a long term basis. Second, it serves only to strengthen the bureaucracy headed by the municipal commissioner vis-a-vis the elected set up represented by a weak mayor. His term must, therefore, be coterminous with that of the commissioner. A mayor elected for only one year naturally finds himself ineffective and weak in his relationship with the commissioner who outstays him. A one year term for a mayor against a four or five year term for the council and a five year term for the municipal commissioner appears anomalous.[15]

In order to ensure that he does not remain merely a dignified cipher, he needs to be endowed with executive authority. But surprisingly the Rural-Urban Relationship Committee (1966) while examining this issue had not favoured the grant of executive authority to him and had observed as under, 'If the Mayor is to exercise more executive authority, his term, must, of necessity, be longer, possibly coterminous with the life of the council. As the chief executive authority, the mayor must necessarily be made removable by a vote of no-confidence, which would be derogatory to the dignity and position of the mayor. If the Mayor was to handle the executive function, he is likely to be subjected to intense party and political pressures which again would lower his prestige. Moreover, the city administration today is a full-time job requiring expertise and experience. The committee therefore, did not favour any substantial increase in this power of the Mayor.' Even then his position needs to be strengthened and in this respect it had suggested that: (*i*) he should be made the sole channel of communication between the corporation and the government; (*ii*) he should be made *ex-officio* chairman of the standing committee; this will involve him more closely and intimately in important legislative and executive matters of the corporation; (*iii*) he should be consulted by the government for the appointment of municipal commissioner; (*iv*) he should be empowered to write the confidential report of the commissioner; (*v*) he along with the chairman of the various committees should constitute an appellate tribunal to hear appeals against the decisions of the municipal commissioner.[16]

Separation of Deliberative and Executive Functions: Rationale and Critique

The distinctive feature of corporation government is what is commonly known as the separation of executive and deliberative powers. The corporation lays down broad policies, frames by-laws, sanctions budget and keeps a general watch over executive administration. But the entire executive authority is vested in the commissioner, who is appointed by the state government. He occupies the status of a coordinate authority and derives powers directly from the law.

The credit for conceiving of the institution of municipal commissioner goes to Sir Firoz Shah Mehta who held a definite view 'that the municipal council is not to administer and govern for which it is radically unfit and to vest executive authority in it would be a retrograde step, the only safe and efficient way of disposing of the executive authority is to vest it in a single responsible officer.'[17] His scheme is accordingly enshrined in Bombay Municipal Corporation Act, 1888. The Royal Commission on Decentralisation (1907) had also recommended that an elected chairman of the council should be its presiding officer and spokesman and the task of administration should be entrusted to a full time appointed official subject to the control of the council and its standing committee. 'Such an arrangement', the commission wrote, 'would meet the argument that the elected chairman of a large city municipality who might be a busy professional man, would not have the time or the experience to administer it satisfactorily.'[18] Government of India's Resolutions of 1915 and 1918 had lent further support to the philosophy of keeping the deliberative and executive functions in separate hands in the larger interests of efficient municipal administration. This scheme was thought to be the fittest one in the interest of the imperialist powers.

As the presidency towns of Calcutta, Madras and Bombay were the main centres from where imperial power used to radiate, the retention of bureaucratic control was consistent with the ethos of colonial rule. The executive in the corporation governments of these cities was therefore conceived in terms of the politics of imperialism. City government was firmly in imperial hands through the appointment of commissioner just as distinct administration was in direct government control through the posting of the collector.[19] With the achievement of independence, the bureaucratic control of corporation government should have logically come to an end. But strangely enough, instead of rejecting the colonial structure, the design of city government in the big cities was more and more fashioned after the old model. It is a pity that Rural–Urban Relationship Committee (1966) also failed to appreciate the meaning of the great political change in the country since independence and recommended that the commissioner should be retained in the old form, the mayor should be kept informed of all going-ons in the corporation and an appellate committee should be set up to review decisions when appeal would be received. This is the entire mole hill that the Rural–Urban Relationship Committee could produce.[20] The system of separation of deliberative and executive wings has been criticized on the following grounds:

1. The structure of corporation government seems to have been designed on the assumption that 'policy' and 'administration' are two distinct and divisible functions which can be entrusted to two separate authorities. But in the practical world of governance, especially in the realm of local government, policy and administration are inextricably intertwined.

2. The retention of the government appointed commissioner as a coordinate and independent authority in a democratic polity is hardly justified as it involves an unwarranted trespass intc the domain of the representative local council. A state appointed functionary to administer a self-governing community has been considered to be an assault on the time honoured principles of democracy and autonomy. The late Professor W.A. Robson had denounced such a system of civic administration in these words, 'The regime in Bombay provides for the executive power to be concentrated in the municipal commissioner, an official appointed by the state government. We cannot regard Bombay as fulfilling the essential conditions to qualify as a self-governing city, namely, that not only the deliberations of policy, the passing of ordinances and the control of finance, shall be within the ambit of an elected council, but also that executive power shall belong either to the council or to an organ appointed by the council or to officers directly elected by the citizens.'

3. The statutory division of deliberative and executive powers has been a constant source of conflict and friction between the commissioner and the corporation.

4. The commissioner's attempt to run the executive administration without political interference is thwarted by pressures from the corporation; the councillors, on the other hand, complain that since they are to share the blame for the deficiencies and failures in civic administration, they should have the statutory responsibility for executive administration.

5. This fragmented structure and splitting of authority has resulted in nobody's concern for planning the development of the city, mobilization of resources and enlisting popular support for civic development.

6. A commissioner may be a very efficient administrator but he cannot be expected to play the role of a political leader, which should indeed be assigned to the elected mayor and the councillors who in the present scheme are not capable of performing it as they are bereft of executive powers.

The deficiencies and failures of the separation of deliberative and executive function are beautifully summed up in the analysis of the functioning of the scheme in Calcutta city government as follows:

> 'The dual government of Calcutta based on a separation of powers between the councillors and the commissioner is indefensible on many grounds. It is essentially inappropriate as a tool for civic planning and development. The provision of an independent commissioner has repeatedly been

> demonstrated to provide at best only a negative check on the parochialism and bias of the councillors with the result of either a cold war between the councillors and the commissioner or the subservience of the latter to the former. Under the present system, there is no institutional device, machinery or agency to absorb or reconcile the differences between the councillors and the commissioner to their mutual advantage and the benefit of the city.

More important still, the lack of cooperation between the commissioner and the councillor deprives the city of leadership—the corporation-in-council cannot, because of its size, itself satisfy the need for leadership, no standing committee can presently fill the void, the mayor functions as speaker and ceremonial head, and the commissioner is prevented from giving executive leadership in view of his official background and appointment. If he is lucky, the commissioner can at best be an effective and routine administrator, he cannot hope to be an effective innovator, pioneering new and radical measures, without the support of the councillors and the social forces they represent.[21]

The Committee on Budgetary Reforms in Municipal Administration (1974) while discussing the weaknesses of the existing structure of municipal authorities which were mainly responsible for their malfunctioning, had *inter alia* observed, 'The separation of deliberative and executive wings in the municipal corporations had resulted in strained relations between these two important wings. Quite often the deliberative wing which is the final authority for passing the estimates took unilateral decisions to inflate the figures of revenue estimates presented by the executive wing. Ultimately when these expectations were not fulfilled, as was to be expected, the executive wing was blamed for failure to attain the targets. This makes the executive wing more conservative. On the other hand, the deliberative wing would complain of not only deliberate pegging down of estimates of income but also of indifference to the policy of deliberative wing on the part of the officials—the deliberative wing sometimes considered the chief executive as an agent of state government purposely planted in the local authority resulting in alienation. There appears to be some element of mutual distrust in the relationship of the two wings. This is perhaps so because the deliberative wing as well as the chief executive are recognized as executive authorities in municipal acts.[22]

The anomalous and archaic executive structure of corporation government as a result of the separation of deliberative and executive function has been highlighted by several research studies also.'[23]

Remodelling the Structure

The system discussed above results in operational inefficiency which creates more tensions and weakens the system. There is therefore, the need for remodelling the structure and trying other models and testing their efficiency, for instance, strong mayor system, mayor-in-council system etc. In the strong mayor form, the mayor is to be the sole executive, guided and controlled in matters of policy and finance by the council of elected representatives and assisted and supported by the commissioner in administration. Mayor-in-council form of corporation government is favoured by the mayors and corporators of important corporations.[24]

As a concrete measure, the Metropolitan Council of Delhi had passed a Bill in 1966 proposing a mayor-in-council form of municipal government for Delhi. The mayor-in-council scheme was proposed as a part of the comprehensive plan to reorganize the set up of Delhi Municipal Corporation and a Bill to amend the Delhi Municipal Corporation Act (1957) to this effect was introduced in the Parliament in 1966, but it could not be passed due to the dissolution of the Parliament for holding general elections and it was not re-introduced thereafter. According to the provisions of the Bill, mayor-in-council was to consist of a mayor elected by members of the corporation and two deputy mayors appointed by the Lt Governor of Delhi on the mayor's advice. The mayor-in-council was *inter alia* to exercise certain executive powers now vested in the corporation council, to take over powers and functions of the standing committee, to appoint with the

Lt Governor's approval municipal commissioner who was to be the chief executive officer of the corporation, and to exercise supervision and control over the corporation work. The mayor was removable by an absolute majority vote of the total membership of the corporation. Thus, the scheme sought to introduce a sort of cabinet system and project the mayor as a sort of prime/chief minister in the city corporation of Delhi and aimed at abrogating the old duality in corporation administration.

A seminar held under the auspices of the Indian Institute of Public Administration at New Delhi in September 1969 had also discussed the Cabinet system in municipal administration in India,[25] but it remained only an academic exercise and no state government came forward to introduce mayor-in-council system. It was the United Front Government which came into power headed by CPI(M) in West Bengal in 1977 that it went ahead with its programme of effecting reforms in municipal government and passed the Calcutta Municipal Corporation Bill, 1980, providing, for among other things a mayor-in-council as the political executive in the new corporation wherein the corporation, the mayor-in-council and the mayor would constitute the new trinity of the municipal authorities for the municipal government of Calcutta. The executive power shall be exercised by the mayor-in-council and the commissioner shall function under the supervision and control of the mayor. The mayor-in-council would be a small body, consisting of the mayor and six to 10 members who shall be nominated by the mayor and allocated responsibility by him and could be removed from office by his written order. The mayor-in-council shall be collectively responsible. A resolution carried by a majority of not less than two-thirds of the total number of elected members of the corporation will be necessary for the removal of the mayor or the deputy mayor or both. In the words of Shri Prasanta Sur, Minister-in-charge, Local Government, West Bengal, who had introduced and pioneered the bill, the mayor in addition to his role as the first citizen of Calcutta, and not the commissioner, shall provide executive leadership too. And so that he can be effective as a leader in a city with perhaps the greatest political awakening and political consciousness anywhere in the country, we have opted for the *strong mayor system* whereby only the mayor would be elected by the elected councillors, and his colleagues in the mayor-in-council shall work at his pleasure—though they would be selected from the elected representatives of the people only.[26] Thus the existing commissioner oriented executive designed originally for the Bombay Municipal Corporation towards the end of the 19th century was replaced by the mayor-in-council form of executive in the two municipal corporations of Calcutta and Howrah in 1981. The implications of this new experiment with the executive system in the municipal corporation in West Bengal are monumental for the municipal government in the country and this experiment may be attempted in other states as well in the times to come.

Municipal Commissioner

The municipal commissioner is the chief executive officer of the corporation. He is the kingpin of the municipal administration and as such is at the apex of the municipal administrative hierarchy. He is entrusted with the responsibility of keeping the entire administrative machinery under his control, giving it necessary guidance and direction. If the American City Manager and the British Town Clerk embody great contributions to the art of city government made by the countries concerned, the municipal commissioner is the Indian contribution.[27] The municipal council is the legislative body laying down policies for the civic governance of the city and the administration of these policies is the responsibility of the commissioner. Thus the office of the commissioner is based on the philosophy of keeping policy making functions separate from its administration. The credit for conceiving the institution of municipal commissioner goes to Sir Firoz Shah Mehta. He had a definite view 'that the municipal council is not to administer and govern for which it is radically unfit and to vest executive authority in it would be a retrogressive step the only safe and efficient way of disposing of the executive authority is to vest it in a single responsible officer.' His scheme was enshrined in the Bombay Municipal Corporation Act of 1888. The separation of policy making from its execution was commended by the Royal Commission on Decentralization (1907), which recommended an elected chairman of the council to be the presiding officer and spokesman of the council as a whole and the tasks of administration to be entrusted to a full time state appointed official subject to the control of the council and its standing committee. Such an arrangement, the Commission wrote, 'would meet the argument that our elected Chairman of a large city municipality, who might be a busy professional man, would not have the time or the experience to administer it satisfactorily.' The Resolutions of 1915 and 1918 of the government of India had lent further support to the philosophy of keeping of these two functions in separate hands in the larger interests of efficient municipal administration.

Appointment of the Commissioner

The Punjab state government appoints the commissioner from amongst its Class-I officers having a minimum of 10 years' service in that class. It is also provided in the Punjab Municipal Corporation Act that no officer who has attained the age of superannuation shall be appointed as commissioner. The state government had three proposals with regard to the class and status of officers to be appointed as commissioners. The first proposal had emanated in the cabinet sub-committee meetings, suggesting that IAS officers in super time scale with the status of divisional commissioner should be appointed as municipal commissioner. It was contended that the corporation authorities have to seek assistance from police, judiciary, district administration, and other government departments for its proper functioning and only an officer of a status higher than that of a deputy commissioner could get things done from the local officers as well as at the level of the government. Second, the local government department had proposed IAS officers in the senior scale for these appointments, for the reason that since the corporations shall be having much higher status and powers as compared to the municipalities, it would be in the fitness of administrative propriety if a person belonging to IAS cadre was appointed; and the third proposal had come from the chief minister who felt that all the senior officers of the state including the PCS officers were equally competent and therefore PCS. officers should not be deprived of these senior positions in the prestigious cities of the state. His proposal was considered to be convincing and was therefore included in the act. But in actual practice only senior officers from the IAS cadre have been appointed to these positions.

Arguments for and Against the Commissioner's Appointment by the State Government

The commissioner's appointment, vested in the state government, has been a subject of great controversy. A state appointed functionary to administer a self-governing community has been considered to be an assault on the time honoured principles of democracy and autonomy. The late Professor W.A. Robson had denounced such a system of civic administration. He wrote, 'The regime in Bombay provides for the executive power to be concentrated in the municipal commissioner, an official appointed by the state government—we cannot regard Bombay as fulfilling the essential conditions to qualify as a self-governing city, namely, that not only the deliberations of policy, the passing of ordinances and the control of finance, shall be within the ambit of an elected council, but also that executive power shall belong either to the council or to an organ appointed by the council or to officers directly elected by the citizens.'[28]

This arrangement is further criticized on the ground that the government appointed commissioner is a generalist having no intimate knowledge of any branch of municipal administration like public education, public health, public works, etc. and that without such knowledge, it may be difficult for him to make decisions in regard to any of these fields. This argument does not sound strong enough, as a specialist in urban affairs may be specialist in any one of the branches of the city government and hence may be incapable of taking care of the others. What an administrator in city government requires is the ability to take an overall disinterested view of all branches of administration, as he shall be having heads of the specialized branches of administration to advise him in their respective spheres of activity.

It is alleged that the commissioner, appointed as he is for a fixed term of three years or so, considers it only a sojourn, a spell of time and by no means a part of career in his cadre, an assignment outside his line to which he is anxious to return as soon as possible.[29] It is also contended that commissioner being a public servant cannot be expected to mobilize popular support and public participation on a large scale which is essentially a function of political leadership.

The protagonists of this arrangement however see in it a pragmatic reconciliation of political democracy and administrative efficiency. They argue that the commissioner being an experienced civil servant enjoying security of service and a fixed tenure is likely to administer the policies laid down by the council in an efficient and impartial manner.

It is an established fact that the state government will not like to abandon its right of appointing a commissioner but it would be advisable if it consults the mayor in making the appointment as this would lead to harmonious relationship between the council and the commissioner; secondly the government should not confine appointment of commissioner to civil servants only, it should develop the practice of appointing to this post persons from the public life also, as having a background of public life, such a person is likely to be more in accord with the elected council and when after serving his term as a commissioner, he returns back to public life, the community shall have the benefit of having in its midst an informed citizen possessing direct experience of civic administration.[30]

Term of the Commissioner

The commissioner is appointed for a period of three years, which can be further renewed by the state government for a term not exceeding three years. The act provides that the state government may recall him at any time by giving a notice of at least one month to the corporation. The government shall have to recall him if the council passes a resolution by a majority of not less than two-thirds of the total number of members, in a specially convened meeting for the purpose requesting the government to do so. Besides, a commissioner may seek his transfer any time before completing his term of three years. The act also provides that if any vacancy occurs in the office of the commissioner on account of death, resignation or removal, the government may appoint another person to officiate as commissioner for a term not exceeding two months, pending the appointment of a regular commissioner.

It has been observed that the transfers or replacement of the commissioners are made too frequently and most of them do not complete even the normal stipulated term of three years. Frequent transfers of the chief executive not only bring about a disruption in the civic administration but also breed delays, corruption and politicking at lower levels. A rational transfer policy subject to the completion of a term of minimum three years is, therefore, required to be evolved and implemented in the interests of the continuation of the policies of administration and their successful implementation.

Powers and Functions of the Commissioner

The powers and functions of the municipal commissioner are many and varied. He is one of the statutory municipal authorities to carry out the provisions of the corporation act. His most important statutory function is to execute the resolutions of the council and of its committees. He is authorized to attend the meetings of the council and of any of its committees. He can participate in discussions and express his views on various points but he has not the right to vote. He is expected to answer a question put to him by any councillor but he may not respond to a query seeking such information as in the opinion of the mayor may be prejudicial to the public interest. He is custodian of all municipal records. He is to prepare the budget estimates and after these have been passed to submit them to the state government for approval. He is to keep the mayor informed of all the official correspondence which he might enter into with the state government.

He has been clothed with a vast variety of powers. He can make appointments to posts carrying a certain grade. The appointments constitute lever of patronage to the councillors who have to oblige their supporters, relatives and other influential sections of the public with their recommendations for jobs, and such recommendations, the commissioner has to take into account in many cases.

All the contracts are made by the commissioner on behalf of the corporation and he himself can also enter into any contract involving an expenditure not exceeding Rs 25,000 or such higher amount as may be fixed by the corporation from time to time. He can delegate to any other municipal official any of his ordinary powers, duties, and functions.

The commissioner has extraordinary powers too. He can take immediate action on the occurrence or threatened occurrence of any sudden accident or unforeseen event involving or likely to involve extensive damage to any property of the corporation or danger to human life, but he has to inform the corporation of the action taken, reasons for the same and cost involved.

The multi-dimensional nature of the activities of the commissioner makes him the pivot of municipal administration. As a whole time municipal officer in charge of municipal administration he is required to spend most of his time even outside office hours, in looking to daily correspondence, planning, designing and reporting for the purpose of improving the welfare of the citizens of the municipal area. His role is hard, the work is heavy and the pressure on him tremendous, yet he can survive and do good work to make the city life clean and liveable.

Functions of Municipal Corporations

Municipal corporations all over the country have been assigned by their respective state governments a long list of functions. As a matter of fact, functions to be performed by the municipal committees and the municipal corporations are similar in nature. The real difference lies in their powers and resources. Their jurisdiction and area of operation increase when the municipalities are raised to the status of municipal corporations. The functions of municipal corporations can be classified into obligatory and discretionary function. The former comprise supply of wholesome water; construction and maintenance of water works; naming and numbering of public streets; road transport services; lighting and cleansing of public streets and other public places, removal and disposal of filth and rubbish; construction, maintenance and cleaning of drains, public latrines, urinals, etc.; removal of obstructions and projections in or upon public streets and other common places; securing or removal of dangerous building or places; establishment and maintenance of hospitals, maternity and child welfare centres; preventive measures and checking of dangerous diseases; vaccination and inoculation; registration of births and deaths; regulation of places for the disposal of the dead and provision of places for this purpose; provision of primary education; maintenance of fire brigades; control and regulation of eating places, and publication of the corporation's reports.

The discretionary functions include construction and maintenance of public parks, gardens; public housing; plantation and care of trees and flowering bushes on road sides and elsewhere; destruction or detention of stray dogs and other animals causing nuisance; survey of buildings and lands; reception of VIP's; celebration of national days; registration of marriages; organization and management of fairs and exhibitions; relief of destitute and disabled persons, etc.

The obligatory functions as enumerated above can be epitomized into four main types—public health, public safely and convenience, medical relief and public works which when spelt out comprise sanitation and conservancy. These functions have to be necessarily performed and for which budgetary provision has to be made; and failure to perform these functions can empower the state government to dissolve it.

Performance of the Functions: An Appraisal

Municipal corporations, with some exceptions, have failed to perform their obligatory functions. Potable water is not available to the whole of the city and wherever available, it is found to be unfit for human consumption; the sewerage system covers only a few localities and wherever it exists, it is not properly maintained, its construction is found to be defective, sewage overflows manholes which are at some places uncovered and are responsible for the deaths of people; sewage keeps stagnating in congested lanes and commercial centres; sewers are not properly cleaned and several deaths take place because of the poisonous gas generated by them; at some places sewerage practically collapses in the absence of any disposal channels; slums are growing at alarming rate and no improvement is visible in the living conditions of slum dwellers; sanitation is conspicuous by its absence, huge heaps of garbage in congested lanes and busy business centres are a common sight, there is overpowering stink in the interior localities,[31] the roads and footpaths are in bad shape, dilapidated unsafe buildings are not removed/repaired, etc.

This pathetic performance of the corporations, however, does not belittle their efforts to do their best for the development of the city and the provision of services and facilities to their inhabitants within the resources at their disposal. We cannot afford to be oblivious of the fact that they are confronted with gigantic task of developing the city and providing basic amenities to their people as a result of tremendous increase in their population and area and rapid industrialization. They have been able to accomplish various schemes of development; provided water supply and sewerage to vast areas of their cities, laid new roads and widened the old ones, provided road dividers to regulate traffic flow, built several by-pass roads to divert the traffic coming into the city, constructed flyovers to reduce the traffic congestion inside the city, constructed roundabouts at various crossings of the roads to avoid accidents and beautified them and also the roads converging into them, with ornamental trees and flowering plants. They have also provided numerous parks and recreation sites, libraries, and reading rooms both mobile and immobile; set up health centres, dispensaries and first-aid posts, and electric crematoria in different parts of the city. Their anxiety to make the lives of the citizens healthy and happy can be appreciated but their main constraint is lack of financial resources. Some of the corporations have reached a state of virtual bankruptcy and the state governments do not come to their rescue in the desired measure by providing them the necessary financial help in the form of grants or sharing with them some share of the taxes collected on their behalf by the corporations. The state finance commissions as required to be constituted by the Constitution (74th Amendment) Act, 1992, may perhaps bring them out of this impasse by recommending financial allocations to them appropriate to their requirements.

Erosion of Their Functions

It is surprising that even after more than 60 years of independence, the municipal bodies including municipal corporations can undertake only such functions as have been assigned to them by state legislatures. In this respect, we follow the British method of specific grant which means that no local authority may do anything which it is not definitely entitled to do by virtue of statute.

In other words, their functions are limited by the state government. This restrictive approach to municipal functions no longer holds good in the changed political context and needs of the country. The Punjab Local Government (Urban) Enquiry Committee had accordingly expressed the hope that, in the new set-up, local bodies as instruments of national policy would be used more and more and there would be steady enlargement of their functions.[32] In the First Five Year Plan, the Planning Commission's thinking was that the general direction of policy should be to encourage self-governing bodies and to assist them in assuming responsibility for as large a portion of the administrative and social services as possible.[33]

But on the contrary, there has been an increasing tendency on the part of the state governments to take over more and more local functions either directly or by creating special purpose agencies. The local finance enquiry committee had deplored the tendency to transfer functions from local bodies to the state government in the fields of elementary education, public health and communications and expressed the opinion that wholesale transfer of functions from the local bodies to the state governments, are a retrograde step and should be avoided. Whatever be the criteria for demarcation of functions between the state governments and local bodies, the desperate financial position of the latter should not be made a ground for reducing them to practical impotence.[34]

The transfer of functions is not only a retrograde step but also anachronistic. It could have some justification in the pre-Independence era when the central government worked to spread its tentacles in every sector of life but not in the post-Independence era when we are free from all alien pressures.[35] The Rural–Urban Relationship Committee was also of the view that the remedy for the inefficiency and non-performance of their duties does not lie in depriving the municipal bodies of their functions but in improving and strengthening their organizational and administrative set up, allocating to them adequate resources and giving them expert and technical help in the discharge of their functions.[36]

The argument of incapability or inefficiency of municipal governments has proved to be a handy argument for the state governments in favour of demunicipalization of the management of certain local services.[37] Thus, the rise of competitive bureaucratic urban local institutions and state take over of municipal functions have led not only to erosion of municipal functions but also created an atmosphere of distrust with regard to urban local government.[38]

Despite the need for increasing the functions of municipal governments in the context of the problems of urbanization and the state increasingly assuming a welfare and socialist orientation, these have been gradually decreased.[39] The state governments have been setting up special authorities to perform functions of a certain type such as improvements and development of towns, housing, water supply and sewerage and control of pollution, etc. For example in Madras, the state government has set up a number of special purpose authorities like the Slum Clearance Board, Housing Board and Madras Metropolitan Development Authority.

In view of the lack of the sufficient resources for these specialized agencies, the question of their continuity needs serious consideration. There can be three alternatives in deciding their future: (i), they should be abolished and merged with the concerned municipal body as has been done in Uttar Pradesh, Delhi and other states; (ii) all these organizations should be put under a unified administrative control of the city council to secure coordination in their working; (iii) an urban development authority should be set up to ensure better coordination among the various agencies and to raise more institutional finances. The finances of municipal corporations in their various aspects, such as their sources of revenues, heads of expenditure, budgets, accounting and audit as also the question of state government supervision and control over municipal corporations, its need and justification, its forms and mechanism have been discussed in detail separately in the chapters entitled 'Urban Local Government Finances' and 'State Control over Urban Local Governments' of this book.

NOTES AND REFERENCES

1. *Encyclopaedia of Social Sciences* (New York: Macmillan Co., 1935), xi p. 86.
2. *Ibid.*
3. Report of the National Commission on Urbanisation, 1988, Vol. II, p. 155.
4. S.R. Maheshawari, *Local Government in India* (Agra: Lakshmi Narain Aggarwal, 1999), p. 212.
5. G.P. Krishna Rao, *Nagarlok* 6, no. 3 (New Delhi, IIPA, 1974), p. 20.
6. Report of the Rural-Urban Relationship Committee, Vol. I, Ministry of Health and Family Planning, June 1966, para 4, 11.
7. Constitution (74th Amendment) Act, 1992, Article 243-Q.
8. Mayor's Newsletter, Vol. XI, No. 1, January, 1983.
9. The Constitution of India, Article 243-T.
10. *Ibid.,* Article 243-R.
11. *Ibid.,* Article 243-S.
12. *Ibid.,* Article 243-ZE.
13. G. Ram Reddy, in A. Avasthi (ed.), *Municipal Administration in India* (Agra: Lakshmi Narain Aggarwal, 1972).
14. S.R. Maheshwari, *Local Government,* p. 174.
15. *Ibid.*
16. Report of the Rural-Urban Relationship Committee, *op-cit.*
17. Pardeep Sachdeva, *Dynamics of Municipal Government and Politics in India* (Allahabad: Kitab Mahal, 1991), p. 62.
18. Royal Commission on Decentralisation, 1907.
19. Mohit Bhattacharya, 'The Mayor-in-Council System', *Nagarlok* 13, no. 4 (October–December, 1981), p. 3.
20. *Ibid.*
21. Ashraf Ali, *The City Government of Calcutta: A Study of Inertia* (Bombay: Asia Publishing House, 1960), 77.
22. 'Report of the Committee on Budgetary Reforms in Municipal Administration', Government of India, Ministry of Works and Housing, New Delhi, June 1979, p. 37.
23. David, R. Rosental, *The Limited Elite: Politics and Government in two Indian Cities,* University of Chicago Press, 1970.
24. Report of the Rural-Urban Relationship Committee, Vol. II, 1966.
25. Refer to Cabinet System in Municipal Government: 'Proceedings of the Seminar', 15–16 September 1969, Centre for Research and Training in Municipal Administration, The Indian Institute of Public Administration, New Delhi, 1970.
26. Extract from the speech by Shri Prasanta Sur, Minister-in-charge, Local Government and Urban Development, Govt. of West Bengal, before the Legislative Assembly on April 29, 1980 while introducing the Select Committee Report on the Calcutta Municipal Corporation Bill, 1980.
27. M.A. Mutalib, 'Municipal Commissioner', *Indian Journal of Public Administration* (Autumn, 1987): 287.
28. W.A. Robson, *Great Cities of the World* (London: George Allen and Unwin, 1954), 51–54
29. Gyan Prakash, 'Organising City Government', *Indian Journal of Public Administration* 15, no. 3 (1968): 489–500.
30. S.R. Maheshwari, *Local Government,* p. 182.
31. According to Mrs Maneka Gandhi, Former Environment Minister, Government of India, while inaugurating the Fifth Pollution Control Camp at Anand Parbat in New Delhi on 21 March 1991, among the industrial cities, Ludhiana, the Manchester of India, is the dirtiest city in the state of Punjab, Delhi is one of the three worst polluted cities in the world despite the fact that the Central Pollution Control Board is spending the maximum on the city to keep it pollution free.
32. Report of the Punjab Local Government (Urban) Enquiry Committee, 1957, p. 98.

33. Government of India, Planning Commission, First Five Year Plan, p. 141.
34. Report of the Local Finance Enquiry Committee, 1966, p. 16.
35. *Ibid.*, pp. 955–56.
36. Report of the Rural–Urban Relationship Committee, p. 16.
37. Ashok Makhopadhaya, *Municipal Government and Urban Development: A Study of the Reforms in West Bengal* (New Delhi: Indian Institute of Public Administration), 6.
38. Anil Bhatt, 'Municipal Government in Gujarat: Structure, Process and Style', in Abhijit Datta (ed.), *Municipal and Urban India* (New Delhi: IIPA, 1980), 35.
39. T.N. Chaturvedi, in S.K. Sharma and V.N. Chawle (eds.), *Municipal Administration in India*, p. iv.

Urban Local Government Personnel Administration

Efficient and effective functioning of any organization depends mainly on the competence of the staff employed for implementing its policies and programmes. Herman Finer has rightly observed, 'adequately organized the political philosophy, high leadership and command, these would be of no effect without the body of official experts in applying the accumulated supply of power and wisdom to the particular cases permanently and specially employed to do so.'[1] It is more so in the case of municipal governments, as they are intimately concerned with and are responsible for the provision of facilities so vital for healthy living. An efficient administrative, professional, and technical staff at the municipal level is, therefore, the *sine qua non* of vigorous and efficient municipal government.[2] Being a service-oriented organization with the minimum of mechanization in its operation, municipal bodies are to depend heavily on the competence and devotion of their staff in the performance of their tasks.[3] Again, the success of local representative governments may very largely be attributed to the effective combination of the different qualities that are contributed by elected representatives and non-elected employees.[4] The pace of decentralization will be conditioned by the availability of a competent staff and it is very much the performance of the staff that decides whether more functions will be delegated to the local bodies or their existing functions will be taken away.[5] Besides, in developing countries local bodies have the potential of serving as engines of economic development. If any breakthrough is to be achieved in economic development through the agency of local bodies, it is the staff that will have to act as a catalyst in that process.[6] Municipal personnel system, thus, needs to be a sound one.

According to a study made by the United Nations, the Municipal Personnel system can be classified into three categories.[7]

1. Separate Personnel System
2. Unified Personnel System
3. Integrated Personnel System

Separate Personnel System

A separate personnel system is one in which each local authority has the power to appoint and administer its own personnel, who are not transferable to any other jurisdiction by a central body. In the past, municipal bodies in most states in India practiced the separate personnel system. This system has been in vogue in various countries like USA, UK, Japan and New Zealand.[8] The merits and demerits of this system are the following:

Merits

1. Under this system, the municipal body is obliged to ensure the inhabitants for its employee's effective performance.
2. The employees recruited locally are supposed to be familiar with local conditions and thus can develop their greater interest in local affairs as compared to the employees recruited from outside.
3. The prospects for continuous employment in their own area can attract more talented persons to enter the municipal services.
4. The separate personnel system enhances the status of the municipal body by granting more powers regarding recruitment and management of its personnel.
5. The system being confined to local employees, local community and local problems restricts outside interference.

Demerits

1. The system is not suitable for small municipalities to scale minimum standards and to recruit competent persons.
2. It suffers from the disadvantages of nepotism, political interference and insecurity.
3. The chances of promotion are limited. The officials on higher posts may frustrate this due to the lesser number of higher posts to which they can expect promotion.
4. The relations between political leaders and the officials can hamper the smooth functioning of the local body.
5. Political pressures can penetrate into every aspect of administration involving officers in factional politics.
6. The limited financial resources of a local body hinder employment of suitable and competent persons.
7. An elected council cannot act impartially for recruitment of its personnel but is likely to be influenced by various factors, especially political ones.

In short, the system affords such advantages as recruitment of local people who possess better knowledge of local conditions, have keen interest in local affairs and are committed to the achievement of the welfare of their community. But its disadvantages outweigh its advantages. The Rural-Urban Relationship Committee (1966) had opined 'Under this system, Municipal bodies had misused their autonomy in matters of appointment and disciplinary control; chances of promotion were limited, feeling of insecurity among the staff was acute and political pressurization had penetrated into every aspect of administration involving officers in factional policies.'[9] The Punjab Municipal Employees Pay Committee (1969) had endorsed this view and observed:

> There is evidence that in several municipal committees, posts have been created for no valid reason on extraneous considerations, such as the desire to provide cushy posts for protégés and relatives of the dominating ruling groups and powerful individuals; that no qualifications have been prescribed for administrative and ministerial persons; that no legal procedure has been laid down prescribing method of recruitment; appointments are made by direct recruitment or by promotion on *ad hoc* basis; nor is

> there any clear articulation of basis of selection for recruitment by promotion, often promotions are made on extrinsic conditions without regard to merit and order of seniority of the eligible employees, lack of definite basis of promotion leads sometimes to the appointment of persons who are unfit for their roles and free rein to nepotism, favouritism and jobbery and other malpractices detrimental to efficiency and morale; that one of the most glaring deficiencies in the present system of municipal personnel administration is the lack of security of tenure which throws municipal employees at the tender mercies of municipal commissioners and exposes them to the baneful impact of group and party polities, municipal employees are hired and fired at the whim of dominating ruling groups often for extraneous and improper considerations.[10]

The Municipal government has become a by-word for inefficiency, corruption, nepotism and favouritism. Indeed, for all known administrative deficiencies, inefficient personnel, which is the product of separate personnel system, is the root of all these ills.[11]

UNIFIED PERSONNEL SYSTEM

The Unified Personnel System or provincialization of municipal services was considered to be a remedy for the ailments of the prevailing municipal personnel system. Under a unified personnel system, all or certain categories of local authorities form a single career service for the entire state. It is distinct from the state/national civil service, and it is the State Government which administers and controls the service. The employees are transferable between local governments within the state. Local governments, thus, get divested of the authority to recruit and administer personnel. The countries which have adopted this system include Ireland, Thailand, Nigeria and Ghana.

Merits

1. The system proposes the creation of a national or state wide career service based on the principle of merit.
2. It reduces the chances of favouritism in the recruitment of personnel.
3. The smaller local bodies can obtain the services of more qualified persons.
4. This system helps the personnel to acquire experience in different local bodies and in different circumstances, which gives them a much wider approach to the problems of local government and a much greater competence to tackle individual problems.
5. It supplies a framework for promotion from one grade to another, which sustains the interest of the personnel in the services.
6. Persons transferable from one local body to another can have a feeling of greater freedom of operation without any inhibition that their entire career will be at stake if they offend the non-officials of any particular local body.
7. The system gives the personnel prestige in the public eye, self-confidence and compulsive efficiency.[12]

Demerits

1. This system is not completely conducive to the principle of local autonomy.
2. A few small municipal bodies, due to their limited resources, may find it difficult to bear the cost of state-wide cadres, which have to be paid at a higher level.

3. The possibility of transfer from one municipal to another can restrict an employee to develop a sense of loyalty and belonging to a local body.
4. The system reduces the agency's power over recruitment, promotion and discipline, which ultimately results in making the staff non-responsive to the municipal committee.
5. Where the municipal councils have to bear the cost for the training of staff, the situation can further deteriorate due to shortage of funds.
6. The system does not provide any solution for promotional opportunities as a few large municipalities only can afford to maintain higher posts.

Integrated Personnel System

In the integrated personnel system, the personnel of the state government and those of local government form part of the same service and in which vertical as well as horizontal transferability is possible. In other words, the state government may constitute an integrated service for some or all categories of personnel for the urban government. The integrated personnel system exists in various under-developed countries like Nepal, Taiwan and Morocco.

Merits

1. This system provides uniformity in regard to salaries, conditions of service and retirement benefits for civil servants.
2. The officials, under this system, are free from local politics and pressures.
3. Horizontal and vertical transfers make it possible to have the services of more competent staff.
4. The system provides wider possible career opportunities in public service.
5. Personnel can be acquired in accordance with the technicalities of the problem.

Demerits

1. The employees may not be as responsive, loyal and committed as they would be to a local body.
2. It is possible that some inefficient persons may get an opportunity to enter municipal service at the behest of the State Government.
3. There is a danger of conflict between municipal councillors and officials belonging to integrated service.
4. Under this system, the employees will have to work under dual control, on the one hand, the control of state government with regard to appointment, promotions and disciplinary action, and on the other hand, the control of municipal authorities in regard to day-to-day administration.
5. The local bodies will become training centres for the employees. As soon as they will gain some experience in the field of local administration, they will be transferred to the state government departments.

Position in India

In India, all three systems, namely, separate, unified and integrated, are followed in various states. The integrated system is followed in Tamil Nadu and other southern states wherein officers serving municipal government are transferable horizontally between municipalities and also vertically between national, state, and municipal governments. The unified model is in vogue in Rajasthan, Uttar Pradesh, Punjab, and Haryana where municipal services have been unified up to the supervisory and clerical levels, but the lowest level employees continue to be recruited and controlled at the municipal level. The Separate personnel model is obtainable in West Bengal, Maharashtra, and Gujarat, where the municipal authorities enjoy exclusive competence to recruit and manage their own personnel, subject to the rules framed by the concerned state governments to control certain aspects of the management of municipal personnel. Thus, the personnel system of urban local government in our country differs from state to state and even in the same state, as therein the unified personnel system operates where higher echelons of municipal services are concerned, and the separate personnel system works in the case of services at lower levels.

Provincialization of Municipal Services

Provincialization of municipal services has been stressed and emphasized by various forums and government committees from time to time. The first conference of Local Self Government Ministers held in August, 1948, had adopted the following resolution:

> In view of the fact that provincial cadre would facilitate recruitment of suitable personnel from a wide field and provide a more efficient and contented service, this conference is of the opinion that there should be provincial cadres for the higher executive and technical staff employed by local bodies.

The second conference of Local Self Government Ministers held in 1954 had reiterated the same suggestion. The Central Council of Local Self Government in conjunction with the Fourth Conference of Ministers of Town and Country Planning, held in 1963, had recommended the provincialization of administrative, health, engineering, and town planning services of the municipalities in the interest of better and more efficient administration. The Rural-Urban Relationship Committee (1966) had observed that it would be more convenient and advantageous to have a combined integrated service for public health engineers, town planners, and medical and health officers, as also of Accounts and Audit Officers, in order to attract and to ensure a steady flow of qualified and competent persons.[13] In its report the Task Force on Management of Urban Development appointed by the Planning Commission (1983) held that personnel development had been the weakest aspect of urban management in India and suggested the formation of state cadres for key positions in municipal management like chief officers, engineers, accounts officers, and revenue officers, and opined that the separate personnel system would be of greater advantage with respect to the lower levels.[14]

In pursuance of the recommendations of various commissions/committees, various state governments, including Punjab and Haryana, had provincialized municipal services by making necessary amendments in their respective municipal acts. The Punjab Government, for example, in order to put a check on the misuse of their powers by the municipalities and to have a uniform pattern by regulating certain posts created by different municipalities, amended the Punjab Municipal Act of 1911 in 1973 in order to provincialize certain services in the municipalities. The amendment provides that notwithstanding anything contained in the Act, the state government may, by notification, constitute in the prescribed manner, all or any of the following municipal services: (*i*) Punjab Service of Municipal Executive Officers; (*ii*) Punjab Service of Municipal Engineers and Section Officers; (*iii*) Punjab Service of Municipal Health Officers; (*iv*) Punjab Service of Municipal Secretaries; (*v*) Punjab Service of Municipal Accountants; and (*vi*) such other municipal service as the state government may decide.

The state government can also make rules for regulating the recruitment and conditions of services of the members of the municipal services and for the classification of such services. In 1975, the Punjab Government provincialized only seven municipal services but by the end of July 1976, the number had risen to twenty-four. Thus, the state government has provincialized the municipal services from the post of Assistant and above, and also laid down rules regarding their recruitment, promotion, and conditions of service. The government is also empowered to transfer any member of the municipal service from a post in one municipality to a post carrying the same scale of pay in another municipality. In this way, the state government has assumed complete authority for the creation of posts, appointment, transfer, and other conditions of service of the personnel working in the municipal services, despite the fact that they get the salary, allowances, gratuity, annuity, pension, and other payments from the funds of their respective municipality.

The municipalities have been left with the power to appoint personnel belonging to non-provincialized service, the clerks and Class-IV employees. Thus, there are two types of personnel, those (*i*) belonging to provincialized services and (*ii*) those employed by the municipality.

Similarly, the state government has constituted the (*i*) Punjab Service of Corporation Engineers and Sectional Officers, (*ii*) Punjab Service of Corporation Health Officers, (*iii*) Punjab Service of Corporation Secretaries, and (*iv*) Punjab Service of Corporation Accounts Officers and Accountants, and is empowered to constitute such other corporation services as it may decide. The state government has so far constituted twenty-one municipal corporation services and framed detailed rules for regulating the recruitment and the conditions of service of the members of the Corporation services, to transfer any member of a corporation service from a post in one corporation to a post carrying the same scale of pay in another corporation. The salary, allowances, gratuity, pension, and other payments required to be made to the members of the Corporation services are charged from the concerned Corporation funds. It is also provided that every person who immediately before the creation of corporation services was serving in a city on a post in relation to which a corporation service is created shall become a member of the corresponding corporation service if he is found fit by an authority appointed by the government in this behalf for becoming such a member on the basis of his qualifications and service record. If he is not found fit, the post which he is serving shall be deemed to have been abolished.

The power of creating posts and making appointments to them other than the corporation services is vested in the commissioner if the maximum of the grade of a post does not exceed Rs 500 and in the corporation if it so exceeds provided that no post the maximum of the grade whereof exceeds Rs 1,000 shall be created save with the approval of the government.

The powers of the appointments of personnel in a municipal corporation are thus shared by the state government, the commissioner and the corporation. Appointments to the post of commissioner are made by the state government from amongst its senior IAS officers and those of joint and assistant commissioners from amongst its IAS and senior PCS officers, respectively.

Recruitment of Municipal Personnel

Recruitment constitutes the cornerstone of the whole personnel structure[15] for it determines the tone and calibre of public services. On it rests the nature and degree of usefulness of the administrative machinery.[16] Dimock and Dimock rightly observe, 'The fundamental operation in building a strong public service is recruitment. If original selection is carelessly or inadequately performed, weakness is carried with the staff which time and training may never cure.'[17] The municipal administration, close as it is to the public, can inspire respect and confidence only if it is manned by efficient civil servants.[18] It is, therefore, essential that municipal bodies should have a sound policy and system of recruitment in order to get competent staff.

The state government makes recruitment to the provincialized municipal services on the recommendations of a Selection Committee,[19] which is constituted by it and consists of five members, out of whom three are officers of the government and two non-officials having sufficient experience of urban local bodies.

At least one of the members of the selection committee must belong to Scheduled Castes. The Selection Committee, keeping in view the nature and duties of the post required to be filled, can associate not more than two members who are experts in the field concerned. The person to be associated should not be less than the rank of a superintending engineer in the case of the selection of an engineer and not below the rank of joint director of health services in the case of selection of medical staff.

In Punjab, at the time of constituting municipal services and their provincialization it was decided that all employees with the requisite qualifications, working in different municipalities would be absorbed against the corresponding equivalent posts they hold in the municipality. After filling these vacancies, the remaining and new posts sanctioned by the state government were to be filled in by direct recruitment and promotion in the ratio of 50:50.

The selection committee is to follow the policy of the government regarding the reservation of seats for Scheduled Castes and other backward classes while recommending appointment to the municipal services. Provision has also been made to make appointments by transfer/deputation from other departments if suitable candidates are not available by direct recruitment or promotion.

The state government also makes appointments to the municipal corporation services such as those of executive officers, secretaries, municipal engineers, and municipal health officers on the recommendations of a selection committee.

It is evident that a municipal corporation does not enjoy any autonomy worth the name in the recruitment of personnel for the management of senior and middle level positions. For recruitment to lower posts, the corporation and the commissioner have to abide by the rules and regulations which may be framed by the state government. Besides, the commissioner has no say in the selection of officers to be appointed against posts in the provincialized cadre. The constitution of selection committees does not inspire confidence in regard to its independence. They are dominated by officials nominated by the government. It is suggested that the recruitment should be made by a ,municipal service commission on the pattern of Calcutta Corporation or by State Public Service Commission. Alternatively, it is desirable that a member of the State Public Service Commission should also be included in the Selection Committee who should act as its *ex officio* chairman. This will go a long way in building the image of the Selection Committees as independent recruiting agencies in the field of municipal administration.

Promotion of Municipal Personnel

Promotion is of great significance in personnel administration. Competent and promising employees must have avenues for advancement in the service to ensure not only effective and better utilization of available human resources but also to retain those who have demonstrated professional competence and administrative abilities.[20] Promotion is thus an incentive and should be based on sound principles of merit and seniority.

The provincialization of municipal services has increased the opportunities for promotion as it has been provided that 50 per cent of posts will be filled by promotion. This has brightened the chances of promotion, and whenever there is a vacancy in a higher grade, a person from lower grade can be promoted. Moreover, as the employees can be transferred from one municipality to another, it has further widened the sphere of promotion, for even when an employee does not get a chance in one municipality, he can be sent to another municipality whenever a vacancy in higher grade occurs there. In order to regularize the system of recruitment and promotion at the time of provincialization, certain qualifications for different posts in municipal services and channel of promotion were laid down. Even then, promotions are few and far between in actual practice for reasons of limited number of higher positions, the complications involved, and the delay caused in finalization of combined seniority list of erstwhile municipal personnel.

In a municipal corporation, promotion avenues are also very meagre. All the top and middle level administrative, executive, professional, and technical positions are held by the personnel belonging to the Corporation provincialized services, which are completely controlled by the state government, whereas all the subordinate and Class IV posts fall within the ambit of non-provincialized services. The employees of the latter cadre have no chances to hold positions in the former service and ordinarily they cannot occupy any positions in any department of the Corporation beyond the level of superintendent or its equivalent.

Seventy-five per cent of the posts of lower division clerks, upper division clerks, superintendents and other corresponding posts are filled through promotion on the basis of seniority while 25 per cent of the posts are filled from outside. This apparently rosy picture pales into insignificance when we discover that promotions were given to only 11 persons out of about 7,000 employees of a corporation only during 1987–88 since its inception in 1977. This is attributed to the cumbersome and lengthy procedure and apathy on the part of corporation authorities. The employees are naturally frustrated.

Even the executive officers of the municipal corporations and municipal committees are an aggrieved lot. They complain that there are no further promotion avenues for them and apart from stagnation in service, they are sore over the fact that more often than not, their subordinates have better pay scales, thereby affecting their status and authority. They, therefore, demand that their pay scales should be revised with 1968 as the base; selection grade be provided for them; and a quota for promotion into PCS and IAS cadres be fixed for them as is done in the case of BDPOs. They should be given 'gazetted status'; at least three posts of deputy directors at the headquarters and regional deputy directors should be kept reserved for senior executive officers, who should be promoted on a seniority-cum-merit basis and similarly the posts of deputy and assistant commissioners of corporations should be made available to them.

Training of Municipal Personnel

An important aspect of municipal personnel administration which is yet to receive adequate recognition is the need and importance of training. Training achieves twin objectives of competence and responsiveness of the officials to democracy.[21] The employees of local bodies also need to be exposed to outside developments and major national problems so that their vision widens and they adopt a comprehensive approach to the problems confronting them.[22] While in countries like England, USA, Canada, Netherland, West Germany and Sweden education and training in municipal government has made significant progress, the Government of India has shown little interest in this regard. Before independence some universities—Nagpur, Allahabad, and Lucknow—instituted courses in municipal administration and the Institute of Local Self-Government, Bombay (1927), made excellent pioneer work in training municipal officials.[23] The Centre for Training and Research, now known as Centre for Urban Studies, an organ of the Indian Institute of Public Administration, has done commendable work in this regard. It was only in 1963 that the Government of India appointed a Committee known as Nur-Uddin Committee on the training of municipal employees. The Committee emphasized the need for imparting training to the municipal personnel in different types of municipal bodies. Professionalization of municipal administration was considered necessary in view of the increasing complexities of urban administration. The Committee recommended the setting up of training institute at the central level which would organize high level, imaginative training programmes, and coordinate the training activities throughout the country and promote necessary uniformity in the programmes of different state level institutes. The committee observed, 'it would be one of the central institute's major responsibilities to prescribe the standard of training and research and it should serve as a model in this respect. The committee did not rule out the need for setting up state institutes but it was felt that lack of adequate resources, equipment and faculty might stand in the way of simultaneous development of a number of state institutes in different parts of the country.'[24]

Rural-Urban Relationship Committee (1963–66) also stressed the urgency of setting up training and research institutions in the field of municipal administration. As a sequel to these recommendations, the central institute was attached to the Indian Institute of Public Administration, New Delhi, and the regional centres were set up at Lucknow, Hyderabad, Bombay, and Calcutta. The institutional linkages of these centres differ from place to place. For example, the Lucknow and Hyderabad centres were located within the department of public administration of the local universities. Later, the Hyderabad centre came out of the University of Hyderabad, Department of Public Administration, but retained its existence under the overall university umbrella. The Bombay regional centre was set up as a wing of the All India Institute of Local Self Government, while the Calcutta Regional Centre was located within the Indian Institute of Social Welfare and Business Management. Of these regional centres, the Calcutta unit has been since wound up.[25] Another central institution set up by the Ministry of Works, Housing and Urban Development, Government of India, is the National Institute of Urban Affairs.

It is clear from the description of the institutional development in the field of training that it is exclusively focused on the municipal employees and it does not cater to the needs of the personnel of the other urban institutions such as Urban Development Authorities, Improvement Trusts, Water Supply and Sewerage Authorities, Slum Clearance Boards and Housing Boards, which also operate in the urban areas and require properly trained personnel for the efficient performance of their functions in their respective fields. Institutional coverage is, therefore, needed to be extended to the personnel of these urban institutions as well. Moreover, the training programmes have to be designed in such a manner as to suit the requirements of the elected functionaries, the generalists and the specialists.

In the North Western region of the country, including Punjab and Haryana, there is no institute as such to impart training to municipal employees. The Punjab Local Government (Urban) Enquiry Committee (1957), had, among other things, recommended for the establishment of a training institute for municipal personnel. And though the Government had accepted the recommendation, it did not take any steps to implement it. Both the Punjab and Haryana governments are of the view that their personnel can be imparted the required training in their respective Institutes of Public Administration at Chandigarh and Gurgaon and at the Indian Institute of Public Administration, New Delhi. But they have hardly instituted any training programmes for their municipal personnel at their institutes of public administration, or deputed their officers for training at IIPA, New Delhi.

It is desirable that state governments should establish a Centre for Research and Training in Municipal Administration at one of their universities to serve as a nucleus for the regional centre, which can be financially supported by the central government like other regional centres.

In the absence of any arrangements of their own for the training of municipal employees, the state governments in this part of the country are failing in their duty to ensure trained personnel for the efficient functioning of their municipal institutions. It is, therefore, imperative that the state governments should take immediate steps to set up a centre for training of municipal and other urban institutions' personnel as an independent government sponsored institution or in collaboration with the universities. The activities of such a centre would be as follows:

1. To collect data on municipal and urban problems and create a data bank for use by public authorities and researchers.
2. To undertake research on urban and municipal problems such as municipal finance and taxation, budgets and personnel, water supply, roads and sanitation, slums, and urban planning and development.

3. To conduct training programmes on urban and municipal problems for the benefit of the employees of the various urban institutions.
4. To conduct a postal course for in-service employees and others in urban development and municipal administration.
5. To build up a library and documentation centre on municipal and urban literature.
6. To disseminate information on urban and municipal problems through journals and other periodical publications.
7. To hold seminars and conferences on urban problems for higher level government personnel, legislators and political leaders.

Once the centre is set up, it can develop into a regional centre to cater to the needs of the states of Jammu and Kashmir, Himachal Pradesh, Haryana, Punjab, and Rajasthan and get financial support and patronage of the central government on the pattern of other regional centres in the country.

Transfers

Transferability is claimed to be a virtue of provincialization of municipal services, but it can prove to be a vice also if exercised arbitrarily and indiscriminately, affecting a large number of employees, resulting in the dislocation of their settled life patterns, and disturbance of education of their children if affected in mid-session, etc.

Transfers are sometimes made on a mass scale in municipal committees and Corporations. These wholesale transfers cause great resentment among the employees and protests among the public, as these are alleged to be ordered without following any rational policy and raise the suspicion of money having changed hands also. Another drawback of the system of transfers is that it encourages manoeuvring and intriguing among the officers and officials to be transferred to a municipal body of their choice. This leads to corruption, managing of political pressures and approaches to ministers. There have been many instances of securing transfers to prize stations and to their home towns through the employment of such means.

Service Benefits

The members of the municipal services are, with respect to leave, travelling allowance, joining time, suspension, medical facilities, fees, honoraria, house rent allowance, dearness allowance, fixation of pay, grant of increment, crossing efficiency bar, deputation and other matters not expressly provided in the Punjab Municipal Service (Recruitment and Conditions of Service) Rules 1975 are governed by the corresponding provisions in the rules applicable to the Punjab Government employees. Some of the major benefits available to municipal employees are the following:

(1) Provident Fund: They are entitled to contribution to the Provident Fund of the municipal committee where they are employed for the time being, provided that on transfer from one municipal committee to another, the balance of Provident Fund at their credit along with interest accrued thereon up-to-date shall be transferred to the municipal committee to which they have been transferred.

(2) Gratuity: They are also entitled to gratuity at such rates as may from time to time be notified by the government or to the amount of gratuity to which they may be entitled under the conditions of service applicable to them immediately before the provincialization of services, whichever is more beneficial to them, provided that the total service of a member under different municipal committees he has served shall be taken into account for calculating the amount of gratuity due to him, provided further that on transfer from one municipal committee to another, the gratuity to which he may be entitled to claim the entire amount of the gratuity payable from the municipal committee last served and the incidence of gratuity on the funds of the concerned municipal committee shall be in proportion to the length of service in each such municipal committee.

(3) Pension: The municipal employees unions have been asking for pensionary benefits also as are available to Government employees but the Punjab Municipal Employees Pay Committee, while sympathising with the demand, had stated that the introduction of pensionary system would be beyond the financial capacity of most of the municipal committees and it would involve many administrative and financial implications. The Rural-Urban Relationship Committee also had not favoured the provision of pension. But despite the above mentioned difficulties, the state government has accepted the demand of the municipal employees for grant of pensionary benefits in July 1991 and authorized the municipal bodies in this regard from their own resources without causing any financial liability to the state government. The Haryana Government has also followed suit in the interest of their municipal employees.

Conduct and Discipline

The need for inculcating in the municipal employees a spirit of single-minded devotion to the service of the local bodies and loyalty to them without any regard to the political complexion of the party in power can hardly be over-emphasized. The people expect from municipal employees high standards of honesty and good conduct and the municipal personnel should always endeavour to live up to the expectations of the people. To achieve this objective, generally the municipalities formulate and enforce a code of rules to regulate the conduct of their employees. The representatives of the municipal employees unions had suggested to the Punjab Municipal Employees Pay Committee in 1969 that the Punjab Government Employees (Conduct) Rules should be made applicable to them provided that there should be no bar to legitimate trade unionism. After the provincialization of municipal services in 1975, the Punjab Civil Services Conduct Rules have been adopted by the municipal bodies as the Municipal Employees Conduct Rules. These rules regulate, *inter alia,* proper behaviour towards official superiors, code of ethics in officials' private and domestic life, political activities, including public speaking, writing in the press and publications, and above all their honesty and integrity by prohibiting acceptance of gifts, engaging in private trade or business, contracting of debts, acquisition and disposal of property, etc.

These rules constitute not only a code of ethics but are also obligatory to be observed scrupulously. Unfortunately, these are more often breached than observed. Integrity among the municipal employees is conspicuous by its absence; corruption is rampant, obliging the public to demand 'vigilance enquiry' into various corrupt practices and scandals in different departments of the municipal bodies.

Corruption in some of the municipal bodies assumes such alarming proportions that the state government is obliged to order an enquiry by the CBI into the affairs of the municipal body concerned.

Besides corruption, there are other violations of conduct rules by municipal personnel such as derelictions from duty, inefficiency, insubordination, immorality, lack of integrity, indebtedness, appearing in public in an intoxicated condition, and failure of their deference to official superiors.

The violation of conduct rules by municipal employees should result in disciplinary action because if misconduct and fault go unpunished, it would encourage other employees to commit the same wrong and may corrupt the whole administration. The State Government has, therefore, provided that the Public Civil Services (Punishment and Appeals) Rules, 1975, as amended from time to time, as far as they are not inconsistent with the provision of the Punjab Municipal Act, 1911, shall apply to the members of the municipal services. Consequently, the power to take disciplinary action regarding all the provincialized posts, namely, of assistants and above, has been transferred to the state government who exercises this power itself or through its officers. In the case of the executive officer, secretary, engineer, town planner, accounts officer, etc., the authority to take disciplinary action and award punishment lies with the state government, while in the case of remaining provincialized posts like superintendents, assistant superintendents, accountants, section officers, stenographers, draftsmen, etc., this power has been vested with the director of local bodies. However, in the case of punishment awarded by the director of local bodies, an appeal can be made to the state government, whose decision is final in all the cases. In the case of the remaining non-provincialized posts like those of clerks, typists and Class-IV employees, the president and the municipal council retain the right to take disciplinary action and award punishment. Regarding the provincialized posts, the municipal committee can only convey to the state government through the director of local government its displeasure about the working of its employees and recommend that suitable disciplinary action be taken against them.

When a municipal employee is to be dismissed, removed or reduced in rank, he is to be given a reasonable opportunity of giving a show cause against the action proposed to be taken in regard to him as stipulated in Article 311 of the Constitution of India. Sometimes, the state government does not follow the required procedure and when its action is challenged in a court of law, it has to be rescinded.

Similarly, every corporation officer and employee is liable to have his increments or promotion withheld or to be censured, reduced in rank, compulsorily retired, removed or dismissed for breach of any departmental regulation or indiscipline or for carelessness, unfitness, neglect of duty or other misconduct, after being given a reasonable opportunity of giving show cause against the action proposed to be taken in regard to him. But a show-cause notice need not be given where an officer or other employee is removed or dismissed on the ground of conduct which has led to his conviction on criminal charge, or where the authority empowered to remove or dismiss such officer/employee is satisfied that for some reason to be recorded by that authority, it is not reasonably practicable to give that person an opportunity of showing cause.

Conclusion

Before the provincialization of municipal services, the power to take disciplinary action used to be vested in the municipal committees. It was then seen that political considerations determined the nature and quantum of punishment; persons commanding influence with politicians used to go unpunished or were awarded minor punishment for serious faults, etc. The provincialization of services under which the power of taking disciplinary action has come to be vested in the government, has lowered the position of municipal committees. It militates against the principle of self-government which should entitle the municipal government to enjoy the power to recruit and control its personnel. It has, on the other hand, created an anomalous situation, a municipal committee now cannot take any action against its own employees, it can only request the government to take disciplinary action against a particular employee if he acts in violation of a code of conduct.

In the case of municipal corporation also, the state government is empowered to take disciplinary action against erring officials and officers. The municipal commissioner and the corporation have no role in the appointment of personnel of corporation services or any part in taking disciplinary action against them. The commissioner can, however, suspend only some members of these services. The position of the commissioner, therefore, needs to be strengthened by giving him more powers of administrative control.

In conclusion, it may be observed that the earlier separate municipal personnel system wherein the municipal bodies enjoyed some autonomy, had resulted in favouritism and inefficiency. The new system ushered in by provincialization of municipal services has also not been conducive to the efficiency of municipal administration for the reason that though the municipal bodies are responsible for the expenditure incurred on their staff, they have no control on them. It is, therefore, worth considering if it would be advisable to revert to the old system of separate personnel system. Ashok Mukhopadhyaya's comparative study of Unified and Separate Personnel System in Municipal Administration in Rajasthan and Gujarat respectively, although based on limited evidence, comes to the conclusion that a unified or integrated system is not *ipso facto* better than separate personnel system and the latter when suitably reformed would not only be an efficient instrument for serving the locality but would also be in conformity with the basic values of the municipal government.[26] Abhijit Datta observes,

> Caderization' is no panacea and one could expect salutary results if the state government regulates the salaries, service benefits, qualifications, recruitment and disciplinary procedures, etc. of local government staff.' 'This is the most prevalent arrangement in many countries and the compromise of having a unified cadre really falls in between the two stools and is unsatisfactory to both the controlling authority and the local elected executive.[27]

NOTES AND REFERENCES

1. Herman Finer, *Theory and Practice of Modern Government* (London: Matheu and Co. Ltd, 1965), p. 723.
2. S.R. Maheshwari, *Local Government in India* (Agra: Lakshmi Narain Aggarwal, 1984), p. 247.
3. Ashok Makhopadhyay, *Municipal Personnel Administration*, (NewDelhi: New Delhi Centre for Urban Studies, IIPA, 1985), p. 1.
4. Humes and Martin, *The Structure of Local Government throughout the World* (The Hague: Martina Mijhoff, 1961), p. 150.
5. K. Venkatraman, 'Creation of a Cadre of Local Civil Service Personnel', in T.N.Chaturvedi (ed.), *Local Government* (New Delhi: IIPA, 1984), p. 156.
6. K. Venkatraman, 'Local Finance in Developing Countries', *Journal of Local Administration Overseas*, London, July, 1965.
7. United Nations, Department of Economic and Social Affairs, Public Administration Branch, *Local Government Personnel Systems* (New York, 1966).
8. G.S. Badhe, 'Provincialisation of Municipal Services in India', in O.P. Motiwal, *Changing Aspects of Public Administration in India* (Allahabad: C. Publications, 1976), p. 140.
9. Report of the Rural-Urban Relationship Committee, 1966.
10. *Report of the Punjab Municipal Employees Committee*, Chandigarh, Controller, Government Press, 1969, pp. 6, 13, 18, and 21.
11. S.R. Maheshwari, *Local Government in India* (Agra: Lakshmi Narain Aggarwal 1984), p. 247.
12. Henry Maddick, *Democracy, Decentralisation and Development* (Bombay: Asia Publishing House, 1963), pp. 184–85.
13. Report of the Rural-Urban Relationship Committee, 1966, Vol. I, para 8.08, pp. 76–77.
14. Planning Commission, Report of the Task Force on Management of Urban Development (New Delhi: Government of India, 1983).
15. Glen Stahl, *Public Personnel Administration* (New York: Harper and Row Publishers, 1966), p. 59.
16. E.M. Gladden, *The Civil Services: Its Problems and Future* (London: Staples Press, 1945), p. 64.
17. M.E. Dimock and G.O. Dimock, *Public Administration* (New Delhi: Oxford and IBH Publishing Company, 1970), p. 198.
18. F.W. Marx, *Elements of Public Administration* (New Delhi: Prentice Hall of India Pvt. Ltd., 1968), p. 510.
19. The Punjab Municipal Services (Recruitment and Conditions of Service) Rules, 1975, rule 5 (3).
20. Pigos Paul and Myers Charles, '*Personnel Administration—A Point of View and Method* (New York: McGraw Hill, 1965), p. 419.
21. D.R. Sachdeva, *Local Government Services in India*, (Jalandhar: Raj Publishers, 1974), p. 111.

22. Hargopal and A.V. Satya Narain Rao, 'The Problem of Training in Municipal Administration,' *Nagarlok* 3, no. 3: 5–6.
23. R.B. Das, 'Pre-Entry and Post-Entry Training for Municipal Employees,' *Nagarlok* 3, no. 3: 5–6.
24. Henry Maddick, 'Democracy, Decentralisation and Development', p. 175.
25. Report of the Committee on the Training of Municipal Employees, New Delhi, Ministry of Health, 1963, p. 7.
26. Mohit Bhattacharya, 'Training for Urban Management', *The Indian Journal of Public Administration* 34, no. 3 (July–September, 1988): 635–636.
27. Ashok Mukhopadhyay, *Municipal Personnel Administration* (New Delhi: Centre for Urban Studies, Indian Institute of Public Administration, 1985), pp. 104–105. See also, Abhijit Datta, in *Introduction' to Local Government*, edited by T.N. Chaturvedi and Abhijit Datta (New Delhi: Centre for Urban Studies, IIPA, 1984), p. xi.

9

Urban Local Government Finances

The significance of finance is too obvious to need any elaboration as no organization can exist, much less achieve its objectives, without at least a minimum of finances. That is why Kautilya, the great Indian philosopher, remarked, 'all undertakings depend upon finance, hence foremost attention should be paid to the treasury.'[1] Every administrative act has its financial implications, either creating a charge or making a contribution to the treasury. The importance of finance is so great in administration that Llyod George is said to have once remarked that 'government is finance'.[2] In fact, finance constitutes the backbone, the life and blood of government; it provides fuel to the administrative machinery. Sound fiscal policy is, therefore, of crucial importance to the government whether central, state or local. Imprudent financial management not only brings discredit to the government, but also alienates it from the people, and may endanger its very existence. Felix A. Nigro has rightly observed:

> Financial administration is of great importance today because of the tremendous increase in the amounts of money expended for government services. Everything government does requires money. It is utterly essential that sound principles and techniques of financial administration be employed.[3]

The responsibilities of municipal bodies have tremendously increased as a result of the rapid increase in urbanization and adoption of welfare state as the ultimate goal of our polity. In any multilevel pattern of government the effectiveness with which the lower units would operate is determined to a large extend on how their finances are organized in relation to their functional responsibilities.[4] Local government finance thus assumes great importance. In order to be able to discharge their obligations in respect of development and improvement of their respective areas, provision of civic amenities and welfare services, municipal bodies require adequate financial resources commensurate with the tasks assigned to them. But unfortunately municipal authorities in our country are proverbially deficient in financial resources. As far back as in 1925, the Indian Taxation Enquiry Committee had noted that the finances of local bodies were inadequate for the services they were required to perform. The Municipal Acts set out an impressive list of obligatory and discretionary functions entrusted to the local authorities. And, besides these legally allocated functions, their responsibilities have been growing in the wake of rapid urbanization causing continuing and mounting pressure on the civic facilities and amenities. It is regrettable that the importance of these obligations with adequate resources has never been sufficiently recognized.[5] Since independence, this aspect has been enquired into by numerous Central and state commissions and committees but their recommendations have not been matched with adequate follow-up action towards implementation. The decentralization movement of the post-independence period has not radically adhered to financial conditions of local government and they continue to suffer from paucity of resources,[6] and the gap between their finances and desired level of services is continuously widening.

Powers of Taxation of Local Government

Local governments in India do not have the inherent power of taxation—the constitution does not specify any taxes for their exclusive use. It may, however, be mentioned that the Scheduled Tax Rules framed under the Government of India Act, 1919, contained an exclusive list of taxes to be utilized by or for the local authorities. These rules were repealed with the abolition of the distinction between provincial and local taxation in the new federal scheme embodied in the Government of India Act, 1935, putting every local tax into the basket of the tax resources of the provincial governments. The present Constitution of India has inherited and sanctified the same arrangement. As such, local governments are empowered to levy only such taxes as have been approved by the state government. Consequently, they are at the mercy of the state government in respect of their finances. A demand has been often made that they should be given a separate list of taxes on the lines of the Union and the State lists, and the constitution amended accordingly. The question was examined by the Local Finance Enquiry Committee in 1951, and it had recommended a list of thirteen taxes, viz. (*i*) terminal tax on goods or passengers carried by railway, sea, or air; (*ii*) tax on land and buildings; (*iii*) tax on mineral rights; (*iv*) octroi; (*v*) tax on vehicles other than those mechanically propelled; (*vi*) tax on animals and boats; (*vii*) tax on professions, trades, callings, and employment; (*viii*) tax on advertisements other than those published in newspapers; (*ix*) tax on goods and passengers carried by road or inland waterways; (*x*) tax on the consumption or sale of electricity; (*xi*) capital tax; (*xii*) tax on entertainment; and (*xiii*) tolls for exclusive utilization by the local government but had disapproved of the idea of inclusion of this list in the constitution. Similarly, the Taxation Enquiry Commission (1953–54) had suggested a list of ten taxes to be reserved for local government which the state government could increase also but had argued against their incorporation in the constitution. The commission had observed as follows:

> While we do not consider that a constitutional amendment is called for, we very strongly recommend to the state governments that the taxes which we indicate should be allowed to be developed only by the local bodies or for them, and that where the state governments are at present exploiting any of those taxes for appropriation of state revenues, they should gradually withdraw from the field and meanwhile allot the proceeds from the taxes to the local bodies concerned.

The commission had further stated:

> Although constitutional amendment may not be a feasible proposition, the earmarking of an area of taxes for exclusive utilization by local government will keep it unaffected by the changing moods of the state government and ensure definite and elastic sources of revenue. This requires specific provisions in the municipal legislation.[7]

But these recommendations have not been given the consideration they deserved and the local governments continue to depend on the whim and will of the state governments for their financial resources.

Municipal Budget

Municipal budget is the annual financial statement of the anticipated income and expenditure of the concerned municipal body. Budget preparation is usually the occasion for determining the levels of taxation and the ceilings on expenditure. The main objective of the budget is to ensure that funds are raised and money is spent by the executive departments in accordance with rules and regulations and within the limits of sanctions and authorizations by the municipal council. The councillors look at it as an opportunity to advance interests of their constituencies and to appraise policy fulfilments. In the state governments' view it is a method of exercising control and enforcing uniformity in the interest of efficient functioning of local government institutions.

The responsibility for preparing the budget rests with the Executive and it is often considered by the finance sub-committee before it is put before the council for discussion and approval. The approval of the budget is granted by the state government in the case of Class-I and the deputy commissioner in case of Class-II and HI municipalities. Municipalities are required to submit the budget for approval to the government before the 25th of February every year. It is not feasible for the authorities to scrutinize the budget in a short span of one month and is therefore approved in a hurry. As a matter of fact, the budgets are treated as routine communications and are examined mostly at the clerical levels and passed with certain routine remarks. In most cases the approval is accorded even without properly examining the documents. Detailed examination is conducted only in case the state government has received complaints about serious irregularities.[8]

The system of approval of budget by the state government either directly or through its functionaries is not conducive to efficient management of municipal affairs as quite often the process of approval is time consuming and till the formal approval is received, the municipal government is run on a slender budget. Consequently, no worthwhile activities are undertaken in the first three to four months. The delay also occurs unwittingly on the part of the state government because of the fact that the Department of Local Government and the Directorate of Local Government are not adequately equipped to make such scrutiny quickly and comprehensively.

But the state government had its own reasons to have the right to approve the municipal budget, chief among them being its concern in ensuring proper financial health of the local government for which it is accountable to the legislature on the one hand and to the people on the other; it gives substantial grants to the municipal bodies for a number of activities and it would naturally be interested in ensuring proper utilization of such grants.

The via media could be that the state government should retain indirect control over the budgets of the local bodies. It should assume powers under the municipal statutes to issue guidelines in sufficient details and the municipal bodies be left free to formulate and finalize their budgets within the framework of the provisions laid down thereunder. Similarly, the controls like laying down certain conditions at the time of giving loans and grants with a view to gain some leverage for providing guidance would be preferable to the direct and negative ways of control.

Sources of Income of Municipal Bodies

Constitutionally, local bodies in India as discussed earlier have not been provided with a separate list of taxes and they are, therefore, at the mercy of the state government for their financial resources. Consequently, there is a universal complaint that local bodies, which are responsible for managing city services, do not have adequate resources to justify their existence. The existing sources of income of municipal bodies can be classified into four categories:

1. Local taxes/tax revenue;
2. Non-tax revenue;
3. Grants-in-aid;
4. Loans/borrowings.

Local Taxes

Local taxes constitute the major portion of municipal income resources. It is about two-thirds of the revenue collected by the municipal bodies. A municipal committee can impose a number of taxes, such as octroi tax, tax on property, tax on vehicles (other than motor vehicles) tax on property, and advertisement tax.

The scope of taxation is somewhat larger in the case of a municipal corporation in view of the broader functions it is expected to perform. The taxes, levied by it are: tax on land and building, octroi, tax on vehicles and animals, tax on advertisements (other than advertisements published in newspaper), tax on buildings, tax on professions, trades, callings, and employments and any other tax which the state legislature has power to impose under the constitution, subject to the prior approval of the government. Though the tax heads of a municipal corporation are not very extensive as compared to those of a municipal committee, they are exploited more intensively. In the following are listed some of the taxes which a local body can levy: property tax, registration fees, fair tax, animal tax, market tax, ctroi tax, terminal tax, turnover tax, toll on new bridges, vehicles tax (non-motorized), betterment tax, conservancy tax, lighting tax, sanitation tax, scavenging tax, water tax, advertisement tax, entertainment tax, profession tax, pilgrim tax, special education tax, etc.[9]

Non-tax revenue of municipal bodies consists of receipts from fees and fines, incomes from remunerative enterprises and miscellaneous sources. The primary purpose of collecting fees and fines is regulation and control of trade, markets, industrial establishments, and eating places, rather than resource mobilization. Revenue from remunerative enterprises comprises incomes derived from leasing out market places, slaughter houses, commercial buildings, exhibition grounds, stadia, swimming pools, and other municipal properties.

Of all the taxes levied by municipal bodies the most important from the point of view of revenue are discussed as follows:

Octroi: Case for Its Abolition or Retention

Octroi is the tax on entry of goods into a local area for consumption, use or sale therein. Its origin can be traced to the *chungi* of the Mughal period, the Sikh *dharat* and the *Muhtaraja* of Maratha towns. A municipal body initiates a proposal by adopting a special resolution to levy a tax and the state government may sanction the same or refuse to sanction it or return if for reconsideration. The state government can also instruct a municipal body to levy octroi on a particular item, at a particular rate. It can also grant exemption to private institutions from payment of octroi. But this power is likely to be misused for political and 'vested interests' reasons. For instance, a writ petition challenging the exemption of octroi granted to Nikki Tasha India Ltd, Faridabad (Haryana) by the commissioner, Ambala Division was admitted by Punjab and Haryana High Court on January 10, 1989. The petition was filed by Mr Nanak Chand Sabharwal, a social activist in public interest litigation who apprehended that exemption might be made operative under political pressure which had earlier been stayed by the High Court in a writ petition filed by the chief administrator, Faridabad, by withdrawal of the writ petition. He submitted that in case the writ petition is withdrawn by the administrator, the exemption becomes operative, the Faridabad complex would lose an income of more than Rs 1 crore and may have to refund Rs 4 crore already collected from the company as per the impugned order of the commissioner. The government in order to bring uniformity in the rates of octroi, may also adopt schedule of octroi rate, on some of the items.

Octroi constitutes the single largest source of income of municipal bodies but hardly has a tax attracted such scathing criticism as the octroi,[10] mainly due to the reasons that it constitutes a major hindrance to the free flow of traffic and trade and hence it retards the growth of commercial and industrial activities;[11] that it is a regressive tax as its incidence falls mainly on articles of common man's use; that its administration is atrociously cumbersome and vexatious;[12] that it is assessed and collected by low paid municipal staff and is liable to generate corruption among them; that it necessitates multiple check posts involving enormous expenditure on the maintenance of police, etc.[13] There has been therefore a demand for its abolition. Some states like Tamil Nadu, Madhya Pradesh, and Bihar, and recently Haryana (1999) have already abolished it. But others are reluctant to follow suit unless they are assured adequate alternative resources.[14] The Committee on Augmentation of Financial Resources of Urban Local Bodies (1963) was also of the view that bad, as octroi is, as a form of local taxation, it cannot be abolished outright unless alternative sources of taxation which should compensate for the consequential loss of revenue are developed.[15] It is rightly felt that the abolition of octroi without any clear substitute seems to be fraught with danger and without it municipal bodies cannot function.[16] Octroi constitutes the financial backbone of municipal bodies; its overwhelming importance in the tax structure had therefore led the Punjab Local Government (Octroi) Committee to observe 'the Municipal Committees will be thrown on the verge of bankruptcy if this source of income is withdrawn'.[17] Shri Surjit Singh Barnala, former chief minister of the state had stated on the floor of the House:

> Octroi constitutes as much as 60 per cent of the income of municipal bodies. Most of them were already in the red and found it difficult to make both ends meet. If octroi was abolished, their condition would go from bad to worse unless they were provided money from another sources.

He had further observed that:

> Abolition of octroi would also render about 5,000 employees jobless and although the centre had made recommendation to abolish it, the Punjab Government was not in a position to implement it because it would necessitate mobilizing alternative source of revenue for municipalities.[18]

Other arguments which can be given in favour of retention of octroi are: that the proposed alternatives such as entry tax, toll tax and surcharge on sales tax have their own disadvantages, while the entry tax and toll tax would suffer from the same disadvantages and cause more or less the same hardship to the people as octroi, surcharge on an existing tax would be relevant only to some of the municipal committees having jurisdiction over big cities. Revenues from octroi accrue to the municipal bodies and fall in their coffers on day to day basis. This considerably improves their liquidity position and enables them to meet their day-to-day requirements. If they are to look to the state government for reimbursement of surcharge on sales tax, that might be imposed in lieu of octroi, their fate would be the same as it is in relation to getting reimbursement of additional excise duty on liquor in lieu of octroi imposed by the state government. Scarcely additional excise on liquor is reimbursed to them before the fag end of the year and that too in driblets. Further, any surcharge imposed in lieu of octroi may not have the advantage of elasticity. At present, the municipal bodies are free to rationalize their octroi schedules and rates having regard to their requirements which would be lost if octroi is substituted by surcharge.

Property Tax

Property tax is levied on buildings and lands on the basis of their rental value instead of their capital value as the former is easier to determine on the basis of market rent and is not subject to wide fluctuations as the capital values of the properties are. A municipal body by a resolution passed at a special meeting and confirmed by the state government can impose, suspend, reduce, or abolish the tax or exempt in whole or in part from the payment of any such tax, any person or class of persons or any property, or description of property. Under these provisions, the state government may grant exemption from payment of house tax to newly constructed residential buildings for three years from the date of their application. It may also exempt all charitable, philanthropic and religious buildings and institutions like schools, colleges, hospitals, and orphanages from the levy of this tax. Exemption may also be granted to serving or ex-servicemen of the armed forces and freedom fighters who have been honoured with *Tamra Patras* from the payment of this tax in respect of their property provided their annual income from all sources does not exceed a specified amount per annum.

The state governments are also empowered to issue directions to the municipal bodies to impose and notify the tax rate payable on buildings and lands according to certain norms, mainly fixing varying percentages on their rental values. The state governments are also empowered to allow rebate to the house tax payers provided the payment of the tax is made within a stipulated period from the date of issue of a bill, for instance, a rebate of 20 per cent is allowed if the payment is made within 10 days from the date of receipt of the bill and of 10 per cent if the payment is made within 15 days of the receipt of the bill.

Central government buildings and lands are however exempted from this tax. Article 285 (1) of the Constitution of India lays down that properties of the Union government are exempted from all taxes imposed by a state or by any local authority within the state unless Parliament by law provides otherwise. This is inequitable in view of the inadequacy of finances of local government. Parliament should pass the necessary legislation to enable the municipal bodies to impose the tax on Union properties too. Again the rental value of the property is always under-assessed by the petty municipal officials in collusion with the landlords and the provision of appeal against the assessment to the elected council itself leads to another scandalous situation. This underlines the need for an independent, impartial, and trained administrative machinery to secure fair assessment.[19] The Committee on Augmentation of Financial Resources of Urban Local Bodies (1963) had recommended the setting up of a Central Valuation Department to get the work of assessment of properties in different municipalities done.[20] The Rural-Urban Relationship Committee (1966) had also lent support to the need for a central valuation agency and suggested the appointment of a chief valuation officer in the Directorate of Local Government who should lay down principles for assessing the annual value and supervise and control the valuation officers.[21]

Profession Tax

Profession tax is levied on trades, professions and callings and may be termed as local income tax. It is elastic as it automatically increases with increase in income and population.[22] Moreover, since it is a personal tax, it assures quick and easy payment.[23] The Constitution of India had prescribed a limit of Rs 250 per annum[24] of this tax in 1949 but this ceiling was increased to Rs 2,500 per annum in 1988 by the Constitution (60th Amendment) on the representation of some state governments to the Centre that the ceiling needed to be revised upwards in view of the price rise and other factors. This would enable the states faced with a resource crunch to raise additional funds. It may, however, be noted that the Central government had observed that the raising of the ceiling was an enabling provision; that the state governments were to decide which section of society was to be taxed and whether salaried classes and industrial workers were to be excluded or not; and that the Central government was not to issue any guidelines to the states regarding the collection of the tax.[25]

This tax is criticized on the ground that it constitutes another additional income tax which the citizens grudge to pay. Municipal bodies, therefore, avoid levying it lest they incur the annoyance of their constituents. As a matter of fact, even those municipalities which had initially levied it have abandoned it and the state governments have not taken any note of it, obviously for political considerations, despite the fact that it is an obligatory tax. Municipal bodies need to muster courage to levy this tax to augment their revenues.

Entertainment Tax

Entertainment tax is levied on programmes and luxuries including betting and gambling.[26] Generally entertainments for charitable, religious, and educational purposes, as also for advancement of agriculture, industry, and public health are exempted. The tax is determined, imposed and collected by the state government and after the close of each year it is reimbursed to the municipal body concerned in whole or in part. The Committee on Augmentation of Financial Resources of Urban Local Bodies had suggested that entire proceeds from this tax, which at present go to the state exchequer, should be earmarked for local bodies as it has a local basis and can also be best administered by a local authority with a certain degree of autonomy.[27]

Advertisement Tax

Municipal corporations are empowered to levy tax on advertisements other than those published in the newspapers with the prior sanction of the state government. Anyone who displays an advertisement on any land, building, post, or structure or in any vehicles plying within municipal area, or by means of cinematograph, has to pay this tax. However, any advertisement relating to public meetings or election to Parliament or state legislature or the corporation is exempted from such tax. The state government can also direct a municipality to levy this tax.

Grants-in-Aid

Grants-in-aid form an important constituent of municipal finance. A payment made from the treasury of the state government to a local authority for the purpose of assisting that authority in carrying out a part or all of its activities is known as grant-in-aid.[28] The revenues of local bodies are inelastic in relation to their needs and as a result there is a tendency for the gap between the two to go on widening. This gap is narrowed down as far as possible by the provision of more finances by the state government in the form of grants-in-aid. When the state governments assign more and more functions to the local authorities, they are under a moral obligation to assist them to carry out these functions, particularly when the principal sources of revenue have already been tapped by them.[29] The Rural-Urban Relationship Committee had rightly observed, 'The system of grants-in-aid has the advantage that the grants can be related to the needs and the resources of urban local bodies.'[30] Grants-in-aid can be given for general or specific purposes. The general purpose grants are intended to augment the revenue of the local bodies for discharging their normal functions, whereas specific grants are tied to specific purposes such as medical and public health and road maintenance. These are designed to induce local action in desired fields as part of national or state level policy and in providing the required measure of control over the quality of the services. The amount of grants is generally determined on the basis of matching formula, population, per capita income and expenditure, revenue gap, and other considerations. There is, however, no uniform criteria for current fiscal transfer from the state to local bodies.[31] Grants are thus *ad hoc* and discretionary in nature depending largely on the availability of funds with the states. These need to be codified to ensure continuity and certainty. Municipal bodies have been receiving general and specific grants from the state government but they have not been adequate for their needs. It is regrettable that even these inadequate grants are not fully utilized by the fixed time and have therefore to be refunded. It is substantiated by the observations made in the audit reports of various municipal corporations and municipal committees. This constitutes a sad commentary on the performance of municipal bodies in regard to the utilization of grants. They should avoid such lapses to improve their image with the government and the public.

Loans

Municipal bodies are obliged to borrow from state government and other agencies to meet emergencies and for capital expenditure which they cannot afford out of their revenues.[32] Their borrowings are regulated by central law known as the Local Authorities Loan Act, 1914. Based on this act, their exact borrowing powers are defined in the respective municipal laws detailing the limits and purposes of their borrowing.[33] But all proposals relating to loans are required to be cleared by the Reserve Bank of India. These restraints have been imposed lest the local governments should indulge in reckless borrowing and thus land themselves in a perilous financial situation.[34]

There are some significant differences in some of the salient features of the borrowing operations of municipal corporations and municipal committees. First, municipal corporations can borrow only for developmental activities and for payment of debt charges. But municipal committees are permitted to raise loans for capital works, for relief work during times of famine or scarcity and for the prevention of dangerous epidemic diseases as well as for discharging previous debts. Second, the maximum period for which loans can be borrowed by municipal corporations is 60 years as compared to 30 years in the case of municipal committees. Third, municipal corporations can raise loans on the security of their immovable property and all or any of their funds by issuing debentures but municipal committees can borrow on the security of their funds only.

Municipal governments find it difficult to raise loans because of their poor image in the eyes of the people. It is only when the state government assists them by guaranteeing payment of loans along with interest that the public can take the risk. The Punjab Local Government (Urban) Enquiry Committee had accordingly recommended:

> In view of lack of prospects of local bodies securing capital in their names for development purposes, the state government should be prepared to give guarantee for loans floated by municipal committees (Class I), and for small committes, the state government should provide enough funds as loans for productive schemes and loans as well as subsidies for essential services.[35]

Municipal corporations and municipal committees have been raising loans which have not been commensurate with their needs but even some of these loans have not been properly utilized by the stipulated period and have not been paid back in time resulting in the liability for the payments of penal interest. It is desirable that the municipal bodies should utilize the loans as per time schedule and strictly in compliance with their terms and conditions to justify their needs.

Municipal Expenditure

The various municipal acts lay down priorities in respect of expenditure of municipal committees. The first charge on the municipal fund is the repayment of loans followed by various other items of expenses in the following order:

Contributions not exceeding 1 per cent of the income for the financial year preceding the year, towards the cost of the directorate/inspectorate as the state government may establish for advising, assisting, and supervising the work of municipal bodies; charges of establishment including police; audit fees; maintenance of homes for paupers and lunatics; water works; drainage, sewerage, and other works; annual payment to the state government equivalent to the total provision made in the budget for the year (when the educational institutions run by the municipal bodies were provincialized) under the main head 'Education', excluding provisions relating to public libraries, reading rooms, and museums; construction and maintenance of public streets, bridges, drains, latrines, urinals, tanks, and water courses; hospitals and dispensaries, rest houses, *sarai*s, poor houses, markets, and other works of public utility, relief works in times of famine, floods and scarcity, public parks and gardens, holding of fairs and exhibitions; and all acts and things which are likely to promote the safety, health welfare, and convenience of the inhabitants.

The Municipal Corporation Acts provide for the application of moneys from the corporation fund in payment of all service charges and costs necessary for carrying out the provisions of the act, and on all acts and things which are likely to promote the safety, health, welfare, or convenience of the inhabitants for meeting the cost of the local government, directorate, or its sub-offices and for the execution of any work certified by the secretary of the local government department of the concerned state to be urgently required in public interest.

Most of the expenditure incurred by municipal bodies relates to the charges of establishment, payment of loans with interest and very little percentage of revenue is left for meeting expenditure on the provision of the minimum needs of the citizens of their respective localities and hardly any amount for development activities and the finer needs of enrichment of life. Invariably the municipal bodies suffer from acute financial stringency and most of them reach a critical state of bankruptcy. Most of the municipal corporations/committees owe crores of rupees to contractors, their development works are at a standstill, there is deterioration in the sanitation work, the sewerage system remains choked, the residents do not get adequate piped water supply, roads are in bad shape, street lighting is poor, pollution causes big health hazards, and so on. They have to, therefore, approach the government for substantial financial aid which is not made available promptly, with the result that the civic conditions of the city suffer further deterioration.

Accounting and Auditing

Accounting and auditing occupy a place of importance in any organization, public or private. In a local body they function as custodians of the public money and are responsible for ensuring proper custody, accounting and expenditure in accordance with the rules and regulations and provisions in the budget.[36]

Accounting reflects accurately the day-to-day financial transactions, the receipt of revenues and the payment of expenses. Municipal bodies are required to maintain accounts in the form and manner as prescribed by the state government and to follow the Accounts Code which *inter alia* describes the duties of the officials connected with the financial transactions and lays down the procedure for disbursement of money.

The audit is a tool of financial control. Its function is to ensure that all financial transactions are conducted according to the rules, that all receipts are duly credited to the proper accounts, and that no amounts are paid without proper authorization. It is required to take into account the principles of financial property, i.e. of faithfulness, wisdom, and economy. Accordingly, Nigral has defined the audit as an analysis of proposed or past expenditure with respect not only of its legality but also to its desirability.[37] Ashok Chanda describes its role aptly:

> In all recognised democracies, audit is not just tolerated as necessary evil, but is looked upon as a valued ally which brings to notice procedural and technical irregularities and lapses on the part of individuals, whether they are errors of judgement, negligence or acts and intents of dishonesty. The complementary role of audit in administration is accepted as axiomatic, being essential for toning up the machinery of government.[38]

The audit of the municipal bodies is generally conducted by the Examiner of the Local Fund Accounts. It can either be post-audit or pre-audit. In the former case, a test audit is conducted of a part of the financial transactions of the year and if it discloses serious irregularities, faults and mistakes, the government may order a special audit. The post-audit is not considered to be of any value as it is a post-mortem of the expenditure which has already been incurred and is like locking the barn after the horse is stolen.[39] The pre-audit system, on the other hand, is regarded to be a more effective instrument of financial control. The state government introduces the pre-audit system in selected municipal bodies and places at their disposal the services of one resident audit officer representing the examiner of the local fund accounts assisted by a number of junior auditors. The auditors draw their salary from the government, which charges its audit fee from the municipal body concerned. They pre-audit all the payments, whereas accounts of income, stock, etc. are subject to post-audit check in accordance with the quantum prescribed from time to time in respect of each account. Pre-audits are, however, criticized on the ground that they curb initiative and lead to delay in the process of implementation.[40]

The audit prepares reports on the annual audit which consists of (*i*) audit notes dealing with serious irregularities requiring particular attention of the local and higher authorities and (*ii*) objection statement relating to technical irregularities, mistakes and defects. The council is required to consider both the audit notes and the objection statement and to express its opinion on them to the examiner. In case a particular loss is incurred due to the negligence or misconduct of a particular councillor or officer, the examiner issues a certificate of surcharge and transmits it to the state government, who alone has the power of ordering surcharge and realizing it from the councillor/officer concerned.

Objections of various kinds are raised by the audit. Instances of some of them are: municipal bodies do not put up the records asked for by the audit. It leads the audit to feel that non-production of records was intended to conceal serious financial irregularities committed by the officers; temporary advances remained outstanding against government departments or agencies and municipal employees. Many of the employees had either been transferred or had retired from service. It was intriguing how the last pay certificates were issued to them without getting the advances adjusted; the arrears of various taxes were not worked out and carried over in the new registers nor the statements supplied to audit to enable it to depict their up-to-date positions; no attention was paid towards the settlement of outstanding objections which had piled up over the years. Even the objections relating to the recoveries had not been attended to. Action on them might not be possible at this late stage being time barred under the Indian Limitation Act and similar other regulations. It is a matter of great concern that the deliberative and executive wings of the municipal bodies do not take the audit reports and objections seriously. This is alleged to be quite natural in view of the inherent defects in the system. The audit objections are usually directed against the decisions of the councillors themselves who cannot be obviously expected to take action against own selves. The result is that an unconsciously long time is taken for reports to be put up for consideration and still longer to act upon the audit recommendations and with the passage of time, their value is considerably diluted.

Municipal bodies, on the other hand, are highly critical of the negative attitude of the audit, which has resulted in curbing initiative and creating friction between the deliberative and executive wings on the one hand and within the executive wing on the other. They feel that audit should not only be progressive and enlightened in outlook but also appreciative of the difficulties in implementation of the schemes. There is enough weight in the observations of the municipal bodies and it is, therefore, desirable that the audit should give greater emphasis on evaluation of efficient performance rather than just confining itself to the regulatory aspect as is the case at present.

As mentioned earlier, it has also been observed by the audit that innumerable audit objections have been pending for a number of years, some being as many as over two decades old. The continuation of audit objections in such large numbers and for such a long period undoubtedly casts a reflection on the performance of the municipal bodies concerned but the keeping of these objections alive for so long is also of no value. Evidently the remedial or corrective value of these objections has ceased to exist. All longstanding audit objections therefore need to be dropped.

In conclusion, it may be observed that the controversy regarding the role of audit is largely due to lack of appreciation on the part of the auditors and councillors or the executive of each other's importance.

Reasons for Critical Financial Condition of Urban Local Bodies

The urban local bodies as discussed above suffer from acute scarcity of finances. The reasons for their critical financial condition are as follows:

Unjust Distribution of Revenue Sources

The sources of income assigned to municipal bodies are inadequate as compared to their functions. These bodies are allocated taxes like octroi, terminal tax and house tax. The proceeds collected from these taxes are not sufficient for the municipal bodies to perform their functions effectively. The taxes which are highly payable like customs, excise duties, sale tax, income tax, and land revenue have been included either in the Union List or are levied by the state governments. Therefore, injustice has been done with the urban local governments as far as sources of income are concerned. The functions of these bodies are always on the increase but the higher governments have never paid any attention in regard to their sources to make them proportionate with their functions.

Defective Budgeting

The system for preparing municipal budget is defective. Balance is not kept between income and expenditure. Sometimes expenditure exceeds the proposed income and the municipal bodies have to face a crisis which ultimately results in breakdown of services. Some municipal bodies start certain projects even before the budget is prepared. When the budget is prepared and placed before the competent authority for approval, those projects even do not figure in the budget and therefore the municipal bodies have to suffer financial loss.

Hesitation to Impose New Taxes

The local authorities have been empowered to impose certain taxes. The elected members who constitute the local council are always afraid of imposing new taxes on people because they feel that this will result in their unpopularity and resentment among the people and they will not vote for them in the next elections.

Defective System of Grants

The grants provided by the state government is an important part of municipal finance. But it is unfortunate that these grants are inadequate, unmatched to their needs, irregular, unsystematic and uncertain. There is no uniform criterion to provide grants to the municipal bodies and generally these are *ad hoc* and discretionary depending upon the availability of funds with the state governments.

Rigid Government Attitude

The attitude of the state governments towards municipal bodies is quite rigid. In some states like Punjab and Haryana, the state government has taken over some of the municipal functions and has set up specific purpose agencies to perform those functions. But the expenditure in regard to these functions is borne by the municipal bodies. This kind of attitude is totally unfair.

Defective Accounts and Audit System

Accounting and auditing have an important place in municipal administration. Both are instruments for keeping a check on utilization of public money. In various municipalities audit objections remain pending for many years and in some municipalities audit is not conducted regularly. The accounts rules and regulations framed by the respective state governments are not followed, resulting in financial losses and embezzlements.

Limited Borrowing Powers

The municipal bodies have been provided with very limited borrowing powers. These borrowing powers are governed under the central legislation known as Local Authorities Loans Act, 1914. The state government has the power to sanction borrowing of up to Rs 5 lakh in the open market with a condition of repayment in 30 years. The approval of the central government is required if the amount exceeds Rs 5 lakh. The rate of interest charged is also generally higher than the market rate. By and large, the attitude of the state or the central government is not in favour of municipal borrowing.

Faulty Tax Administration

The system of municipal tax administration suffers from various defects. The administrative machinery for collection of taxes is inefficient and ineffective. The concerned personnel are not equipped with adequate training and requisite skills for the purpose. The financially, starved local bodies cannot pay their employees adequate salaries. In order to meet their needs and requirements the employees indulge in corrupt practices, which results in leakage of revenues, mounting size of uncollected dues, evasion in taxes and further widening the gap between resources and expenditure.

Poverty

Poverty among Indian people is one of the most crucial factors responsible for critical financial condition of urban local bodies. The per capita income of an individual is much low as compared to other prosperous countries of the world. The Union and state governments exploit this limited taxable capacity of the people to the fullest extent, leaving very little scope for the local government. The rapid growth of urbanization has further aggravated the situation and has made the services provided by the municipal bodies more expensive.

Suggestions for Augmenting Municipal Finance

Municipal bodies all over the country are in great financial crisis. Municipal finances, therefore, need to be improved urgently to enable the urban local bodies to perform their multifarious duties and functions effectively.

One of the reasons for poor municipal finances is the shyness on the part of local government to levy taxes and when it has to, it keeps the rate quite low; added to this is the sluggish and partial collection of whatever taxes are levied. Local fund audit reports are replete with instances of poor collection and heavy arrears. The causes for the failure to levy and collect taxes are the reluctance on the part of the elected council to incur the displeasure of the electorate,[41] loose administration, and unwillingness on the part of municipal authorities to make use of the coercive process provided for by the law. The Taxation Enquiry Commission had viewed inefficiency in assessment and collection of taxes as one of the greatest drawbacks of local bodies and recommended as a solution that all municipal bodies should have chief executive officers empowered to invoke all coercive processes to enforce recovery of taxes; that there should be provision for incentives also in the form of rebates for prompt payment, and that a person in arrears of the municipal dues should be disqualified from seeking election to the local body.

The services of municipal police can be made use of in collecting the taxes, preventing encroachments, and checking the evasion of octroi. Every municipal committee or corporation is required to maintain a sufficient police establishment for police requirements within the municipal limits and for the performance of duties imposed on it by the Act.[42] The municipal police is, however, not a separate cadre nor is it recruited by the municipal body. A municipal council sends a requisition to the district superintendent of police, who in consultation with the district authorities sends a small contingent to the municipality on deputation.

Although the utility of municipal police is quite obvious, no definite policy has been evolved by the state governments in respect of making it obligatory on municipal bodies to avail themselves of its services.

The following additional measures may be suggested for augmenting the resources of municipal bodies:

Maximum Utilization of Existing Resources

Property tax should be earmarked for exploitation by municipal bodies and evaluated by a Central government agency as is done by the Inland Revenue Authorities in UK. It should be made mandatory, freed from shackles of the Urban Rent Restriction Law, and the Central government property should not be exempted from this tax.

Octroi on agricultural produce should be re-imposed, as its exemption has resulted in heavy loss of revenue. Industrial goods should be exempted from octroi for a limited period only and the municipal bodies equitably compensated by the government for the loss. Goods belonging to state undertaking, including the state electricity boards should not be exempted from octroi. Before granting any exemption from taxation or reduction in the level of any tax, the municipal body concerned should be consulted. The levy of octroi on uniform scheduled rates should be made compulsory, which should be periodically revised in keeping with the rise in prices in consultation with the municipal bodies.

Assignment/Sharing of Proceeds of Certain Taxes Levied by the State Government

The urban local bodies should be assigned the entire proceeds of entertainment tax, which is essentially local in incidence; at least 20 per cent of the proceeds of motor vehicle tax on the basis of population and mileage maintained by the local bodies; total proceeds of theatre and show taxes; at least 15 per cent of the land revenue on the pattern of Maharashtra; not less than 33 per cent of proceeds of sales tax and market fee in view of the fact that most of the commercial transaction take place in cities and towns; 25 per cent of income from registration of transfer of immovable property; 5 per cent of the income from local bus services; and entire receipts from the fines in the cases of breach of municipal laws as well as in prosecutions under state and Union laws administered by local authorities such as the Prevention of Food Adulteration Act after a deduction, say, of 5 per cent as administrative costs.

Commercial Undertakings

Municipal bodies should take up remunerative enterprises which would create permanent assets, yielding perennial non-tax revenue. For this purpose they should be given liberal loan assistance on low interest rates and rendered necessary technical assistance free of cost. The debt of remunerative enterprises should be a charge on the revenue derived from them. There should be relaxation of dates for payment of instalments for the repayment of loans at least for such period till the enterprise really becomes remunerative, subject to a maximum of five years.

Need for Maximum Economy

The expenditure on general administration and collection of revenue of municipal bodies is on high side. For example, it is 24.9 per cent in Rajasthan and 24.4 per cent in Punjab, against the all-India level of 11.6 per cent. This shows that the administrative and revenue collection machinery is an expensive one and there is a great deal of extravagance on establishment. The state governments, therefore, should direct the municipal bodies that they should not incur more than a certain percentage of expenditure (12.5 per cent) on general administration and collection of revenue and for good and sufficient reasons to be placed on record a committee may raise this limit by another 2.5 per cent. This stipulation needs to be strictly enforced by invoking the provisions of relevant sections of the Municipal Act in cases where persuasion fails to achieve the desired results. Economy can also be effected by setting up an independent agency (the Municipal Works department under the local government) for the execution of municipal works as at present a substantial amount of their income (13.0 per cent) is spent as departmental charges of the public works department. Similarly, by providing centralized system of municipal purchasing of supplies, material and equipment through a state agency, the state government can ensure economy and the availability of goods of highest quality. Municipal bodies should also be equitably exempted from contribution to provincialized schools in view of their extremely precarious financial position coupled with the fact that they have no share in the administration of these institutions.

Utilization of Resource Potential from Municipal Fees and Property

Municipal fees should be made an effective instrument of municipal finance and their rates should be adequately increased on uniformity patterns. Licence fees in particular for offensive and dangerous trades should be levied on a sliding scale. Steps should also be taken for effective assessment and collection of fees and to plug leakage of revenue. Similarly, in order to utilize the resource potential from municipal properties to the maximum, municipal bodies should raise the rents on municipal properties particularly (say, every five years) in view of the rise in the level of prices, collect them on the basis of prescribed rates, avoid unreasonable remissions, and take all coercive measures for their realization.

Revolving Fund

It is also suggested that the state governments should seriously consider the setting up a revolving fund to assist local governments in financing programmes of urban development such as acquisition and development of land, construction of houses, widening of existing roads, construction of new ones, supply of utility services, provision of open spaces, parks, playgrounds, etc. All these entail huge initial capital which is evidently beyond the capacity of even big municipal corporations. Revolving fund basically means to revolve the initial working capital in such a way that it yields a handsome return on investment which along with the working capital is again ploughed back with a view to securing increasing return in each cycle of investment.[43] In the jargon of accountancy, it means 'a fund from which moneys are continuously expended, replenished and expended'.[44] The idea underlying a revolving fund is that the completion of a programme or scheme financed out of it makes possible the recovery of the original outlay, which then becomes available for financing new schemes. And so, the fund revolves. The swifter the speed at which the fund revolves, the larger shall be the volume of schemes executed from it over a period. If the fund brings back to itself, as it must, something extra in the form of interest and profits, it continually enlarges itself and is thus enabled to undertake business on a still higher scale. It is obvious that only such schemes as are truly remunerative in the strict business sense shall be chosen to be financed out of the revolving fund.[45]

Municipal Finance Corporation

The Rural-Urban Relationship Committee has suggested the setting up of a Municipal Finance Corporation in each state to advance loans to the municipal bodies to meet the capital needs of municipal enterprises such as city transport, milk supply, electricity, cinemas, hotels and the like. The Corporation could have an authorized capital of rupees 10 crore or more to be subscribed by the Government of India, the Reserve Bank of India, the Life Insurance Corporation, commercial banks, and other financial institutions as also the local bodies. It should be run on commercial lines and should have the power to issue debentures and raise market loans under the guarantee of the Union Government.[46]

Urban Development Finance Corporation

An Urban Development Finance Corporation could also be set up to finance the municipal development plans and programmes. It is argued that such a corporation would be better equipped to tap additional resources and to give special attention to the requirements of municipal programmes. The United Nations has also supported the demand for such a central loan agency and observed: 'Such an agency would not only provide loans to local authorities at reasonable rates but could also give technical advice on individual projects and spur long term physical planning at the local level.'[47]

In the final analysis it is to be accepted that the above-mentioned arrangements would be useful to a limited extent of financing the remunerative and self-liquidating projects, but for financing the social infrastructure investments in the field of education, health, housing, etc., what is needed is combination of loans and grants which can be provided only by the Central and state governments.[48]

Municipal Finance Commission

The problem of inadequacy of finances of municipal bodies has been seriously discussed by numerous commissions and committees appointed by the Central and state governments from time to time. A joint meeting of the Central Council of Local Self Government and the Executive Committee of the all India Council of Mayors organized by the Ministry of Works and Housing had suggested to set up a municipal finance commission. The Rural-Urban Relationship Committee which made a detailed study *inter alia* of finances of urban local bodies had also, keeping in view the provisions of Article 280 of the Constitution of India, recommended that well before the appointment of the Central Finance Commission by the President, the governor of each state should appoint a body to be known as the Municipal Finance Commission to examine the financial obligations for various obligatory services and development schemes. 'The state governments', the committee observed, 'may include the financial obligation arising from the recommendations of the Municipal Finance Commission in their proposal of the Central Finance Commission.' In this way, the finances of local bodies will become an integral part of the overall national finances. This procedure will not only act as a financial insurance for local bodies and protect them against arbitrary incursions of the State government but also act as a stimulus for them to make the best use of the taxes allocated to them.

To begin with the state governments did not evince interest in the proposal. However, as a result of persistent demand made at the meetings of the Central Council of Local Self Government, a number of state governments have set up Municipal Finance Commissions, Maharashtra (1973) being the first, followed by Orissa (1975). Every state would be obliged to set up such a commission if there is a constitutional mandate.

There is no denying the fact that when the state governments themselves are frantically searching for additional sources of revenue, it is but natural that they would pay scant attention to the needs of local authorities. They have, in fact, been not only reluctant to part with such resources which are patently local but have even been tempted to encroach upon municipal tax resources by levying identical and parallel taxes. The Taxation Enquiry Commission (1953–54), as has been mentioned earlier, had suggested reservation of specified tax resources in favour of local government but as usual the suggestion has remained on paper only.

The state governments are constantly looking to the centre for their resources and as a result of the recommendations of the Central Finance Commission, their share and allocation in the revenues of the union government have been increasing from time to time. It would not be too much, therefore, to stress that the state governments should be prepared to devote at least a proportionate share from the increased allocations to the urban areas. After all, the local and state governments are partners in the endeavour of promoting the welfare of the people and their financial relationship should also be based on this principle.

State Finance Commissions

The Constitution (74th Amendment) Act, 1992, *vide* Article 243 (I) provides that the governor of a state, as soon may within one year of the commencement of Constitution (Amendment) Act, 1992, and thereafter at the expiration of every fifth year, constitute a finance commission to review the financial position of the municipalities and make recommendations to him as to

(*a*) the principles which should govern

 (*i*) the distribution between the state and the municipalities of the net proceeds of the taxes, duties, tolls and fees which can be levied by the state which may be divided between them and the allocation between the municipalities at the level of their respective shares of such proceeds,

 (*ii*) the determination of the taxes, duties, tolls, and fee which may be assigned to and appropriated by the municipalities,

 (*iii*) the grants-in-aid to the municipalities from the consolidated fund of the state,

(*b*) the measures needed to improve the financial position of the municipalities;

(*c*) any other matter referred to the Finance Commission by the governor in the interests of sound finance of the municipalities.

The governor shall cause every recommendation made by the Commission together with an explanatory memorandum on the action taken thereon to be laid before the legislature of the state.

In compliance with this constitutional stipulation, all the states had set up their state finance commissions. Most of the state finance commissions have submitted their reports to the concerned state governments. Some of them are yet to examine and accept them.

Punjab was, perhaps, the first state in the country which had moved fast once the 73rd and 74th Constitutional amendments became effective. It passed the Punjab Finance Commission for Panchayats and Municipalities Act, 1994 on 19 April 1994. The Finance Commission was constituted on 22 April 1994, with Mr J.P. Gupta, a retired IAS Officer, as its chairman. The Commission submitted its report to the Governor of Punjab on 31 December 1995. Thus Punjab became the first state in the country to have received the commission's report.

The Commission, *inter alia,* had recommended that 20 per cent of the net proceeds of at least from taxes collected by the state should be shared with the municipalities and Panchayati Raj institutions. These taxes were stamp duty, Punjab motor vehicles tax, electricity duty, entertainment tax and entertainment tax (cinematograph). In respect of the entertainment taxes, the share recommended for municipalities was 80 per cent and for Panchayati Raj institutions 20 per cent.

The Commission also listed several user charges which the municipalities could levy. It recommended extension of surcharges to water supply, sewerage, parking, slots, solid waste management, etc. It also observed that the state must also provide 'specific purpose' grants for additional coverage of population by core services.

Referring to expenditure on establishment, the commission had said that for improving core services and reducing expenditure progressively, work should be off-loaded to private agencies, besides keeping establishment expenditure to the minimum.

The commission has also recommended that municipalities must check and plug revenue leakage and bring economy in expenditure. The cost of collection of revenue should not exceed 5 per cent of the total collection. Punishment for evasion of octroi should be made more stringent. Municipalities could sign MoUs with gram panchayats or *samitis* for inspection of warehouses or storage space in their jurisdiction. To avoid congestion and ensure flow of traffic, the municipalities should evolve a system of 'composite permit'.

There should be no exemptions on octroi. If these were given, the government must compensate municipalities. In respect of property tax, the commission recommended that it be forthwith delinked from rentals to increase yield and reduce litigation. There should be a higher rate of taxation to allow use of vacant land for social functions and entertainment. There should be a surcharge at the rate of 50 to 100 per cent on commercial, industrial, and other non-residential establishments and polluting industries involving hazardous processes.

The municipal committees should have 'valuation committees' to hear objections and all records relating to assessment be made available to the public on payment of a fee. Voluntary filing of statements by persons liable to assessment should be made obligatory. Failure to file it should be made punishable.

Regarding water supply and sewerage, the commission recommends that all stand-posts be abolished unless water bills were paid by the community and consumers collectively. Water rates are to be linked to power tariff in addition to the annual hike of 10 per cent to offset cost escalation. Sewerage charges are to be made equal to the water charges. There should be differential rates of water for commercial and industrial consumers and connections. The entire water supply is to be metered. There is need to progressively privatize maintenance of water supply, billing, and collection of revenue. For augmentation of resources the Commission has recommended tax on professions, trade, calling and employment, tax on advertisements and hoardings, sub-soil rights (licensing of private tube-wells and corresponding fee), revision of non-tax rates, and reducing state controls on fixing of local tax rates.

The Commission recommended per capita grant-in-aid to 'weak' municipalities besides specific purpose and incentive grants. There was need for streamlining the system of pre-audit and setting up of accounts committees in each municipality, besides a state-level public accounts committee. How effectively and sincerely the government implements these recommendations needs to be seen.

NOTES AND REFERENCES

1. Kautilya, *Arthashastra*, translated by Shomasastri (Mysore: Raghuveer Printing Press, 1956), p. 65.
2. Quoted by M.P. Sharma, *Public Administration: Theory and Practice* (Allahabad: Kitab Mahal, 1978), p. 449.
3. Felix A. Nigro, *Public Administration—Readings and Documents* (New York: Rinehart and Co. Inc., 1951), p. 312.
4. S.K. Sharma and V.N. Chawla (eds), *Municipal Administration in India—Some Reflections* (Jalandhar: International Book Company, 1975), p. 175.
5. 'Report of the Committee on Budgetary Reform in Municipal Administration', Government of India, Ministry of Works and Housing, New Delhi, 1974, p. 22.
6. M.J.K. Thavraj, 'Finances of Local Government in India', *Indian Journal of Public Administration* 24, no. 3 (1978).
7. 'Report of the Taxation Enquiiy Commission (1953–54)', Ministry of Finance, Govt of India, 1955, p. 363.
8. 'Report of Committee on Budgetary Reforms in Municipal Administration', p. 20.
9. Entry 52 of the State list Seventh Schedule, Constitution of India.
10. Refer to Proceedings of a Seminar on 'Octroi and Terminal Taxes', *Nagarlok* (October–December, 1977), Special Issue on Administration of Octroi.
11. Report of the Rural-Urban Relationship Committee, p. 94.
12. S.R. Maheshwari, *Local Government in India,* p. 273.
13. Kundanlal and S. Bhargava, 'Octroi Levy', *Business Standard,* February 28, 1979.
14. Report of the Taxation Enquiry Commission, p. 273.
15. 'Report of the Committee of Ministers on Augmentation of Financial Resources of Urban Local Bodies', 1963, pp. 48–49.

16. Hoshar Singh, 'The Place of Octroi in Municipal Finance in Rajasthan', *Nagarlok* 2–3 (July-September, 1976).
17. 'Report of the Local Government (Octroi) Committee', Chandigarh, Government of Punjab, 1967, p. 4.
18. Statement of Mr Surjit Singh Barnala, the then Chief Minister, in the Punjab Vidhan Sabha on 9 March 1986.
19. 'Report of the Taxation Enquiry Commission', Vol. III, p. 292.
20. 'Report of the Committee of Ministers on Augmentation of Financial Resources of Urban Local Bodies', 1963, p. 39.
21. Report of the Rural-Urban Relationship Committee, pp. 98–99.
22. K.K. Sinha, *Local Taxation in a Developing Economy* (Bombay: Vora and Co. Publishers Pvt. Ltd.), pp. 96–97.
23. Gyan Chand, *Local Finances in India* (Allahabad: Kitabistan, 1947), p. 130.
24. The Constitution of India, Article 276.
25. Statement of Mr. S.B. Chavan, Finance Minister, Govt. of India, in Lok Sabha, on 30 November 1988.
26. Entries 33, 34 and 62 of State List, Seventh Schedule, Constitution of India.
27. 'Report of the Committee on Augmentation of Financial Resources of Urban Local Bodies', p. 54.
28. Venkata Rao, *Local Self Government in India* (Delhi: S Chand & Co. 1960), p. 236.
29. 'Report of the Committee on Augmentation of Financial Resources of Urban Local Bodies', p. 56.
30. Report of the Rural Urban Relationship Committee, Vol. I, p. 103.
31. M.J. Tharvaj, 'Finances of Local Government in India', in T.N. Chaturvedi (ed.), *Local Government* (New Delhi: Indian Institute of Public Administration, 1984), p. 127.
32. Gyan Chand, *Local Finances in India*, pp. 202–203.
33. Refer to Punjab Municipal Corporation Act, 1976, Sections 158 and 159.
34. S.R. Maheshwari, *Local Government in India*, p. 277.
35. 'Report of the Local Government (Urban) Enquiry Committee', Government of Punjab, 1957, p. 56.
36. 'Report of Committee on Budgetary Reform in Municipal Administration', *op. cit.*
37. Felix, A. Nigral, *Modern Public Administration* (New York: Harper, 1970), p. 397.
38. Ashok Chanda, *Indian Administration* (London: Alien and Unwin 1967), p. 243.
39. R.K. Khanna, *Municipal Government and Administration in India*, p. 163.
40. 'Report of Committee on Budgetary Reforms in Municipal Administration', p. 106.
41. This is corroborated by the stand taken by municipal committees in Haryana against the recent hike in octroi, water rates, stamp duty and development charges ordered by the state government to improve the finances of urban bodies on the recommendations of the Resources Committee (Local Bodies). The Bharatiya Janta Party which shared power with the Lok Dal in the Government opposed the increase in civic taxes for fear of losing ground in the towns and municipal commissioners of many municipal committees such as Yamuna Nagar refused to endorse the government notification enhancing the various taxes. The government ultimately had to withdraw the notification.
42. Refer to S.K. Sharma and D.R. Sachdeva, 'Municipal Police: Role and Responsibilities', *Indian Journal of Public Administration* 34, no. 1 (1978): 209–16.
43. Gangadhar Jha, 'Revolving Fund as a Technique of Financing Local Development : A Critique', in K.S.R.H. Sharma (ed.), *Financing Urban Development in India* (New Delhi: Indian Institute of Public Administration, 1984), p. 159.
44. Kohler, *Dictionary of Accountants*, quoted from J.P. Shah's *Revolving Fund: A Technique for Financing Public Housing Programmes*, Selected Papers from Symposium in Housing Finance, New Delhi, February 1–3, 1985, pp. 102–05 (NBD and U.N. Regional Housing Centre [SCAFE]).
45. S.R. Maheshwari, *Local Government in India*, p. 279.
46. Report of the Rural-Urban Relationship Committee, pp. 107–108.
47. United Nations, *Decentralisation for National and Local Government* (New York, 1962), p. 65.
48. Abhijit Datta, *Issues in Municipal Finance*, p. 229.

State Control over Urban Local Governments

There are two antithetical views about the supervision and control of state government over municipal bodies. The advocates of populism who are staunch supporters of unbridled municipal democracy are opposed to any sort of interference by state government. They believe that the control and supervision of the municipal institutions is unwarranted, unnecessary and fraught with mischief; and that self-government would cease to be so if it is made subject to external control and supervision.[1] They further contend that decentralization implies complete autonomy without any outside restrictions and limitations, that centralization of powers would tend to transform local government into local administration; and that the strength of a central government that tries to keep local government weak is an illusive strength.[2]

Proponents of paternalism, on the other hand, hold the view that municipal bodies have to be regularly controlled, supervised, guided, and occasionally punished for their acts of omission and commission.

Arguments in Favour of State Control

It is argued that since, constitutionally, municipal government falls within the province of the state government, the latter has the power to determine their structure, functions, and financial resources.[3] In other words, being infrasovereign bodies created by the state government, they are amenable to its control and their autonomy is limited.[4] In their opinion, the autonomy of municipal bodies implies the degree of self-government within the ambit of their functions but it does not mean their unlimited authority and freedom. They therefore hold that some measure of control of state government over the municipal institutions is not only desirable but also necessary. They contend that 'ever since the inception of statutory institutions of local government, the state government has reserved the right to regulate their structural autonomy and has not treated decentralization as something sacrosanct but as a device to aid the achievement of the ends of government'.[5]

State control over municipal bodies is favoured for other reasons also. It enables the government to put into operation a policy which individual local institutions may find irksome or unduly restrictive of their initiative. The state government can also lay down certain minimum standards of administration below which the services of the local authorities should not be allowed to fall.[6] State control is also needed for proper direction, unification, and coordination of the civic services and for securing consistency and continuity both in the formulation and the implementation of the national policies.[7] The Taxation Enquiry Commission had accordingly observed, 'The state government constituting the representative governing authority in a state has the responsibility to see that local bodies are efficiently organized; that they perform their functions properly, and that they take adequate part in the development of the country.'[8]

According to Prof. M.P. Sharma:

> The Central or State Governments are ultimately responsible for the financial solvency of the local bodies. They cannot leave a local body threatened with bankruptcy to its own fate because that would mean the cessation of certain vital services like water supply and sewerage in its area. If the central or state governments are to be responsible for the financial soundness of local bodies, they must have the power to exercise financial control in a measure sufficient enough to prevent mismanagement. The government gives grants-in-aid to the local bodies and to enable it to ensure that the grants are properly and usefully utilized local bodies must be subject to the control of higher authorities.[9]

Moreover, the local bodies, after all, form a part of the greater whole, i.e. the state, and there must be some higher authority to intervene when any local body ignores the fundamental canons of sound administration or sacrifices in any other way the interests of the people.[10] It has been rightly observed by late Prof. P.A. James that in the absence of any control, the local bodies are prone to work in an erratic way, defeating the very purpose for which they were set up. And complete autonomy to local bodies would spell anarchy.[11]

Planning provides another rationale for state control over municipal bodies. According to the latest thinking on planning, the rural and urban local bodies are to be involved both in the formulation and implementation of plans for their respective areas.[12] As such, the state governments are to provide the required guidance to the local bodies in the formulation of plans, and exercise supervision and control on them in their execution.

From the foregoing discussion, it is clear that the state control over municipal bodies is justified on the grounds that it is conducive to the maintenance of a reasonable degree of efficiency; that it helps in weaning away local bodies from vested interests; that it aids in augmentation of financial resources of the local bodies which are generally reluctant to impose direct taxes; that it makes for minimizing regional imbalances and ensures stability and uniformity in administration; that it safeguards national interests in their embryonic stages and that it facilitates sounder socio-economic planning.[13]

Forms of Control

Municipal bodies are subject to the legislative, executive, and financial control of state government and also amenable to judicial control.

Legislative Control

Legislative control is exercised by the state government by virtue of its inherent right granted to it by the constitution and according to which it has the exclusive power to make laws in respect of local government institutions and decide their functions and powers.[14] That is why Prof. R.K. Gooch observes, 'Legislature is in a position theoretically and potentially to treat local government in any conceivable way.'[15] C.A. Cross remarks, 'All formal control which the government exercises stems from a specific statutory provision.'[16] Accordingly, municipal bodies in a state are the creation of the respective state legislature and derive their powers from the statutes pertaining to them. The legislature can also empower the government to make rules and regulations for all municipal matters such as elections, personnel, accounts, taxation, etc.

The state legislature can also make amendments in the municipal Act from time to time and legislate separate Acts also to deal with some matters of importance instead of making minor changes in the existing Act.

Means of Legislative Control

From among the various means of legislative control such as discussions and debates and different kinds of motions like call attention, adjournment, and privilege, questions asked by the members of the legislature during the question hour constitute the most powerful means of soliciting information about different aspects of municipal administration from the minister concerned. The questions raised in the assembly generally relate to issues like municipal elections, including preparation of electoral rolls, election petitions, gazette notification of elected members, removal of members, writs filed in the High Court, supersession and abolition of municipal committees, personnel, finance, and day-to-day administration of municipal bodies.

Legislative control over municipal bodies as discussed above, is of great significance, but it cannot be exercised in an effective manner owing to paucity of time at the disposal of the legislators, technical nature of municipal administration and political considerations, biases, and prejudices of the ruling party.

Administrative Control

Administrative control over municipal bodies is the most effective type of control extending to every aspect of municipal administration. Baker Benjamin has termed it as the technical direction of municipal affairs by the state administrative authorities.[17] It comprises of determination of criteria for the creation of different kinds of municipal bodies; defining, increasing or decreasing their territorial limits; fixing the number of the elected members and the seats to be reserved for the Scheduled Castes and Scheduled Tribes, conduct of free and fair elections; delimitations of wards; co-option of members of certain categories of people not represented through elections; appointment of associate members and officials advisers; extension of the term of office of members or its reduction due to supersession, disposal of election petitions, removal of members and office bearers such as president and vice-president, etc.

The state government exercises administrative control over municipal bodies as follows:

1. Power to Approve By-Laws: The state government is vested with the power to approve by-laws and rules framed by the municipal bodies; to issue memoranda, circulars, and directions containing advice, suggestions, instructions, and directives; to sanction specific schemes; to prescribe service standards; to lay down procedures and norms; to conduct enquiries and inspections; to obtain periodic reports and to require the municipal bodies to obtain prior approval of the government for undertaking certain kinds of functions or for imposing any tax; etc.

The state government is also vested with the power to annul resolutions passed by the municipal bodies if these are felt to be in excess of the powers conferred on them by law or are contrary to the interests of the public or are likely to cause waste of municipal funds or lead to a breach of peace, or encourage lawlessness.

2. Control over Personnel: The state governments have assumed complete authority over the municipal personnel since the provincialization of municipal services from the post of an assistant and above. It is now the government which creates the posts, lays down definite qualifications for different posts and channels of promotion, makes appointment on the recommendations of a selection committee constituted by it, orders transfers from one municipality to another and determines their conditions of service, though the salary, allowances, gratuity, pension, and other payments are made by the concerned municipal body. The government is also vested with the power to take disciplinary action against the personnel of municipal services. The municipal bodies enjoy the right to employ only clerks, and class-IV employees subject to the approval of the state government. The president and the municipal committee concerned can take action against personnel employed by the municipality but an appeal against it can be made to the government, whose decision is final. The state government, on its own, can also demand punishment or dismissal of any servant of the committee who in its opinion is unfit for employment.

Similarly in the case of municipal corporations, the commissioner, in whom the entire executive power is vested, is appointed by the state government. And since all cadres of municipal corporations drawing a prescribed minimum salary per month have been provincialized, the state government has been empowered to exercise complete control over the personnel of municipal corporations with respect to their recruitment, transfer, promotion, conditions of service, conduct and discipline, etc.

3. Power of Inspection: The state government is also vested with the power to conduct inspections of the activities performed by the municipal bodies. The inspections are conducted by the representative of the state government at the district level, and in the state where the directorates of local bodies have been set up, the local inspectors are appointed for this purpose.

The purpose of inspection is to ensure that the municipal bodies are functioning within the framework of the Municipal Act. The state government issues suitable directions to the concerned local body in order to make it more efficient and to streamline its functioning and the inspection is intended to ensure that these directions are being observed meticulously.

4. Reports and Enquiries: The municipal bodies are obliged to send periodic reports to the state government regarding their functioning. The reports can be quarterly, half yearly or annual. These reports include information concerning financial, administrative, and statistical matters. This is a tool in the hands of the government to get acquainted with the latest state of affairs of municipal bodies. The government can initiate any enquiry on the basis of these reports and can also extract any kind of information from the municipal body.

5. Default Powers: A municipal body is obliged to perform its functions within a specified period. If a municipal body fails to perform a particular function within a specified period, the state government can issue directions to finish the work in the stipulated time. If the municipal body still fails to perform that function, the state government can get that work done on its own but the expenditure for that work is to be incurred by the concerned municipality.

6. Appellate Powers: There is a provision in various state municipal acts for making appeals to the state government against any municipal decision. Some of these decisions are concerned with issue of licences, refusal for construction at a particular site, demolition of a building, and disciplinary actions.

7. Powers of Dissolution and Supersession: Of all the administrative powers of control that state government exercises over municipal bodies, the power to dissolve or supersede a municipal body is the most drastic—a sledge hammer type of power.[18] Dissolution connotes terminating a council and giving a chance to the electorate to elect a new council within a specified time limit. Supersession, on the other hand, means suspension of the council and placing the entire control of the municipal body in an administrator appointed by the state government. Dissolution is thus less severe than supersession. Dissolution stems from lack of confidence in the competence of the councillors and penalizes them, while supersession amounts to punishing the electorate because it deprives them of their representatives in a municipal body. The state governments have been vested with the power of suspension and supersession of municipal bodies. It is provided in municipal acts of various states:

> That if in the opinion of the state government, a committee is not competent to perform or persistently makes default in the performance of the duties imposed on it under the Act or exceeds or abuses its powers, the state government by an order published in the official gazette, together with the statement of reasons thereof can declare the committee under suspension for a period not exceeding one year. But after the expiry of the period of suspension, if the committee again acts in a similar manner, the state government by a similar order can supersede the committee. Before making an order of suspension or supersession, the state government is required to give an opportunity to the committee to show-cause why such one order should not be made, but such an opportunity is not necessary where it is not reasonably practical to do so.

The state governments have been frequently resorting to supersession of municipal bodies on the grounds of incompetence, persistent default in the performance of their statutory duties and abuse of powers. The reasons usually given by the state government for their supersession have been: the sanitary conditions in the municipal area of the committee were most deplorable and no proper arrangement for the removal of garbage had been made and, as a result of that, the city was stinking; the committee did not make adequate arrangements for the supply of drinking water in the newly constructed colonies on the outskirts of the town and the constructions therein were mostly unauthorized due to non-adoption of model building by-laws by the municipality; in the matter of providing street lights, the position was highly unsatisfactory; the municipal committee had failed to take proper care of municipal roads and almost all the roads within the municipal area were in a bad shape, which was not only a cause of annoyance to the public using vehicles but also to the pedestrians; the municipal committee had resolved to stop the Public Health Department from executing sewerage works in the city which was against the public interest; the maintenance of accounts in the municipality was unsatisfactory and the committee had practically taken no action for the clearance of old requisitions and objections of the audit which were hundreds in number; the financial position of the committee was not satisfactory; it had raised loans but the amount of recoverable arrears of various taxes and fees was substantial which clearly indicated that due attention was not being paid by the committee towards realization of arrears.

These charges appear to be quite common and can be easily levelled against any municipal body. High Courts when approached quash the decisions of the state government to supersede the municipal body concerned, motivated as they are by the political and partisan considerations.

The provisions for the supersession of municipal corporations are generally similar to those for the supersession of municipal committees with the difference that the period of the supersession of the former is not to exceed two years as against the stipulation of no time limit in the case of the latter. The consequences resulting from the supersession of a corporation would also be the same as in the case of a municipal committee, viz. that all councillors shall on such date as may be specified in the order, vacate their offices without prejudice to their eligibility for election; that during the period of supersession of the corporation, all powers and duties conferred and imposed on the corporation shall be exercised and performed by such officer or authority as the government may appoint in that behalf; that all property vested in the Corporation shall, until it is reconstituted, vest in the government; and that before the expiry of the period of supersession, elections shall be held for the purpose of reconstituting the corporation.

Critical Analysis of the Power of Supersession

The provisions governing supersession of municipal bodies are questionable due to their lack of objectivity and absence of definite criteria for determining efficiency or defaults:

1. In the first instance, the words 'in the opinion of the government' make it clear that it is the opinion of the government that counts. It is well known that judged by the known standards opinion can never be objective. Nowhere has it been mentioned in the Act or under the rules as to how this opinion is to be formulated or arrived at.[19]
2. Secondly, it is no possible to define competence in precise terms and to assess it objectively. A municipal council may be very competent in performing some functions but quite inefficient in performing other functions.
3. Again, competency of a single council independently assessed will be something very different when it is assessed in relation to other councils.
4. Moreover, a council may not be able to exhibit competency in the performance of its multifarious duties in view of the fact that the finances of the municipality are not commensurate with the functions entrusted to it.
5. Further, competency is judged both by the directorate and the secretariat. Different officers are associated with this process at different levels. It cannot be denied that what is considered competent by one officer may not be considered as such by another. Subjectively assessed competence cannot therefore be a real ground justifying the supersession of a municipal body.[20]
6. Maladministration may further be due to the lapses on the part of individual councillor, the president, the executive officer, and the council in its collective capacity. The government generally cannot pinpoint the responsibility squarely and it is unfortunate that the committee as a whole should be punished for the fault of one or the other of its constituents.
7. 'Default' is another ambiguous term. There have been municipal councils in default in relation to certain functions but it is highly doubtful whether all such cases come under the category of persistent default.
8. Incompetence or default in performance needs to be proved for which evidence has to be produced. What actually happens is that all of a sudden, for one reason or other, the decision to supersede is taken, and then efforts are made to collect information and evidence to lend support to the decision already taken. Hence it is commonly held that most supersession decisions are politically motivated.[21]
9. As a matter of fact, party politics has been a major factor in the supersession of municipalities. In municipal committees in which the interests of the party in power at the state level are safely looked after no such drastic action is taken even if their administration is in poor shape.[22] The decision to supersede, therefore, is a political one and occasionally partisan.[23]
10. Lastly, the view that if a municipal council abuses its powers or is considered incompetent to perform its functions it should be superseded is mistaken, as mankind has not yet and cannot ever contrive a foolproof legislation or, for that matter, any foolproof human organization. If that were so the judiciary would not have declared so many state and even parliamentary acts *ultra vires* of the Constitution. The decisions of the high courts are sometimes rescinded by the Supreme Court. Many actions of the bureaucrats who, as a class, tend to regard themselves as the acme of wisdom and uprightness, have invited the wrath of the judiciary.[24]

Supersession of municipal bodies is therefore not a proper remedy for the maladies from which they generally suffer. It is a short-term palliative dealing with the symptoms rather than the disease itself.[25]

This drastic action by the government has been disapproved by almost all the committees and commissions which have probed into the affairs of municipal bodies. The Simon Commission had significantly pointed out that where a spur or rein was needed the ministers were only given a poleaxe.[26] The aim of the government should be to rectify and remedy the evils progressively and to improve the councils from within by infusing greater enthusiasm for self-government and civic responsibility among the inhabitants of the civic community rather than to pronounce the capital sentence of them.[27] Every suspension is a setback to the cause of the development of responsible local government and it should be avoided so far as possible on that ground alone.[28] Supersession, dissolution or action in default by the state government should, therefore, be applied rarely and as a last resort after all means of advice and persuasion have been exhausted.[29]

The incompetence of municipal bodies in performing their functions can be attributed to the weaknesses of their structure, which include the absence of a strong and independent executive, undue interference by the councillors in executive matters, inefficient and unqualified municipal personnel, inadequate resources, losses due to improper assessment, faulty collection of taxes, and wasteful expenditure. And unless these defects are removed through necessary changes, a council cannot be expected to perform its duties efficiently and effectively. It is on such changes that attention needs to be focused. Political supersessions of municipal bodies do not take the system anywhere towards achieving the objectives of municipal government.[30]

Despite the disapproval and condemnation of supersession by various committees and commissions as discussed above, it is surprising that it is still in vogue in an unabated manner. Its continuance may be explained by reasons: first, that it may be purely conventional and hence taken for granted; second, the application of supersession as a controlling device seems to be inextricably linked with politics of one kind, or the other, councils belonging to a different political party or even of the same party but of a different or opposite groups can be superseded on one pretext or the other; third, supersession is resorted to for arresting a deteriorating situation and toning up the administration of a municipal body to a particular standard and then to hand it over to the elected representatives of the people.[31] Finally, the mistrust entertained by the government that local bodies at any time may go wrong, in which case the government will have to assume responsibility and the notion that it is best discharged by recourse to supersession has led to its continuation.

Conclusion

Whatever the reasons prompting the government to supersede municipal bodies, it is in the fitness of things that municipal governments having been elected by the freely expressed choice of the people should be allowed to run their full course set out in the governing act itself. Suspension or dissolution of elected local government amounts to a supersession of democracy itself. And setting at naught the people's choice by force of a mere executive fiat is adding insult to injury.[32] A local government should be inflicted punitive actions such as suspension or dissolution only by the people's representatives at a higher level. According to Prof. G. Mukherjee, 'The statute which creates local bodies and gives them all powers is enacted by the people's representatives in the state legislatures. Logically, therefore, it is that body alone which can decide as to whether a local body should be superseded or not.'[33]

Control Mechanism: Agencies of Control

The state government exercises supervision and control over municipal bodies through state level and local agencies. The former comprise the Department of Local Government, Directorate of Local Government, and technical departments, and the latter consist of the deputy commissioner and the sub-divisional officer.

In other words, three segments of administration are concerned with local bodies, *viz.* (*a*) the secretariat, (*b*) the department, and (*c*) the regional and field officers. The Secretariat is basically a policy formulating body and the field offices and subordinate offices are the regional or field agencies for policy implementation. And in between these two, comes the institution of 'directorate' which caters to the policy formulation needs of the secretariat and also ensures proper and effective implementation of policies by the subordinate field offices. The institution of 'directorate' is normally technical in nature and as such gives technical advice to the secretariat on matters falling within its jurisdiction.

Department of Local Government

The Department of Local Government exercises control over municipal bodies by laying down the major policies of local government and issuing directions and orders to municipal bodies. The department is also concerned with some major issues of local government such as delimitation of the wards of a municipal body, fixing the number of members to be elected and nominated, extension of term of a local body, and elections to municipal bodies.

Not all states have a separate department of local government. In some states the department of local government has been merged with another department. For example, Maharashtra has one department for urban development, public health and housing; in Andhra Pradesh a common department exists for public health, housing and local government. But there are also some states like Punjab, Haryana, and Rajasthan which have separate department of local government.

The Department of Local Government is headed by a cabinet minister or a minister of state holding independent charge. He lays down the major policy of the department and decides major policy issues. A senior IAS officer is the Secretary of the department. He is assisted by joint secretary, deputy secretaries, under-secretaries and the supporting staff.

The Directorate of Local Bodies in Punjab, for instance, is headed by a Joint Secretary who is the *ex-officio* director of Directorate of Local Government and is assisted by a joint director. The post of the joint director is held on *ex-officio* basis by one of the three deputy secretaries of the department. There is one deputy director (headquarters) assisted by an assistant director and other clerical staff. The directorate has its regional offices at Amritsar, Jalandhar, Ludhiana, Patiala, and Ferozepur under the charge of a deputy director to provide guidance and advice to the municipalities at their door step. The regional deputy directors exercise almost the same powers as were being exercised previously by the deputy commissioners in their respective districts.

Functions of the Directorate

1. The directorate plays an important part in the formulation of municipal policies by the state government. This is facilitated by the fact that the joint secretary and a deputy secretary of the department perform the functions of the director and the joint director, respectively. Actually the secretariat branches of the department of local government are situated within the building premises of the directorate and function under the direct supervision of the director (joint secretary) and the joint director (as the deputy secretary).
2. The directorate advises the government on all policy issues concerning municipal administration such as creation and classification of municipalities, their structure and functions, taxation, loans and financial grants, creation of state municipal services and their recruitment, training and promotion, and state-municipal relations. Besides, it also functions as a controlling agency for all municipal and urban institutions in the state. The control pertains to municipal elections, approval

or repeal of municipal resolutions, appointment, promotion, and transfer of certain categories of municipal employees and disciplinary action against them and the supersession or dissolution of a municipal body.

3. The director and the joint director being preoccupied with policy making functions, the inspection work is usually taken up by the deputy director (headquarters) and the five regional deputy directors as also by the deputy commissioner. Sometimes enquiries are also conducted by the directorate into the affairs of the municipal bodies either on public demand or on its own.
4. The directorate formulates rules and regulations and communicates these to the municipal bodies. It also issues circulars with a view to explaining government orders, tenders advice on specific cases and elaborated procedural matters. Many a time, municipal bodies approach the directorate to help them in specific cases such as asking a functional department for the expeditious sanction of their cases.
5. The directorate, sometimes, also undertakes the execution of specific services under extraordinary circumstances.
6. Besides performing the above functions, the directorate ensures inter-departmental coordination, interprets and relaxes, if necessary, existing rules and orders of the government, examines the municipal inspection reports, conducts research on local government problems, etc.

Technical Departments

Due to financial constraints, most of the municipal bodies, especially the small ones, cannot afford to engage technical experts to advise them on technical aspects of their schemes of water supply, sanitation, health, roads, public works, etc. They have to depend on the state technical departments for preparation, scrutiny, technical sanction, and even sometimes for the execution of their schemes. Their dependence on the technical departments thus naturally establishes a relationship between the municipal bodies and the technical departments. The municipal bodies submit their schemes to the respective technical departments through the regional directors or the director of the Directorate of Local Government. The technical departments concerned examine the proposals and accord their technical sanction. The Director of Local Government works as a link between the municipal bodies and the technical departments.

Under this arrangement, municipal schemes are often held up because of delay in securing technical sanction from the department concerned. It has, therefore, been suggested that the Directorate of Local Government should have an engineering cell to render assistance and advice to the municipalities in purely technical[34] matters and the cost of the cell be met from what municipalities are now required to pay to the technical departments for investigation work, preparation, and implementation of schemes. Alternatively, a purposeful coordination among the different state functional departments can be achieved by a coordination committee, consisting of nominees of various functional departments, with the Director of Local Government as the chairman. This committee would serve as a technical staff agency for advice and if any problem is beyond the solution of this committee, the Department of Local Government can take it to the sister secretariat departments for necessary consultation and decisions.

Local Level Agencies

Role of Deputy Commissioner in Municipal Administration

Once the divisional commissioners and deputy commissioners enjoyed vast powers of supervision and control over municipal bodies. And though the powers of the commissioner have been curtailed, the deputy commissioners continue to exercise substantial powers in respect of civic bodies even after the establishment of the Directorate of Local Government. Deputy commissioner can enter and inspect any immovable property occupied by a municipal committee, inspect any work in progress, call for any document, return, statement, account, report, and proceedings of the committee. He has also the power to suspend in writing the execution of any resolution or order of a committee if it is contrary to the interest of the public or is likely to cause waste or damage of municipal funds or property or is likely to lead to a breach of peace or encourage lawlessness. In case of an emergency, he may provide for the execution of any work that is considered to be necessary for the service and safety of the public and may direct that the expenses of the execution of the work be paid by the committee. He has the power to order performance of duties in case of default.

He is the in-charge of municipal elections starting from preparation of voters lists, receiving nomination papers and conducting elections of councillors, chairman, and vice-chairman. Election petitions must be presented to him within 14 days of the result of an election. He can extend this period also on the basis of sufficient grounds for such extension.

He approves the budgets of municipal committees of Class-II and Class-III. He is empowered to prevent extravagance in municipal establishments. If, in his opinion, the number of persons employed by a committee in services other than those in respect of which a municipal service has been instituted, or the remuneration assigned to them is excessive, he may require the committee to reduce the number of persons or the remunerations as the case may be.

He also hears appeals against the assessment or levy of any tax or against the refusal of refund of any tax under the Act. He also decides the appeals against compensation awarded by a municipality in certain cases. The sites for slaughter houses can be fixed only with his approval.

The sub-divisional officer, who is the in-charge of a sub-division in a district, enjoys the same powers in a sub-division as the deputy commissioner does in a district, the only difference is that of jurisdiction. The deputy commissioner is supervising and controlling authority of all municipalities in the district, whereas a sub-divisional officer is authorized to supervise and control only the municipalities situated in his area. Another distinction is that a sub-divisional officer has not been delegated the powers in emergency or in case of default.

The description of the powers of the deputy commissioner as given above clearly brings out his role in supervision and control of municipal bodies. The state government still finds in him an expedient and effective instrument to exercise control over municipal administration. Those who subscribe to the view that he cannot be relieved of the supervisory and controlling powers over municipal bodies hold that the municipal authorities do not have the expert knowledge even to frame their budgets properly and manage their finances and administration efficiently and therefore the district machinery has to be utilized to tone up municipal administration;[35] that the directorate has not appointed field officers at the district and tehsil levels; that the deputy commissioner carries enormous influence in the public on the one hand and with the functional departments of the government on the other, and therefore, he alone, not the chairman of the municipal board, can ensure smooth and efficient functioning of municipal administration with the support and cooperation of district officers.[36]

Those who disapprove of the deputy commissioner being entrusted with supervising and controlling powers over municipal bodies aver that the Directorate of Local Government should have separate field agencies of its own, as the deputy commissioner—revenue and general administrative officer as he is—does not possess any special knowledge or training in municipal administration. Second, he is on all accounts an overworked official, more than that, he is the most harassed official.[37] Such an official can hardly be expected to devote the requisite time and attention to municipal affairs. He, therefore, entrusts this work to the sub-divisional officer for whom, this is an additional responsibility and he, in turn, perforce leaves it to be handled by a senior clerk who again does it in addition to his duties. Thus at the district headquarters, there is not even a single senior clerk whose whole time business is to manage this aspect of deputy commissioner's work.[38] The Punjab Local Government (Urban) Enquiry Committee had rightly observed that 'Deputy Commissioners owing to their multifarious duties do not find sufficient time to guide the municipal officers or help them in the formulation of their programmes and their implementation'. It had therefore underlined the need for an experienced and expert field agency directing, guiding and supervising the affairs of the local bodies.[39]

Rationale for the Establishment of Directorate of Local Government

The need for the establishment of a Directorate of Local Government was emphasized by the Punjab Local Government (Urban) Enquiry Committee (1957). It had observed:

> The directorate is needed to exercise control and supervision over the municipal bodies, and to help and guide them in the performance of their activities and to undertake inspections to ensure that their performance is bettered.[40]

The Committee on Augmentation of Financial Resources of Urban Local Bodies (Zakaria Committee) had also recommended the setting up of municipal directorates. It stated:

> Every state should have a directorate of municipal committee under the charge of a senior officer with considerable knowledge of and experience in local administration. The directorate would exercise close supervision over the working of the chief executive officers and also give necessary guidance to the local bodies. It will also function as the Inspectorate of Local Bodies and by frequent inspections ensure that the performance of the local bodies is upto the mark.[41]

The Central Council of Local Self-Government, in its meeting held in February 1965, also urged the state governments to establish the directorates to keep a watch on the implementation of its resolutions and those of the conferences of mayors of municipal corporations, and to ensure the execution of the local government schemes. The executive committee of the Central Council, too, endorsed these recommendations and suggested the formations of planning cells to help and guide the urban local bodies in the preparation of five year plans.[42] The Rura–Urban Relationship Committee was also of the opinion that a well organized directorate at the state level with effective regional inspecting staff should go a long way towards improving the system of direction, supervision, and control of local bodies. It should guide and advise local authorities in the solution of their current and future problems and advocate their cause with the relevant departments.[43] The study team on district administration of the Administrative Reforms Commission also advocated the setting up of a directorate at the state headquarters along with the inspectorate attached to it.[44]

The Punjab Government had set up a directorate of municipal inspection and Guidance in 1962. It had appointed divisional inspectors at Patiala, Ludhiana, and Jalandhar. But it was realized that the system of divisional inspectors for the supervision and guidance of local bodies was not sufficiently effective, and that the establishment of a directorate of urban local bodies was the only way out to achieve the desired objectives. It was felt that:

1. At present the activities of the local government, by and large, were restricted to what may be called 'police functions', that is, prevention of misuse of powers by local bodies through audit and inspection by the divisional inspectors and deputy commissioners in the form of removal of members, supersession of incompetent local bodies, etc.

2. The local government department greatly felt handicapped without a field organization on the pattern of the directorates of other departments.
3. The department was overburdened with their workload, much of which could be processed and dealt with at the directorate level, thereby ensuring speedy disposal of cases.
4. There were only three divisional inspectors and the work of control, supervision, and guidance at the district and sub-divisional levels was left with the busy collectors and sub-divisional officers whose hands were already full with multifarious duties pertaining to revenue, development, and general administration and who could not therefore deal with the problems of urban local bodies effectively.
5. The majority of the members of municipal bodies were ignorant of the laws and rules governing municipal administration, and therefore there was an urgent need to have an organization for educating them in civic responsibilities and duties, and that only a properly organized directorate could undertake this job.

Major arguments in favour of setting up the directorate thus have been a general dissatisfaction with the existing state machinery for municipal supervision and control, the need for reducing the congestion of work at the secretariat level, the need for a field organization on the pattern of the directorates of other departments, and the utility of a well-equipped state machinery which could act as a bridge between the municipalities and the state-level institutions.

The Punjab Government prompted by these considerations had established the Directorate of Local Government in 1966.

Appraisal

The directorate was established with the express purpose of making the supervision and control over local bodies more effective by reducing the scope of powers and control exercised by the district authorities in relation to municipal administration. That is why more and more powers have been delegated to the regional deputy directors. Despite this, a comparison of the powers of the regional deputy directors and the deputy commissioners shows that the former have been assigned much less authority and they do not enjoy any appellate, emergency or special powers. Besides, the delegation of powers to the director/regional deputy directors does not deprive the deputy commissioner of the original jurisdiction under the Act. Two sets of officers operating in the same area, empowered with the same authority, may cause confusion and create problems due to conflicting opinions about their jurisdiction and powers. It appears that the directorate has not clearly defined the role of its own regional officers and that of the traditional state field administration. To cite an example of this ambiguity, the power of suspension of municipal resolution or orders were, to begin with, delegated to the regional deputy directors, but these have since been withdrawn and are exercised by the deputy commissioner. Again, the director has been delegated some important financial powers of sanctioning of budgets, re-appropriation from one hand to another and regulation of expenditure in the case of Class-I municipalities but similar powers in respect of Class-II and Class-III municipalities have not been delegated to the regional deputy directors and these are still exercised by the deputy commissioner.

Because of the overlapping jurisdiction of the directorate and the deputy commissioner, an element of competitiveness between the two is bound to erupt which may result in belittling the importance of the directorate, discouraging its expansion, and its abolition altogether. It would be improper to replace the directorate by the district administration, for it involves a comparison between incomparable agencies. The directorate is a state level agency with statewide jurisdiction, functions, and responsibilities while district administration is purely a field level organization.[45] It is the director and not the deputy commissioners in the different districts who can ensure uniformity in state supervision and control over the municipal bodies.

If at all a comparison is to be made, it should be between the district administration and the regional offices of the directorate,[46] who constitute as much a field agency as the latter. From the municipal administration point of view, the relationship between the directorate and the deputy commissioner is of vital significance; coordination, and cooperation between the two is therefore very essential as any conflict between them will jeopardize the development and smooth functioning of municipal administration in general.

In addition to the inherent structural and operational defects in the directorate organization vis-a-vis the position and role of deputy commissioner in municipal administration, the functioning of the directorate has been further criticized on the ground that it has acted more in an autocratic and authoritarian manner in exercising supervision and control over municipal bodies, not in any way different from what the municipal bodies had been subjected to prior to its establishment, and less as an agency for providing advice, guidance and help to them, which was precisely the major role expected of it.

It is also alleged that the directorate has been a source of delays in disposal of cases of municipal bodies. For example, the budgets of 24 class 'A' civic bodies for 1987–88 had not been approved by the directorate before 31 March 1986 and the plea given by it was that its officers had been busy, overworked and hard pressed for time due to their preoccupation with the session of the Assembly since 11 March 1987.

Another inadequacy of the directorate has been that its directors have not had a fixed tenure. They have been transferred too frequently. These have been instances when the directors have held the office for a few days or months only. This is detrimental not only to the overall efficiency of the directorate, but also to its routine functioning, as an officer with short tenure cannot be expected to formulate any policy, much less to implement it and to be committed to the objectives of an organization.

The directorate has thus not been able to produce the desired impact. It is rather felt that it has proved to be superfluous and the earlier arrangement, when the deputy commissioner had a direct control over the civic bodies and the remaining work could be properly managed from the secretariat itself, was a better one. The Haryana Unit of the BJP had demanded abolition of the directorate in a memorandum submitted by its five-member committee with Mr Ram Lal Wadhawa as Convener, to the Local Self Government Minister, Mr Sampat Singh on 8 September 1988. It may be mentioned that the Directorate of Local Bodies, Haryana, which was bifurcated from Punjab at the time of the reorganization of the states was wound up on 31 December 1968. It was set up again on 1 April 1983 after a lapse of 15 years. In between there had been no directorate to coordinate and control the working of the municipal committees. It would therefore be no surprise if it is abolished again and a demand for the abolition of directorate is put forth in Punjab also sometime.

Financial Control

As discussed earlier, urban local bodies are always at the mercy of the state government in regard to their finances. This financial dependency of local bodies on state government provides an opportunity to the latter to exercise control over the former. The state government also lays down various rules and regulations for the audit and maintenance of accounts. Therefore, it becomes obvious for the funding agency (state government) to ensure that the funds are not misutilized and the guidance regarding audit and accounts are properly followed. All of this necessitates the state control over municipal finance.

Financial control manifests itself in (*a*) regulation of municipal income derived from taxes, fees, loans, and grants; (*b*) regulation of expenditure; (*c*) budget; (*d*) accounting; and (*e*) auditing.

Regulation of Municipal Income

A municipal body can levy taxes, modify and abolish them only with the approval of the state government. The state government can also require a municipal body to levy a tax, rate or fee or exempt a particular class of tax payers from their payment. During emergency, the state government has the power to impose tax at rates to be determined by it even when a municipal body does not want it and does not need it.[47] The Punjab Municipal Corporation Act, 1976, gives a list of taxes which it is obligatory for the corporation to levy and at such rates as may from time to time be specified by the government by notification.[48] And if the corporation fails to impose tax so ordered by the state government, the government is authorized to impose the tax and the order so passed shall operate as if the tax has been duly imposed by the corporation.[49]

The state government awards grants-in-aid to the municipal bodies to enable them to meet their ever growing needs and therefore exercises control over them to ensure that the grants are properly utilized and not misappropriated or diverted to functions other than those for which they were sanctioned. The state government also advances loans to them or allows them to raise these from other financial institutions and stands surety for them. It also determines the rate of interest on loans.[50] The state government ensures that the loans are utilized for the purpose for which they are received, the unspent amount is refunded and these are paid back along with interest as per agreed time schedule.

Regulation of Expenditure

The state government regulates municipal expenditure by fixing limits on expenditure to be incurred on various items, laying down regulations and procedures for incurring expenditures, for example, of inviting tenders or quotations to avail the benefit of market competitive rates on the purchases to be made, requiring the local bodies to obtain administrative and technical sanction from the competent authorities if the work involved exceeds a particular limit of expenditure.

Municipal Budget

Municipal bodies are required to prepare their budgets in the forms prescribed by the state government and get the same approved by it. Sanction of the state government is also required for re-appropriation from one head to another head of the budget. The state government, while approving the budget, has to see that the concerned municipal body has a minimum closing balance and necessary provision for the repayment of loans.

Accounting

Accounting constitutes the main ingredients of a sound financial administration. Mere imposition of taxes does not improve the financial position of the municipal bodies if taxes are not fully realized, the account books are not properly maintained and supervision over collection and expenditure is not exercised. In Punjab, the municipal bodies are required to follow the Punjab Municipal Accounts Code, 1930, which lays down detailed procedures for all sorts of financial transactions. The form and manner in which the accounts are to be maintained are generally prescribed by the Accountant General and any departure from these can be made only with the sanction of the state government.

Auditing

Municipal accounts are subject to annual audit conducted by the Examiner of the Local Fund Accounts to ensure that financial transactions are properly carried out, that amounts to be collected are duly realized and credited and that no amounts are paid without proper authority and provisions of funds in the budget. The audit reports point out irregularities pertaining to non-regularization of expenditure in excess of budgetary provision, non-adjustment of loans raised, non-recovery of taxes, irregular and wasteful expenditure, embezzlement and misappropriation of municipal funds, non-observance of works rules, and the like.

Judicial Control

Judicial control is intended to safeguard the rights of individuals against their encroachment by municipal authorities and those of municipal bodies against infringement by the state government. Judicial control is not only limited to the right of an aggrieved individual to sue a local authority for damages, there are, in addition, remedies available to secure the performance by local authorities of their statutory duties or to restrain them from acting outside their jurisdiction. The remedies available are in the form of various kinds of writs such as injunction, certiorari, prohibition, mandamus, and quo-warranto:

1. Injunction is a writ issued by a court requiring a person or a party to refrain from doing a thing, e.g. the Municipal Committee of Ludhiana was stopped from demolition of a part of building (*Municipal Committee Ludhiana v. M/s S.R. Saini Brothers.* Court Regular appeal No. 1254 of 1968, decided on 22 January 1980).
2. Certiorari enables a superior court to send for the record of the proceedings and orders of a lower court to enquire into its legality and to quash the order if found beyond its jurisdiction.
3. Prohibition is issued by a superior court to an inferior court and also to an authority exercising judicial or quasi-judicial functions for the purpose of preventing it from usurping jurisdiction with which it is not vested.
4. The writ of mandamus is in the nature of a command issued by a court to any person or public body to do something which is a part of their official duty.
5. The writ of quo-warranto can be applied for by any member of the public to challenge the rights of a person to hold a public office and to get him ousted if he has unlawfully usurped or intruded into such office.

Judiciary has the power to interpret laws governing the local government, by-laws and rules made thereunder and declare them *ultra vires* if they contravene the constitution or some provisions of other laws. The courts, however, do not interfere in municipal administration on their own. They intervene only on the initiative of the aggrieved party and when they are satisfied that errors of law, fact finding, jurisdiction and procedure have been committed.

The courts have entertained and decided hundreds of cases relating to the constitution of municipal committees or municipal corporations, election and removal of their members and office bearers, conduct of business, delegation of powers, punishment and dismissal of officers and servants, taxation, supersession, etc.

The judiciary thus plays an important role in providing justice to the aggrieved parties against the arbitrary and unlawful actions of the municipal bodies and the state government. But judicial control is not very effective because, first, the judiciary never takes the initiative, but intervenes only on being approached by the aggrieved citizen or by some one interested in the case, consequently many cases are never brought to the notice of the courts; second, litigation is a very expensive affair which a private citizen of moderate means can ill-afford; third, the judicial process is very lengthy, dilatory, and time consuming and is therefore very discouraging and frustrating for the persons concerned to take recourse to court of law; fourth, municipal acts and the municipal corporation acts of some states bar the jurisdiction of the courts in certain cases.

In order to make the judicial control more effective, necessary reforms need to be brought about in the prevalent judicial system, which is confined to the redress of wrongs already committed and does not provide for preventive justice, which should authorize the courts to define or declare disputed rights and duties before any suit involving them is contested in the courts. Second, the courts have no power to enforce their decisions and they have to depend upon the executive branch of the government to carry them out. Hence, there is need for ensuring complete cooperation of the executive in the execution of the decisions of the courts. Third, special municipal courts exclusively dealing with municipal laws need to be established for speedy disposal of suits. Some municipal bodies have experimented with the institution of municipal magistracy for quick disposal of cases successfully. It is desirable that other big municipal committees and corporations should revive or introduce this system to render speedy justice to the public.

CONCLUSION

The mechanism of control has been inherited from the British Government, which for obvious reasons favoured a restrictive local government in India and therefore had imposed a system of checks resulting in an exceptionally high degree of regulation, control, and interference in the affairs of local government, thereby rendering the local government impoverished and emasculated. But in free India the role of the state government towards grassroots democracy is to be essentially different from what was designed by the alien government. Now the local government is to be recognized as a part of the responsible governmental system of the country and is allowed to play its role as such in the development of the lives of people and the promotion of their welfare. In the words of Ursula Hicks:

> The kind of relationship between central [which means state] and local governments that has to be aimed at, is neither control of local government by central government nor such concurrent powers as would be appropriate for the units of a federation. Rather, the optimal relationship would be a partnership of the active and co-operative members, but with the central government definitely the senior partner.[51]

Similarly, the Taxation Enquiry Commission had observed:

> The state government constituting the representative governing authority in a state has a vital role to play in ensuring the proper functioning of local bodies. It is its responsibility to see that local bodies are efficiently organized, that they perform their functions properly and that they take adequate part in the development of the country. The role of the state government is therefore not merely of a negative aspect *viz.* the prevention of the misuse of powers by local bodies through audit and periodical examination but a positive one, *viz.* active encouragement and development of local bodies. Government control and help should, however, not be so meticulous or minute as to destroy the autonomy or self-reliance of local bodies. The goal of state efforts as well as the purpose of state control should be the development of local self governing institutions into efficient instruments of administration, capable alike of formulating policies and of execution them.[52]

The Punjab Local Government (Urban) Enquiry Committee (1957) had also emphasized that 'the conception of government role must change from that of a controller to that of an adviser, guide and help'.[53] In fact, control should be so designed as to generate respect in the people for their local government and to sustain and enhance the pride of city fathers.[54] In other words, if municipal institutions have to be retained and promoted at the grassroots level, state control has to change from restriction to facilitation.[55]

NOTES AND REFERENCES

1. Shriram Maheshwari, *Local Government in India* (Agra: Laxmi Narain Aggarwal, 1984), p. 35.
2. Mohit Bhattacharya, 'State Control over Municipal Bodies', *Indian Journal of Public Administration*, 22 (1976): 465–71.

3. Mohit Bhattacharya, *State-Municipal Relations* (New Delhi: Indian Institute of Public Administration, 1972), p. 6.
4. Hume and Martin, *The Structure of Local Government Throughout the World* (The Hague: Martimes Nizaff, 1961), p. 2.
5. United Nations, *Decentralization for National and Local Government,* 1962, pp. 5 and 22.
6. Golding, *Local Government* (London: The English Universities Ltd., 1964), p. 43.
7. R.L. Khanna, *Municipal Government and Administration in India* (Chandigarh: Mahindra Capital Publishers, 1976), p. 166.
8. Report of Taxation Enquiry Commission, 1953–54, Vol III, p. 34.
9. M.P. Sharma, *Local Government and Finance in U.P.* (Allahabad: Kitab Mahal, 1954), p. 71.
10. R. Argal, *Municipal Government in India* (Allahabad: Aggarwal Press, 1960), p. 147.
11. P.A. James, 'State Control through Supersession and Dissolution', in S.K. Sharma and V.N. Chawla (eds.), *Municipal Administration in India: Some Reflections* (Jalandhar: International Book Co., 1975), p. 175.
12. Prime Minister Rajiv Gandhi's address to the Sammelan of the members of Panchayati Raj bodies of the North and Western states held at New Delhi on 21–24 January 1989.
13. R.B. Das, 'State Supervision and Control', *Nagarlok* (October–December, 1970): 57. Also refer to Hoshiar Singh, *State Supervision over Municipal Administration—A Case Study of Rajastnan* (New Delhi: Associated Publishers, 1979), p. 3.
14. Article 246 (3) States, 'The Legislature of any state has exclusive power to make laws for such a state or any part thereof with respect to any of the matters enumerated in List-II in the seventh schedule in the Constitution referred to as the state list.'
15. R.K. Gooch, quoted in Anderson, W. (ed.), *Local Government in Europe* (New York: 1939), p. 72.
16. C.A. Cross, *Principles of Local Government Laws* (London: Sweet and Maxwell, 1959), p. 155.
17. Baker Benjamin, *Urban Government* (New Delhi: Affiliated East-West Press Ltd., 1965), p. 329.
18. V.R. Rao, *A Hundred Years of Local Self Government in Assam* (Gauhati: Bani Parkash, 1965), p. 520.
19. P.A. James, 'State Control through Supersession and Dissolution', p. 180.
20. *Ibid.,* p. 182.
21. Mohit Bhattacharya, 'State Control over Municipal Bodies', in T.N. Chaturvedi and Abhijit Datta (eds.), *Local Government* (New Delhi: IIPA, 1984), p. 62.
22. Hoshiar Singh, *State Supervision over Municipal Administration* (New Delhi: Associated Pub. House, 1979), p. 99.
23. Donald B. Rosenthail, *The Limited Elite: Politics and Government in Two Indian Cities* (Chicago: University of Chicago 1970), p. 19.
24. S.R. Maheshwari, *Local Government in India* (Agra: Lakshmi Narain Aggarwal, 1984), p. 287.
25. Report of the Rural-Urban Relationship Committee, 1966, p. 118.
26. Report of the Indian Statutory Commission, para 35.
27. T. Appa Rao, 'State Administrative Control over the Major Municipal Corporations in South India', *Journal of the Society of State Governments* 3 (1970): 20.
28. Ursula K. Hicks, *Development from Below* (Oxford: Clarendon Press, 1961), p. 457.
29. Report of the Rural–Urban Relationship Committee, 1966, p. 118.
30. Partap Singh, 'Supersession of Municipal Committee', *Economic and Political Weekly* (8 April 1972): 747.
31. Venkat Rao, V. 'Control of Municipal Administration in the Madras Presidency', *Quarterly Journal of Local-Self government Institute,* Bombay, 17 (1947): 414.
32. S.R. Maheshwari, *Local Government in India,* p. 287.
33. R.B. Dass (ed.), *Deliberative and Executive Wings in Local Government* (Calcutta: Oxford and IBH Publishing Co., 1968), p. 77.
34. Mohit Bhattacharya, 'State Directorate of Municipal Administration', in T.N. Chaturvedi and Abhijit Datta (eds.), *Local Government* (New Delhi: IIPA, 1984), p. 31.
35. *State Machinery for Municipal Supervision,* Proceedings of the Seminar held at Indian Institute of Public Administration (New Delhi, 7–8 March 1970), p. 51.

36. Gian Parkash, *District Administration and Urban Local Bodies,* p. 583.
37. A. Avasthi, 'The Changing Role of the Collector/Deputy Commissioner', in A. Avasthi and S.N. Verma (ed.), *Aspects of Public Administration* (New Delhi: Allied Publishers, 1964), pp. 84–85.
38. A. Avasthi, 'Role of the Collector in Municipal Administration', *Nagarlok* (April–June, 1970).
39. Report of the Punjab Government (Urban) Enquiry Committee, (1957), pp. 8–9.
40. *Ibid.,* p. 18.
41. Report of the Committee on Augmentation of Financial Resources of Urban Local Bodies, 1963, p. 44.
42. Mohit Bhattacharya, *State Directorates of Municipal Administration* (New Delhi: IIPA, 1969).
43. Report of the Rural–Urban Relationship Committee, Vol. I, 1966, p. 120.
44. Report of the Administrative Reforms Commission (1967), p. 76.
45. Mohit Bhattacharya, 'State Directorates of Municipal Administration', p. 51.
46. *Ibid.*
47. Satya Pal Dang, 'Attack on Powers of Local Bodies', *Mainstream,* 19, no. 26 (February 28, 1991): 207.
48. Punjab Municipal Corporation Act, 1976, Section 90 (1) and (2).
49. *Ibid.,* Section 90 (5).
50. Local Authorities Loan Rules, Punjab, 1927, Rule 11.
51. Ursula K. Hicks, *Development from Below,* p. 437.
52. Report of the Taxation Enquiry Commission, p. 374.
53. Report of the Punjab Local Government (Urban) Enquiry Committee, p. 42.
54. S.R. Maheshwari, *Local Government in India,* p. 384.
55. Mohit Bhattacharya, 'State Directorates of Municipal Administration', p. 14.

Special Purpose Urban Authorities

Urban local governments mainly comprise municipal corporations and municipal councils to administer the local affairs and provide civic amenities for the well-being of the citizens of their respective areas. The former are constituted by the state governments concerned for bigger towns having a minimum population of three lakh and the latter for cities/towns that are not too big. These are periodically elected on the basis of adult franchise and perform the functions assigned to them under the statutes. But there also exist some other urban institutions in the municipal areas that are required to perform some of the municipal functions like improvement and development of the towns, housing, water supply, sewage and pollution control. Such urban institutions are: (*i*) Improvement Trusts, (*ii*) Housing Development Boards including urban estates, (*iii*) Water Supply and Sewerage Boards, and (*iv*) Pollution Control Boards.

These institutions are located in the urban areas and are a mix of single-purpose and multipurpose organizations. A single purpose agency is called as such because it addresses itself to the realization of a single purpose specified in the concerned statute under which it is set up, whereas multi-purpose agencies cater to more than one purpose. Of the above-mentioned urban authorities, the housing board and urban estates for instance can be termed as single purpose authorities, while the other institutions are multipurpose bodies.

Reasons for the Creation of Special Purpose Agencies

The reasons usually advanced for the creation of these urban institutions and specific purpose agencies are that: (*i*) the municipal authorities have neither the necessary administrative machinery nor resources to tackle the problems arising out of rapid urban growth;[1] (*ii*) the rules and by-laws of the municipalities stand in the way of shouldering responsibilities attached to the developmental activities;[2] (*iii*) the municipal corporations and municipal committees are by and large centres of inefficiency, corruption and political nepotism, most of these are bankrupt and cannot in any way tackle big problems;[3] (*iv*) certain activities are so technical and complex that they require concentrated attention and specialized effort, which the municipal bodies are not in a position to afford, already overburdened, as they are, with numerous functions.[4]

In short, the creation of uni- or multi-functional agencies is justified on the plea of the inefficiency of local authorities and their being inadequately equipped to perform these tasks.[5]

The state governments, therefore, have been setting up special authorities to perform functions of a certain type. For example, in Chennai, the state government has set up a number of special purpose authorities like the Slum Clearance Board, the Housing Board and the Madras Metropolitan Development Authority. Uttar Pradesh has a Housing Board and a Water Supply and Drainage Board for the entire state. In Delhi, there is Delhi Development Authority and in Kolkata, there is the Kolkata Development Authority and similarly in Punjab and Haryana, Improvement Trusts, Housing Board, Water Supply and Sewerage Board and Pollution Control Board, etc. have been set up which have been assigned the tasks customarily falling within the sphere of action of municipal governments.

Improvement Trusts

It is the local governments' accepted responsibility to plan for the improvement and development of the areas under their jurisdiction, but with the tremendous increase in the growth of urban areas, as a result of rapid urbanization, being too pre-occupied with the maintenance of civic services and lacking adequate financial resources and necessary technical personnel, it has been felt that they are incapable of meeting the challenges of planning and execution of major urban development projects and therefore the task of improvement and development has to be entrusted to a separate agency such as Important Trusts.

The agency charged with the responsibility of improvement of cities and towns was first created in India in 1864 and it bore the name of the Sanitary Commission. In that year sanitary commissions were set up in Bengal, Bombay and Madras as a response to the recommendations of the Royal Sanitary Commission, which had been appointed in 1859 to give advice and assistance in all matters relating to public health and sanitation, to advise on the sanitary improvement of native towns and on prevention and mitigation of epidemic diseases. Bombay Improvement Trust was the first to be established, in 1898, when the outbreak of bubonic plague in 1896 had compelled the government to adopt measures for the removal of unsanitary dwellings, prevention of over-crowding and carrying out much needed sanitary improvements in the city with a view to securing better living conditions for the people. The Calcutta Improvement Trust was set up in 1912. Encouraged by the examples of Bombay and Calcutta Improvement Trusts, other provinces also began setting up such agencies. The Punjab Town Improvement Act was passed in 1922, but it could not be given effect to until 1936 when the first Improvement Trust was created at Lahore, then Capital of joint Punjab. At present Punjab and Haryana have 21 and 11 improvement trusts, respectively.

Constitution

An improvement trust comprises a chairman and officers appointed by the state government and representatives of concerned municipal body. The improvement trusts in Punjab, for instance, consist of a chairman, three officers serving under the state government, one of whom should be a town planner, the other an officer not below the rank of an extra assistant commissioner and the third an engineer not below the rank of an executive engineer taken from the Buildings and Roads Branch or the Public Health Branch of the Department of Public Works of the state government, three members of the municipal committee or the corporation as the case may be, and three persons, one of whom should be a member of the scheduled caste, all to be appointed by the government. The chairman and the members are appointed for a renewable term of two years. The higher personnel of the Trust belonging to the provincialized services of the Improvement Trusts are recruited and controlled by the state government whereas the lower employees are recruited and controlled by the trust.

Functions

An improvement trust is a statutory body constituted for the specific purpose of city improvement. Its functions include improvement and expansion of the city, opening up of the congested areas, provision of open spaces for purposes of ventilation and sanitation, improving building sites, laying out or altering of streets, re-housing for poor and working classes, acquisition of land to re-house persons displaced by execution of schemes, control of speculation in land, particularly of sub-urban one.

Finances

Sources of revenue of the improvement trusts are sale of land, share of stamp duty on transfer of immovable property, betterment fees, contributions by municipal committee or corporation, borrowing and grants-in-aid by the state government.

Criticism

Improvement trusts, are criticized mainly on the following grounds:

1. Their setting up for the performance of municipal functions, and being dominated by bureaucrats is nothing short of an assault on the philosophy of local government.
2. There is no *prima facie* case for constituting adhoc bodies for the execution of town planning and improvement schemes, though there is a great deal to be said for the government exercising a certain measure of control over the preparation and execution of schemes for improvement and development and to maintain a separate development fund and to distinguish clearly between its capital and revenue accounts. Yet there is no necessity for creating a semi-officials body for carrying out the schemes of improvement.[6]
3. A committee of the municipal council can, with the assistance of a few co-opted engineering, public health and financial experts, be trusted to do work as efficiently as any adhoc body especially constituted for the purpose.
4. In the eyes of the local government, a special purpose agency like the improvement trust, which takes away one of its functions and, what is more, which is financed in part by it, carries the image of a trespasser.[7]
5. In the words of Rural–Urban Relationship Committee, it has been gradually realized that Improvement Trusts engaged in town improvement in a limited piecemeal and haphazard way, without attempting to conceive the overall plan and development requirements of the city in the regional context cannot meet the requirement of town planning and development.[8]
6. They have not proved successful as they were functioning more or less as colonizers for new areas without caring for the core areas and the impact of their schemes on the services in the city as a whole.
7. They lacked long-term perspective and had reduced themselves to a position of a 'department concerned with constructing housing colonies without ensuring adequate provision of civic and social services for the new areas.'[9] It is a mistake to style Improvement Trusts as local bodies because they lack the characteristics of a local body, which are, first, that they are composed of representatives elected by the local people, and second, that they undertake the programmes and determine their priorities on the basis of the felt needs of the citizens.
8. The improvement trusts on the other hand are stuffed with politicians and bureaucrats nominated by the government, accountable to none but the government.

9. Financially, too, they are not viable. They do not have adequate financial resources to undertake development projects and have to resort to borrowings which they are not in a position to pay back on time inviting penal interest.
10. Their image with the public has been that of poor performance because of allotment of residential and commercial sites on concessional rates out of their discretionary quota by the ministers to their favourites, time-consuming process in the allotment of plots and inordinate delay in delivering their possession to the allottees, non-development of the concerned areas for years on end, exorbitant prices as compared to the compensation paid for the acquisition of land, red tapism, inefficiency, and, above all, rampant corruption.
11. The relationship between the representatives of the municipal committee or corporation and the bureaucrats as members of the improvement trusts has been that of alienation and hostility as the former believe that their rights have been usurped by the latter.

The remedy for this malady could be found in the merger of the improvement trust with the concerned city corporations and their amalgamation with the housing board in the case of other towns, as the aims and objects of both the organizations are more or less similar.[10]

A provision to this effect exists in the Punjab Housing Development Board Act, 1972 which reads: 'The state government may be notification abolish an improvement trust from such date as may be specified in the notification and all its assets and liabilities shall stand transferred to and vested in the Board.' The Act further provides that even during its existence, if so directed by the state government, the improvement trusts may function as agents of the Board in respect of any scheme and shall for the execution of the scheme, work under the direction and control of the Board. Alternatively, the state government may dissolve the improvement trust and consequently all properties, funds and dues which are vested in or realizable by the trust and the chairman, respectively, shall vest in and be realizable by the municipal committee of the town concerned and all liabilities which are enforceable against the trust shall be enforceable only against the concerned municipal committee. Accordingly, the improvement trusts had been or are being abolished or transferred into the new development authorities. For instance, the Bombay Improvement Trust was abolished in 1937 and its function devolved on the corporation itself. Similarly, the Madras Improvement Trust was amalgamated in 1958 with the Housing Board, which had been formed in Tamil Nadu in 1956. The Kanpur Improvement Trust was replaced by the Kanpur Development Board in 1945 and with the establishment of Nagar Mahapalikas (municipal corporations) in KAVAL cities in 1959, this Board and the improvement trusts in Kanpur, Allahabad, Varanasi, Agra, and Lucknow were altogether abolished. The concerned municipal corporations are now empowered to perform planning and development functions.

Housing Development Boards

Housing is a basic human right and necessity and providing reasonable shelter to all is a global problem. In the words of Javier Perezde Cuellar, former UN Secretary General:

> Homelessness was a growing global problem affecting the rich and poor countries. If unsolved the problem poses a threat, both immediate and long term to the welfare of the peoples and development proposals of the international community as a whole, in most of the developing countries we see the twin forces of rapid population growth and increasing urban poverty converging into a crisis which may assume monumental proportions in the coming decades. Only action now, concerted, bold and imaginative, can help relieve the current pressure and avert the future shock. Let us bear in mind that a society is judged not so much by the standard attained by its most affluent and privileged members as by the quality of life which it is able to assure for its weakest citizens."[11]

Even the most developed countries like the USA and USSR are facing a shortage of housing stock. The problem of homelessness also exists in the most affluent country, Canada, where the homeless have been demonstrating for homes. A fraction of the people in such affluent communities is forced to live in ghettoes because possessing a decent house is beyond their means. The situation in the Third World countries is more alarming.

Position in India

1. In India, nearly two-thirds of the population lives below the poverty line and more than one million are shelterless. From nine million units in 1951, the shortage of housing stock in India had increased to about 25 million in 1985. In 1971, about 10.4 million units were identified as unserviceable dwellings but these are still being used by those who cannot afford alternative accommodation.[12]
2. Another distressing factor is the existence of slums in sub-human conditions, where there is no provision for drinking water or toilets, and other basic amenities are also pathetically lacking. The First Five Year Plan stressed the need for slums clearance but later it was observed that slum-dwellers did not prefer better housing because of non-availability of employment at or near the new housing location. That is why emphasis has now been shifted from relocation and removal of slums to upgradation of slums.
3. There is also a need to build houses which are less costly and suited to our economic environment.
4. Finding funds is an important factor of housing policies. Investment in housing involves both public and private institutions. The existing agencies like HUDCO and LIC are, therefore, being strengthened, and housing cooperatives and building societies are being encouraged to accelerate building activity because providing shelter to all requires massive efforts on the part of government, housing finance bodies, cooperative and private builders.
5. United Nations had declared 1987 as 'International Year of Shelter for the Homeless' and reminded and warned the nations that any inertia in this regard can create an alarming situation threatening social and political stability. Late Rajiv Gandhi, former Prime Minister of India was seized of the problem and had observed: 'We have always laid special emphasis on the provision of housing for the poor. The new 20-Point Programme (1986) lays particular emphasis on housing for the poor people along with provisions of basic facilities.'[13] In the words of Ms Mohsina Kidwai, former Minister of Urban Development, Government of India, 'Housing is high on our list of priorities. The magnitude of the problem would need innovative strategies, mobilization and utilization of resources. The government of India has set up a National Housing Bank with initial capital outlay of Rs 100 crore (1987–88) to facilitate availability of housing finance.'[14]

For meeting the growing demand for housing, the Planning Commission in the First Five Year Plan had recommended the setting up by the central government, of agencies to subsidize construction of houses and the central government had, in turn, stressed on the setting up of housing boards at the state level also. Accordingly, the Government of India had established Housing and Urban Development Corporation (HUDCO) in 1971 with the prime objective of providing shelter to the poor. Up to 1988, it had promoted over 2.5 million housing units in the country, over 90 per cent of which were for the economically weaker sections and low income groups. These achievements though impressive in themselves are insignificant in relation to the magnitude of the problem being faced by the poor in the country. The achievements of HUDCO in real terms have been: (*i*) creating awareness and sharing experiences about the complex nature of the shelter problems and their solution, (*ii*) improving availability of sites and promoting self-built affordable housing related to the needs and life style of the people, (*iii*) supporting projects through a financing system favouring the poor, (*iv*) promoting the use of traditional low cost building technologies and their improvement, and (*v*) evaluating projects to study their replicability and consolidating these into policies and programmes.[15] HUDCO also took the major initiative of establishing its Human Settlement Management Institute where experiences are shared, problems researched, results documented and information disseminated.

Housing Development Boards in the States

The housing development boards in various states are constituted by the state government concerned under specific Acts passed by its legislature. Their constitution, powers and functions follow more or less the same pattern. The Housing Development Board in the state of Punjab is discussed as an instance representative of housing boards in other states.

To undertake the housing programme systematically, the Punjab Housing Development Board was set up on 9 May 1983. The Board is an autonomous body subject to general control by the state government. It consists of a Chairman and three whole time nominated members: (*i*) Housing Commissioner, five *ex-officio* members, namely Secretary Housing and Urban Development Department (if he is not appointed as Chairman), Secretary Finance Department, Secretary, Local Government Department, Chief Town Planner, and Chief Engineer, Public Health and not more than five persons from amongst those persons who have wide experience in Housing and Urban Development to be nominated as part-time members. At least one of the nominated whole time members should be a member of scheduled castes while at least two of the non-official part-time members should be members of the scheduled castes or backward classes. The Punjab Housing Development Board (Conditions of Service of Chairman and Members) Rules, 1973, provide for the qualifications and other service conditions of the Chairman and members of the Board.

All citizens of India except those owning a house or a plot in colonies established by Punjab Housing Development Board, urban estates, improvement trusts, or private colonies registered under the Colonies Act in the urban area of Punjab or Chandigarh are eligible for registration with the Board for the purchase of a house. The Board constructs houses of various categories for different income groups, viz., economically weaker sections (EWS), low income group (LIG), middle income group (MIG) (Lower), middle income group (MIG) (Middle), and middle income group (MIG) (Higher), and higher income group (HIG), and allots the houses to the registered persons by drawing lots.

There is however a provision for reservation of houses for different categories (except for ESW and LIG houses) such as Scheduled Castes or Scheduled Tribes (8 per cent). Defence personnel including BSF/GREF (5 per cent), widows of defence personnel and BSF personnel belonging to and settled in Punjab (2 per cent), employees of Punjab Housing Development Board (2 per cent), retired police personnel (2 per cent), police personnel (5 per cent), discretionary quota of the Minister for Housing (5 per cent), discretionary quota of Secretary, Local Government, Housing and Urban Development (1 per cent), discretionary quota of the Board for hard deserving cases (5 per cent), inter-caste married couples (0.5 per cent), blind and physically handicapped persons (1.5 per cent), Indians settled abroad or those returned to India permanently who can pay full money in lump sum in foreign exchange (3 per cent), employees of Punjab Government/Government of India domiciled in Punjab including retired state government or Government of India employees (2 per cent), freedom fighters discretionary quota (2 per cent), couples undergoing terminal operation (2 per cent), terrorists victims (4 per cent), and general (50 per cent).

While there may be justification for reservation for different categories, the discretionary quota of the minister and the bureaucrat (Secretary to Local Government) has been criticized for its having been misused on political and nepotism considerations resulting in the cancellation of the allotment of houses when challenged in courts of law. This reservation therefore needs to be done away with. Since its inception, the Board has made great strides in ameliorating the housing problems of the people from all walks of society, particularly the poor, by providing shelter to them.

By and large, the Board adopts the low cost techniques and new innovations evolved by various research organizations of India such as CBRI and NBD. In addition, great emphasis is laid on proper quality control to ensure construction in accordance with the prescribed specifications and as per time schedule.

Numerous house building cooperative societies are also engaged in house building activities such as HOUSEFED (The Punjab State Federation of Cooperative House Building Societies Ltd) instituted in 1970.

Urban Estates

To meet the shortage of housing in the state, Directorate of Housing and Urban Development in various states including Punjab and Haryana have set up urban estates in some select fast growing cities and towns wherein residential plots are offered to the public at reasonable rates. The estates have been provided with modern amenities such as metalled roads, street lighting, drinking water supply, drainage, sewerage, parks and open places and beautified with ornamental trees, and shrubs planted along the roads. There is, therefore, a big demand for residential plots in them. Consequently, the Directorates do not only undertake the expansion of the existing urban estates, but also set up new urban estates from year to year to satisfy this demand.

The construction of buildings in the urban estates in various states is regulated under the respective Urban Estates (Development and Regulation) Acts, and the rules framed thereunder. No plot holder is authorized to construct his house in an urban estate without getting the plans approved by the Estate Office.

Other Steps Taken for Provision of Houses

1. To boost the construction activity in the Urban Estates, loans are advanced to the plot-holders for the construction of houses.
2. Under the subsidized Industrial Housing Scheme, houses are constructed for allotment to the eligible industrial workers.
3. The cooperative and the employer sectors are given financial assistance for the construction of houses in the form of loan and subsidy.
4. Under the Low Income Group Housing Scheme, loans are advanced to individuals as well as the cooperative societies.
5. Houses are also constructed under Crash Housing Scheme for allotment to the government employees posted at the district or tehsil and other places. The shortage of houses has given rise to high rents. which the employees with fixed income find very difficult to pay. The houses constructed by government are allotted to various categories of employees and 10 per cent of the pay is charged as rent, which is very nominal as compared to the rent prevailing in the market.
6. Various central and state government departments, public undertakings and industrial concerns also provide houses to their employees in their respective housing colonies such as Defence, Central Excise, Posts and Telegraph, Railway, Power, LIC, Bank, and Police.

The housing facilities provided so far touch only a tip of the iceberg. Building activities, therefore, need to be accelerated at the top speed to meet existing and growing demand for houses by availing of the institutional finance facilities provided by National Housing Bank, nationalized banks, Life Insurance Corporation, Housefed, Unit Trust of India, public sector organizations, and the private sector.

Conclusion

The main function of the three institutions, viz. improvement trusts, housing board and urban estate is to provide more houses to meet the shortage of the households. Moreover, their pattern of functioning is also similar. It is, therefore, felt that in order to avoid duplication or triplication of institutions for the performance of the same function which involves unavoidable heavy expenses on establishment and other paraphernalia including equipment, etc. it would be better if by merger of all of these institutions a single agency is created for housing purposes. Among other things such a step will solve the problems of acquisition of land, raising of funds, etc. and render the process of house building easier, economical and speedier. The Punjab Government accordingly merged urban estates with the housing board in May 1991 transferring all its assets and liabilities to the latter, notwithstanding the protests of the employees of the urban estates against such a move as they felt that their careers would be jeopardized.

The Water Supply and Sewerage Boards

The obligatory functions of municipal bodies *inter alia* include the provision of two essential basic amenities, potable water supply and efficient system of waste water disposal for the protection and promotion of health of people in their urban areas. These functions have been carried out generally by the state public works department (Public Health Department) out of funds made available by the local bodies partly from their own sources and partly by raising loans and grants from the state government. It is regrettable that after more than 60 years of Independence, the people in urban areas were either not being served with safe potable water supply or even if they were having some kind of water supply, it did not provide them with adequate quantities essentially required. The conditions on the sanitation front were even worse. In spite of sincere efforts on the part of the state governments, the most inhuman practice of carrying night-soil as head-loads by a section of society still continued. The governments, therefore, realized that unless an autonomous agency is set up it may be impossible to improve and provide safe drinking water supply to the entire urban population in their respective states as also to provide safe and satisfactory methods of disposal of human wastes and thus to raise not only the health standards but also the living standards of the urban population. Accordingly, the Water Supply and Sewerage Boards have been set up in various states including Punjab and Haryana to make a breakthrough in this rather vital field where very little progress had been achieved earlier.

The Board is constituted in terms of the legislation enacted by the state legislature concerned. It consists of a chairman and directors, generally secretaries to the government, Local Government Department, Health and Family Welfare Department, Public Works Department (Public Health); a director of the Local Government Department; a chief engineer of the Public Works Department (Public Health branch), and its managing director.

The board plans and formulates water supply and sewerage projects and carries out their implementation by arranging institutional finance both from within and outside the country from agencies like the International Development Authority (World Bank), Life Insurance Corporation (LIC), and the Housing and Urban Development Corporation (HUDCO), etc. The board's endeavour is to cover maximum cities and towns under their schemes of potable water supply and underground sewerage depending on the financial resources available for the extension of the schemes.

The Agriculture Ministry, Government of India, had floated a very comprehensive programme for development and utilization of organic manurial resources within the country during the Fifth Five Year Plan with the twin purposes of increasing food production and to prevent pollution of underground water, rivers and streams due to dangerous industrial and human wastes. The Government of India used to meet one-third of the estimated cost of the scheme as central subsidy. The Punjab Water Supply and Sewerage Board had prepared 61 sewage and sullage utilization schemes at a total cost of Rs 3.45 crore and got them sanctioned from Government of India with a total central subsidy of Rs 1.15 crore, and led all the states in the country in this respect. The Government of India had since transferred the sewage and sullage utilization schemes to the state governments which had agreed to finance the ongoing schemes. In addition, the board has also been carrying out water supply and sewage works in towns other than those covered under IDA, LIC and HUDCO projects according to the deposit of funds by various local bodies.

The demand for water supply and sewerage connections has been increasing over the years with the awareness on the part of the people to avail of these basic facilities. But the boards have not been able to cope with the growing demand due to not only financial scarcity but also their organizational and functional weaknesses and deficiencies which may be discussed below, taking the Punjab Board as representative of boards in other states.

Weaknesses and Deficiencies of the Water Supply and Sewerage Boards

1. The boards suffer from paucity of funds. They depend upon the various funding agencies for the supply of funds by way of aid and loan which may not be available continuously. Therefore, as soon as one installment of funds is exhausted they have to discontinue their operations and take them up only when the next installment is received. In the meantime, the staff has to be retrenched resulting in their frustration and agitation; and great inconveniences to the residents of the city or town concerned due to incompletion of the works which sometimes remain partially completed due to non-availability of funds. The Punjab Board, for example, had almost completed the IDA projects about three years ago and it was trying to keep itself going by getting the second development phase with the World Bank aid and also getting the transfer of water supply and sewerage work from all the municipal bodies to itself to ensure regular flow of money supply. According to the chairman of the Board, an ambitious Rs 600 crore project was on the anvil for bringing rural areas of the state under the umbrella of sewerage and water supply for which the government was approaching the centre for World Bank aid and loan from the LIC and HUDCO. A total sum of Rs 1,200 crore was required for covering all the towns of the state under the sewerage and water supply projects. If both these projects were put into operation in due course of time, the Board would have its hands full.

2. In addition to the inadequacies of finances, the boards have been a target of criticism for their imperfect administrative organization due to two separate sets of personnel, persons on deputations and the Board's own employees, procedural improprieties and malpractices resulting in bad performance and corruption charges. The boards are not provided with technical staff of their own at the time of their inception. For instance, three circles of the Public Works Department (Public Health) were turned over to Punjab Board and eight executive engineers and 30 assistant engineers were drafted on deputation from the Public Health Department to the Board along with the subordinate staff. The Board made its first expansion two years later by opening three additional circles and recruiting a few assistant engineers and the clerical staff. About 60 per cent of the Board's 3,500 employees were on deputation from the Public Works Department (Public Health) and the rest were direct recruits. The usual tug of war goes on between the persons on deputation and the regular employees of the Board which is detrimental to the efficiency of the Board.

3. The boards are charged with other derelictions of their duties also. For instance, water closets are installed at several sites where houses have not even been built. In a bid to make the most of the job assigned to them, the contractors give connections indiscriminately.

4. Although the economically weaker house owners are to be provided with a sewer connection on a deferred payment basis, all categories of people including income tax assessees and gazetted officers take advantage of the scheme. In many cases, house owners are never told that they would be required to pay the cost of the connection in installments. They are simply made to sign a form which is filled in by the contractors in most cases.

5. The boards do not fix the monthly sewer service charges on some rational basis and decide these to be equivalent to the drinking water supply charges retrospectively, with the result that house owners are confronted with heavy arrears of sewerage charges which they are unable to pay in a lump sum. Such absurd decisions of the boards are challenged in courts which rescind them and the boards have to suffer heavy financial losses.

6. The water supply is erratic, irregular and undependable due to the inadequacy of water reservoirs and the frequent failure of electricity required to energize the tube-wells. The residents other than those of ground floors sometimes do not get water supply the whole day and even those living on the ground floors complain about non-supply of water when taps go dry due to breakdown of electricity. The remedy lies in providing alternate source of power by installation of generators for uninterrupted energization of tube-wells.

7. The sewerage works executed by the boards are of poor quality resulting in their breakdown which do not only cause health hazards but require massive financial investments to repair them and sometimes to reconstruct them.

8. The boards have earned notoriety for corruption. In some places the citizens have been obliged to approach the state governments to institute enquiries by the Central Bureau of Investigation (CBI) into scandals involving embezzlement of money of the boards and that of the municipal bodies. The corruption has assumed such high proportion that even the employees of some of the boards themselves have submitted a memorandum against the corrupt practices of the boards especially of their chairmen and offered to provide vital information in this regard and asked for a high level enquiry into the functioning of the chairmen and their removal.

In conclusion, it may be observed that the performance of the water supply and sewerage boards has not been up to the mark. That is why some states have been considering about their abolition. But it is hard to find some other organization as their substitute. The best way is to revamp their organization and functioning and not to let them starve of funds so that they could meet the most essential water supply and sewerage disposal needs of the urban and rural populations of the country.

Pollution Control Boards

Pollution caused by water, air and noise constitutes one of the greatest challenges to urban governments. The central government Water (Prevention and Control of Pollution) Act, 1974 defines 'Pollution of water as such contamination of water or such alteration of the physical, chemical or biological properties of water of such discharge of any sewage or trade effluent or of any other liquid, gaseous or solid substance into water (whether directly or indirectly) as may, or is likely to create a nuisance or render such water harmful or injurious to public health or safety or to domestic, commercial, industrial, agricultural or other legitimate uses, or to the life and health of animals or plants or of aquatic organism.' The Central Government Air (Prevention and Control of Pollution) Act, 1981, defines air pollution as any solid, liquid or gaseous substance present in the atmosphere in such concentration as may be or tend to be injurious to human beings or other living creatures or plants or property or environment.

Rapid urbanization and industrialization have resulted in the deterioration of the environment. The technological and industrial revolution, though providing immense benefits and prosperity to mankind, has brought in its wake the colossal problems of pollution, which constitutes a grave threat to the very survival of the human race and civilization. Pollution by industry alone through the smoke it emits and the liquid effluent it generates causes incalculable damage to the environment and health of people.

Environment and its pollution has been the concern of the entire world, and as a manifestation thereof, an international conference on environment was organized at Stockholm in June 1972 under the auspices of United Nations, in which India had also participated. Decisions were taken to take appropriate steps for the preservation of natural resources. The Government of India, in order to implement these decisions, enacted the Water (Prevention and Control of Pollution) Act, 1974, and the Air (Prevention and Control of Pollution) Act, 1981. It was felt that there should be an integrated approach for tackling environment problems relating to pollution. It was, therefore, proposed that the central board for the prevention and control of water pollution constituted under the former Act would also perform the functions of the Central Board for the Prevention and Control of Air Pollution. These acts also provided for the constitution of the state boards for the prevention and control of water pollution, and state boards for the prevention and control of air pollution. Accordingly, various states such as Punjab and Haryana had constituted boards for the prevention and control of water pollution which are subsequently also authorized to exercise the powers and functions of the State Board for Prevention and Control of Air Pollution. Punjab had, for example, constituted the board for the prevention and control of water pollution by an enactment of the state legislature on 30 July 1985, and vested it with the powers and functions of the board for prevention and control of air pollution from 15 May 1986.

The boards generally consist of a chairman (having special knowledge or practical experience in respect of matters relating to environmental protection), two officials to represent the government, three members from amongst the members of the local authorities, two persons to represent the interests of agriculture, fishery, industry, trade, or any other interest which in the opinion of the state governments ought to be represented, and two persons to represent the companies or corporations owned, controlled, or managed by the state governments. All these persons are nominated by the governments for three years. The governments also appoint a full time member-secretary of the board. The boards may also associate any person whose assistance or advice they may desire to obtain in performing any of their functions but he or she will not have a right to vote. The state governments may remove any member of the board before the expiry of his term of office, after giving him a reasonable opportunity to show cause why he should not be removed. And it may also supersede the board for a period not exceeding one year after giving it a reasonable opportunity if it feels that the board has persistently made default in the performance of its functions, or that circumstances exist which render it necessary in the public interest to supersede it.

The main functions of the board are to plan a comprehensive programme for the prevention and control of pollution in the state and to secure the execution thereof; to encourage, conduct, and participate in investigations and research relating to problems of pollution, to collaborate with the central Board in organizing the training of persons engaged in programmes relating to pollution and to organize mass education programmes relating to pollution.

In addition to these functions, the boards may establish or recognize a laboratory or laboratories for the analysis of samples of water or of any sewage or trade effluent; inspect air pollution control areas at such intervals as it may think necessary, assess the quality of air therein and take steps for the prevention and control of air pollution in such areas, lay down standard for emission of it pollutants into the atmosphere from industrial plants and automobiles or for the discharge of any air pollutant into the atmosphere from any other source whatsoever not being a ship or an aircraft.

The boards have their own funds comprising the sums which may, from time to time, be paid to them by the state government concerned and other receipts by way of gifts, grants, donations, benefactions, fees, fines, etc. The central government levies and collects a cess from every person carrying on any specified industry, and from every local authority, calculated on the basis of the water consumed. The proceeds of the cess are credited to the Consolidated Fund of India and the central government by appropriation made by law, pays to the central board and every state board from out of such proceeds, with regard to the amount of cess collected by the state government concerned.

Urbanization is taking its toll in almost every city. The cities which were once called 'city of gardens' and considered to be the cleanest cities have lost that claim. The gardens have been devoured by residential and commercial activities. III-planned and ribbon growth on the outskirts and congestion in the old cities have put a great strain on the public services and created major ecological hazards. Lack of proper and adequate collection, and treatment and disposal system of the cities wastes have aggravated the pollution problem. The boards have been persuading the concerned municipal bodies to treat the sewage before letting it on the land for irrigation, so that it is not a health hazard for residents of the city eating vegetables grown with it.

One of the major causes of air pollution in the cities is the exhaust fumes from the automobile traffic. Monitoring carried out by the Boards have revealed 80 to 85 per cent of the buses and 40 to 45 per cent of other vehicles plying in the cities emit gases beyond permissible limits. The boards have, therefore, requested the state transport commissioners to amend the motor vehicles rules in order to control these emissions. The boards also propose to install an air quality monitoring station in various cities to continuously monitor the quality of air.

With increased industrialization, the menace of pollution is assuming alarming proportions in industrial cities and towns. Ludhiana, the industrial capital of Punjab has come to be described as the most polluted city in the state. The atmosphere there has already got polluted 200 per cent to 300 per cent above the norms laid down by the Central Pollution Control Board. Here the skyline is characterized by dark blast smoke emitted by chimneys. The roads are almost choked with traffic and there are frequent traffic blocks. The location of railway station and the loco-shed in the heart of the city has added to the serious problem of pollution. It is feared that the incidence of high blood pressure, respiratory and eye diseases, tuberculosis, and cancer will rise in the city if effective steps are not taken to check industrial pollution.

Due to the efforts of the Pollution Control Board, the problem is being tackled in various ways. Some industrial units have been persuaded to modify their processes to minimize pollution; some industries have installed gravity separation chimneys to arrest particulate matter; those industries which were major users of rice husk have improved their furnaces with better efficiency furnaces; other major industries have substituted their old boilers with new ones based on efficient suspension burning. But much more needs to be done to combat the evil of pollution.

It is felt that pollution control systems are not within the means of small units and therefore a new system needs to be developed keeping in view the constraints of such units. In view of the magnitude of the problems, realistic steps need to be taken by the government and municipal bodies. It should be obligatory on the part of the municipal bodies to install treatment plants for industrial effluents. Municipal corporations are criticized for not discharging their duties in spite of the fact that they collect crores of rupees from the industrial sector in form of taxes. It is alleged that the pollution control boards are interested only in the prosecution of industrialists, and they do not come forward in helping the industrial sector in installing pollution control devices.

Anyhow, it has to be realized that the task of rehabilitation and preservation of environment is stupendous. It cannot be left to the pollution control boards or government agencies alone. It is for the people of every city to resist unplanned growth and pollution activities in their respective cities and to restore them the glory they deserve. In some of the cities environment societies have been set up for creating awareness about environment among the citizens by organizing essay competitions, declamation contests, exhibitions, etc. and formulating plans for the maintenance of neglected parts and round-abouts by involving youths.

CONCLUSION

A study of the various urban institutions entrusted with municipal functions attempted above clearly brings to light the following:

1. The functions assigned to them are overlapping, as for instance, housing development is the task of three agencies, viz. urban states, the housing board and the improvement trusts, without any perceivable coordination among them. There is thus a strong case for amalgamating these agencies into one or restricting this activity exclusively to one agency only. Similarly, the functions of town development are vested both in the municipal bodies and improvement trusts and provision of water supply and sewerage have been entrusted both to municipal bodies and the improvement trusts who, in turn, are the clientele of the Water Supply and Sewerage Board, which could perhaps render better services if it were to prepare and execute schemes for the entire areas of concerned cities instead of taking them up piecemeal as is inevitable under two separate jurisdictions. In the same way, environment improvement is the responsibility of the concerned municipal body, the Pollution Control Board and the Sewerage Board but the supply of water and the disposal of the sewerage is that of municipal body concerned. And since the operations of these are seldom synchronized, the citizens have to suffer.
2. The creation of these agencies has diffused and disintegrated the system of urban local government and lowered its prestige and significance.
3. The citizens have been put to a lot of inconvenience for getting their various needs fulfilled by approaching multiple organizations.
4. The multiplicity of organizations has diluted the responsibility of each and it has become difficult to fix responsibility for the lapses and failures in the performance of local tasks which are obviously interlinked.
5. These agencies, composed of bureaucrats as they are, are not amenable to popular control and are therefore responsible for negation of local democracy.
6. The municipal bodies which contribute to the budget of these agencies have no control over them or their policies.
7. These agencies suffer from paucity of funds (some of them are even bankrupt) and therefore unable to adequately perform their tasks.

The question of the continuity of these agencies therefore needs serious consideration. There can be three alternatives in deciding their future; first, they should be abolished and merged with the concerned municipal body as has been done in Uttar Pradesh, Delhi, and other states as mentioned earlier, and their finances should consequently be restored to the municipal bodies which would naturally be strengthened with requisite financial resources and technical expertise to perform their tasks; second, all these organizations should be put under the unified administrative control of the city council to achieve coordination in their working, and lastly, an urban development authority should be set up in the concerned state to ensure better coordination among various agencies involved in urban development as well as to raise more institutional finances. Accordingly Haryana had set up Haryana Urban Development Authority (HUDA) in 1971 and Punjab also set up Punjab Urban Development Authority (PUDA) in 1995.

NOTES AND REFERENCES

1. D.S. Chaudhary, *Municipal Administration in Rajasthan* (Jaipur: Romesh Book Dept, 1970), p. 135.
2. R.K. Khanna, *Municipal Government and Administration in India* (Chandigarh Mahindra Capital Publishers, 1967), p. 98.

3. Ashish Bose, *Studies in India's Urbanisation* (New Delhi: Tata MacGraw Hill, 1973), p. 252.
4. K.K. Puri, An Analytical Study of Improvement Trusts in Punjab, unpublished PhD thesis, Punjabi University, Patiala, 1980.
5. 'Report of Committee on Budgetary Reform in Municipal Administration', Government of India, Ministry of Works and Housing, 1974, p. 13.
6. Gyan Chand, *Local Finance in India* (Allahabad: 1947), p. 239.
7. S.R. Maheshwari, *Local Government in India,* p. 219.
8. Report of the Rural–Urban Relationship Committee, p. 50.
9. Report of the Committee on Budgetary Reform, p. 15.
10. First Five Year Plan, Government of India, Planning Commission, 1952, pp. 609–11.
11. U.N. Secretary General's New Year's Message on 1 January 1987.
12. Francis Cherunilan and Odeyar D. Beggade, *Housing in India* (Bombay: Himalya Publishing, 1987).
13. Rajiv Gandhi in his message on the occasion of the 'International Year of Shelter for the Homeless', 18 May 1987.
14. Mohsina Kidwai, Minister for Urban Development, Government of India, in her message on IYSH, 87, 18 May 1987.
15. Statement of S.K. Sharma, Chairman and Managing Director, HUDCO, dated 21 May 1987.

Urban (Town) Planning

The process of urbanization in our country is going on at an accelerated pace. The urban population, which was 5 crores in 1947, has increased to 28.5 crores according to the 2001 census, and the number of cities with a population of more than one million (ten lakhs) has gone up from 12 in 1981 to 40 in the year 2001. During 1990, the 218 Class-I cities (with a population of more than one lakh) accounted for more than 60 per cent of the total urban population of the country. Out of 20 crore of the urban population, 12 crore lived in Class-I cities and 5 crores 60 lakhs in metropolitan cities. The unprecedented population pressure caused by population explosion and migration of people from rural to urban areas has resulted in unplanned and haphazard growth of cities. Our urban physical structure is characterized by irrational land-use dispositions, inefficient land development and utilization, acute housing shortages, and above all, environmental degradation. While the smaller urban centres remain impoverished and unable to provide even a minimum level of infrastructure and services, the larger ones suffer from acute inadequacy of services and distribution creating zones of extreme urban deprivation. They face the challenges of inadequate feeding, educating, housing, and employing a large and rapidly growing number of under-nourished, semi-literate, semi-skilled, under-employed, and impoverished city dwellers, living on pavements, in poorly serviced chawls, in unhygienic slums, in illegal squatters' colonies, and in other forms of degraded and inadequate settlements.[1]

All these maladies of urbanization and urban growth can be attributed to the lack of urban planning which has to be resorted to earnestly in appropriate measures in pursuance of the urban policies and programmes of the central and state governments in order to have planned growth of our cities and towns to make them liveable places.

Definitions of Urban (Town) Planning

Urban planning, or town planning, as it is popularly termed in our country, is concerned with spatial development of urban settlements—the use and development of land. The concept and practice of modern town planning has its origin in Britain, where urbanization in the wake of industrialization process started in 1801 and led to rapid and haphazard growth of urban areas in the latter part of the nineteenth century; to combat this, the British government had enacted the Housing and Planning Act of 1909. This Act covered both the urban and rural areas; as Britain is a small and compact country it was felt that any attempt to plan and develop urban areas only would be futile unless the non-urban areas were also included in the scheme. Hence land use planning, etc. was extended were to towns and villages in the entire country and the term used in England was 'Town and Country Planning'. This very term is used in India also whereas the term 'City and Regional Planning' is used in the United States of America.

Another concept for orderly development and redevelopment of cities according to predetermined plan is expressed in the term 'Master Plan' which has developed during the first quarter of this century and has acquired legal expression during the last two or three decades. It is called 'Comprehensive Development Plan' in the USA and 'Town Development Plan' in the UK. The term 'Town Development Plan' (Master Plan) found statutory expression for the first time in the UK in the Town and Country Planning Act, 1947. An urban development plan is a programme for investment of all types of resources in the economic, social, and physical infrastructure of a city or town, thus integrating the traditionally separated fields of economic, social, and physical planning.

Town planning has been defined in various ways: Thomas Adam defines 'Town Planning is the art of planning the physical development of urban communities with the general object of security, healthy and safe living and working conditions, providing efficient and convenient forms of circulation and advancing the general public welfare. It aims at the preservation of natural beauty as essential to healthy living conditions, and leads to the promotion of beauty in buildings as a by-product of sound social and economic growth.'[2]

John T. Howard defines Town Planning as the guidance of the growth and change of urban areas. As such, it is aimed at fulfilling social and economic objectives which go beyond the physical form and arrangement of buildings, streets, parks, utilities and other parts of the urban development.'[3]

The Bhore Committee in its Report (1946) had observed 'The purpose of town and country planning is to utilise the available land to the best advantage of the community, taking into consideration its various needs such as the provision of land for residential purposes, the development of agriculture and industries and the creation of recreational facilities.'[4]

According to Lewis Mumford, 'City planning involves the coordination of human activities in time and space, on the basis of known facts about place, work and people. It involves the modification and correlation of various elements in the total environment for the purpose of increasing their service to the community, and it calls for the building of appropriate structure, dwellings, industrial plants, markets, water works, drains, bridges, villages, cities—to house the activities of community to assist the performance of all its needful functions in a timely and orderly fashion.'

In its main essentials, the development of city includes an orderly, planned and coordinated layout and expansion; slum prevention; determination on future populations and densities; allocation of land for industry, housing, commerce, recreation and other essential uses; means of communication; adequate water supply; electricity; transport, and other civic amenities.

Aims and Objects of Modern Town Planning

It is evident from the definitions of town planning given above that its aims and objects are: an orderly arrangement of the various parts of a town, residential, commercial, and industrial, so that each part could perform its functions with minimum cost and conflict; an efficient system of circulation both within and outside the city, providing for optimum use of all means of transportation; the provision of housing, educational institutions, dispensaries and hospitals, water supply, sewerage, public utilities, and services, community services, and recreation facilities.

It is also clear that the concept of town planning is not confined to the orderly development of towns and cities only and it covers larger areas—a district and a region as well—to ensure the orderly development of the entire physical environment.

Nature and Scope of Urban Planning

Town planning is generally conceived to concern itself with the land use pattern of a town. But it is too narrow a view of town planning. It has a wider scope of arranging the layout of a town in such a manner that it promotes the social and economic well-being of the community to enable it to live a healthy and wholesome life. Town planning makes continual adjustment with political, sociological, and economic factors prevalent in a community. Moreover, town planning is now being defined in broader terms and it is so interpreted as to include larger areas—regions and the state. The scope of town planning thus includes multi-purpose and multi-dimensional use of land in the best interests of the community and the nation and it is ever widening with the growing complexities of urbanization. Its scope may be discussed in details as follows:

1. Planning for Regulation of Land Use: Urban planning is concerned with spatial development of urban settlements—the use and development of land which is a limited resource in urban areas in relation to the demands made on it. Also the location of an activity, particularly an industry, can have a profound effect on social, economic and environmental issues. It is, therefore, imperative that the use and development of land is regulated in a manner that would take account of social, economic and environmental objectives.

2. Planning for the Best Use of Land: The many and varied interests involved in land-uses, the competing demands for land and the growing importance of ensuring that land is put to the best use by virtue of its quality, its contents and the location make the need for urban planning (physical planning) all the more urgent.

3. Planning of Land Use in the National Interest: Urban planning is also to assess present and future requirements of land for various forms of human activity; to design the physical framework within which all forms of development will take place in a planned, orderly, and as effective a manner as possible in the national interest.

4. Planning for Realization of Social Values: While in planning, the physical base is no doubt important, all improvements in physical environment have a higher purpose, namely, the realization of certain social values. Therefore, it is necessary to understand the relationship between social, economic, and spatial aspects. Physical growth must be in harmony with well defined social and economic needs and ends. This is only possible when the three essential and complementary aspects of development—social, economic, and physical are considered together and coordinated from the very beginning.

5. Urban Planning for Economic Growth: At the city level, urban planning is subject to man-made factors involving relationships such as that between intra-urban transportation pattern and work and living places. It involves the specifics of land use patterns and the functional requirements of individual cities. Unless the city provides an efficient environment for carrying out its trade and productive activities, the erosion of the economic growth may result. Therefore, land use planning at the city level is just as concerned with economic growth as are national and state planning.

6. Planning Approach for Generation of Employment: Urban planning should aim at devising ways and means to increase the economic productivity of urban population and improve urban efficiency of eliminating bottlenecks and breakdowns in the delivery of urban services. This necessitates a dynamic and entrepreneurial approach to urban planning. An essential aspect of such an approach is the generation of employment. Employment creation must be synchronized with plans for promoting housing, infrastructure and mass transportation.

7. Planning to Conform to Urban Development Objectives and Principles: Urban planning can make a positive contribution to our national development if it shifts from its present emphasis on land use planning to guiding the very complex, interrelated processes of social and economic change. A prerequisite for this change is the formulation of urban development objectives and principles in precise terms so as to promote appropriate guidance for land-use planning and regulations.

8. Planning Objectives for the Urban Poor and the Lower-middle Class: The poor constitute over half the total urban population. They live in *bustees* and shanty towns. Their living conditions are deplorable. One of the planning objectives should be to provide employment opportunities for them and a minimum living environment by making available potable water, a system of sanitary latrines, a drainage system, paved and lighted roads and a modest amount of other space, and making social services like health and education easily accessible to them.

The other target group is the lower middle class who has a reasonably secure employment but whose incomes are only slightly better than those of the poor. In a tight and inadequate housing market in our large cities, their housing options are severely circumscribed. They scramble for admission for their children in over-crowded educational institutions, health services serving them are disjointed, they have inadequate water supply and live with a generally unhygienic drainage. For most, the journey to work is a nightmare. It is imperative that they should live in conditions that enhance rather than depress their productive capacity. The planning objectives for this target group must be to provide an adequate stock of modest housing, economical, safe and comfortable journey to work, assured supply of potable water, adequate sanitary drainage and waste disposal, education up to the secondary level, preventive and curative medicine, and opportunities for sports, recreation, and cultural activities.

9. Improving Urban Scenario: The urban scenario, especially in our major cities, reflects that they are subject to rapid demographic growth and uncontrolled physical expansion, the urban poor constitute over 50 per cent of their population and have no access to housing and civic services; mass transportation is poor; physical decay characterizes the central districts and old residential areas; and finally archaic local system government prevails, resulting in poor urban management and grossly inadequate finances. Moreover, our cities are where evils such as sub-human conditions in shanty towns, functional chaos, environmental degradation and pollution, unemployment, and under-employment, hunger, diseases, illiteracy, and a general lack of skills come to a head in monstrously visible concentration of human misery.[5] Urban Planning is to concern itself with all these hard realities and to provide remedies to mitigate/eliminate these ills which affect urban areas.

Principles of Town Planning

The haphazard manner in which our cities and towns are growing underscores the need for an urban philosophy and planning principles and objectives to guide urban expansion along desired lines of renewal and development. The structuring of urban settlements should proceed according to a plan which must express the basic principles and standards which should shape the physical form of our cities and towns, their general land use pattern, the transportation system, various urban facilities and services. Some of the principles to be observed in town planning are:

1. Cellular Character of Urban Structure: The urban structure should be cellular in concept, based on the principle of hierarchy of functions performed by the city. Not all the functions of the city can be satisfied in a central area. There are many that can be fulfilled in the residential precincts. Therefore, the cellular organism of the city must start from the small shops around the corners in housing clusters and residential neighbourhoods, and from these move to bigger quarters—community centres and district centres, and to the city centre and metro which provide more basic functions and services and goods of higher grade.

2. Reduction of Enforced Movement to a Minimum: A city should be planned in such a manner that enforced movement is reduced to a minimum. This can be achieved by relating all compatible types of urban functions, in the most intimate manner with each other, within urban sub-units of a size which establishes desirable workability thereby reducing the need for the use of motorized transport to a minimum, resulting in saving of vast areas of land required for urban motorized ways and parking.

3. Neighbourhood Unit for Community Life: Town planning must give due regard to the neighbourhood unit in the urban structure of a city which has been the traditional pattern of our community life. Town planning which ignores the human scale and human values inevitably erodes the urbanity of our cities.

4. Town Planning Legislation Should Not Be Restrictive but Liberal: The present zoning regulations and development controls with respect to major functions and land use are restrictive; they should be more positive and liberal.

5. Planning Should Take Aesthetic Aspects into Consideration: Urban planning is not merely a matter of allotting land for various kinds of activities and uses. It is also very much concerned with the quality of physical environment that is produced by such allotments. Real improvement of urban environment through physical planning can be achieved only through planning that takes into consideration not only the human fundamental needs but also the need for aesthetic satisfaction. Hence, as in the case of social and economic objectives, aesthetic objectives must also be expressed and steps taken for their achievement as an integral part of physical planning process in cities and towns.

6. Planning to Take Proper Care of Transportation: Our cities are plagued with traffic congestion. The rapid increase in automobile traffic has had a profound and bewildering influence on our cities with far reaching social and economic implications. Pollution from automobiles has become a health hazard. Planning must, therefore, be so envisaged as to provide for transportation system in a way as to ensure its conformity with improvement of urban environment.

7. Urban Renewal as a Part of Planning Process: Urban renewal aimed at rebuilding the old parts of the city should not be taken up on a piecemeal basis in a haphazard manner but should be planned and progressed as an integral part of the urban planning process.

8. Planning Should Be the Responsibility of the City Government: Urban planning should emerge from the people themselves. If this responsibility is placed on the city government, it is probable that the development plan that emerges will prove more acceptable and easier in implementation.

9. Planning Is a Continuous Process: Urban planning is much more than mere preparation of a master plan, because urban planning is not an event but a process. Once begun, it is a continuous process of preparing plans, sanctioning plans, and finally implementing plans.

10. Need for a Permanent Planning Structure in City Government: The urban planning process evolves with the rapidly changing social and economic structure of our society. It is, therefore, important to set up a permanent urban planning structure within the city government which will secure the continuity of the planning process.

11. Need to Make Urban Management Efficient and Responsive: Urban planning involves the specifics of land-use patterns and functional requirements of individual cities. Therefore, at the city level there is an urgent need to make urban management more efficient and responsive to urban demands. Urban planning is not a detached activity but an integral part of the whole business of the city government. The needs and activities of other departments must be taken into account by the urban planning department and reconciled with its policy and proposals.

12. Plan to Be Practical and Economical: The function of urban planning is to create a well-balanced synthesis of what otherwise might be a mere collection of separate policies and claims, to combine them into one consistent policy for the use and development of land within the urban area, to devise the means of translating this policy in the physical conditions of that area into a plan that is practical, economical, and aesthetically pleasing, and to organize the implementation of the development for which the plan was provided.

13. The Planning Function to Vest in the Chief Town Planner: Under the existing planning acts, urban planning becomes a state concept—regarded primarily as the preparation of a plan, the other aspects being left to be pursued independently by other departments. This results in the value of urban plans being lost. Therefore, if urban planning is to be properly formed, the organization of a local planning authority should be such as to vest in the chief city planner the full responsibility for handling the planning function.

14. Need for Restructuring of City Governments: The existing institutional structure of municipal governments, inherited from the British Raj, has proved to be inadequate in managing contemporary urban problems. It is not structured to cope with rapid urban growth or to manage cities of several million inhabitants. The system of city governments therefore needs to be restructured and revamped to provide proper organization for urban planning.

15. Agency for Consultancy to Small and Medium Towns: While the Class-I cities with populations of one lakh and above may develop their own urban planning capability in terms of qualified staff, the state town planning organization needs to set up a special wing for providing consultancy services in urban planning to small and medium towns.

16. Town Planning is of an Interdisciplinary Nature: Urban planning shares substantive concerns for the quality of life and environmental amenities with a number of other groups. Town planners must, therefore, work in teams with other disciplines. Because of the inter-disciplinary nature of town planning, the traditional structure of town planning, which has been dominated by architects, civil engineers, and surveyors, must allow the inclusion of economists, sociologists, geographers, etc.

17. Planner's Responsibility to Improve the Quality of Life for All: An urban planner's primary responsibility is to be concerned with the arrangement of physical space in the human environment so as to improve the quality of life for all.

18. The Planning Process Involves Preparation, Sanctioning and Implementation of Plans: Urban planning is much more than the mere preparation of the plan for city development; once begun, it is continuum of preparation of plan, getting it sanctioned by government and finally implementing it. The activities connected with preparation of a plan consist of research—compilation of facts about the planning area which bear on its development, evaluation of present needs and resources of the area and drawing up development objectives. The sanctioning of the plan involves review and appraisal by the sanctioning authority and the implementation of the plan requires both regulatory and development and re-development activities.

19. Planning to Be a Detailed Programme of Action: A vital and essential characteristic of a plan is that when it is prepared, it has to be in the form of detailed programme of action.

20. Planning to Be Both Spatial and Functional: A viable plan is both spatial and functional: while the spatial aspect relates to land-use policy, the functional aspect relates to urban transportation and communication system, public housing and public utilities like water supply, drainage, and power supply.

21. Planning a Continuous Process for the Development of an Urban Area: Urban planning can be characterized as a continuous, coordinated, and programmatic process of effecting the development of an urban area.

Chandigarh, conceived and designed as the capital of Punjab in 1950s, was built keeping in view some of the principles of planning enumerated above. In spite of all the derogatory epithets—concrete jungle, soulless, dull, the myth persists that it is the 'City Beautiful'. It is an architectural paradise, a place of vast open spaces and wide avenues. When Chandigarh was conceived, there was practically no architectural or town-planning know-how. It was a wise decision to bring in the best brains of the world to build Chandigarh. Now, we have a large number of professionals who can deliver the goods with confidence. Chandigarh suffers from some problems—it has many slums and new ones are springing up every other day, its famed vehicular arteries are getting choked, and its open spaces are becoming parking lots. It is not a pedestrians' paradise as it was made out to be. The accident rate in the city is very high. It is not a city which responds to the Indian ethos, psychology, economy, and social norms. It is undoubtedly a Western oriented city which it had to be because it was conceived as such. Many new ideas in urbanization are coming up.[6] Town planning of future cities will take these into consideration and avoid the pitfalls of the existing planned cities.

Town Planning in India: Historical Perspective

The evolution of town planning in India can be traced from Vedic times through various periods to the present day as follows:

Town Planning in Ancient India

The concept of town planning is not new to India. It has been practised even in ancient times as is substantiated by planned towns like Harappa and Mohenjodaro. Towns in these times were equipped with streets, sewers, water supply, markets, gardens, tanks, and public buildings and facilities. Hiuen Tsang also made a mention of the wide and high walls and inner gates of Indian cities. The people of the Indus Valley civilization (3000 BC) had the proud distinction of giving to the world its earliest cities, its first urban civilization, its first town planning, its first drainage system and its earliest example of city government.[7]

Improvement Trusts as Agencies of Town Planning

It was in the medieval and later times that the towns began to grow rapidly in an unplanned and haphazard way giving rise to the problems of overcrowding, squalor, and lack of sanitation. As the municipal bodies were too preoccupied with the maintenance of civic services and lacked financial resources and technical personnel to meet the challenges of planning and execution of urban development projects, the need for a special agency to undertake the task of improvement and development of towns was felt and the improvement trusts were set up on the recommendations of the sanitary commissions appointed in all the presidency towns of Calcutta, Madras, and Bombay in 1864. The first improvement trust was created in Bombay in 1894, followed by other cities in various states under enactments passed by the provincial legislatures.

The aims and objectives of the improvement trusts are planning development of areas adjacent to the municipal areas and for improving the present unhygienic and unhealthy conditions of the towns and cities. In most of the cases improvement trusts have worked effectively and contributed to the development of their towns and cities in a satisfactory manner but some of them could not keep pace with the needs of the urban development and had to be abolished.

Modern Town Planning in the Pre-Independence Period

The genesis of modern town planning can, however, be traced to Britain, which enacted a legislation on town planning in 1909, the first of its kind in the world. In modern India, town planning may be said to have its origin in 1912 when New Delhi, as the new capital of the country was planned by its architect Lutyens as the first planned city. The central government had then impressed upon the provincial governments the great and growing importance of town planning and suggested the enactment of legislation on the mode of the British Housing and Town Planning Act of 1909. Accordingly, the Province of Bombay had enacted the town planning legislation in 1915 and set up a Town Planning and Valuation Department to advise on and to prepare town development, improvement, extension and slum clearance schemes. The same year Sir Patrick Geddes had visited India to advise the Madras government on planning and redevelopment of old cities. Legislation on town planning was passed in UP in 1919, Madras in 1920, Punjab in 1922, and so on. Despite this, town and country planning remained almost a neglected item and it made no headway. The interest taken by the Government of India from time to time was an 'occasional burst of insight' and was not sustained and neither was the response.[8] The central and provincial governments had not taken adequate steps even to implement the recommendations made by the Halland Commission in 1918 on the scientific and technical aspects of town planning and by the Whitley Commission in 1919 on town planning legislation. Generally the provincial governments had not shown any active interest in the subject until recently when post was problems came to the fore.[9] The towns continued growing rapidly and haphazardly without any conscious direction and control. In 1941 it was reported by the census commissioner that India was in for urbanization on a big scale and that it would affect pronouncedly the really large towns rather than smaller towns with all the drawback of lack of control, squatter's freedom and general squalor. The Health Survey Development Committee appointed by the central government was struck by a virtual absence of towns and country planning in India. It had observed:

> Progress in town planning has been extremely slow. During the last 20 or 25 years, although certain eminent town planners had visited India and offered advice to provincial governments, and in certain cases, even prepared definite schemes for individual cities, very little action had been taken. In some of the larger cities in the country, improvement trusts had been working for some time and although their specific purpose was to assist in the planning of the cities, the results achieved had been very limited.[10]

Further, even less attention had been paid to village planning than to town planning. Most villages had grown in a haphazard manner, and, in far in too many cases, it would be beyond the capacity of a planner to improve existing conditions to any reasonable extent.[11]

Town Planning in Post-Independence Period

The post-Independence period has witnessed the emergence of planned new townships which were established to resettle the mass exodus of people from Pakistan as a consequence of the partition of the country in 1947, and secondly to provide settlements to the industrial labour in proximity of the public sector projects started as a part of the policy of industrialization which inevitably leads to urbanization. The townships set up for the first category of people, viz. refugees were Rajpura, Faridabad, Nilokheri, and Kalyani, and those of the second category, viz. industrial townships, were single industry township like Rourkela and Bhilai, townships having an industrial complex such as Durgapur, Nangal, Chittranjan, and Ranchi, Heavy Electrical Township near Bhopal, Indian Telephone Industries and Hindustan Aeronautics near Bangalore, Company towns like Sindri, Modinagar, and Pinjore, port towns like Kandla and administrative towns like Chandigarh, Gandhinagar, and Bhubaneshwar.[12] Urbanization since independence was thus marked by growth of small towns, agro-industrial centres, setting up of institutional and administrative centres including places of tourist interest, educational centres and new state headquarters and emergence of new industrial centres and major irrigation and power projects.[13]

These new towns or townships, however, suffer from certain deficiencies and drawbacks which render them bereft of planning concepts and strategies; the industrial townships have led to uncontrolled, sporadic and unsightly developments, in some towns, the original plans have not been implemented properly; intended structures have not been erected for the playgrounds; parks and lawns, etc. have not been provided; various towns lack the provision of housing for all, rehabilitation towns such as Rajpura, Nilokheri, etc. seem to be totally unplanned, no attempt has been made to integrate the displaced persons with the local people. Similarly, in various company towns integration has not been attempted by merging company and non-company dwellings and earmarking sufficient space for housing in the private sector; the capital towns like Chandigarh, the City Beautiful, have not been maintained properly by adhering to the laws and by-laws governing the land-use patterns, hygiene and sanitation standards, etc. with the result that they would gradually lose their identities as planned cities.

On the whole, the towns have been growing haphazardly ringed by suburbs, hemmed in by ribbon growth all along the main roads.[14]

Town Planning in Five Year Plans

With the adoption of planning for socio-economic development of the country since 1951, town planning has become a part of the overall national plan. The first five year plan (1951–56) recognized that the cities and towns were growing haphazardly and were causing deterioration in the conditions of living in them. The plan had, therefore, recommended a National Town and Country Planning Act which would provide for zoning the use of land, control over ribbon development, location of industries in areas considered suitable and the preparation of master plans. The plan also emphasized the importance of regional planning in the context of several river valley projects and rural community development projects, and specifically recommended that regional planning should take into account the population, agricultural conditions, industries, and communications of a region with a view to securing a balance of population between villages and market towns and industrial centres.

The Second Plan (1956–61) which laid emphasis on industrial growth particularly basic industries recognized the impact which location of new activities such as industries, market, irrigation and power development schemes would have on the distribution of population and recommended that all these be coordinated within an overall frame of development drawn up for each region and each state.

The Third Plan (1961–66) specifically provided for the preparation of comprehensive development plans for practically all the major cities and their surrounding areas including industrial centres and also for some of the rapidly growing regions. A beginning was also made for drawing up development plans for metropolitan cities and the regions around them, providing for the growth of secondary centres to reduce pressure on the metropolitan city itself.

The Fourth Plan (1966–71), noting that urbanization is an essential concomitant of industrialization, also pointed to the need for balanced regional development and dispersal of activities. The plan also recommended for a regional approach to urban development and the need for an urban land policy, land values and strengthening the administrative structures of local bodies. The concrete programmes that emerged during the plan period were slum clearance, environmental improvement in slum areas, social housing, urban water supply and sanitation, land acquisition and land development, and preparation of master plans for cities and regions.

The Fifth Plan (1974–79) has as its objectives the augmenting of civic services in urban centres as far as possible with a view to make them fit for a reasonable level of living, tackling the problems of metropolitan cities on a more comprehensive and regional basis, promoting the development of smaller towns and new urban centres to decrease the pressure of increasing urbanization and providing necessary support for the enlargement of the scope and functions of the industrial townships so as to make them more self-contained.

The Sixth Plan (1979–85) provided for the integrated development of small and medium towns and also for a regional or sub-regional spatial plan prior to the selection of towns for development; and cluster of villages approach for provision of roads in the case of hilly, tribal, desert and coastal areas through special planning, which will not only design the optimal regional road network but will also guide the provision of utilities, facilities and services.

The Seventh Plan (1985–90) emphasized the need of preparation of master plans of all the towns and cities; implementation of Perspective Development for Delhi-2001 for the systematic development of the city on the basis of the policy framework and overall land use pattern and development controls provided for therein, implementation of National Capital Region Plan to avoid any haphazard development of the region and achieve a manageable Delhi by 2001; augmenting the finances of HUDCO to enable it to plan for housing needs of the weaker sections of society and provision of urban infrastructure, etc.

Model Town and Country Planning Legislation

The Central Regional and Urban Planning Organization had prepared a model legislation—Model Town and Country Planning Law, in 1960, and circulated it for the guidance of the states. A sub-committee constituted by the Conference of the State Ministers for Town and Country Planning in 1961 to examine it had emphasized that no model legislation could meet the requirements of each state individually, it could at best provide the basic guidance in regard to town planning legislation, leaving it to the states to adapt it to meet their guidelines. The Model Law also visualized an administrative machinery comprising the State Planning Board, the local planning authorities, and the Chief Town Planner as the principal permanent officer of the town planning department of the state.

The West Bengal government had constituted a commission for legislation on Town and Country Planning in 1962 to examine the Model Law in the light of the conditions prevalent in the state and to make recommendations for a suitable legislation.

The Commission had, *inter alia,* suggested five principles to govern town planning, viz. (*i*) the law should be practical and capable of being enforced; (*ii*) that the machinery should not be loosely joined but compact and capable of functioning with the minimum amount of jolting and creaking occasioned by the existence of too many tiers between the top and the bottom, (*iii*) that while planning should be centralized, its execution or implementation should be decentralized; (*iv*) that people's cooperation should be obtained by limiting the areas and range of control to essential things and giving them a real opportunity to voice their opinions and objections with a guarantee that they will be considered; (*v*) that local authorities should not be completely ignored but should be gradually initiated into the meaning and purpose of planning control by being given some responsible duties in enforcement and implementation. The commission had also recommended that there should be a minister in charge of town and country planning, although he may be in charge of other allied department as well, but the responsibility for the administration of town and country planning should not be divided between different ministers; the department of town and country planning should be an independent department with its own secretariat and directorate.

The Committee on Model Planning Legislation constituted by the Fourth Conference of State Ministers for Town and Country Planning in 1964 to examine the Report of the Bengal Commission had reiterated the observations of the sub-committee constituted by the conference of State Ministers of Town and Country Planning (1961) that no model legislation on town planning was capable of meeting, in full, the requirements of each state individually and that it would have to be adapted to suit individual states. It was of the view that the state planning authority of the type recommended in the Model Law was necessary so that there was available an overall plan advisory body to advise the state government and to give realistic appraisal of any plan prepared for a local body; the local planning authority should be flexible enough to permit the state government to give representation to various interests at the local level.

In pursuance of the discussions, suggestions and recommendations at the forum of conferences of State Ministers of Town and Country Planning, several states revised and modernized their town planning legislations.

Metropolitan Planning Organizations and Metropolitan Development Authorities

The central and state governments have set up city development authorities to provide for planned development of the respective cities or/and regions in their jurisdictions. Delhi Development Authority was established by the central government under the Delhi Development Act, 1957, to give concrete shape to the policy of bringing order into building activity in Delhi as per perspective development plan for Delhi 2001.

Similarly the Calcutta Metropolitan Organization was set up in 1961 by the Government of West Bengal to promote the development of Calcutta metropolitan area according to plan; Bombay Metropolitan Regional

Planning Board was constituted in 1967 under the Maharashtra Regional and Town Planning Act, 1966; the Patna Metropolitan Regional Planning Board in 1967, and the Nagpur Metropolitan Regional Planning Board in 1968. All these metropolitan planning organizations, redesigned as metropolitan development authorities, perform identical functions, mainly allocation of land for different uses, general distribution and general locations of land and the extent to which the land may be used as residential, industrial, agricultural, or as forest, or for mineral exploitation; reservation of areas for open space, gardens, recreation; transport and communications, such as roads, highways, and railways; water supply, drainage, sewerage, sewage disposal and other public utilities, amenities, and services including electricity and gas; reservation of sites for new towns industrial estates and any other large scale development or project which is required to be undertaken for proper development of the region or new town; preservation, conservation and development of natural scenery, forest, wild life, natural resources, and landscaping; preservation of objects, features, structures or places of historical, natural, architectural or scientific interest and educational value; areas required for military and defense purposes; afforestation and prevention of erosion; proposals for irrigation, water supply, and hydro-electric works, flood control and prevention of river pollution; and providing for the relocation of population or industry.

Recommendations of the Study Team of Administrative Reforms

Despite the establishment of development authorities entrusted with the task of developing their respective areas on planned basis, preparation of master plans of various cities and towns for their planned development, town planning legislation, etc. town planning does not seem to have made any headway. The study team on the machinery of Government of India and its procedure of work appointed by the Administrative Reforms Commission (1967) had come to the conclusion that town planning could almost be said not to exist and was of the view that there was an urgent need of setting up of an effective nodal agency from where measures for regional planning could be initiated and implementation in the various governmental agencies at the centre and in the states overseen.[15] It had recommended the setting up of a central agency for regional planning in the central government with the following functions:

1. To provide leadership and guidance to the states in the matter of regional planning, to serve as a clearing house of information and experience and to operate as a coordinating agency in respect of central ministries dealing with proposals for regional planning
2. To promote, where necessary, and particularly in big problem areas, the formation of regional boards with representatives of central as well as state interests armed with effective powers to implement plans
3. To advise the location of public sector projects, and particularly to assist in getting integrated development plans prepared in consultation with the state governments for areas surrounding such projects
4. To prepare master plans for metropolitan cities, industrial areas and so on, including the location and planning of new townships
5. Overall policy and programmes of town planning (slums clearance, sanitation, housing, water supply, etc., through local bodies)
6. Aid to state governments—financial and technical
7. Utilization of land
8. Co-ordination in regard to local self-government in urban and rural areas
9. To service a joint council of local self-government and regional planning at national level
10. Policy on powers and functions of local bodies, including personnel policy

Division of Town Planning in Planning Commission

The Planning Commission concerned with national planning and formulating five year plans for various sectors of economy and development has set up a Housing and Urban Development Division entrusted with the task of planning for urban development of various states and regions. Its Task Force on housing and urban development had observed in its report (1983) that the approach to urban development had been piecemeal and desultory and emphasized on the formulation of urban policy at the national level. The Planning Commission thus takes adequate interest in the development of cities and regions on a planned basis.

Other Institutional Arrangements for Town Planning

1. Ministry of Urban Development was set up in 1985 (which was designated as Ministry of Urban Affairs and Employment in 1998) for broad policy formulation and monitoring of programmes in the areas of housing, urban development, urban poverty alleviation and urban water supply. These are essentially state subjects but the central government plays a coordinating and monitoring role and also supports these programmes through central sector schemes, institutional finance and expertise. Its town and country planning organization is the apex technical advisory body on matters relating to urban and regional planning, strategies, research, monitoring and evaluation of central government schemes and development policies.
2. The issues, policies, and administrative structure for town and country planning are discussed at the conferences of state ministers for town and country planning and appropriate decisions taken for implementation in the respective states.
3. Various states have set up full-fledged departments dealing with town and country planning with extensive field organizations. Town and Country Planning Organization (TCPO) and the states' departments of town and country planning play a key role in town planning.

Their organization and functions are therefore discussed in detail as follows:

Towns and Country Planning Organization (Government of India)

The Town and Country Planning Organization (TCPO) was established in 1962 by merging the erstwhile Central Regional and Urban Planning Organization and the Town Planning Organization to address itself to physical planning on the national level under the administrative control of the then Ministry of Housing and Urban Development. It has now been placed under the newly formed Ministry of Urban Development since 1985, redesignated as Ministry of Urban Affairs and Employment in 1998.

Its main functions are:

1. Formulation of national policies concerning urban and regional planning and development to form part of national five-year plans.
2. Pursuance of approved urban schemes and programmes so as to achieve their effective implementation and in this context to render such technical assistance and advice that may be necessary to the central ministries, state governments, and other public and semi-public agencies.
3. To provide active assistance to the union territories in the preparation of plans for development of urban areas as well as regional development.

4. To undertake the preparation of detailed development plans (zonal development plan) within the framework of the Delhi Master Plan, originally prepared by it for Delhi Development Authority (DDA), and to advise DDA and other agencies on the broad policies enunciated in the Delhi Master Plan.
5. To advise specialized agencies like the Department of Tourism, the Atomic Energy Commission, public undertakings such as the Oil and Natural Gas Commission and Damodar Valley Corporation in such matters as integrated planning, planning and development of industrial townships, planning standards, and planning implementation measures.
6. To undertake studies leading to the preparation of regional development plans for important resource regions falling in more than one state in the country.
7. To carry out applied research on specific topics in the socio-economic and physical aspects of urban and regional planning.
8. To undertake studies in industrial development, industrial location, and distribution from the point of view of balanced regional and urban development in the country.

In short, the TPCO is the apex technical advisory body on matters relating to urban and regional planning strategies, research, monitoring, and evaluation of central government schemes and development policies. It provides technical inputs for formulation of urban development and infrastructural development policies to the Ministry of Urban Affairs and Employment and provides consultative services and project assistance to different states and organizations. It is also involved in the appraisal, monitoring, and evaluation of important schemes of the Government of India like the Integrated Development of Small and Medium Towns (IDSMT), Urban Basic Services Programme (UBS), the PM's special grant programmes for Bombay (Mumbai), World Bank assisted State Urban Development Projects and Environmental Improvement of Urban Slums Schemes (EIUS), etc.

A glimpse of the activities of the TPCO can be had from the various types of projects and schemes it has completed or has been engaged in during the last few years. These activities comprise tourism development plans for Gwalior Fort (MP), Golkanda Fort, Hyderabad (AP), Chittorgarh (Rajasthan), Sankisa (UP), etc.; beautification proposal for White Town, Pondicherry; Singrauli Regional Development Plan; Interim Development Plan for Port Blair; study on the Dimensions of Public Investment in Slum Improvement Programmes, its efficacy and impact on quality of life of slum dwellers; analysis of industrial potential in the small and medium towns; study on environmental improvement of Pushkar Lake area; analysis of development of women entrepreneurship in urban areas; study on Appraisal of Urban Land Policies and Programmes in selected cities; management of urban fringe land development in selected metropolitan cities of India; monitoring of urban residential land prices; Report of the Task Force on Urban Poverty Alleviation in the Eighth Five Year Plan; Report on Environmental Improvement of Urban Slums; organizing specialized training courses for the middle and senior level officers associated with the urban development activities in the central, states, local bodies and specialized institutes in collaboration with the Institute of Local Self-Government, Birmingham, UK, etc.[16]

The TCPO is appropriately termed as the technical arm of the Ministry of Urban Affairs and Employment in matters of town planning, regional planning, and urban development.

State Departments of Town and Country Planning

Various states and union territories have set up their departments of town and country planning with almost identical and similar functions but differing slightly in their organization and activities according to their native circumstances and requirements. The organization and functions of the Town and Country Planning

Department of the State of Punjab is given below as an illustration of its counterparts in other parts of the country.

The Town and Country Planning Department was set up by Government of Punjab in 1962 as the state planning agency for physical planning and programming both in urban and rural sectors in the state. It also undertakes programming and monitoring of integrated projects and schemes of various government departments, state corporations and local bodies. It is entrusted with the responsibility and activity involved in formulating policies and strategies in physical planning, urban and regional development at the state, regional, community, block, town, and village level, and the implementation of projects and schemes entrusted to the state and local development and civic authorities.

Organization of the Department

A minister is in charge of the department exclusively or in combination of allied departments like local government since designated as Punjab Urban Development Authority (PUDA), Housing and Urban Estates. The secretariat of the department, headed by a Senior IAS officer as its secretary, advises the minister in policy matters. The head of the department is the Chief Town Planner who is assisted by the Divisional Town Planner at the headquarters and by senior town planners, area planners, divisional town lanners, etc. in the field offices. The function of the department are as follows:

1. To advise the state government on all matters relating to physical planning and development in the state both in urban and rural areas.
2. To advise the various departments of the government such as local government, housing and urban development, colonization, industry, public works, housing board, town improvement trusts, municipal corporations, and municipal council on all planning matters and also to prepare schemes for them.
3. Finding locations for industrial projects and estates; setting up of urban estates, new towns, and alignment of highways near towns; locating of rural growth centres, bus stands, petrol pumps, cinema sites, hospitals, educational institutions; beautification of places of pilgrimage and tourist importance, etc.
5. Preparation of master plans for cities and towns.
6. Integrated urban development programme including project reports, monitoring, etc.
7. Preparation of detailed plans for *mandi* townships for the colonization department.
8. Preparation of controlled area plans under the Punjab Scheduled Roads and Controlled Areas.

A Resume of the Activities of the Department

The activities undertaken by the department in pursuance of the functions assigned to it may be summarized as follows:

1. *Preparation of master plans*: Due to rapid industrialization and urbanization, the cities and towns are growing rapidly in an unplanned and haphazard manner. Master plans of cities and towns are prepared to guide their development in a systematic manner. They contain proposals for future development of a town during the next twenty years and identify areas for meeting the long term requirements of land for different uses, viz. residential, industrial, commercial, traffic and transportation, and public utilities and services.

2. *Preparation of layout*, etc. of town planning schemes of municipal corporations and municipal committees.

3. *Preparation of development schemes*: Surveys plans, layout plans and demarcation plans of the schemes of the improvement trusts under the provision of the Punjab Improvement Trust Act, 1922.

4. The work relating to various urban estates set up under Punjab Urban Estates (Development and Regulation) Act, 1964, viz. preparation of survey plans, layout plans, demarcation plans, numbering plans, zoning plans, and building and architectural control.

5. *Controlled areas*: Selected areas are declared as controlled areas by the state government under the provisions of the Punjab Scheduled Roads and Controlled Areas (Restriction of Unregulated Development) Act, 1963, to prevent haphazard development around towns and important places. Under the provisions of the Act, the building construction and development in the controlled areas is to be carried out in accordance with the development plan prepared and notified under the Act. The department carries out the various planning works, viz. surveys, preparation of existing land-use plans, proposed land-use plans, and draft notification relating to declaration of controlled areas and their development plans.

6. The office of Divisional Town Planner, Mandi Division of the Departments carries out planning works, viz. preparation of layout plans, building control sheets of grain markets and new mandi township set up under the Punjab New Mandi Township (Development and Regulation) Act, 1960, for the colonization department.

7. *Government and semi-government projects and schemes*: For the development of towns of religious and historical importance, state level and district level development boards have been constituted by the government. The department prepares development plans in pursuance of the decision of the various city development boards and coordinates with other departments in this regard. For example, the department prepared plan showing commercial buildings and buildings from security point in a diameter of 30 m to 100 m around Golden Temple Complex at Amritsar and also the plan showing SGPC and religious buildings in a diameter of 30 m to 100 m around Golden Temple Complex at Amritsar. The department also prepares project reports for administrative complexes at the district, tehsil, and sub-tehsil.

8. *Building applications*: The department tenders advice on building applications for construction of buildings, in the schemes of municipal corporations, municipal committees, improvement trusts, urban estates, controlled areas and on the applications for the grant of 'No Objection Certificate' for setting up of petrol pumps, storage of petroleum products, construction of cinemas, and installation of brick kilns. Similarly, reports are sent to the competent authorities under the Urban Land (Ceiling and Regulation) Act, 1976, on applications or cases referred by them. This technical advice is tendered after detailed site inspection and examination of the case under the relevant provisions of various schemes and rules and acts applicable in the particular case or the area.

9. The Environmental Research, Planning and Design Organization of the department is entrusted with the programming, planning, evaluation, coordination, and monitoring of integrated urban development programmes of selected cities and towns, especially the small and medium towns; implementation of low cost sanitation schemes introduced by the Government of India since 1983–84; integrated development programmes of bigger cities aimed at their development and to generate employment so that these cities serve the regional population effectively; environmental improvement of urban slums; setting up of environmental parks in small towns in commemoration of Jawaharlal Nehru Centenary (UNICEF aided Urban Basic Services Programme for which UNICEF, Government of India and state government provide grants-in-aid in the ratio of 40 : 40 : 20); construction of improved crematoria under the 100 per cent centrally sponsored scheme; preparation of comments on recommendations of

National Commission on Urbanization; preparation of base maps in collaboration with the Survey of India; preparation of traffic operation plan; and monitoring and implementation of schemes regarding removal of encroachments for major roads in certain towns.

10. *Area planning and regional planning*: The integrated area planning strives to study the needs and potentials of a given area and to identify prospective growth centres for providing the necessary infrastructure and economic activities. The aim is that the entire development activity in the given area is properly integrated so that best results are achieved. The area planning units of the department prepare physical development plan at the regional, district, and block levels and undertake preparation of development plans for villages under the Integrated rural development programme.

In addition to its basic specified works the department also formulates Human Settlement Structure Plan–2001, sustainable development of environmentally critical mandi areas falling in river Beas and Sutlej; Chandigarh Inter-State Capital Region plan, etc.[17]

Deficiencies in Town Planning Practice and Impediments in Its Implementation

Town planning strategies and practices suffer from certain weaknesses and deficiencies. Their implementation has also not been able to achieve the desired objectives. The causes responsible for the inadequacies of the planning processes and the impediments in their implementation may be discussed as follows:

1. Urban Planning Is Predominantly Land-use Oriented: Urban planning is predominantly land-use and physical change oriented, and socio-economic planning is yet to be blended with the kind of physical planning that is in vogue in the major cities and towns.[18]

2. Urban Planning Not a Part of National Planning Process: The plans prepared for the development of urban centres have remained mainly regulatory and the positive development envisaged in these plans has never materialized; they have not yet become a part of the mainstream of the national planning process.

3. Master Plans Restricted to Land-use Allocation Only: Master plans or comprehensive development plans prepared for various towns and cities indicate the manner in which the land is proposed to be used and prescribe development control measures for enforcing the land-use plan. These master plans with their rigid land-use and development controls have proved extremely poor instruments for regulating the dynamic process of urban growth. The core problems of urban planning are not only spatial but also functional. The preparation of master plan as the principal activity of urban development is a static concept, whereas urban planning must be seen as a dynamic, adoptive, interactive, and continuing process of anticipating planning and managing social and economic change brought about by the economic development of the country.

4. Absence of Statutory Backing of Master Plans: An analysis of the various town planning Acts prevailing in different states by and large reveals that no statutory backing of the development plans exists in the states of Jammu and Kashmir, Punjab, Orissa, and West Bengal; only limited statutory backing is available in Uttar Pradesh and Haryana; quite a number of master plans are prepared without legal sanction; no comprehensive town planning act exists in the states of Punjab, Haryana, West Bengal, and Uttar Pradesh.

5. Development Plans Lack Phasing of Programmes and Mode of Financing: Generally development plans prepared in the country neither give any specific programme for implementation nor spell out their phasing and mode of financing.

6. Absence of Single Authority for Implementation of Plans: No proper administrative responsibility has been entrusted to any single authority for the implementation of development plans. Every development agency works in isolation and without coordination, resulting in poor results and benefits to the target group. A comprehensive town planning act should be enacted which should be operative both in municipal limits as well as controlled areas. A single urban development agency may take the responsibility to implement the plan in phased manner.

7. Separate Agencies for Preparation and Implementation of Plans: The planning of towns and cities and the implementation of plans are vested in two separate agencies. The planning function is generally discharged by the town and country planning organization of the states while the local bodies are responsible for their implementation. The local bodies by virtue of their constitution, are not able to have a clear and proper perspective in focus and a positive development aspect. Further there is multiplicity of agencies to implement the plan and each agency tries to interpret the development in its own way. This pinpoints the need for a combined agency which can handle the twin functions of planning and implementing of a city development plan. Delhi Development Authority has successfully interwoven these two functions.

8. Urban and Rural Planning Not Interlinked and Integrated: The economic planning and spatial planning (locational—suitable location for different activities) have not been interlinked or integrated, which is crucial for establishing a balanced urban–rural relationship. The Rural–Urban Relationship Committee (1966) and other expert bodies had accordingly recommended that the planning process should aim at a balanced and integrated development of urban and rural areas. This is imperative for the removal of regional disparities in the country. With this purpose, the Planning Commission has accepted the district as a unit for planning because at this level a complete integration of urban and rural development can be achieved and both can be made to act as complementary and supplementary to each other in development.[19] Consequently, district level planning as an integral part of the national planning process has been getting wide recognition at the level of the Planning Commission and within state governments and a series of recommendations and guidelines for institutionalizing district level planning have been issued as Planning Commission documents.[20]

9. Encroachment on Public Lands: Another factor responsible for the failure of planning effort is the ever-increasing encroachment on public land and the mushrooming of unserviced, unplanned, and unauthorized colonies. It is estimated that approximately 650 unauthorized colonies in Delhi occupy 4,000 hectares of land and have a population of about a million—this picture is universal to all urban centres of any reasonable size. So widespread is the problem that in Delhi, from time to time, unauthorized colonies are regularized. In Madhya Pradesh, the government decided to regularize all encroachments in 1984, about two million of them; and in Patna the situation is accepted as a normal way of life. So long as government fails to ensure easy and affordable access to land and so long as the policy to regularize that which is illegal continues, every city planning effort is bound to fail.

10. Land Not Used As Economic Weapon for Furtherance of Development: The existing town planning practices are largely aimed at controlling land-use patterns rather than authorizing land-use in terms of economic returns, employment generation, provision of shelter and the raising of additional resources for city development. In other words, under zoning, land is not used as an economic weapon for the furtherance of development.

11. Land-use Planning to Match Demography to Land Availabilities: Our land-use planning tends to be an exercise in matching demography to land availability. Even in the Plan for Delhi 2001, the operational part of the plan is that, by 2001, Delhi will have a population of 12.2 million to accommodate which another 2,400 hectares of land will have to be acquired. The whole planning exercise relating to land, therefore, boils down to relating land needs to the projected population and does not pay proper heed to the availability of social infrastructure such as employment, shelter, education, health recreation, and other similar activities.

12. Development Planning Acts Deficient in Planning Administration: The urban development planning acts currently in operation are seriously deficient in respect of planning administration. The complexity and dimensions of contemporary urban development problems are too formidable to be tackled within the framework of existing urban planning laws; to make the urban planning process more responsive to the changing needs of the rapidly growing cities, the urban development acts are in urgent need of review and revision in the light of a realistic conception of urban planning.

13. Coordination of Plan Preparation by Urban Planning Authority with that of Functional Public Agencies: In the urban planning process, every major functional agency in a city whose activities significantly affect the development of the planning areas is, in a way, a plan preparing agency. A multiplicity of such functional agencies, such as housing boards, water supply and sewerage boards, electricity boards, inter-city road transport corporations, public works departments, railways, port trusts and the like exist in most cities. Each such agency prepares its own plan for its activities. But such plan-making is by itself inadequate for dealing with the complex problems of development of a city as a whole. A central planning authority at the city level with wide perspective, specialized physical planning skills and sufficient resources has, therefore, to be set up to prepare and maintain a comprehensive development plan for the city, revising where necessary the functional agencies plans. A close and continuous coordination must therefore exist between the central planning authority and the functional agencies. Further, the central planning authority which is required to coordinate plan preparation must also coordinate the implementation of plans and provide direction and guidance within the framework of a comprehensive development plan and other plans.

14. Scarcity of Open Land for Planning: The cities and towns have not been left with much open space which could be planned. As mentioned above, whatever little vacant land is available has been illegally occupied by the vested interests with the connivance and abetment of municipal authorities and used for construction of residential houses rendering the preparation of town planning for such areas of no consequence.

15. Dilatory Process of Acquisition of Land: Town planning schemes suffer due to the dilatory process of acquisition of land to be covered by such schemes. Moreover, the prices of land in the periphery of towns and cities is prohibitively high which the local bodies are unable to afford due to their extremely weak financial position.

16. Intervention by Politicians: Lastly, the town planning schemes are violated with impunity because of the intervention of the politicians who in order to appease their constituents lend them every conceivable support to have their way in carrying on their building activities and not to bother about the town planning stipulations. Thus political parties and politicians offer formidable obstruction to implementation of town planning schemes.

Conclusion

Population explosion, industrialization, migration from rural to urban areas have accelerated urbanization in India in recent years on an unprecedented scale. The urban population, which was 50 million in 1947, has increased to 28.5 crores as per the 2001 census. It means that by the end of the current decade, the urban areas will hold a population equal to the total population of the country at the time of independence. The number of cities housing a population of over ten million is projected to increase from a dozen in 1981 to 40 in 2001. Degradation of human life resulting from the process of urbanization cannot be overlooked. The National Commission on Urbanization has drawn pointed attention to the most brutal and inhuman living conditions in urban areas with large section of population living in squatter settlements. This frustrating and gloomy scenario in urban areas is attributed primarily to unabated and uncombated growth and concentration of population in the few metropolitan cities, which has led to acute exploitative conditions, not only within their confines in terms of access to land, economic opportunities and income distribution but also in a wider area in thwarting the growth of second and third order urban centres. Urban planning is, thus, of crucial importance to check further deterioration of cities and towns and to ensure orderly and planned urban expansion.

Town planning is generally to concern itself with the land-use pattern of a town but it is too narrow a view of it. It is now being defined in wider terms to include larger areas, districts, regions, and the whole of the state and the development of land to achieve social, economic, and environmental objectives.

Town planning is to be guided by certain principles and national objectives such as a cellular character of urban structure, reduction of enforced movement to a minimum, positive and liberal planning in place of negative and regulatory planning, consideration of aesthetic aspects, proper care of transportation system, urban renewal, planning as a continuous process, planning to be the responsibility of the city government with a permanent planning agency which will be headed by the Chief Town Planner, planning consultancy services to be introduced in small and medium towns, and finally planning to be both spatial and functional.

New Delhi was the first city to be planned in 1912. The town planning legislation was thereafter enacted in many provinces. The Health Survey Development Committee of the central government had regretted woeful absence of planning in towns and especially of villages. The movement of town planning, however, got a momentum in the post-independence period with the establishment of new industrial towns and the concern expressed for its lack in the various Five Year Plans and the provisions made for it in the setting up of the Central Town and Country Planning Organization for the preparation of a Model Town and Country Planning legislation which was given due consideration by the state ministers of town and country planning and adapted by the various states to suit their native requirements; establishment of metropolitan planning organizations; the recommendations made by the study team on the Machinery of Government of India and its Procedure of Work appointed by the Administrative Reforms Commission (1967); establishment of a Division of Town Planning in Planning Commission; and Town and Country Planning Organization at the centre and departments of town and country planning in states; and finally the setting up of the Central Ministry of Urban Development in 1985 as the nodal agency to oversee the planning processes and practices in pursuance of the urban policies through its apex technical advisory body, TCPO.

Despite all the paraphernalia provided for town and country planning in the form of legislation and the institutional agencies, the implementation of town planning schemes has not been satisfactory due to their inherent weaknesses and certain impediments such as planning being predominantly land-use oriented, and its not being a part of national planning process; absence of statutory backing of master plans, and existence of separate agencies for preparation and implementation of plans without any coordination among them; absence of interlinked and integrated rural and urban planning; encroachment of public lands; and political intervention and politician's role in encouraging the violation of planning regulations and thus frustrating the efforts of planners to plan for the planned development of urban and rural areas.

The remedies for making the town and country planning exercise worthwhile lie in providing for an effective town and planning organization in each state. Whereas Madhya Pradesh has a powerful directorate of Town and Country Planning and the Environment Planning Coordinating Organization (EPCO), Orissa has only a rudimentary one, there was virtually no town planning organization available even to prepare plans for newly developed resource specific industrial towns. Town and country planning is a discipline which has yet to achieve the status of some other disciplines such as public works, irrigation, and forestry. This does affect the weightage given to the advice rendered by a directorate on issues relating to settlement planning. Town planning needs to take care of conservation of historic towns, areas and monuments, and the architectural fabric of urban areas. Conservation must, therefore, be recognized as an integral part of the town planning process, that is, of land-use plans, building regulations and development policies.

In most states, the Directorate of Town and Country Planning languish at the level at which they were originally created, when during the Third and Fourth Five Year Plans the central government gave states some assistance for preparing urban plans. Traditional organizations such as TPCO, NBC, OBRI and NEERI are extremely diffused. This has seriously impaired their effectiveness both as research organizations and organizations which can render high level technical advice in the urban fields.

Finally, the schemes for town and country planning need to be formulated in the right perspective taking into consideration the present and future needs of the country, and should be implemented with a strong political will to ensure a planned development of land and other infrastructure.

NOTES AND REFERENCES

1. R.P. Misra, *Million Cities of India* (New Delhi: Vikas Publishing House, 1978), p. 16.
2. 'Report of the National Commission on Urbanisation Vol. I', Ministry of Urban Development, Govt. of India, New Delhi 1988, p. 1.
3. Census of India, 1961, Vol. 1, Part-II A(i), p. 51.
4. Mohit Bhattacharya, 'Urbanisation and Urban Problems in India: Some Policy Issues', *Nagarlok* 7, no. 4 (October–December, 1975): 4.
5. Report of the National Commission on Urbanisation, Vol. II, p. 1.
6. National Institute of Urban Affairs, Status of India's Urbanisation, 1986.
7. Report of the National Commission on Urbanisation, p. 5.
8. Statement of Shri V.S. Chaudhary, Haryana's Director of Census to T.N.S., 22 August 1991.
9. Dolly, Harbhajan Singh, *City Life Beckons All, The Tribune,* 4 October 1991.
10. S.R. Maheshwari, *Local Government in India* (Agra: Lakshmi Narain Aggarwal, 1984), p. 155.
11. Report of the National Commission on Urbanisation, p. 2.
12. R.K. Bhardwaj, 'The Problems of Urban Development in India', in S.K. Sharma (ed.), *Dynamics of Development,* Vol. II (Delhi: Concept Publication, 1978), p. 662.
13. Kingsley Davis, The Origin and Growth of Urbanisation in the World, *American Journal of Sociology,* March 1953: 429.

14. United Nations, Planning of Metropolitan Towns and New Areas, quoted in Francis Cherunelam, *Urbanisation in Developing Countries : A Socio-economic and Demographic Analysis* (Bombay: Himalaya Publishing Co., 1984), p. 65.
15. Report of the Ministry of Urban Development, Govt. of India, 1990–91, pp. 45–47.
16. *Ibid.*, p. 37.
17. Decision taken at a meeting of the Consultative Committee attached to Ministry of Urban Development at New Delhi on 11 November 1991, chaired by Mrs Sheila Kaul, Union Minister for Urban Development.
18. Towards Rural Prosperity—A Paper prepared by FICCI, New Delhi, 3 Feb 1992.
19. Town and Country Planning Organisation, National Urbanisation Policy: An approach. Proceedings of the meeting of Expert Group on National Urbanisation Policy 28th Jan. 1975.
20. S.S. Bhatti, *How to Combat Urbanisation,* The Tribune 22 July 1991.

Ministry of Urban Development

The subjects of urbanization, urban development and urban local government have been under the charge of various ministries in the past, and lately under the Ministry of Works and Housing. The Government of India, alarmed at the increase in the process of urbanization at a rapid pace and the consequent challenges posed by it, established a separate Ministry of Urban Development in 1985, which was renamed as Ministry of Urban Affairs and Employment in 1998. It is headed by a cabinet minister or a minister of state who is assisted by a minister of state or a deputy minister. Its executive and administrative head is the Secretary of senior IAS rank. He is assisted by two additional secretaries and four joint secretaries. The ministry has been allotted the following subjects for policy formulation and its execution and implementation:

1. Properties of the union, whether lands or buildings, with the following exceptions: (*i*) those belonging to the Ministry of Defence (*Raksha Mantralaya*), the Department of Railways and the Department of Atomic Energy and the Department of Space; (*ii*) buildings or lands, the construction or acquisition of which has been financed otherwise than from the Civil Works Budget; and (*iii*) buildings or lands, the control of which has at the time of construction or acquisition or subsequently been permanently made over to the other ministries and departments
2. All government civil works and buildings including those of union territories, excluding roads and excluding works executed by or buildings belonging to the Railways, P&T and the Department of Atomic Energy and the Department of Space
3. Horticulture operations
4. Central public works organization
5. Administration of government estates including government hostels under the control of the ministry; location or dispersal of offices in or from the metropolitan cities
6. Allotment of accommodation in Vigyan Bhavan
7. Administration of the Requisitioning and Acquisition of Immovable Property Act, 1952 (30 of 1952)
8. Administration of Delhi Hotels (Control of Accommodation) Act, 1949 (24 of 1949)
9. The Public Premises (Eviction of Unauthorised Occupants) Act, 1971 (40 of 1971)
10. Administration of four rehabilitation markets, viz. Sarojini Nagar Market, Shankar Market, Pleasure Garden Market, and Kamla Market

11. Issue of lease or conveyance deeds in respect of government-built properties in Delhi and New Delhi under the Displaced Persons (Compensation and Rehabilitation) Act, 1954 (44 of 1954), and conversion of lease deeds, allotment of additional strips of land and correctional areas adjoining such properties
12. Formulation of housing policy and programme (except nodal responsibility for housing for landless rural labour which is assigned to the Department of Rural Development; review of the implementation of the plan schemes; collection and dissemination of data on housing, building materials, and techniques; general measures for reduction of building costs
13. Human settlements including the United Nations Commission for Human Settlements and International Cooperation and Technical Assistance in the field of housing and human settlements
14. Stationery and printing for Government of India including official publications
15. Planning and coordination of urban transport systems, with technical planning of road based systems being subject to items 22 and 23 under the Ministry of Surface Transport, and technical planning or rail based systems being subject to items 1 and 2 under the Ministry of Railways, Railway Board
16. Urban development including slum clearance schemes and the jhuggi and jhonpri removal schemes; international cooperation and technical assistance in this field
17. Town and country planning; matters relating to the planning and development of metropolitan areas; international cooperation and technical assistance in this field
18. Schemes of large scale acquisition, development and disposal of land in Delhi
19. Delhi Development Authority
20. Master plan of Delhi, coordination of work in respect of the master plan and slum clearance in the Union Territory of Delhi
21. Erection of memorials in honour of freedom fighters
22. Administration of the Delhi Development Act, 1957 (67 of 1957)
23. The Delhi Rent Control Act, 1958 (59 of 1958)
24. Development of government colonies
25. Local government, that is to say, the constitution and powers of the municipal corporations (excluding the Municipal Corporation of Delhi); municipalities (excluding the New Delhi Municipal Committee), other local self-government administrations excluding Panchyat Raj institutions
26. The Delhi Water Supply and Sewage Disposal Undertaking of the Municipal Corporation of Delhi
27. Water supply, sewerage, and drainage (excluding rural water supply which is assigned to the Department of Rural Development); supply of drinking water and sanitation; international cooperation and technical assistance in this field
28. The Central Council of Local Self-Government
29. Allotment of government land in Delhi
30. All attached or subordinate offices or other organizations concerned with any of the subjects specified in this list
31. Public sector projects falling under the subject included in this list, except such projects as are specifically allotted to any other department
32. The Urban Land (Ceiling and Regulation) Act, 1976 (33 of 1976)
33. Delhi Urban Art Commission, Delhi Urban Art Commission Act, 1973 (1 of 1974)
34. Administration of Rajghat Samadhi Committee

35. All matters relating to planning and development of the National Capital Region and administration of the National Capital Region Planning Board Act, 1985 (2 of 1985)
36. Matters relating to the Indian National Trust for Art and Cultural Heritage (INTACH)
37. National Co-operative Housing Federation

Under its administrative control, the ministry has attached and subordinate offices, public sector undertakings and statutory or autonomous bodies as follows:

Attached Offices

Central Public Works Department, Directorate of Printing, Directorate of Estates, National Building Organization.

Subordinate Offices

Controller of Stationery, Controller of Publications, Land and Development Office, Town and Country Planning Organization.

Public Sector Undertakings

National Buildings Construction Corporation Ltd, Housing and Urban Development Corporation Ltd, Hindustan Prefab Ltd.

Statutory and Autonomous Bodies

Delhi Development Authority, Delhi Urban Arts Commission, National Capital Region Planning Board, National Institute of Urban Affairs

The Central Public Works Department is the principal agency of Government of India for construction and maintenance of all central government projects.

The Directorate of Estates is mainly responsible for the administration of government estates and hostels in addition to managing the central government lands in Delhi.

The Land and Development Office administers Nazul rehabilitation leases in Delhi.

The Town and Country Planning Organisation is the technical arm of the ministry in matters of town planning, regional planning and urban development.

The Central Public Health and Environmental Engineering Organization provides the technical inputs in the sphere of urban water supply and sanitation.

The National Building Organization disseminates information in respect of housing and building construction, with particular emphasis on promoting innovative and low cost technology.

The Directorate of Printing, with its 21 presses in various parts of the country, caters to the printing requirements of the central government ministries and departments.

The Stationery Office performs a similar function in respect of the stationery requirements of the central government offices.

The Publication Department, located in Delhi, stocks and sells government publications.

The Housing and Urban Development Corporation, established in 1970, is the premier housing finance institution in the public sector. It undertakes only indirect financing through housing agencies like the state housing boards, development authorities, municipal corporations, cooperatives, etc. Its operations are oriented to serve particularly the poorer sections of the society.

The National Building Construction Corporation is a civil construction agency which has major clients both in India and aboard. It has a number of turn key projects to its credit including bridges, flyovers, industrial structures, water treatment plants, hostels, TV towers, hospitals and railway buildings, etc.

The Hindustan Prefab Ltd is engaged mainly in the manufacture of pre-stressed cement concrete poles, railway sleepers, wooden joinery items, pre-cast concrete components, water storage tanks, Vayutan (light weight autoclaved cellular concrete) blocks for insulation, partitions, etc.

The Delhi Development Authority has statutory jurisdiction over all development and land-use in the union territory of Delhi and the *Delhi Urban Arts Commission* has statutory mandate to preserve and develop the aesthetic quality and environment in Delhi.

The National Capital Region Planning Board, constituted in March 1985 under the NCR Planning Board Act, 1985, has two important goals to be achieved, viz. (*i*) involving harmonized policies for the control of land-use and development and infrastructure in the NCR so as to avoid any haphazard development of the region, and (*ii*) achieving a manageable Delhi with a futuristic approach.

The National Institute of Urban Affairs (NIUA) was set up in 1976 as an autonomous organization, registered under the Societies Registration Act, 1860, for carrying out urban research in the country and collecting, processing, storing, and disseminating information relating to urban local bodies, their functioning, management, finances, development programmes, and personnel training.

Functions of the Ministry of Urban Development

The functions of the Ministry of Urban Development also includes the organization, functions and activities of the various offices attached and subordinate to it and also the public sector undertakings and statutory and autonomous bodies under its administrative control. These are discussed in detail as follows:

Housing and Human Settlements

Housing is a state subject but the central government is responsible for the formulation of policy with regard to programmes and approaches for effective implementation of the social housing schemes, particularly those pertaining to weaker sections of the society.

National Housing Policy

The draft National Housing Policy was placed before the Parliament in May 1988 and was adopted by the Rajya Sabha in November 1988. In January 1990, the government decided to reformulate the policy in order to take account of subsequent developments and to make it responsive to the needs of different income groups in urban and rural areas, particularly to the poorer sections of the community, women, and vulnerable groups. Accordingly, the draft National Housing Policy was reformulated and the ministry arranged for its widespread consultation and interaction with central ministries, state governments, governmental and non-governmental organizations, professionals and different sections of the population in various fora including four regional conferences at Madras, Bombay, Calcutta, and Delhi. The draft policy document was endorsed by the state governments and union territory administration in the conference of the ministers for housing, urban development, local self–government, held in New Delhi in October 1990. Meanwhile, the state governments had been requested to prepare action plans for the achievement of time bound physical and financial targets in housing within the context of the Eighth Plan.

National Housing Bank

With a view to augment the flow of institutional finance to the housing sector and to promote and regulate housing finance institutions, the National Housing Bank was set up as a subsidiary to the Reserve Bank of India in July 1988. The ministry is closely involved with various initiatives of the National Housing Bank for mobilizing resources and channelizing funds for various forms of housing activities and infrastructure within the framework of the National Housing Policy. The bank is operating a 'Home Loan Account Scheme' for the mobilization of savings from the general public linked to guaranteed loans and preferential allotment of a house. The National Housing Bank is operating refinance schemes for supplementing assistance by commercial banks, state or regional level home financing institutions (HFIs), a scheme for refinancing land development, and shelter schemes of public agencies and cooperatives. It is refinancing HUDCO's operations in respect of public agencies. Its schemes are targetted at dwelling units of less than 40 sq m.

Essentials of National Housing Policy

Parliament's decision to review the draft National Housing Policy for amendments and changes is a welcome step. The complex housing problem increases year after year mainly because of high birth rate and large influx of people into urban areas. Shelter being one of the most crucial human needs the demand for housing has always been exceeding the supply. In metropolitan cities of Mumbai, Calcutta, Delhi, and Chennai, one-third of population lives in deplorable conditions due to lack of adequate housing and absence of essential services. In rural areas, the condition of essential services is worse and most of the houses are unsafe or unfit for habitation.

A survey conducted by the National Building Organization has revealed that of the total demand of 15 crore houses, about 25 per cent is still unfulfilled which means 4 crore more houses to provide shelter to every household. Of this shortage of 4 crore houses, the rural shortfall amounts to 2.5 crore. With the mass inflow of rural people into cities, the rural and urban shortfalls are likely to become equal by the end of this decade.

Government of India took some measures to counter the problem of housing shortfall during the Seventh Five Year Plan. Two major measures taken were the laying down of the National Housing Policy and the creation of the National Housing Bank. These steps, though commendable, need further improvement for producing desirable results and for successful implementation.

While the success of the National Housing Policy lies in motivating the maximum people to invest in housing, in maximizing housing and in providing essential services of water-supply, sewerage, and lighting, the National Housing Bank should be able to attract people towards its housing schemes and in providing financial assistance to them.

The National Housing Policy needs a review of the resources and to match the priorities of the Tenth and Eleventh Five Year Plans. The following suggestions need to be incorporated in the national housing policy to make it more effective in the achievement of its targets:

1. The private sector should also be taken in the ambit of the National Housing Policy. Housing Development Financial Corporation on its own has done a tremendous job in the field of housing. With the government support, the private sector shall be able to better mobilize the resources for housing.
2. The policy should declare housing construction as an industry so that various concessions available to the industries may be available to the housing also.

3. More emphasis on raising multi-storeyed buildings needs to be laid in the policy. The population explosion in the country is gradually restricting the land available to each household. Since the cities already developed cannot be dismantled and rebuilt, separate areas in and around cities have to be planned for raising multi-storeyed residential buildings. It shall also be a step forward to promote group housing.
4. The number of small-size plots should be increased in the planning under land development schemes by the developing agencies like HUDA, DDA, and others. This will accommodate more people in each of the newly developed locality in each city.
5. The National Housing Policy must lay emphasis on use of low cost techniques in housing. National Building Organization has been working on the development of a number of cost reduction techniques and has made successful efforts in this direction. What is essentially required is that these techniques developed by the National Building Organization are to be better promoted at state and national level by imposing them on PWDs, housing boards, and housing authorities. The research institutions like CBRI, NBO, and others should be encouraged to continue their research work on cost reduction techniques. Engineers, architects, and builders who come forward with new ideas, proposals, and designs should be rewarded under a special clause in the policy.
6. Public sector undertakings should be asked to develop housing colonies for their employees. The employees should be provided accommodation during their service at various stations of postings and on retirement they should be given ownership of a house at the station of their choice. The cost of the house may be recovered from the employee gradually during his service period. In short, instead of house building loans, houses should be provided. Finances for such housing colonies can be arranged from HUDCO which has evolved a number of such schemes for grant of loans to public bodies. The policy should liberalize and enlarge the scope of HUDCO. The HUDCO schemes should envisage return of loan by collecting monthly recovery installments from the employees. Such schemes will solve the housing problem to a large extent. The group housing colonies so developed will have better hygienic conditions and the houses shall cost much lesser than that each employee will incur individually in building one's house. Cost reduction techniques shall also have better scope in such schemes.
7. Another feature of the National Housing Policy should be the compilation of a separate price index for building materials. The all India consumer price index (CPI) does not truly reflect the increase in prices of building materials. (The last CPI shows that there is an increase in the cost of building materials which does not correspond with actual increase in cost of building materials which has been more than 12 per cent). Building materials price index (BMPI) will enable the government to exercise a better control over prices of building materials as well as save a number of real estate projects from shelving mid-way as the builder initially calculates the cost of each unit on the basis of CPI and later finds it difficult to cope with the increase in prices of building materials.
8. Home loan account scheme floated by the NHB should also be reviewed. The scheme aimed at collecting Rs 240 crore by June 1991, but could gather Rs 30 crore only. To attract more investors, the NHB should provide better concessions.
9. The National Housing Policy should be made a part of the Five Year Plans. Targets fixed thus can be better monitored. This will also necessitate regular survey of the demand for houses in rural and urban sectors and thus a realistic demand versus supply chart of housing can be prepared.

With the above measures, it will be easier to cope with housing scarcity and today's pipe dream of providing 'shelter to all'.

Building Centres and Technology Extension

The national network of Nirman or Nirmiti Kendras (building centres) is being established with central assistance through HUDCO under a central scheme. These centres impart training to artisans in low cost construction skills and produce building materials and components including fly ash bricks and established mud blocks through innovative techniques. The scheme has been in operation since 1988–89. Under the scheme, a central grant of Rs 2 lakh is given to each centre and this is supplemented by HUDCO loan at a low rate of interest. So far 160 centres have been identified out of which 50 had become functional till 31 December 1990. Some states have set up state level units for running these centres and are entrusting various construction works to them. The products of these building centres have been exempted from excise on the recommendation of the ministry.

Building Materials and Technology Promotion Council

In order to bridge the gap between research and development and to promote large-scale application of innovative building materials and technologies, an organization named 'Building Materials and Technology Promotion Council' has been set up as a society under the aegis of the Ministry of Urban Development. The union minister for urban development is the president of this council. The Board of Management has representatives from concerned central ministries, state governments, housing finance and industrial development promotion institutions like the NHB, HUDCO, IDBI, IFCO, ICICI, etc. The council was inaugurated by the minister for urban development on 24 July 1990. The council is structured to undertake the task of extension and application of technologies and materials developed by research institutions on the ground, especially by public agencies like CPWD, to promote the manufacture of building materials from industrial and agricultural wastes, to encourage entrepreneurs in this sector and to ensure appropriate changes in specifications and standards to make available low cost technologies to individual households. The council has already taken a lot of initiative in utilization of fly ash and other wastes, introduction of new specifications by CPWD and BIS and to increase the entrepreneurs interface with financial institutions and research agencies.

Pavement Dwellers Scheme

This scheme was introduced to provide shelter to the footpath dwellers and the absolutely shelterless in metropolitan and large cities. Under the action plan of the government, announced in January 1990, the central scheme sought to provide night shelter and sanitation facilities to foot path dwellers at a per capita cost of Rs 5,000 with 20 per cent subsidy from the central government and 90 per cent loans from HUDCO. The scheme is now applicable to all urban areas, wherever the problem of footpath dwellers exists.

Central Government Employees Welfare Housing Organization

A new organization for providing housing to central government employees was set up as a society under the aegis of the ministry of urban development to meet a long felt need of central government employees. The society started functioning from October 1990 and has since then executing housing schemes for central government employees in different parts of the country.

Social Housing Schemes

The social housing schemes, namely (*i*) Housing Scheme for EWS, (*ii*) Housing Scheme for LIG, (*iii*) Housing Scheme for MIG, (*iv*) Rental Housing Scheme for state government employees, (*v*) Rural Housing Sites-cum-Construction Assistance Scheme for landless workers are being implemented in the state sector with state plan provision and loan assistance from HUDCO and other financial institutions.

Urban Employment Through Housing and Shelter Upgradation

As a component of the Nehru Rozgar Yojna, HUDCO has launched a scheme for urban employment through housing and shelter upgradation in all cities and towns with a population between one lakh and twenty lakhs, for beneficiaries with an annual household income of less than Rs 7,300. The financing pattern of the scheme provides that HUDCO will finance upto Rs 3,000 as loans for each dwelling unit which will be dovetailed with a central government subsidy of Rs 800. In addition, a subsidy of Rs 200 will be provided by the state government or the concerned local body. Under this scheme, HUDCO had sanctioned 170 schemes. In order to derive maximum benefits from this scheme and also to make it fully operational, grants are provided under NRY through HUDCO towards training for upgrading the construction skills of the beneficiaries through local bodies and selected training centres at the rate of Rs 1500 per trainee with other forms of support.

National Cooperative Housing Federation of India (NCHF)

The National Cooperative Housing Federation (NCHF) of India was set up in 1969 as a national level organization spearheading the entire cooperative housing movement in India and is supported by the Ministry of Urban Development as part of the government's encouragement of cooperative housing. Its aims are to coordinate the apex cooperative housing finance societies, and to promote and develop cooperative housing societies in the country. Till 1989–90, out of 25 state-level apex societies and federations, 23 had become members of the NCHF. The state-level apex societies had advanced loan of Rs 1889.56 crores to the primary cooperative societies for the construction of 1,975,910 houses till 31 March 1990, and have mobilized considerable savings for construction in the process. They are now securing refinancing from NHB and loans from HUDCO for enlarged operations. Nearly 60 per cent of the units are meant for low income groups. So far the government's contribution towards paid up share capital is Rs 15.25 lakh. During the year 1989–90, a grant-in-aid of Rs 3.90 lakh was sanctioned for NCHF by the central government. NCHF also takes up training schemes for the personnel for cooperative housing societies. It has formulated a model law for cooperatives for the guidance of state governments.

International Cooperation

United Nations Centre for Human Settlements

United Nations Centre for Human Settlements (UNCHS) is an inter-government body established through a resolution of the UN General Assembly for guiding the habitat activities. India is a member of UNCHS and has been contributing 1 lakh US Dollars since 1976. Half of the annual contributions is payable in Indian currency. India was re-elected as a member of UNCHS is 1988 for a period of four years. Thus, India continues to be a member of UNCHS till 31 December 1991.

Urban Development

Urban development is a state subject and the central government performs an advisory and coordinating role apart from providing technical and financial assistance for promoting orderly urbanization, as is reflected in the schemes mentioned as follows:

Centrally Sponsored Scheme for Integrated Development of Small and Medium Towns (IDSMT)

The Scheme of IDSMT was launched during the Sixth Five Year Plan in 1979–80 with an outlay of Rs 96 crores to reduce the migration of population from rural areas to major urban areas; to generate employment by creating resource generating ventures in the small and medium towns and also to provide sufficient infrastructure facilities in these towns so that their hinterland is served better. The scheme continued during the Seventh Five Year Plan with an outlay of Rs 88 crore. Under this scheme, central assistance was given to towns where population was less than one lakh during 1971 census for the Sixth Plan and during 1981 census for the Seventh Plan. However, certain towns with a population above one lakh, as identified by the National Commission on Urbanization for priority development, were also considered under the scheme during the Seventh Plan.

In the Scheme during the Sixth Five Year Plan, each town was given a maximum central assistance of Rs 40 lakh on 50 per cent matching basis, with an additional sum of Rs 15 lakh for low cost sanitation (LCS) provided the state government made arrangements for another Rs 12 lakh for the same. During the Seventh Plan the pattern was changed as follows: Central assistance on matching basis to the tune of Rs 46 lakh for infrastructure, Rs 8 lakh as compulsory LCS component, and Rs 6 lakh as an optional LCS component. During the Sixth Five Year Plan, 235 towns were covered and central Assistance of Rs 63.57 crore was given. During the Seventh Five Year Plan, central assistance of Rs 80.05 crore had been released which included not only the assistance for 145 new towns but also subsequent instalments for the towns which were approved during the Sixth Five Year Plan. By the end of the Seventh Five Year Plan the state governments had reported a total expenditure of Rs 195.22 crore. The scheme is continuing with timely amendments and modifications:

Objectives of the Scheme

1. Improving infrastructural facilities and helping in the creation of durable public assets in small and medium towns
2. Decentralizing economic growth and employment opportunities and promoting dispersed urbanization
3. Increasing the availability of serviced sites for housing, commercial and industrial uses
4. Integrating spatial and socio-economic planning as envisaged in the Constitution (74th Amendment) Act, 1992
5. Promoting resource generating scheme for urban local bodies to improve their overall financial position

For the year 1998–99, central assistance of Rs 35 crore were earmarked under this scheme.

Infrastructure Development in Mega Cities

Keeping in view the recommendations of the National Commission on Urbanization (NCU) and in response to persistent demands made by the state governments for central assistance to undertake the development of infrastructure in mega cities, the centrally sponsored scheme for infrastructural development in mega cities was initiated during 1993–94. The primary objective of the scheme is to enable the mega cities to build a revolving fund by the end of the Ninth Plan for sustained investment in urban infrastructure through adoption of direct and indirect cost recovery measures. The main features of the scheme are as follows:

1. The scheme is applicable to Mumbai, Calcutta, Chennai, Bangalore, and Hyderabad
2. The funds under the scheme are channelized through a specialized institution or a nodal agency at the state level
3. The sharing between the central government and the state government is at 25 : 25 : 50, with the larger proportion to be met from institutional finance or the capital market
4. The projects under the scheme consist of a suitable mix/basket of (*i*) remunerative, (*ii*) user charge-based, and (*iii*) basic services projects
5. The nodal agencies are required to provide project related finance for urban infrastructure including water supply, sewerage, drainage, sanitation, city transport networks, land development, slum improvement, solid waste management, etc.

Projects by Foreign Countries

The central government has negotiated for a line of credit to HUDCO and HDFC from the KFW of Germany and the OECF of Japan. The KFW will provide assistance by way of a loan of DM 30 million to HUDCO for undertaking housing schemes for EWS. In addition, in understanding for providing a grant of DM 10 million to HUDCO for its building centres programmes has been reached. The KFW has agreed to provide DM 25 million to HDFC for financing EWS housing programmes. Proposals have been sent for loan assistance from OECF, Japan to HUDCO for financing urban infrastructure projects.

Ministry of Urban Development had close interaction with the ESCAP activities and participated in two important and policy level Seminars on 'Innovative Community based Housing Finance and Credit System for Low Income Households and Developing the Building components Industry through the Application of Modular Coordination Rules' held at Bangkok during 1990.

World Bank Assisted Urban Development Projects

The World Bank (IDA) is assisting various states in urban development programmes. These projects are currently under implementation in the states of West Bengal, Madhya Pradesh, Maharashtra, Gujarat, Uttar Pradesh, and Tamil Nadu. Slum upgradation, water supply and sanitation, shelter upgradation, area development, transportation, etc. are the components for which the World Bank assistance is given. These projects are monitored by the ministry. The ministry is also in the process of getting additional project reports from the state governments of Kerala, Himachal Pradesh, Orissa, Maharashtra, Andhra Pradesh, Karnataka, and Madhya Pradesh for placing before the World Bank.

Urban Transport

The responsibility of coordinating the urban transport system throughout the country rests with the Ministry of Urban Development. Urban Consortium Fund has been created to assist various state governments and union territories in taking up studies for the improvement of the transport network in urban areas. The ministry extended assistance to the Delhi administration for conducting a feasibility study on Mass Rapid Transit System for Delhi and had sanctioned funds to the governments of Karnataka, Tamil

Nadu, and Rajasthan in connection with carrying out transportation studies for Bangalore, Madras, and Jaipur, respectively.

URBAN LAND (CEILING AND REGULATION) ACT, 1976

The Urban Land (Ceiling and Regulation) Act, 1976, came into force on 17 February 1976 in the states of Andhra Pradesh, Gujarat, Haryana, Himachal Pradesh, Karnataka, Maharashtra, Orissa, Punjab, Tripura, Uttar Pradesh, and West Bengal and in all the union territories. The act was subsequently adopted by the states of Assam, Bihar, Madhya Pradesh, Manipur, Meghalaya, and Rajasthan. The state governments. union territories have so far acquired 29,751.53 hectares of excess vacant land and approved 2406 schemes for the construction of 319,951 dwelling units.

Regional Centres for Urban and Environmental Studies

The ministry assists the three regional centres for urban and environmental studies in Bombay, Lucknow, and Hyderabad in addition to the Centre for Urban Studies, IIPA, New Delhi, by releasing grants-in-aid from the non-plan and plan funds, for enabling them to conduct training programmes and seminars and workshops for policy makers and officials connected with urban development and local self-governments.

Training in the Field of Urban Development Under the Colombo Plan

The ministry is allotted training slots in the field of urban development of subjects like housing, urban transport, urban finance, management of urban development, management of urban renewal, etc. for technical cooperation training programmes Fellowships under the Colombo Plan. The ministry nominates suitable officers for such training courses. Moreover, in order to strengthen the municipal governments and to enable them to improve their performance considerably, a draft municipal training plan has been finalized by the ministry in consultation with All India Institute of Local Self-Government, Bombay. The main emphasis under the first phase of implementation of the Municipal Training Plan (MUNTP) is to upgrade the skills of the staff working in the larger cities.

WATER SUPPLY AND SANITATION

Water supply and sanitation are state subjects. The Ministry of Urban Development is responsible for policy formulation, coordination of the International Drinking Water Supply and Sanitation Decade Programme, technical guidance, organizing conference and seminars, manpower development, research activities, management information system, and in securing international cooperation and assistance. The activities of the ministry in this respect may be summarized as follows:

1. International Drinking Water Supply and Sanitation Decade: The United Nations had declared the period 1981–90 as the 'International Drinking Water Supply and Sanitation Decade' with a view to provide safe drinking water supply and adequate sanitation facilities to all the member countries by 1990. The 'decade' programme was launched in India on 1 April 1981 with the objective of increasing the urban population coverage with water supply facilities from 72.25 per cent in 1981 to 100 per cent in 1991 and with sewerage and sanitation facilities from 25.04 per cent in 1981 to 80 per cent in 1991. During the Seventh Five Year Plan, an outlay of Rs 2935.64 crore under the state sector and Rs 39.11

crore under the central sector had been provided for urban water supply and sanitation as against the projected requirement of Rs 5997.7 crore. Keeping in view the outlay provided, the decade targets in respect of urban water supply and sanitation were scaled down to 90 per cent and 50 per cent, respectively. The Working Group for the formulation of the Eighth Five Year Plan (1990–95) has envisaged requirement of funds for urban water supply sanitation sector, including solid waste management to the tune of Rs 14,094 crores in order to achieve coverage of 100 per cent for urban water supply (Rs 8,850 crore), 75 per cent for sewerage and sanitation (Rs 5,000 crore), solid waste management facilities in 40 towns with more than 5 lakh population (Rs 200 crore) and support programmes for manpower development, research activities, etc. (Rs 44 crore). In view of the resource constraints prevailing in most of the states and urban local bodies, the ministry has been concentrating in augmenting and expanding the base for urban infrastructure financing through the Housing and Urban Development Corporation (HUDCO).

2. Urban Low Cost Sanitation: Separate schemes had been under implementation for the elimination of scavenging through construction of low cost sanitation units through the Ministry of Welfare, Ganga Action Plan, Integrated Development of Small and Medium Towns, and loans from HUDCO. These schemes have since been integrated for the elimination of manual scavenging to maximum possible extent in the Eighth Five Year Plan. Under the scheme, 500 towns with population of less than 5 lakh (1981 census) are to be declared scavenger free annually. This would be achieved on a whole town basis through urban local bodies in the state governments and union territories by replacing existing dry latrines or construction of low cost sanitation units where open defecation is resorted to and rehabilitation of the scavengers thereby liberated. The scheme is being operated through HUDCO by providing a mix of subsidy from the central government and loans from the HUDCO in a synchronized manner to the state governments and union territories where the problem persists as per the following financing pattern subject to availability of fund: EWS (45 per cent subsidy, 50 per cent loan and 5 per cent beneficiary contribution), LIG (25 per cent subsidy. 60 per cent loan and 15 per cent beneficiary contribution), MIG/HIG (Nil subsidy, 75 per cent loan and 25 per cent beneficiary contribution).

Training Programmes

The ministry provides assistance for conducting postgraduate, short-term and refresher courses in selected key areas for the benefit of all categories of personnel engaged in urban water supply and sanitation. It also arranges technical study tours for various WHO fellows of neighbouring countries. The ministry had sponsored officials from the states and the union territories for training programme in different disciplines on water supply and sanitation in UK under the Colombo Plan and for training-cum-study tours abroad under the WHO Fellowship programme. The ministry also organizes seminars and workshops and research activities on various aspects of water supply and sanitation management, and tries to secure international cooperation and assistance from UNDP or the World Bank for various schemes.

Central Public Works Department

The Central Public Works Department (CPWD) is the principal agency of Government of India for construction and maintenance of all central government projects, except those of Railways, Communication, Atomic Energy, Defence, Airports (National and International) and All India Radio. The activities of the CPWD cover a wide spectrum of area and encompass selection of sites, geotechnical investigations, architectural, structural, electrical, air-conditioning and landscape planning, design, execution and monitoring, quality control and post-completion maintenance, contract management and arbitration cases, etc.

The CPWD handles a wide range of projects like housing and commercial complexes, educational institutions, sports complexes, hospitals, workshops, factories, hostels, foodgrain storage structures, roads, bridges, etc., and until recently, airports, too. It also undertakes works of public sector undertakings and autonomous bodies as 'deposit works'.

The CPWD has developed considerable expertise in the field of civil, electrical, mechanical, and air-conditioning engineering, architecture, horticulture, and landscaping. It has a Central Design Organization to undertake complex structural design work with the help of computers and to provide consultancy services. The department has also introduced computerization in other areas like architectural design, project scheduling and monitoring, schedules of rates, payroll and personnel management, inventory control, etc. The Central Public Works Department specifications and schedules of rates are comprehensive and reflect the experience gained over nearly six decades. These are updated periodically and find wide acceptance among several departments, public sector undertakings, and even private architects.

The CPWD has field units spread all over India to take up construction works even in remote parts of the Country. The Department also undertakes works abroad for India-aided projects and Indian embassies.

Directorate of Estates

The Directorate of Estates is mainly responsible for:

1. Administration of government estates (residential/office accommodation) under the control of the Ministry of Urban Development at New Delhi, Mumbai, Calcutta, Chennai, Shimla. Nagpur, Faridabad, Ghaziabad, and Chandigarh;
2. Allotment of accommodation in Vigyan Bhawan;
3. Administration of: (*i*) Requisitioning and Acquisition of Immovable Property Act, 1952, and (*ii*) Public Premises (Eviction of Unauthorised Occupants) Act, 1971;
4. Control and administration of Grand Hotel, Shimla, and government hostels;
5. Administration of markets in government colonies in Delhi, Faridabad, and Ghaziabad;
6. Administration of holiday homes for central government employees at Kanyakumari. Mussorie, and Shimla.

A separate Ministry of Works and Estates had been carved out of the Ministry of Urban Development and was placed under the charge of a cabinet minister on 22 October 1999.

Earmarking of Residential Accommodation for the Union Council of Ministers

While allotting residences to the cabinet ministers or minister of state or deputy ministers, it has to be ensured that the building has sufficient accommodation to take care of the functional needs of the minister. The first functional necessity is office accommodation preferably in a separate block. The second functional necessity is vast open space to receive a large number of visitors. Besides, in recent past security has become another important prerequisite so that necessary security arrangements can be made in the ministerial bungalows. In brief, these three basic requisites for ministerial bungalows have to be ensured on a permanent basis involving considerable expenditure. Consequently, it is necessary to ensure that the bungalows with these facilities are always allotted to them.

This can be achieved by earmarking bungalows for the ministers. Therefore, it had been decided to approach the cabinet to earmark bungalows for the Union Council of Ministers. The cabinet decided that the proposal may be given effect to through a resolution and legislation may be brought about subsequently. They also directed that the leaders of opposition in both the Houses of Parliament should also be included in the said resolution. Accordingly, a Resolution dated 30 May 1990 was published in the Gazette of India earmarking 68 bungalows for the Union Council of Ministers and leaders of opposition in both the Houses of Parliament. More accommodation is to be sought for them.

National Buildings Organization

The National Buildings Organization (NBO) was established in 1954, and is engaged in the promotion of substitute or new building materials such as clay pozzolana, cellular concrete strength bricks, plastic pipes, secondary species of timber, the materials based on industrial and agricultural wastes like fly ash bricks, wood board, coir waste, roofing sheets, bamboo materials, roofing, etc. It has been propagating the use of dehydrated lime for saving cement for building construction. The organization has also been engaged in the promotion of pre-fabricated housing system for mass housing. The NBO and its 15 regional housing development centres organize training courses also.

In the light of the establishment of the Building Materials and Technology Promotion Council, a restructuring exercise for NBO has been taken up in order to make it complementary to the extension functions of the council and to emphasize the role of NBO in building up the housing information system and promotion of research.

Town and Country Planning Organization

The Town and Country Planning Organization (TCPO) is the apex technical advisory body on matters relating to urban and regional planning strategies, research, monitoring and evaluation of central government schemes and development policies. It provides technical inputs for formulation of urban development and infrastructural development policies to the Ministry of Urban Development and provides consultative services and project assistance to different states and organizations. The TCPO is involved in the appraisal, monitoring and evaluation of important schemes of Government of India such as the Integrated Development of Small and Medium Towns (IDSMT), Urban Basic Services programme (UBS), PM's special grant programme for Bombay, World Bank assisted state urban development projects and Environmental Improvement of Urban Slums Schemes (EIUS), etc.

Directorate of Printing

The Directorate of Printing is primarily responsible for executing printing jobs for all ministries and departments of the central government. Apart from government publications, printing of forms for civil and defence purposes, stocking and distribution of forms amongst various government departments as per their needs are also primary and important functions of this directorate. The directorate has under its administrative control 21 printing presses' including three textbook presses, spread throughout the country and a forms store and an outside printing establishment at Kolkata.

Stationery and Publications

Government of India Stationery Office is responsible for the procurement and supply of paper, paper made articles and other stationery items to the departments and offices of the government including various missions abroad, union territory administration and a few quasi-government organizations. The headquarters of the department is at Calcutta with three regional depots in New Delhi, Mumbai, and Chennai.

The Department of Publications is responsible for the stocking, sale, and distribution of government publications (including periodicals, the *Gazette of India*, and *Delhi Gazette*) of about 185 departments and ministries, attached and subordinate offices of the central government and autonomous bodies.

Statutory and Autonomous Bodies

Delhi Development Authority

Delhi Development Authority was established under the Delhi Development Act, 1957, to provide for planned development of Delhi and to give concrete shape to the policy of bringing order into building activity in Delhi. The Authority is a body corporate having perpetual succession and a common seal with power to acquire, hold, and disposal of property, and to contract. It can sue and be sued.

Delhi Urban Art Commission

The Delhi Urban Art Commission was set up by an Act of Parliament with a view to 'advise the Central Government in the matter of preserving, developing and maintaining the aesthetic quality of urban and environmental design within Delhi and to provide advice and guidance to any local body in respect of any project of building operations or engineering operations or any development proposal which affects or is likely to affect the sky-line or the aesthetic quality of surroundings or any public amenity provided therein.' The Act came into force with effect from 1 May 1974.

Primarily local bodies like Delhi Development Authority, Municipal Corporation Delhi and New Delhi Municipal Committee refer to the commission for advice, the plans of schemes submitted to them by practising architects before according approval. The projects and schemes are analysed and deliberated upon by the commission in its regular meetings in which the concerned architects are also afforded an opportunity to interact with the commission and explain their concept. The advice given by the commission is communicated to the local bodies for further necessary action. The commission is also designed to undertake *suo-moto* projects and studies relating to certain specific projects of wider interest for the development of Delhi.

National Capital Region Planning Board

The National Capital Region Planning Board was set up in March 1985 to prepare a statutory plan for the National Capital Region undertaking a series of in-depth studies and consultations at various levels. The statutory enforcement had commenced on 23 January 1989. The National Capital Region (NCR) Plan is a statutory plan of its own kind in the country providing for planned development of an inter-state region, which has been prepared with the active involvement of not only the participating state governments of Haryana, Rajasthan, and Uttar Pradesh and the union territory of Delhi Administration, but also includes proposals which have been prepared in consultation with the concerned central ministries.

The NCR Plan, 2001 has laid primary stress on development of infrastructure, both at regional and local levels, and large-scale employment generation in the identified priority towns to prevent continued migration.

National Institute of Urban Affairs

The National Institute of Urban Affairs was set up in 1976 as an autonomous organization registered under the Societies Registration Act, 1860, for carrying out research in urban development and administration and collecting, processing, storing, and disseminating information regarding urban local bodies, their functioning, management, finance, development programmes, and personnel training. The ministry has been assisting the institute by providing annual grants. The institute regularly interacts with national and international agencies also.

The institute sponsors research projects on the topics of great significance and relevance such as the Informal Finance for the Urban Housing Status and Prospects; Municipal Corporation of Delhi: A Study of its Finances; Slum Improvement and Upgradation Projects for Trivandrum, Cochin and Calicut; Women, Urban Poverty and Economic Development; Urban Child: Factors and Processes of Marginalization; Index and profiles of innovations in Delhi; A Directory of Non-governmental Organizations in India; Accessibility and Adequacy of Basic Services to the Urban Poor; Women in the Urban Informal Sector, etc. The institute also carries out studies on subjects such as Formulation of National Urban Policy (Draft Report); Women in the Urban Informal Sector, etc., and organizes training-workshops, conferences, and seminars in different cities all over the country on such themes as: Women in the Urban Informal Sector; training-workshop on 'Planning and Management of Urban Services'; symposium on 'Urban Policy and Development: Agenda for the 1990s'; a symposium on 'Strengthening of Municipal Government', etc.

The Institute publishes *Urban India*, a bi-annual journal which caters to the needs of academics, administrators, and public men and agencies dealing with urban planning and development issues.

National Building Construction Corporation Limited

The National Building Construction Corporation is engaged over the last 40 years in the execution of a wide variety of civil construction works all over the country for various government departments, public sector undertakings, autonomous bodies, and also for overseas clients. The entire works of the corporation have been divided into two groups, viz. conventional works and specialized works. The specialized works are those works which come from the trust areas of the corporation, which are by nature high technology works. To improve the financial viability, the corporation has entered into the real estate sector. This would be a major thrust area in the future.

Housing and Urban Development Corporation

The Housing and Urban Development Corporation (HUDCO) was set up as fully owned Government Company in April 1970 as an apex techno-finance organization with a view to providing loans and technical support to state and city level agencies and other eligible organizations for various types of housing activity and infrastructural development.

Hindustan Prefab Limited

Hindustan Prefab Limited is a Government of India enterprise functioning under the administrative control of the Ministry of Urban Development since 1955. The company is managed by a Board of Directors.

The company's activities are divided into (*i*) factory products—pre-stressed concrete electric poles and railway sleepers, precast reinforced or pre-stressed concrete building components and light weight concrete blocks, wooden doors and windows, fly ash bricks; and (*ii*) construction works using partial pre-fabrication techniques.

Achievements of the Ministry of Urban Development: An Overview

The Ministry of Urban Development has two distinct sets of responsibilities. One pertains to the construction and maintenance of central government buildings, including residential accommodation, with the exception of those under the ministries of Defence, Railways and Posts and Telegraphs. It is also responsible for the management of central government land and property, most of which is confined to Delhi and some of the metropolitan cities. Their functions are discharged through the agencies of the Central Public Works Department which has field organizations spread all over the country and the Land and Development Office located in Delhi.

The other set of responsibilities pertain to the broad policy formulation and monitoring of programmes in the areas of housing, urban development, urban poverty alleviation and urban water supply. These are essentially 'state' subjects but Government of India plays a coordinating and monitoring role and also supports these programmes through central sector schemes, institutional finance, and expertise.

As it is estimated that a large section of India's population would be living in urban and semi-urban areas within the next decade, the role of the Ministry of Urban Development, from that of mere house-keeping work, has changed to that of planning and policy formulation. With the addition of the subject of urban transport, after the submission of the report of the National Commission on Urbanization and follow-up action thereon, and the formulation of the comprehensive National Housing Policy, the working and function of this ministry has undergone a new re-orientation. The ministry also administratively controls the central government departments of Printing, Stationery, and Publication.

The National Housing Policy continues to formulate short-term and long-term perspectives in the field of housing with necessary assistance from the National Housing Bank for grant of loans. One of the most important challenges facing the country is the task of adequately feeding, educating housing, and employing a large and rapidly growing number of impoverished city dwellers. Though efforts were initiated in the Fifth Five Year Plan to tackle the problem of urban poverty, it is only during the Seventh Plan period that concerted efforts were made to directly solve the problem in a coordinated manner. In the post-Independence period, for the first time an integrated view has been taken for the alleviation of urban poverty by developing a package of programmes such as Nehru Rozgar Yojna, Urban Basic Services for the poor, Environmental Improvement of Urban Slums, Low Cost Sanitation, etc. The Nehru Rozgar Yojna designed to promote self-employment ventures and wage employment was launched in October 1989. The Scheme of Urban Basic Services for the Poor envisages support for bias services, especially social services. The Environmental Improvement of Urban Slums aims at promoting basic physical amenities in the urban slums. These schemes have since been replaced by the Swarna Jayanti Shehari Rozgar Yojna in August 1997.

In order to bridge the gap between research and development and to promote the large-scale application of innovative building materials and technologies, an organization named 'Building Materials and Technology Promotion Council' had been set up as a society under the aegis of the Ministry of Urban Development. The council is structured to undertake the task of extension and application of technologies and materials developed by research institutions, to promote the manufacture of building materials from industrial and agricultural wastes, to encourage entrepreneurs in this sector, to ensure appropriate changes in specifications and standards and to make available low cost technologies to individual households. The council has taken a lot of initiative in utilization of fly ash and other wastes, introduction of new specifications by CPWD and BIS, and to increase the entrepreneurs' interface with financial institutions and research agencies.

Construction of office and residential buildings constitute the bulk of the workload of the Central Public Works Department. The Master Plan for Delhi with perspective development plan till 2001 came into force on 1 August 1990. Under its special projects, the DDA have undertaken planning of three more schemes at Rohini. For the Dwarka Project which is planned to accommodate about 10 lakh population, detailed sectoral plans and services plans had been finalized. The development of the Narela Project on 450 hectares of land is also nearing completion.

A new organization for providing housing to the central government employees has been set up as a 'society' under the administrative control of the Ministry of Urban Development. This meets a long felt need of central government employees. The society started functioning from October 1990 and has executed housing schemes for the central government employees in different parts of the country.

Night Shelter Scheme for footpath dwellers, initially introduced in the metropolitan cities, has now been extended to all urban areas to improve the shelter conditions of vulnerable target groups.

Implementation of the integrated scheme of Low Cost Sanitation and Liberation of Scavengers, introduced in 1989, has been accelerated.

Suggestions for Revamping the Ministry

Despite the achievements of the ministry, it suffers from certain infirmities which need to be rectified in order to make it a more effective instrument for better development of urban areas and their management. The following suggestions were made by the National Commission on Urbanization in this regard.

1. Ministry Should Be Relieved of Extraneous Work: The Ministry of Urban Development must be the nodal ministry for all settlement issues in general and urbanization in particular. It should be shorn of all extraneous work, including the Delhi Division, the Central Public Works Department, the Printing and Stationery Office, the Directorate of Estates, and the Land and the Development Office. These could be transferred to a separate Ministry of Works and Estates.

2. Need for Creating Additional Divisions: The Ministry of Urban Development should, apart from Divisions of Housing, Urban Development, Public Health Engineering, etc., also have two separate divisions of urbanization and urban poverty alleviation, each under a joint secretary or an additional secretary. It is only thus that the implementation of the report of the National Commission on Urbanization, the monitoring of its implementation and review of policies relating to urbanization could become possible and a vigorous effort could be made to deal with the problem of urban poverty.

3. Setting up of National Urbanization Council: Because urbanization is a vital and desirable element of society and the economy, it is but appropriate that, at the national level, a strong and properly structured framework for urbanization should be created. It has been the experience that in any area where new ground has to be broken, the bonds of routine administration have to be untied, and dynamic organizations, capable of decision-making, created. The Atomic Energy Commission, the Electronics Commission, the Council of Scientific and Industrial Research, the National Council of Educational Research and Training, and the Indian Council of Agricultural Research, to name just a few, are governmental organizations which stand outside the normal departmental structure and yet provide impetus to both research and action in specialized field. Urbanization, encompassing, as it does, vast agglomerations of people and a myriad of complex activities, is one such specialized field. The National Commission on Urbanization strongly recommends the setting up of a high-powered full-time National Urbanization Council (NUC). An urbanologist of note, who has practical experience in the field of urban planning and administration, should be its chairman. The council should not only oversee all research in urbanization, but should also firmly guide policy and its implementation. In the matter of settlement planning and management, the council would combine the types of functions performed by the ICAR, in applied research, and the AEC in implementation.

4. Inclusion of a Full Time Urbanization Member in the Planning Commission: The Planning Commission too must have a full-time Urbanization Member. It would be fitting if he is a well-known urban planner. Not only would this bring a high degree of professionalism to settlement planning at the national level, but would also give due importance to the discipline of town planning by according a high status to a planner. The member should be assisted by a full-time Advisor, who would head the urbanization division in the Planning Commission.

5. Role of the Central Town and Country Planning Organization: The Central Town and Country Planning Organisation (TCPO) should be transferred to the control of the proposed National Urbanization Council. It would then have the same relationship *qua* the council as the Indian Agricultural Research Institute has with ICAR, it would be the organization through which the NUC would undertake field work, monitoring and evaluation, and programme formulation. In fact, there is a good case also for transferring the NBC) and the regional centres which impart training to the NUC. The TCPO should move away from its present function of low-grade plan preparation. Its chief planner should have a status equivalent to that of the Director General of the CSIR, and he should be the Director General and Chief Technical Advisor of the NUC. Basically the TCPO should organize a research programme and oversee it. It should help in the formulation of broad urbanization policies and should be the focal point for inter-state discussions at official level on urbanization issues. It should develop long-term perspectives of settlement patterns, even to the extent of indulging in futurology. It must develop a deep understanding of urban processes, so that the levers which can manipulate processes and trends can be identified and activate. In actual planning the TCPO should confine its inputs to large-scale regional plans, support to state departments of town and country planning and the evolution of planning techniques and methodologies which may, from time to time, be appropriate. What it must not do is to get involved in microlevel planning exercises in individual cities. This is best left to state and city planners.

Once the NBO and other research organizations come under the National Urbanisation Council, their research can be given a new direction. While the CBRI may continue to be autonomous, it must develop new thrusts in building-technology research so that mass housing at affordable prices becomes a reality. An efficient information system, easy to set up, easy to upgrade and easy to access, should be developed as an aid to planning and monitoring. A very strong applied bias to research, with different approaches being developed to suit regional needs, could then be ensured. The touchstone for judging the efficacy of research would be the extent to which the government, industry, development agencies, and individuals adopt its results. If the products of the CBRI are snapped up as eagerly as seed developed by, for example, the Punjab Agriculture University, Ludhiana, the research effort could be judged as being worthwhile.

If these suggestions are given due consideration by the government and implemented as far as feasible, the ministry will be better organized to execute its functions, which should be so designed as to belong to the realm of its proper jurisdiction exclusive of extraneous tasks assigned to it as present, and thus to achieve proper urban development and ensure improved basic civic amenities for the inhabitants of urban areas in general and for the disadvantaged sections of society in particular.

Urban Poverty Alleviation

There is no definite criterion to determine the extent of poverty in our country. According to the Planning Commission, 29.9 per cent of the population was living below the poverty line in 1987–88 and the poverty ratio for rural and urban areas was 33.4 per cent and 20.10 per cent respectively. The estimates are derived by drawing the poverty line at Rs 49.9 per capita per month (1973–74 prices), corresponding to a daily caloric requirement of 2,400 per person in the rural areas and an income of Rs 56.44 per capita per month, corresponding to a calorie requirement of 2,100 per head in the urban areas. These figures are, however, contestable as the United Nations Human Development Report (UNHDR) for 1990 found 48 per cent of the country's population living below the poverty line and a report by the Operation Research Group (ORG) put the number at 52.9 per cent in 1989–90. A foolproof criterion to determine the various levels of poverty was therefore required to be laid down to arrive at reliable approximate estimates of people living below the poverty line. Bihar has 3.65 crore of people living below the poverty line representing 49.5 per cent of its total population. Madhya Pradesh with 2.54 crore of people living below the poverty line has as much as 46.2 per cent of its population in this category. Uttar Pradesh ranks third with 45.3 per cent or 5.30 crore of its people being in this hapless section. Manipur had the least percentage of people living below the poverty belt—12.3 per cent or 1.9 lakh people.

Strategies to Deal with Poverty

Removal of poverty has been the main plank in the platform of planning in India and with this objective in view, the Sixth Five Year Plan had set out a two pronged strategy to deal with the scourge. Emphasis was laid on accelerating the pace of agricultural development since it was felt that this would have a beneficial effect on raising the standard of living of the poorer sections of the society. Simultaneously, it was felt necessary to strengthen and expand the scope of beneficiary oriented anti-poverty programmes in rural areas. Consistent with this approach, the Seventh Five Year Plan laid emphasis on accelerated agricultural growth and anti-poverty and employment generation programmes, mainly in the form of the 20-point Programme.

The 20-Point Programme

The 20-point programme was launched on 1 July 1975 as a 'Garibi Hatao' programme to alleviate the conditions of the poor sections of the society. A revised programme was announced on 14 January 1982. The basic objective of this programme was to continue its focus on the provision of better living conditions of the weaker sections of the society while aiming at all round improvement in productivity. The revised 20-point Programme (TPP-82) had been under implementation from 1982–83 onward. The New 20-point Programme 1986 (TPP-86), prepared under the guidance of the late Prime Minister Shri Rajiv Gandhi was laid on the tables of both the Houses of Parliament by the minister of Programme Implementation on 20 August 1986. It was restructured in the light of the experience gained in the implementation of the 20-Point Programmes of 1975 and 1982. While some of the items of the earlier programmes were dropped, its scope had been extended to bring within its ambit other items having a closer and more direct link with the nation's assault on poverty.

The coverage of the programme had been broadened and included a number of major areas of social concern such as the provision of clean drinking water, health facilities, acceptance of family planning, expansion of education equality for women, justice to Scheduled Castes and Scheduled Tribes, new opportunities for youth, housing for the under-privileged sections of the society, improvement of slums and the protection of environment. Besides eradication of poverty, the other important goals sought to be attained related to enhanced agricultural production and productivity, reduction in income inequalities, removal of social and economic disparities and in general, raising the quality of life. The TPP-86 renewed the government's commitment to the eradication of poverty, the raising of productivity, the reduction of income inequalities and the removal of social and economic disparities; in general, it aimed at improving the quality of life of the people. It was not a declaration of intent but a Charter of Emancipation for the poor.

The outlays for different items of the programmes were not fixed separately and specifically and these were derived from the relevant plan heads under states/UTs and plans of concerned central ministries. The financing of various schemes under the programme showed a close partnership between the central and state governments in the spheres of economic planning in general and the implementation of anti-poverty programmes in particular. The 20-Point Programme formed an integral part of the plans of the state governments/UT administrations and central ministries. However, some schemes like RLEGP and the family welfare programmes were funded entirely by the Central government. Other programmes, namely, IRDP, NREP and Bonded Labour Rehabilitation were joint financed from central and state resources on a 50:50 basis.

Magnitude of Urban Poverty

India has witnessed population explosion after independence. The total population of the country had doubled from 350 million in 1947 to 800 million in 1980. During the same period, the urban population had increased four-fold from 50 million to 200 million. By the turn of the century, total population had touched 1,000 million and urban population 350 million. Though there are many challenges posed by urbanization trends, the most demanding of them is urban poverty.

According to official estimates, approximately 27.7 per cent of the urban population lived below the poverty line in 1987–88; it meant at least 5.7 crore people, or more than one out of every four urban citizens. The National Commission on Urbanization had drawn pointed attention to the most brutal and inhuman living conditions in urban areas with large sections of people living in squatter settlements. According to a study conducted by National Institute of Urban Affairs, 68 per cent of the urban poor were women and children. If one adds to this the aged and the disabled, the customary perception of the urban poor changes. More recently, this aspect has been forcefully brought out by a distinguished authority on human settlements from Argentina, Mr. Jorge E. Hardoy, in one of the publications of the International Child Development Centre of UNICEF based in Florence, Italy. According to him, the most vulnerable urban group in future will be children. Tens of millions of children will be struggling to survive alone or with their families unless a massive effort is launched to create conditions that substantially reduce the number of households leading lives of deprivation, without stable or adequate income, without access to the most indispensable services, and constantly facing fear as urban violence grows. He says:

> The future cities of the Third World will be very different form the cities we know. They will be different not only in size and population but also on account of their age and labour structures. They will be cities of adolescents and children. Many will work before the minimum age established by law because their incomes are crucial for their families and for their own survival. Most will not complete primary school even though completing school is a family aspiration. Many will die young or live in poor health and will abandon their homes and live on their own on the city streets threatened by violence and the process of dehumanization. Different values and codes resulting from poverty and unemployment, combined with the massive presence of children and adolescent and of households headed by single woman, will give rise to a mixture of aggressiveness and solidarity of expectations and frustrations.

The signs of what Mr Hardoy has observed are already visible in Indian cities. The phenomenon of urban poverty has altered the landscape, the social fabric and overall character of Indian cities.

Policies and Programmes for Urban Poverty Alleviation

Poverty alleviation, as a dominant objective in India's development strategy, appeared initially in the Fifth Five Year Plan (1974–79). It recognized the existence of large-scale poverty in India and observed that despite the sizable gains of economic development and improvement of living standards over the two decades of planning, 'large numbers have remained poor'. The Fifth Plan, however, made no distinction between rural and urban poverty. It was the Sixth Five Year Plan (1980–85) which marked, in a sense, the commencement of a definite approach to poverty issues. It approached the problem in three stages: (*i*) Identification and measurement, (*ii*) developing realistic targets, and (*iii*) formulation of specific programmes. Like the preceding Five Year Plan, the Sixth Plan also did not directly address urban poverty issues. The Sixth Plan, however, did provide for moving nearly 61 lakh of the total urban poor above the poverty line, essentially through the provision of 'Additional consumption benefits' and better and more equitable distribution of health, education, sanitation, housing, drinking water, and slum upgrading and environmental improvement programmes. The Seventh Five Year Plan (1985–90) constitutes the first conscious attempt to address urban poverty issues directly. It takes explicit note of the 'growing incidence of poverty in urban areas', and points out that the persistent migration from rural areas had led, on the one hand, to rapid growth of slums in many cities and towns, and, on the other hand, to overcrowding in relatively unskilled and low-paid jobs in the informal sector. The Seventh Plan accordingly placed considerable emphasis on improvement in the living conditions of slum dwellers. It further noted that, in order to be effective, the problem of urban poverty would require a major thrust towards employment generation and creation of productive jobs. In line with this major thrust, the Seventh Plan has proposed a strategy that includes provision of gainful employment to the unemployed, particularly women and youth, raising the earnings of those in low-paid jobs, stepping up the productivity and earnings of self-employed workers, and improving the access of the urban poor to basic amenities such as education, health care, sanitation and safe drinking water.

The National Commission on Urbanization had examined the available evidence on the impact of the various programmes—centrally sponsored, state sponsored, and locally initiated. It had also reviewed some of the programmes in the field. The results are mixed but the overall conclusions are: the reach of the programmes is limited; there is a high degree of inflexibility; there is a lack of convergence of programmes, even the main targets are often missed; and, barring the Hyderabad/Vishakhapatnam UCD projects, the programmes are still working on a laboratory scale. At the same time, the commission is aware of the highly effective and innovative programmes in some cities such as the Sites and Slum Improvement Projects in Madras; the Small Loan Programme and Community Health Scheme of the Calcutta Metropolitan Development Authority; the Urban Community Development Projects in Hyderabad and Vishakhapatnam, the Low Cost Sanitation Schemes in Patna and other cities.

The major programmes for amelioration of the conditions of the urban poor may be discussed as follows:

1. Shelter-related Programme: Among the shelter-related programmes, slum eradication had featured as a key approach during the First and Second Plans. In view of resource limitations, resistance of local populations to shifting and maintenance failures, the approach was abandoned in favour of slum improvement and sites and services schemes. About 15.3 lakh slum dwellers are believed to have benefited already under the slum improvement scheme. The Seventh Plan aims at securing coverage of about 90 lakh slum dwellers.

The Economically Weaker Sections (EWS) Housing Programme had succeeded in construction of 65,432 shelter units in the public sector during the Sixth Plan period (1980–85). The National Buildings Organization has estimated that, as on March 1981, about 2 lakh units were needed for the houseless, who should be given first priority, while about 31 lakh units were needed for those who live in *kutcha* units. Besides, the urban poor are concentrated in bustees and chawls and whole families of six to seven people live in congested, one room tenements. The congestion is increasing owing to growing impoverishment, immigration, and population growth from within. Thus, even though the public policy response to the housing needs of the urban poor has improved, it cannot meet more than 10 per cent of the backlog.

2. Nutrition Supplement Programmes: Programmes of nutrition have been significantly expanded in the Seventh Plan. The Special Nutrition Programmes (SNP) and Mid-Day Meal (MDM) are proposed to be integrated with Integrated Child Development Scheme (ICDS). The expected coverage of beneficiaries is likely to be 1.1 crore children and pregnant mothers under SNP and about 50 lakh children under MDM by the end of 1990.

The public distribution system also aims at providing a balanced diet at reasonable prices in the endemically poverty stricken, malnourished and under-nourished parts of the country. Even this limited concept of public distribution is not realized in practice. A review of the literature shows that off-take from the public distribution system is greater in urban areas than in rural area in per capita terms. Andhra Pradesh has used its public distribution system both extensively and intensively to distribute about 5 kg of rice per capita per month to an individual family, subject to a ceiling of 25 kg, along with other essential goods such as sugar, wheat, palm oil (upto a ceiling of 2 kg.), coarse cloth, kerosene, etc. A review of case studies of the public distribution system of Andhra Pradesh shows that the urban poor families meet about 40 per cent of their needs from the public distribution system.

3. Child Development: Among the general programmes of child development, the spread of free education has certainly brought benefits nearer to the urban poor. However, owing to economic and social conditions, the school drop-out rate is higher among the urban poor than the rest of the urban population. Health services have improved in pilot project areas, thanks to intensive efforts of Integrated Child Development Scheme (ICDS), Urban Basic Services (UBS) and Urban Community Development (UCD) projects, but these have still not approached national coverage.

4. Employment Generation and Employment-oriented Training Programmes: Recently Government of India have started a self-employment programme for the urban poor (SEPUP) by earmarking a sum of Rs 200 crore to be distributed to poor urban entrepreneurs whose income does not exceed Rs 600 per month. The maximum credit available is Rs 5,000. The list of economic activities for which loans are available contains 35 items covering activities like hawking on handcart, laundering, welding, cycle rickshaw operation, shoemaking, hairdressing, etc.

5. Participatory Programmes: Urban Community Development (UCD) was started as a pilot project as early as 1969. However, only very few pilot projects survived. In 1981, the Urban Community Development, Low Cost Sanitation, and Small and Middle Town Development Projects, supported by UNICEF, were merged into a new service called Urban Basic Services (UBS). Its aim is to promote citizen participation, strengthen the service capabilities of the local bodies in working with people on commonly felt needs, bring about convergence of services, and coordinate resources of various agencies for the purpose.

6. Schemes of Ministry of Urban Development for the Benefit of Urban Poor: The alleviation of urban poverty, arranging night shelters for footpath dwellers and setting up of a technology promotion council are some of the important achievements of the union urban ministry during 1990–91.

The Nehru Rozgar Yojna was launched in October 1989 to meet the challenge posed by urban poverty and was recast in March 1990. The *yojna* consisted of the schemes of urban micro enterprise, urban wage employment and housing and shelter upgradation.

The scheme of urban wage employment provides wage opportunities to the urban poor by utilizing their labour for the construction of socially and economically useful public assets within the jurisdiction of urban local bodies.

The scheme of housing and shelter upgradation seeks to provide assistance to the economically weaker sections and opportunities for wage employment and upgradation of construction skills. The Housing and Urban Development Corporation (HUDCO) has sanctioned 170 such schemes.

Under the scheme of urban basic services during the Eighth Plan, it is proposed to continue basic services in 169 towns. Another 247 new towns have been identified for the provision of social services under the new scheme.

The scheme of environmental improvement of urban slums aims at ameliorating the living conditions of urban slum dwellers and envisages the provision of drinking water, drainage, community baths, community latrines and other facilities.

The schemes for pavement dwellers was introduced to provide shelter to footpath dwellers and the shelterless in metropolitan cities. The scheme has now been extended to all urban areas. During 1990–91, HUDCO sanctioned six schemes for the construction of night shelters benefiting 4,640 footpath dwellers. Another 22 schemes for the benefit of 2,868 pavement dwellers are under scrutiny and likely to be sanctioned soon.

The master plan for the development of Delhi upto 2001 was revised and came into force on 1 August 1990. Under its special projects, the Delhi Development Authority has undertaken the planning of three schemes in Rohini.

For the Dwarka Project, which plans to accommodate a population of about 10 lakh, detailed sectorial plans are likely to be finalized soon.

Indian policy-makers are aware of the problems of urban poverty but according to NCU, their response has been generally unimaginative, inadequate, half-hearted, and narrowly sectoral. The urban poor are usually equated with slum dwellers. Housing is perceived to be the slum dweller's main problem. Till recently, providing *pucca* houses was perceived as the solution (until the money ran out). Recent new responses like

Sites and Services, Slum Improvement, Urban Community Development (UCD) projects, Integrated Child Development Services (ICDS), Basic Services Approach, Mid-Day Meal Scheme for the school children, and Small and Medium Towns Development Programme, reflect a relatively better assessment of the situation, a more realistic attitude to resource constraints, and probably, a new awareness of social responsibility. However, most of these programmes are at their early, experimental stage, covering not even a small fraction of the people they are meant to benefit. Many are floundering in implementation and some are already showing signs of malfunction. However, these approaches certainly merit proper trial, careful monitoring and evaluation, followed by redesiging and strengthening as may be seen to be necessary. Nevertheless, considering the scale, complexity and gravity of the urban poverty situation and threat it poses to the social fabric and economic well-being of our cities, these measures are woefully inadequate and more effective measures will have to be sought if alleviation of urban poverty is to be achieved within a reasonable time span.

Suggestions for Improving the Lot of the Urban Poor

According to the National Commission on Urbanization, bold, intensive and coordinated efforts are needed to improve the income and consumption levels of the bottom 30 per cent of our population to extend their access to basic environmental and social services, and to ensure their better utilization, and for this purpose it has suggested a thirteen-point programme package for implementation which comprises: (i) national programme of employment training for urban poor youth; (ii) national programme of credit support for expanding micro-enterprises and technological upgradation; (iii) micro-enterprise infrastructure development support (marketing and production centres); (iv) marketing development supports; (v) new programmes of public assets creation for promoting wage employment for the urban poor; (vi) universalization of Urban Community Development (UCD) and Urban Basic Services (UBS) activities; (vii) educational support for extension of family planning and maternal and child health services; (viii) intensification of non-formal education for school drop-outs and working women; (ix) slum improvement shelter upgradation, sites and services schemes, land supply, tenurial security and facilitation through participatory approaches and NGO involvement; (x) extension of public distribution system; (xi) Extension of the family security programme; (xii) support for innovative programmes of voluntary agencies; and (xiii) support for training and action research in urban poverty.

Administrative Setup

Urban poverty removal is going to be a long-term task. Long-term perspective planning, sectoral, and spatial coordination and cumulation through continuity of policies over successive phases will be necessary to make a real impact on the poverty situation. Alleviation of poverty is not the function of a single department. It has to become an orientation for all development departments so that each project which is accepted, and every outlay which is provided is examined in the light of what it means for both the urban and the rural poor. The role of the nodal organ is to provide a common framework for the realization of all sectoral initiatives.

At the implementation level, the nodal ministry is the Ministry of Urban Development. While this ministry can provide coordination of habitant inputs to support the anti-poverty programme, the inputs have to come from many departments and many agencies. The only poverty alleviation services which the urban development ministry was helping state and local governments to establish and monitor were UBS and UCD. They received scant attention because of their miniscule size. A National programme with responsibility for coordinating programme outlays amounting to hundreds of crores every year cannot be accomplished without a strong structure. The minimum which would be necessary is a separate department of Urban Basic Services and UCD within the ministry, with an additional or full secretary at its head. Not only are the tasks to be tackled variegated and challenging, requiring induction of new forms of socio-economic expertise at the central level, but the sheer financial magnitude of the National Urban Works Programme and National Agency for UBS/UCD and citizen participation would also require the support of a full-fledged department. At the state level, it might be necessary to designate senior commissioner to coordinate services for the alleviation of rural and urban poverty. At local government level, the Department of Urban Basic Services and Citizen Participation may be placed under the charge of an additional commissioner. In middle sized towns, a project officer, co-ranking with executive officer, may be needed. In small towns, the differentiation is not necessary. An orientation however, will be needed.

The nodal ministry will be responsible for the urban poverty alleviation programmes and will be mainly responsible for administering the national programme for wage employment for the urban poor, setting up and coordinating the National Agency for Urban Basic Services and Citizen Participation and the interest subsidy schemes for shelter upgradation programmes and micro-enterprises development. As the nodal ministry, it will monitor and coordinate (through inter-departmental committees of secretaries preferably) the entire urban poverty alleviation effort. Its partners will be the Ministry of Labour, Ministry of Commerce and Industry, Ministry of Health, Ministry of Human Resources Development, Ministry of Civil Supplies, and Ministry of Social Welfare. The coordinating financial institutions must direct their loan operations towards the needs of the urban poor.

The process of economic growth and the implementation of anti-poverty programmes both for the rural and urban poor have made a significant dent in the problem of the poverty during the last two decades as reflected in the following table :

	Poverty rate (%)			No. of poor (millions)		
Year	***Rural***	***Urban***	***Total***	***Rural***	***Urban***	***Total***
1972–73	54.1	41.2	51.5	244.2	47.3	291.5
1977–78	51.2	38.2	48.3	253.1	53.7	306.8
1984–85	39.9	27.7	36.9	222.2	50.5	272.7
1989–90	28.2	19.3	25.8	168.6	42.2	210.8

New Schemes for Employment: Jawahar Rozgar Yojna and Nehru Rozgar Yojna

The youth is most vulnerable to economic problems and suffer due to unemployment and under-employment. The government could not of course guarantee government employment to everyone as the right to work would imply. It should, however, grant unemployment allowance to the educated youth at least. Haryana is the first to have introduced the scheme of unemployment allowance at Rs 75 p.m. for matriculates and at Rs 100 p.m. for graduate and postgraduate unemployed youth. The other states should also follow suit. Some states grant free travel to youth appearing for interviews for public jobs. But these are no substitutes for employment. The government should generate employment opportunities for youth to the maximum. Some of the recent plans and programmes to achieve this end are:

Jawahar Rozgar Yojna

The Congress (I) government had launched the Jawahar Rozgar Yojna, an ambitious employment guarantee programme envisaging Rs 2625 crore financial assistance to village panchayat in 1989–90 to guarantee employment to at least one person in a rural family living below the poverty line, for 50 to 100 days a year at a work place near his or her residence. The then prime minister Shri Rajiv Gandhi observed that the Yojna would reach out to all 440 lakh families in rural India living below the poverty line and that all existing rural wage/employment programmes like the Indira Awas Yojna, the Rural Landless Employment Guarantee Programme, the National Rural Development Programmes, and the Integrated Rural Development Programmes would automatically be merged into the Yojna. Under the Programme, any panchayats with a population ranging between 3,000 to 4,000 would get annual financial assistance of Rs 80,000 to Rs 1 lakh. A highlight of the scheme was that 30 per cent of the jobs would be reserved for women. The government hoped to incorporate in the programme integrated schemes to provide employment to the nomadic tribes. The government expected that through the devolution of this programme to panchayats, the benefits of the programme directly reaching the people would be significantly greater than in the past, as thus far, too large a proportion of the funds for such programmes had gone to contractors and intermediaries, there have also been other leakages. Besides, there is scope for economizing on the costs of administration. Central assistance would finance 100 per cent of the programme, the government was structuring the finances in such a way that the states would get their allocation in proportion to the size of their population below the poverty line.

The scheme suffers from snags: The impressive figure of Rs 2625 crore is not the fresh outlay. As much as Rs 1711 crore has been transferred from National Rural Employment Project and Rural Landless Employment Guarantee Scheme, which have been merged in the Yojna, and thus Rs 389 crore is actually the fresh outlay. Out of the total outlay, Rs 2,100 crore or 80 per cent is to come from the Centre and the remaining from the states. It is to be seen how the additional amount of money will be arranged by the Centre and the States. The Yojna is to be implemented by panchayats and each with a population of about 4,000 is to be given Rs 1 lakh to offer jobs. If these villages have only 40 per cent of the residents living below the poverty line—which is the national average—then at least 320 families of five members each will need immediate help. Distributing Rs 1 lakh evenly will mean an annual earning of Rs 1250 for each family of five or Rs 250 per year per individual which is ridiculously little to ensure removal of poverty. Even this calculation may be grossly unoptimistic as a substantial portion of funds will be expanded on providing administrative infrastructure and paraphernalia to manage the scheme and it is the local elite which will benefit from the plans and also a plan share will go to the undeserving sections as has been the experience in the execution of integrated rural development programmes. Lastly, panchayats which have been entrusted with the responsibility of implementing the Yojna, dominated as they are by local landlords and administered by village officials, will not be in a position to hand out justice even-handedly as the elite and the official will join hands to deal roughly with the lowest of the lowly. It is only the actual working of the Yojna which will prove how its benefits have reached the poor.

Nehru Rozgar Yojna

Complementary to the Jawahar Rozgar Yojna, Nehru Rozgar Yojna was launched by Government of India in October, 1989, to provide various employment avenues to the urban poor, mainly the urban youth. The Yojna consists of three components: (*i*) a scheme for setting up of micro-enterprises and providing training and infrastructure set up, (*ii*) a scheme for wage employment for public assets creating, and (*iii*) a scheme of employment through housing and shelter upgradation.

The total financial outlay for the Yojna is of the order of Rs 650 crores, out of which institutional finance amounts to Rs 432 crores. The subsidy element is estimated at Rs 218 crore for which Rs 150 crore and Rs. 68 crore are to be provided by the centre and state or UT governments and urban local bodies, respectively. The share of subsidy between Government of India and the state governments is 50:50 in the case of micro-enterprises schemes and 80:20 in the case of wage employment and employment through housing and shelter upgrading schemes, respectively. Allocation of the central funds to the states or the UTs is on the basis of urban population and incidence of urban poverty. The states and the UTs are in turn responsible to disburse them to different districts and local bodies or implementing agencies on the basis of the urban population of each district.

Nehru Rozgar Yojna expects the municipal bodies to play key role in the entire process which includes selection of employment oriented activities, identification of beneficiaries, provision of necessary infrastructure, assistance in procurement and supply of raw material, facilitating the banks in the recovery of loans through the neighbourhood and mohalla committees, liaison with technical agencies, etc. The Yojna endeavours to open up additional employment avenues in newly established enterprises, service centres, public works programmes, training and shelter upgrading activities, etc.

The objectives of the Yojna are indeed laudable but it suffers from some lacunae: the local bodies may not be able to perform their pivotal role in fulfilling the objectives of the Yojna as constituted they are at present are not able to discharge their present responsibilities because of their weak financial and personnel base and to expect them to perform additional responsibilities requiring higher managerial skills is unrealistic and unimaginative; except the major municipal corporations they not be able even to comprehend the problems and the issues involved in planning and execution of the Yojna. The Local bodies are notorious in failing to collect their own revenues at reasonable level, one wonders how they can be expected to help other agencies in their recoveries. Again the finances to be contributed by the states and local bodies of their own share, will also pose a serious problem due to their incapacity to raise their funds. The beneficiaries will have to raise loans also to provide the needed capitals for their enterprises and it is doubtful if they will be happier or sadder depending upon their capacities to pay back the principal with interest; finally the proposal to set up District Urban Development Agency as an autonomous body to mobilize, administer, and account for Yojna funds does not appear to be viable from the institutional and financial points. This job can be easily entrusted to District Rural Development Authority which has the requisite experience of implementing the rural development programme and thus the present the rural–urban dichotomy which constitutes a major impediment in the process of comprehensive district development can also be avoided.

The success of this Yojna notwithstanding the financial allocations will, to a large extent, depend on the strength of the institutions concerned with its implementation. We can only hope that it will go a long way in affording enormous opportunities for employment to the urban youth resulting in the alleviation of their poverty.

Swarna Jayanti Shahari Rozgar Yojna

This scheme was approved by the Union Cabinet on 5 August 1997. The SJSRY has been launched as a replacement for Nehru Rozgar Yojna (NRY), Urban Basic Services for the Poor (UBSP), and Prime Minister's Integrated Urban Poverty Eradiction Programme. The scheme seeks to provide gainful employment to the urban unemployed or underemployed poor by encouraging the setting up of self-employment ventures and provision of wage employment. The Yojna will be funded on a 75:25 basis between the Centre and the state. The scheme consists of the following:

The Urban Self Employment Programme (USEP)

It has three distinct parts:

1. Assistance to individual urban poor beneficiaries for setting up gainful self employment ventures.
2. Assistance to groups of urban poor women for setting up gainful self employment ventures. This sub-scheme is called The scheme for Development of Women and Children in the Urban Areas (DWCUA).

3. Training of beneficiaries, potential beneficiaries, and other persons associated with the urban employment programme for upgradation and acquisition of vocational and entrepreneurial skills.

This programme will be applicable to all urban towns in India and will be implemented on whole town basis with special emphasis on urban poor clusters.

Salient Features of the USEP

1. Setting up micro enterprises and skill development:

Maximum unit is cost Rs 50,000, subsidy 15 per cent of the project cost, and subject to a maximum ceiling of Rs 7,500. Margin money to be contributed by the beneficiary is 5 per cent of the project cost.

For Joint Venture: Project cost = sum of individual project cost allowable per beneficiary

Subsidy = Total permitted subsidy per person

Training and infrastructure support: Training cost per person = Rs 2,000

Training period = Two to six months, subject to a minimum of 300 hours. The tool kit is worth Rs 600.

Development of Women and Children in the Urban Areas (DWCUA)

DWCUA aims at helping groups of urban poor women in taking up self-employment ventures. The group should consist of at least 10 women. The ceiling of subsidy under the scheme is Rs 1.25 lakh or 50 per cent of the cost of project, whichever is less. Where the group sets itself up as Thrift and Credit Society, in addition to its self employment ventures, it will be eligible for an additional grant of Rs 25,000 as revolving fund at the rate of Rs 1,000 maximum per member. The fund is meant for purposes like purchase of raw materials and marketing, infrastructure support, one time expense on child care activity, expenses upto Rs 500 on travel cost of group members to bank, payment of insurance premium for self or spouse or child by maintaining savings for different periods by a member and any other expense allowed by the state in the group's interest. The revolving fund can be availed by a group only after one year of its formation.

The Urban Wage Employment Programme (UWEP)

The programme shall seek to provide wage employment to beneficiaries living below the poverty line within the jurisdiction of urban local bodies by utilizing their labour for construction of socially and economically useful public assets. It shall apply to urban local bodies, the population of which was less than 5 lakh as per the 1991 census. The material labour ratio for works under this programme shall be maintained at 60 : 40. The prevailing minimum wage rate, as notified from time to time for each area, shall be paid to beneficiaries under this programme.

Funds

The funds remaining unspent in respect of Nehru Rozgar Yojna (NRY), UBSP and PMIUPEP with various states and UTs as on 30 November 1997 was the opening balance for incurring expenditure under the new scheme. In addition, central funds of Rs 98.63 crores had been released for 1997–98 (i.e., 1 December 1997 to 31 March 1998) and allocation of Rs 183.20 crores has been made for 1998–99.

An action plan was also drawn to create self-employment opportunities for the educated unemployed. These included facilitating entrepreneurship in the private sector, self-employment opportunities through public sector and expansion of self-employment opportunities under the existing schemes. The measures for entrepreneurship facilitation include arranging finance, providing various inputs and facilitating licensing, and the like.

The public sector would reserve some proportion of dealership, contracts, and service agencies for the educated unemployed. There were several general suggestions to create immediate employment opportunities without incurring additional capital expenditure. These were: increased use of cloth made by handloom weavers for uniforms, increased use of shoes made by artisans, use of locally made cane basket instead of metal ones. Works in railways and other agencies will be integrated in a right to work programme. Shifts in factories will be increased by reducing the hours of working. Entrepreneurs would be encouraged to use more labour and less capital.

Conclusion

Poverty has assumed serious dimensions in India. It is not confined to rural areas alone. There are stark manifestations of poverty in our cities also. Cities like Bombay, Madras, and Calcutta have such a large population living in slums, shanties, and pavements that almost one-third of these big cities are nothing but slums where the urban poor live. It is estimated that about half of our people are living below the poverty line. The 'Task Force on Projections of Minimum Needs and Effective Consumption Demand', set up by the Planning Commission 1977, had defined the poverty line as the mid point of the monthly per capita expenditure, having a daily calorie intake of 2,000 per person in rural areas and 2,100 per person in urban areas.

Ever since our country embarked on the planning process in 1951, our principal objective has been improving the pace of economic development so as to increase the gross national product by increasing output in all sectors of the economy, The underlying assumption was that if development takes place, its fruits will percolate to all sections of our society including the poor. But the trickle-down effect of development has not reduced the incidence of poverty. Therefore, the policy makers, social scientists, and other thinkers had started thinking that normal process of development could not be depended upon to make a dent on poverty and we must have a direct assault on poverty. Similar feeling permeated our slogan 'Garibi Hatao'. Accordingly programmes to deal with poverty such as Integrated Rural Development Programme (IRDP), National Rural Employment Programme (NREP), The Rural Landless Employment Guarantee Scheme (RLEGS), and Training for Rural Youths for Self-Employment (TRYSEM) were initiated as part of strategy of removing poverty. And earlier programmes of poverty alleviation such as Drought Prone Area Programme (DPAP), Community Development Programme (CDP), Small Farmers Development Agency (SFDA), and Marginal Farmers and Agricultural Labourer Development Agency (MFACDA) were merged in IRD. All the existing rural wage employment programmes like the Indira Awas Yojna, RLEGP, NRDP and IRDP were merged into the Jawahar Rozgar Yojna in 1989. As the basic objective of the Sixth Five Year Plan was the diminishing or reduction of poverty, if not its total elimination and the concern of the Seventh Five Year Plan has also been to reduce poverty further by 14 per cent, it is imperative that the anti-poverty programmes should register significant success.

Reasons for the Failure of the Poverty Alleviation Programmes

The poverty alleviation programmes have, however, not been able to achieve the desired results due to the deficiencies they suffered from. The central government is the dominant force in initiating and planning these programmes as is reflected in the centrally sponsored schemes allowing for little freedom and flexibility at the local level. Gaps in planning are reinforced by an administrative system which has yet to demonstrate its capability to respond adequately and effectively to new challenges. The responsibility for establishing accountability for the achievement of several development schemes at the district level is diffused. There is no single ministry or agency within the Planning Commission and even at state level which integrates the various programmes to form a coordinated whole; over-reliance on bureaucratic administrative machinery to implement anti-poverty programmes has led to the gradual erosion of people's participatory institutions; the failure of the state to implement land reforms and to promote the tiny and cottage industries sectors. Anti-poverty activity was confined to the governmental bodies without participation of either public or other public agencies and voluntary organization. Middlemen exploited the beneficiaries, swallowing the reliefs and not letting them reach the poor people concerned. Other reasons include corrupt practices, lack of adequate facilities for training for different vocations and income generating schemes and job opportunities, the menace of population explosion, illiteracy, unemployment and under-employment leading to migration of rural population to cities, black market, inflation, and corruption.

Measures for the Success of Poverty Alleviation Programmes

Factors which can substantially contribute to the success of anti-poverty programmes should include decentralized planning. Jawaharlal Nehru, the architect of the planning process, had rightly emphasized the significance of the grassroots level institutions at the district level, at the block level, and at the village level for channelizing the peoples' energies not only for plan implementation but also for plan formulation: greater devolution of authority for poverty removal at the district and sub-divisional level; evolving a suitable administrative machinery with simpler procedure to avoid middlemen and corrupt practices; highest standard of devotion; efficiency and integrity from the bureaucracy at both higher and levels; proper coordination and cooperation amongst the different agencies concerned with implementing the programmes and also the normal government agencies to avoid duplication and diffusion of responsibility; linking of the IRDP with the cooperative sector; strengthening of the role of voluntary agencies and social workers; plant over wasteland, which constituted one-third of India's land resources; exploiting the employment potential of land reclamation through land army; implementation of land reforms; initiating programmes for the landless such as those of improvement of public works, for the artisans for raising their skills, of agro-industrialization and establishment of ancillary industries for minimum consumption including that of provision of drinking water; intensifying special programmes for the Scheduled Castes and Tribes and backward classes, for the promotion of education, health and population control; an attack on black money and corruption, a programme of anti-inflation because inflation leads to the erosion of whatever resources the poor possess. Finally, it is imperative that the weaker sections of the community—the tribals, the poor in the urban areas, landless labourers, marginal farmers, etc.—should be awakened and their organizations should be involved in the process of implementation of anti-poverty programmes. Removal of poverty is a herculean task but given the implementation of measures suggested in this chapter, and the political will, it can be mitigated to a very great extent, if not completely eliminated, in not far distant future.

Urban Development Authorities

Urban planning and development, and provision of civic amenities such as water supply, sewerage, and prevention of pollution constitute some of the basic functions of urban local government. But our municipal institutions are alleged to be incapable of performing these functions. The state governments therefore, constitute specialized agencies such as improvement trusts, housing boards, water supply and sewerage boards, and pollution control boards to carry out these functions. The reasons usually advanced for the creation of these urban institutions and specific purpose agencies are that the municipal authorities have neither the necessary administrative machinery nor resources to tackle the problems arising out of rapid urban growth;[1] that the rules and bye-laws of the municipal bodies stand in the way of shouldering responsibilities attached to the developmental activities;[2] that the municipal corporations and municipal committees are, by and large, centres of inefficiency, corruption and political nepotism; most of these are bankrupt and cannot in any way tackle the big problems;[3] that certain activities are so technical and complex that they require concentrated attention and specialized effort,[4] which the municipal bodies are not in a position to afford, already overburdened as they are with numerous, varied functions. In short, the creation of uni- or multi-functional authorities is justified on the plea of the inefficiency of the local authorities and their being inadequately equipped to perform these tasks.[5]

These urban institutions, dominated as they are by nominations made by the government, are anachronistic in the modern age of democracy and are an eye-sore to the municipal bodies as they have eroded their authority, and more so because the latter contribute substantial amounts to them but have absolutely no control over them. Moreover, even the performance of these specialized agencies has not been up to the mark. Improvement Trusts stress more on development and have failed to bring out necessary improvements in the towns and cities. They have been criticized for grave irregularities in the acquisition of land and allotment of plots in their various schemes and for rampant corruption. The Water Supply and Sewerage Boards have failed to provide basic amenities of potable water and sewerage to all the urban areas within their jurisdiction due to financial stringency and other factors and whenever they have been provided, they have been so defective that they have been declared to be beyond repair and have been dismantled and replaced by new ones, thus causing colossal wastage of crores of public money. The Housing Boards have though provided shelter to hundreds of town dwellers but this touches only a tip of the iceberg. Pollution control Board in its drive to check pollution have taken only punitive measures against defaulters but failed to ensure the installation of pollution control devices in all the industrial establishments.

The provision of multiple specialized agencies gives rise to the problem of overlapping of functions and coordination among them. Housing Development, for example, is the function of three agencies viz, the housing board, the urban estates and the improvement trusts. Similarly, provision of water-supply and sewerage is the responsibility of the municipal bodies and the Improvement Trusts, both of whom are in turn the clientele of Water Supply and Sewerage Board. Under such a dispensation, the citizens have to face tremendous amount of inconvenience in reaching the multiple organizations. The creation of these agencies has diffused and disintegrated the system of urban local government and lowered its prestige and significance. They also suffer from a lack of funds.

The predicaments mentioned above can be overcome by abolishing these institutions and merging them with the concerned municipal institutions. In that case their finances would not only be restored to the civic bodies but they would be provided with technical expertise as well; or these institutions should be put under the unified administrative-control of the city council to achieve coordination; or an urban development authority should be set up to ensure better coordination of various agencies involved in urban development as well as to raise more institutional finance. The first two options are not possible due to the lack of finances and technical expertise available with the local authorities. The third option, viz. the constitution of urban development authorities is therefore more desirable, advisable, practical, and realistic for its advantages of a single agency taking an integrated view of the planning and development of the entire urban area under its control and to be responsible for the provision and management of civic amenities therein. Accordingly, the central government constituted urban development authorities, such as Delhi Development Authority under the Delhi Development Act, 1957, and Housing and Urban Development Corporation (HUDCO) in 1971. The state governments have also set up state urban development authorities to cater to the development needs of all the cities/towns in the state. Haryana, for example, has set up the Haryana Urban Development Authority (HUDA) and Punjab has set up Punjab Urban Development Authority (PUDA) for this purpose. Some states have provided for urban development authorities for individual cities, for instance, the Calcutta Metropolitan Development Authority in West Bengal, Kannaur Development Authority in Kerala, etc. Recently, District Urban Development Agencies (DUDAs) have also been constituted in some states, for example, in Kerala (in March 1989) and in Punjab (in April 1991). All urban bodies in the district are the members of DUDA under chairmanship of the district collector/deputy commissioner. The idea has been borrowed from the district rural development agencies. One of the chief objectives of DUDA is to coordinate urban development along desired lines.

Organization and Functions of HUDCO, DDA and HUDA

The organization, functions and activities of the three types of urban development authorities, one operating in different parts of the country (HUDCO), the other confined to a particular city only (DDA), and the third, extending its activities to various cities and towns within the territorial jurisdiction of a state (HUDA) are discussed in detail to get an overview of their operations and achievements in the field of urban planning and development, and provision of services, especially to the weaker sections, as follows:

Housing and Urban Development Corporation (HUDCO)

For meeting the growing demand for housing, the Planning Commission, in the First Five Year Plan, had recommended the setting up by the central government of agencies to subsidize construction of houses.

Housing and Urban Development Corporation, a techno-financial institution was incorporated on 25 April 1970 as an expression of concern of Government of India for the deteriorating housing scenario in the country and its desire to assist the state authorities for its amelioration. HUDCO's prime mandate was to improve the housing conditions of the economically weaker sections and to concretize this, it was necessary to ensure that it would essentially have to be low cost, easily available and require minimum skills. Thus, HUDCO's objectives were outlined to finance and undertake: (*i*) Housing and Urban Development programmes all over the country; (*ii*) the setting up of new or satellite towns either wholly or in part; and (*iii*) the setting up of building material industries.

HUDCO's Programmes and Activities

1. Housing Programmes for the Poor: Keeping in view the acute housing shortage in the country, HUDCO has undertaken comprehensive housing programmes for the poor. It has implemented a differential interest rate policy for various categories of households with special emphasis on the economically weaker sections (EWS) and lower income group (LIG) families. This implies that lower the household income, lower the rate of interest and vice-versa. This policy provides incentives for executing agencies in promoting housing for the less privileged. HUDCO's policies of reaching the target groups has been further intensified by adopting a policy of differential project funding, i.e. the lower the cost of shelter unit, the higher the loan component of HUDCO in proportion to the project cost. This is to help in upgrading of planning design and implementation of the project to be funded by HUDCO. This policy has been consolidated by cutting down on the amortization period, meaning that the lower the monthly family income of the target groups, the higher the amortization period and vice-versa.

2. Augmentation of Basic Community Facilities and Infrastructure Services: For optimum use of resources for the benefit of EWS and LIG families, HUDCO has an overall resource system, plus monitoring and control systems. HUDCO has implemented an array of schemes to give shape to its objectives of providing shelter and thereby ameliorating the conditions of the people of the country. Apart from financing social housing schemes, HUDCO has also attempted to improve the quality of life by augmenting basic community facilities and infrastructural services. It promotes projects involving self help by the beneficiaries by encouraging sites and service, core housing, skeletal housing, etc. It extends financial assistance for basic sanitation schemes on liberalized terms.

3. Environmental Improvement of Slums, Housing Improvement, etc.: HUDCO provides benefits to the masses under the wide canvas of urban housing and rural housing environmental improvement of slums, housing improvement, repair and renewal, social infrastructure, basic sanitation, staff housing, cooperative housing, building materials, land acquisition, and urban infrastructure.

4. Availability of Quicker Finance: To facilitate availability of quicker finance for developmental activities of housing agencies, HUDCO decentralized its operations. Today, it has a regional or development office in almost in every state capital.

To meet its objectives, HUDCO mobilizes funds from various resources such as equity contributions from the government, borrowings from public by the issue of shelter or urban bonds and borrowings from institutions.

5. Infrastructure Projects: HUDCO has financed urban infrastructure projects to a limited extent. To check the deteriorating conditions in cities and towns and to make timely investments in urban infrastructure, the Government of India, pending creation of the separate infrastructure Corporation as HUDCO subsidiary, directed it to extend financial assistance to agencies dealing with the implementation, operation, and maintenance of urban infrastructure. To facilitate this, a separate Urban Infrastructure Finance wing has been created for processing loan proposals for HUDCO financial assistance. Under this facility, HUDCO provides long-term loans for upgradation and augmentation of urban services, supportive activities for the integrated development of specific or whole areas of the metropolitan city or town, support to the development of peripheral areas of a city or new township or growth centres in an integrated regional context and support for innovative urban development schemes of public or private agencies including land development and urban renewal, and leasing of equipment for city level services.

6. Liberation of Scavengers and Nehru Rozgar Yojna: As part of the action plan for implementation of the government's programmes and policies, HUDCO, besides its existing basic sanitation scheme for conversion of dry latrines to water borne latrines, has integrated its schemes with the scheme floated by the Ministry of Welfare and thus introduced an 'Integrated Scheme of the Liberation of Scavengers and Improvement of Sanitation'. The objective of the scheme is to totally eliminate manual scavenging involved in the dry latrines and convert them into low cost sanitation units. Scavengers so liberated would simultaneously be rehabilitated under this scheme by the state governments.

Besides the above, the implementation of the scheme of urban employment through shelter and skill upgradation was also entrusted to HUDCO by the government. This scheme, as a part of Nehru Rozgar Yojna, is designed for promoting employment amongst the urban poor. Loan assistance under this is also available for upgradation scheme in declared slum areas, inner city areas and areas predominantly inhabited by low income group. The scheme should, however, be in line with the shelter and upgradation and development policy of the state.

7. Development Efforts in the North East: HUDCO has been making strenuous efforts to enhance its development work in the North Eastern states. Since the opening of its regional office in Guwahati, HUDCO has increased its loan assistance to this region beyond the normal loan allocation for individual states. Considering the special characteristics of the region, HUDCO has revised its lending norms and increased the ceiling costs by 25 per cent for dwelling units under the EWS and LIG categories. Further, under the urban employment through housing and shelter upgradation programme, schemes have been sanctioned in the states of Assam, Tripura, and Manipur covering the central subsidy allocated to these states to its full extent. It is also proposed to set up an exclusive organization, HUDCO North East Limited, for the development of the region.

8. Promotion of Housing Finance Corporations (HFCs): To step up the effort of the government to create more and more housing finance institutions to facilitate the availability of housing finance to individual home owners, HUDCO has collaborated with Central Bank of India and Indian Bank for setting up of two regional housing finance companies to cater to the needs of people in the central and southern states of the country. HUDCO has provided equity support of Rs 1.25 crores and Rs 2.5 crores to these companies, respectively. The other participants in these ventures are UTI, HDFC, etc.

9. Loan Sanctions: During 1989–90 alone, HUDCO sanctioned 844 projects valuing Rs 1647 crores. Loan commitment for these projects was Rs 907 crores against the target of Rs 760 crores registering an increase of 39 per cent over the previous year's sanctions. Ninety five per cent of total residential units and 85 per cent of plots sanctioned are meant for EWS. These loan sanctions, besides normal housing schemes, included loans for schemes for land acquisition, urban infrastructure, low cost sanitation, liberation of scavengers, NRY, and building material industries. The sanctioned schemes will enable construction and upgradation of 4.6 lakh residential units in urban areas and 2 lakh in rural areas, development of over 0.32 lakh residential plots and conversion/construction of 2.8 lakhs basic sanitation units spread over the length and breadth of the country and also augmentation of water supply and drainage, road improvement facilities, acquisition of 2438 hectares of land and future housing schemes. HUDCO achieved a loan sanction of Rs 6666.67 crores in 1998–99, a massive increase of 118 per cent above the previous year's achievement to Rs 3061.86 crore.

10. Welfare of Weaker Sections and SCs/STs: During 1989–90, HUDCO made significant contribution to the betterment of economically weaker sections and Scheduled Castes and Scheduled Tribes. Over 20 per cent of all dwelling units sanctioned were exclusively meant for SC and ST families. At the end of the year, HUDCO sanctioned schemes envisaged construction of over 1.34 lakh dwellings to benefit SC and ST families exclusively.

11. Two Million Housing Programmes: HUDCO has been assigned a significant role in the implementation of the ambitious programme of the government to provide 20 lakh additional units every year. Of the 20 lakh additional housing units, 7 lakh are to be provided in urban areas involving a total cost of Rs 4,000 crore.

The opening of the retail lending window has inaugurated a new thrust on individuals and has simultaneously given a chance to HUDCO to show its all round abilities to the public at large. Individual Home Finance Division with proper built-in flexibilities and through innovation will try to cater to the needs of all sections of the society.

12. Resource Mobilization: HUDCO raises its finance through government guaranteed debentures, shelter bonds, urban bonds, and capgain debentures and raising term loan from UTI, banks. During 1998–99, it had mobilized Rs 2,150 crores.

13. Promotion of Building Materials and Technologies: As a result of various steps taken by the central and state governments for improving the availability of land, and finance for housing development, it was felt that this will augment the demand for building materials. To meet this increased demand for building materials for low cost housing, HUDCO, since its inception has been making efforts to promote appropriate building materials and technologies for the manufacture of basic, substitute or alternative building materials. In this direction, HUDCO has been extending financial assistance for setting up various building material manufacturing units particularly those utilizing local materials, agricultural, forest, and industrial wastes and also innovative technologies for the manufacture of standard building materials. HUDCO has so far financed numerous building material schemes in various states for dehydrated lime (a substitute for cement); pitch fibre pipes (a substitute for GI and MS pipes); wood working units using secondary species of timber duly treated and seasoned; sand lime bricks replacing the use of clay; and brick making manufacturing units.

14. Building Centres: The Ministry of Urban Development, Government of India, and HUDCO launched a national programme that set up a network of building centres all over the country in the year 1988 for promoting appropriate building technologies through training of artisans. A grant of Rs 2 lakhs is provided by the Ministry of Urban Development and working capital loan upto Rs 4 lakh by HUDCO whereafter the building centres are expected to be self-sustaining. The building centres have trained a number of carpenters, barbenders, etc. Village offices, fishermen markets, and a large number of housing units under Indira Awas Yojna of Rural Housing Programme, and individual homes for all category of people have been constructed by these Building centres.

15. Habitat Engineers: To strengthen its programme of building centres, HUDCO initiated the concept of 'habitat engineer'. This concept is to emphasize the role of the habitat and the habitat engineer to perform as the key functionary of a building centre to enable the promotion of appropriate low cost technologies by supervision and engaging in the execution of the projects and also by providing training to workers and artisans. The habitat engineers are trained over a period of one year in different disciplines before being placed in different building centres for promoting appropriate technologies among workers and others.

16. Studies in Collaboration with TIFAC: The Technology, Information, Forecasting, and Assessment Council (TIFAC) has been established under the Department of Science and Technology (DST) for examining existing technology, the course of future technological developments in various sectors of the economy, ensuring timely availability of requisite technologies, and suggesting strategies for technologies developments in line with socio-economic, environmental, and security needs of the country.

HUDCO has undertaken specific studies along with TIFAC in relation to building technology and skills and different aspects of human settlement planning such as technology for low-rise high density housing, low cost infrastructure, and guided urban development. Based on this work suitable recommendations are being sent by TIFAC to the Ministry of Urban Development for consideration.

17. Design for Housing Scheme for Bhopal Gas Victims: HUDCO's Design and Development Wing, at the request of the MP Housing Board, designed a housing scheme for the Bhopal gas victims. The proposed design is ground plus one-storeyed development with future room facility to each unit at the same level. Houses are organized in cluster condominiums with a single entry point, thus promoting good neighbourhood environment. Low-rise development is proposed in view of the fact that climbing more than one flight may be difficult to most of the gas victims due to their bad health or physical handicap. The cluster condominiums pattern under the scheme was recognized and the Indian Institute of Architects has awarded a certificate for Excellence in Architecture for the proposed HUDCO Design.

18. Training at Human Settlement Management Institute: Human Settlement Management Institute (HSMI) has emerged as a national level training and research institution with a wide variety of programmes of both national and international recognition. The stress of its activities has been on practical aspects of human settlement planning and management with training programmes in the specific subject areas of urban management, housing for weaker sections, slum upgradation, housing finance, computer applications in human settlements, land assembly and development for housing, settlement design, low cost infrastructure, and construction management. A special orientation programme for senior executives of housing and urban development agencies was also initiated in 1989. In the international sphere, HSMI has collaboration with the Institute for Housing Studies (IHS), Rotterdam, Netherlands, for training and research support under Indo-Dutch Technical Cooperation.

19. Habitat Polytech: In order to meet the urgent demand for reorienting technical education to meet the requirement of housing and human settlements, HUDCO in collaboration with Slum Wing, DDA, has established a Habitat Polytech in New Delhi to provide Bachelor courses in Habitat Planning, Habitat Management, Architecture, training for NGO's and training in building skills for artisans. The Polytech provides in-service training to employed engineers in areas related to habitat planning. It is hoped that this Polytech would go a long way in meeting the urgent demand for training field level personnel and voluntary organizations to effectively deal with housing problems of the poor.

20. Human Resource Development: As HUDCO treats its staff as a human resource, it has renamed its Personnel and Administration Wing the Human Resource Development Wing. The HRD Wing, in addition to its usual functions, continuously monitors the training needs of the employees. To meet this it either organizes in-house training courses at HSMI or sponsors names for short term courses organized by reputed professional institutions in the country. In addition, it sponsors its employees for training, study meetings and seminars abroad.

21. UNCHS-Information Dissemination Office, Madras: The United Nations Centre for Human Settlements (Habitat) with its headquarters at Nairobi opened its Information Dissemination Office in Madras on the premises of the southern zonal office of HUDCO on 17 September, 1991. The main objective of the information centre is to undertake the dissemination of UNCHS publications and audio-visual material both within India as well as the neighbouring countries. It is particularly targeted at national and state governments, housing agencies, local bodies, educational institutions, the private sector, and non-governmental and community-based organizations with a view of sensitizing the concepts and objectives of the Global Strategy for Shelter. The UNCHD-IDO will also generate information based on significant contributions in the field of human settlements in India and neighbouring countries for wider global dissemination.[6]

22. SAARC Declaration for Provision of Shelter by 2000: The SAARC heads of states in the fifth SAARC summit held at Male in December, 1990, had declared 1991 as SAARC year of Shelter, with a view to give right focus and arrive at appropriate policies, programmes, and projects which could lead towards the goal of shelter for all by the year 2000. The Male declaration had recognized the imperative need for providing a better habitat to the people of South Asia through optimum utilization of materials, indigenous technology, and skills.

Achievements of HUDCO

Over the last three decades, HUDCO has been consistently working to promote viable settlements, with the prime focus on the economically weaker sections, to maintain a social and economical balance. It encourages indigenous and low-cost building materials and techniques that ensure economic and environmentally appropriate settlements having simple and aesthetic housing designs, thereby reducing costs and bringing housing within the reach of the people. It has established itself as the Nation's premier techno-financing institution in the field of housing and human settlement.[7]

HUDCO sanctioned a loan of Rs 6666.67 crores, provided assistance for the construction of 18.60 lakh dwelling units, over nine lakh sanitation units and 122 urban infrastructure projects throughout the country in 1998–99 and made an approximate profit of Rs 69.71 crores.[8]

In spite of its endeavour HUDCO has yet to achieve a lot to effectively reach the poor communities and a majority still live in shanty colonies with sanitation and civic facilities leaving much to be desired.

Habitat Scroll of Honour 1991 Award to HUDCO

HUDCO was awarded the prestigious award of Habitat Scroll of Honour 1991 by Shri Areot Ramachandran, Under Secretary-General, United Nations, and Executive Director, United Nations Centre for Human Settlement (Habitat), on 17 September 1991 at Madras for innovation, development, and promotion of building material, design, and construction for affordable housing for the poor and training in construction skills. Smt Sheela Kaul, then Minister of Urban Development, Government of India, while receiving the award, had congratulated HUDCO on the conferment of this unique honour and observed that HUDCO has emerged, of late, as a comprehensive human settlement development institution with significant contribution in the field of shelter, urban infrastructure, construction methods and technology, low cost innovative building materials, skill upgradation, and human resources development of the people both in urban and rural areas. She added, 'The award of 1991 Habitat Scroll of Honour by UNCHS to HUDCO epitomizes the international recognition of the role that it is playing in India and this award has also come at the most appropriate time as 1991 has been declared as SAARC year of Shelter.[9]

Delhi Development Authority

Delhi Development Authority (DDA) was set up on 30 December 1957 under an Act of Parliament. Its genesis can be traced to a tiny nazul Office under the deputy commissioner of Delhi in 1922 which was upgraded in 1937 into an improvement trust and finally its transformation into a full-fledged development authority in 1957.

Objects of DDA

The Act defines the objects of the Authority as: 'to promote and secure the development of Delhi according to plan and for that purpose the Authority shall have the power to acquire, hold, manage, and dispose of land and other property to carry out building, engineering, mining and other operations, to execute works in connection with supply of water and electricity, disposal of sewage and other services and amenities and generally to do anything necessary or expedient for purpose of such development and for purposes incidental thereto'.

Delhi, in 1957, had a population of 18 lakh and it was steadily increasing due to the influx of people in search of employment and better avenues of advancement. The growth was haphazard. In order to ensure an integrated and planned development, the Master Plan for Delhi, 1962, provided the necessary framework and guidelines to the DDA.[10] Since its inception, the Authority has endeavoured to ensure growth on the following lines: by creating self-contained zones and divisions and providing residential accommodation and community facilities near the employment centres; by decentralizing the facilities so as to reduce the burden on the public utilities; by providing functionally utilitarian, economically viable and aesthetically satisfying shelters to all the sections of the society as per their family requirements and paying capacity; by ensuring sufficient lung space within the city through the development and preservation of green areas; by preserving the cultural heritage of Delhi and its historical landmarks and at the same time making it a modern city which can withstand the pressures of urbanization for the years to come; by providing recreational/sports centres in all parts of the city; by providing civic amenities and facilities to the unorganized and dilapidated shelters/structures.

Functions of DDA

Far from merely being an agency entrusted with development of land and housing, the DDA has played a role in each and every activity connected directly or indirectly with the development of Delhi as metropolitan city. While it is difficult to compartmentalize the functions of DDA, these can be grouped into: development of land for residential industrial, commercial, institutional and recreational purposes; construction of houses; resettlement of squatters and providing them group facilities; constructing recreational centres and sports complexes; developing and preserving greens; developing infrastructure facilities; constructing commercial facilities for smooth functioning of the city such as bus terminuses and flyovers; constructing commercial centres, convenient shopping centres, etc.; relocation and development of industries to non-farming areas and industrial colonies.

Administrative Organization

The Delhi Development Authority has a multiplicity of functions which it is required to perform in order to fulfil its objectives. The main executive body of DDA is known as 'Authority'. The Authority has 13 members and its constitution is as follows:

1. Lieutenant Governor, Delhi
2. Two representatives of the Municipal Corporation of Delhi
3. Three representatives of the Metropolitan Council
4. Commissioner of the Municipal Corporation of Delhi
5. Three persons nominated by the central government, one of them having experience of town planning and architecture
6. Vice-Chairman, Finance Member, and Engineer Member of the DDA

The Lt Governor, Delhi, is the *ex-officio* Chairman of the DDA. The central government appoints the vice-chairman who is the chief executive, the finance member, engineer member, secretary, and chief accounts officer. The Authority, subject to such checks and balances as may be provided under various rules, may appoint such other officers and employees as are necessary for the efficient working of the organization. The Authority has seven main departments having a number of cells affiliated to each department. The functions of these departments and cells are described as follows:

1. Personnel Department: The Personnel Department is headed by the Commissioner (Personnel). He is assisted by one Director, four Deputy Directors, nine Assistant Directors and secretarial staff. It is responsible for human resource planning and development. It plays a very important role with respect to the recruitment, training, placement and promotion of DDA employees, service matter rules as finalization of seniority, crossing of efficiency bar and confirmation in service.

2. Welfare Department: The Welfare Department looks after the welfare of all categories of employees of the DDA. It also helps in creating healthy employer–employee relations by organizing cultural programmes, social get-togethers, and other allied activities. It also helps in processing case for appointments on compassionate grounds, payment of group insurance, and disbursements from the benevolent fund. In addition to these welfare activities, it runs a departmental canteen that provides clean and healthy food on a no-profit–no-loss basis to all the employees. The Chief Welfare Officer who is the Secretary of the Canteen Managing Committee makes regular inspections of the canteen to ensure maintenance of hygiene in preparation of food stuffs and efficiency and affability in service. The DDA also has a Sports Club which organizes various types of meets and awards prizes to the winners. The welfare section plays an important and effective role in maintaining healthy bonds between the employees and the management. It coordinates and arranges various meetings with the representative of various unions thereby providing a platform for across-the-table discussion. These meetings and discussions help in redressal of grievances.

Parliament and Coordination Branch

Parliament cell processes questions on matters relating to housing, lands, building, administration, horticulture, etc. It replies to the metropolitan council questions as well. It also prepares the annual administration report and other reports.

The coordination committee holds meetings under the chairmanship of the vice-chairman to review progress in various spheres of day-to-day administration and takes appropriate remedial measure wherever necessary. It also disposes time-bound references/queries received from the Directorate of Public Grievances or Cabinet Secretariat or the Ministry of Urban Development.

The Staff Quarters Allotment Branch deals with allotment of staff quarters to the employees of the DDA. After allotment, the staff quarters are inspected to find out if there has been any subletting or violation of the terms and conditions of the allotment. Show-cause notices are issued to the erring allotees and in case no satisfactory reply is given the allotment is cancelled and the allottee is debarred for a period of one year from further allotment.

The Public Relations Cell performs many useful functions such as formulation of advertising policy, fixation of annual advertisement rates, empanelment of advertising agencies, covering of meetings and press conferences, arranging for visits of VIPs, bringing out publicity material, issuing rejoinders to criticism in the media, and organizing public hearings. The DDA being a premier housing and development organization plays host to many delegations visiting India to see the progress made in the realm of urban development.

3. Law Department: The Law Department has been assigned the job of looking after the entire litigation work of the Authority. It also renders advice in all important matters which are referred to it by various departments/sections of the Authority. The Department is headed by Chief Legal Advisor who is assisted by Deputy Chief Legal Adviser, Legal Adviser/Senior Law Officer, Junior Law Officer, and Legal Assistant. The services of advocates on the panel of the authority are also requisitioned from time to time.

The Law Department is organized into seven divisions with the functions enumerated against each as follows:

Division-I: General administration, receipt, and dispatch of notices, summons, general *dak* and coordination with other departments of the Authority.

Division-II: Cases under P.P. Act, LSB (Res.), commercial and industrial plots cases relating to development area, demolition of unauthorized constructions, Nazul land, Wakf land, etc.

Division-III: Cases of Housing, Building and Planning Department, mainly regarding flats, unauthorized construction, cases relating to the Master Plan, etc.

Division-IV: Administration, vigilance, and industrial disputes, cases under Workmen's Compensation Act, Industrial Disputes Act, and Provident Fund.

Division-V: Cases of Engineering Division and Arbitrary Act. These are time bound and thus dealt promptly.

Division-VI: Criminal prosecution for contravention of the Master Plan under Section 29 (2) read with Section 14 of DD Act, 1957 and prosecution for unauthorized construction.

Division-VII: Tis Hazari Court, High Court.

Vigilance Cell

The chief vigilance officer is the head of the Vigilance Department in DDA. He is assisted by one director, four deputy directors, one accounts officer, one section officer, five assistant directors, and one superintendent for the purposes of conducting investigations on non-technical matters and processing of the disciplinary cases against all the employees of DDA. The Vigilance department also has a technical wing for conducting investigation of the cases of technical nature of engineering, horticulture department, etc.

On the technical side, there are two superintending Engineers, eight executive engineers, and six assistant engineers to assist the chief vigilance officer. For the actual conduct of departmental inquiries there is one post of commissioner of departmental inquiries and one superintending engineer (inquiries).

The Vigilance Department is responsible for the implementation of anti-corruption measures and maintenance of integrity in service as per instructions issued from time to time by the Department of Personnel Administrative Reforms, Ministry of Home Affairs and the Central Vigilance Commission. More stress is placed on preventive vigilance, conducting periodical inspections, and surveillance. The defects coming to the notice during the inspections are brought to the notice of heads of departments to plug the loopholes and streamline the procedure wherever necessary. The Vigilance Department examines the existing procedures for the issue of various permits, possession letters and such in order to remove bottlenecks and sources of delay, which are a source of harassment and corruption.

On the engineering side, a constant watch is kept on the cost, quality of material used and the time taken in executing the works. A quality control wing headed by a chief engineer is constantly examining the ongoing work so that there is no compromise on the quality of material used. Surprise checks are done by the technical officers of the Vigilance Department also to detect and prevent malpractice.

The finance and accounts wing of the Authority is headed by the finance member. The accounts of the Authority are maintained in the following six divisions: (*i*) Nazul Account (I), (*ii*) Nazul Account (II), (*iii*) Nazul Account (III), (*iv*) General Department Account, (*v*) Accounts of ISBT at Kashmere Gate, (*vi*) Delhi Lotteries Account.

Nazul Account-I represents the transactions relating to the old Nazul estates entrusted for management by the government to the erstwhile Delhi Improvement Trust under the Nazul Agreement, 1937, and taken over by the DDA in December, 1957, as the successor body. The accounts also include transactions relating to the preparation and implementation of the Delhi Master Plan and zonal development plans.

Nazul Accounts-II comprises transactions pertaining to the scheme of large-scale acquisition, development, and disposal of land in Delhi. The sales proceeds of land and recovery of ground rent realized are accounted for in this account. The surplus of receipts over expenditure incurred on the development of land is remitted to Delhi administration periodically for meeting the liabilities in respect of land acquired or for acquisition of new lands by Delhi administration.

Nazul Accounts-III relates to the Jhuggi-Jhompuri Removal Scheme. This scheme was mainly financed out of the Government grants but has since been transferred to Municipal Corporation of Delhi in June 1988.

General Developments Account is the main account of the Authority. Unlike Nazul accounts, the assets and liabilities arising from the transactions under this account are wholly the property of the Authority as a statutory corporate body. All properties and lands vesting in the Authority are paid for out of the revenues of this account. Under this account the DDA has undertaken housing programmes for the weaker sections, lower income and middle income groups. In addition, the DDA has launched a number of self-financing housing schemes. Commercial schemes like the development of Nehru Place. Bhikaji Cama Place, and the ISBT at Kashmere Gate are also financed from this account.

4. Engineering Wing: The engineering wing is headed by the engineer member. To facilitate smooth working of the wing, the DDA has been divided into six construction zones and each zone is under the charge of a zonal chief engineer. The electrification work of all the six zones is under the charge of a C.E. (Elect.).

The functions of the engineering wing are multifarious and range from developing land for various purposes, constructing various structures over developed land, providing infrastructure such as road, storm water drains, sewerage, water supply and other allied facilities, developing the greens to provide adequate lung space, constructing structures to provide health and recreational facilities. The activities of the engineering wing can be broadly divided into: (*i*) housing, (*ii*) infrastructural development, (*iii*) constructing buildings (non-residential), (*iv*) developing greens (horticulture wing), (*v*) sports complexes and other recreational facilities, and (*vi*) designing various projects.

(*i*) *Housing*: In order to meet the demands of various strata of society, houses of varying accommodation, specification, and cost are constructed.

(*ii*) *Infrastructural Department* involves developing various facilities and amenities such as roads, sewers, drains, levelling of land so as to make it worthy of habitation or construction for various purposes. The work under this head can be sub-divided into various categories: (*i*) development of land by providing infrastructure facilities and making it suitable for allotment as residential plots, commercial plots, etc., (*ii*) development of land and infrastructure for various group housing societies, and (*iii*) development of infrastructure for various residential schemes.

(*iii*) *Construction of Non-Residential Complexes* includes developing and constructing shopping centres which facilitate convenient shopping of various daily necessities to the residents of particular pocket, big shopping centres, commercial centres, industrial sheds, transport centres, community centres, school buildings, etc.

(*iv*) *Developing Green Areas (Horticulture Wing)*: One of the main tasks of the horticulture wing is to develop and maintain large green areas in order to maintain a balanced ecosystem; large green areas are landscaped and developed in the shape of neighbourhood parks, district parks and artificial lakes. Planting of road side tress and maintaining its own nurseries for supply of seed plants are other important activities of the department.

(*v*) *Developing sports complexes and sports facilities at various places in Green areas*: The engineering wing takes up construction of sports complexes at various places with facilities for almost all games. The DDA develops special fitness trails and provides equipment in many of the big parks under its charge to enable the public to practise various types of physical exercises. The DDA develops some parks as special children parks.

(*vi*) *Designing the Various Projects*: The office of the central design organization broadly consists of two units, one pertaining to structural designs and other to service planning.

Quality Control Wing: The function of this cell is to create awareness among the field officers towards the quality of the work and of their responsibilities by making random inspection of the works including random checking of the quality of materials being used in different works. The wing has a full-fledged laboratory of its own for testing the samples of materials drawn from different sites of works during the course of its inspections. In addition to the above tests the wing also investigates complaints received from individual allottees or various residents' welfare associations.

Planning and Architecture and Development Control Wing deals with (*a*) *perspective planning:* perspective plan, urban extension and NCR transportation, walled city and special area; (*b*) *development control and planning:* master plan and zonal plan, planning building section, trans-Yamuna area; (*c*) *projects:* Rohini, Dwarka (Papankalan), Narela, Jasola; and housing and urban projects.

LANDS DEPARTMENT

The Lands Department is headed by the Commissioner (Lands) who is assisted by three directors in the management of the land of the revenue estates entrusted by the Government of India to the erstwhile Delhi Improvement Trust under the Nazul Agreement 1937 and the land placed at the disposal of DDA since 1961 under the scheme of Large Scale Acquisition, Development, and Disposal of Land in Delhi. In addition, this department also administers the land transferred by the Ministry of Rehabilitation. The department functions through the following branches:

Enforcement Branch ensures that most appropriate economical healthy development of the city takes place as per provisions of the master plan and the zonal plans. Where it is noticed that the premises are being used for contravening the provisions of the master plan and zonal plans, the owners or lessees and the tenants are prosecuted under the law, and are punished with fine which may extend to Rs 5,000, and in case of continuing offence, with further fine extended to Rs 250 per day under Section 14 read with Section 29(2) of the DDA Act. Temporary permission is granted under the provision of the special appeal subject to payment of composition fees and fulfilment of other terms and conditions as may be laid down by the authority in this regard.

1. *Lease Administration Branch* disposes of plots through auctions and allotment of alternative plots under the scheme of Large Scale Acquisition, Development and Disposal of Land in Delhi 1961.
2. *Old Scheme Branch* deals with the lease administration of about 14,000 plots leased out by the erstwhile Delhi Improvement Trust, allotment of plots or land under GADGIL Assurance Scheme to the displaced persons, re-development of Kingsway Camp, allotment or auction of MOR land, and regularization of unauthorized occupants on MOR land and old Nazul lands.
3. *Commercial Lands Cell* deals with the disposal of commercial plots. It is also responsible for execution and registration of lease deeds.
4. *Land Protection Branch* protects the vacant lands available with the DDA. The entire state of Delhi has been divided into nine zones headed by the Deputy Director. A mobile demolition squad of the staff strength of 150 persons taken on deputation from Delhi Police assists the Deputy Directors in the discharge of their duties.
5. *Institutional Branch* deals with the allotments of land to government, semi-government and private institutions. The allotment of land to private institutions is made on the recommendation or sponsorship from the concerned department or ministry.
6. *Damages Branch* is responsible for assessment and recovery of damages from the unauthorized occupants squattering on the DDA or government lands. This branch also undertakes eviction proceedings against the unauthorized occupants on government lands or in purchase or cancellation of allotments of staff quarters or those made under various DDA schemes.
7. *Co-operative House Building Societies Cell* deals with 127 cooperative societies out of which one society, i.e. Delhi School Teachers CHBS is being managed by the land building department, Delhi administration, for administrative reasons, the allotment of land to this society was made by the Delhi Administration prior to 1970.

Policies and Guidelines for Redressal of Grievances of Public

DDA has issued appropriate guidelines in consultation with the legal department, to allow mutations where the leasees and allottees have died leaving behind a 'WILL'. Earlier it used to take more than six months to decide these cases but now the work is completed within 10–15 days. To avoid delay in execution of leases, a sub-registrar has been posted to work in Vikas Sadan.

A policy decision has been taken to allow the transfer of plots sold through the Power of Attorney after charging unearned increase. The procedure has been simplified and the mutation is carried out within a week or so of the deposit of unearned increase with DDA.

Possession letters are issued on production of chalaans of payment without their realization being confirmed by accounts. Moreover, arrangements have been made to issue the demand letter on the very next day of auction and possession is handed over immediately on the production of required documents by the purchasers and allotees. Mortgage permission is also now granted along with the possession letters.

5. Housing Department: The allotment of houses constructed by the engineering wing of DDA is entrusted to the housing department. The need for such a department was felt due to the increasing demand for a shelter. Initially the DDA was only developing and disposing of plots for residential, commercial, institutional, and other purposes. But due to large influx of people migrating from neighbouring areas, it was felt that the need for shelter can be best satisfied by constructing flats as per the paying capacity and requirements of different persons. The increases in the number of units necessitated allotment to the right eligible persons and thereby the need for a full-fledged housing department. Apart from allotting number of houses, steps have been taken to simplify the procedure of issuing allotment letters and also to facilitate easy delivery of possession letters to the allottees. Now possession letters are issued across the counter after giving due publicity to the date of allotment and the scheme under which the allotments are being made. Special attention is paid to accommodate retired and retiring public servants.

6. Slum Wing: The slum wing has the main responsibility for improving the quality of life of the slum/jhuggie dwellers. This mandate of the slum wing is carried out by implementing the socio-economic programmes approved by Delhi administration from time to time within the ambit of plan scheme. The qualitative improvement in the life of these disadvantaged settlements brought about by provision of basic minimum amenities also relate to the provision of shelter to shelterless, residential dwelling units to slum dwellers and to the economically weaker sections of the society.

The Slum Areas (Improvement and Clearance) Act, 1959, remained a source of guidance to the various activities of the slum wing with the main stress on the clearance of slums until the termination of the Sixth Five year Plan, 1980–85. Due to some functional problems in pursuing this approach there was a shift from the clearance to the improvement and upgradation of existing slums. The factors that forced for this change were: resistance from slum communities against disruption due to length of stay in the areas; physical and financial constraints to provide alternative housing stock to all the affected families; non-availability of vacant land adjoining the slum areas for relocation; and political overtones in the slum clearance.

The 7th Five Year Plan saw the beginning of definite efforts to restructure or revamp the activities of the slum wing by incorporating innovative and imaginative approaches to solve the physical and other problems of the slum areas. One such major endeavour was to facilitate and promote through access to land, finance and technology for house building by the economically weaker sections/lower strata of society and jhuggie dwellers themselves under the self-help approach, through the formation of co-operative group housing societies. NGOs are also used for motivational efforts for reaching the fits of various welfare schemes of Slum

Wing, to the target group by creating higher receptivity level in terms of acceptance of the programmes and co-operation from the communities.

There are two sources to fund the activities of the slum wing, viz. pre-determined financial outlays provided by Delhi administration under successive annual plans for various projects and programmes and the funds made available from the own resources of the slum wing, from the auctions of the commercial and residential plots and built up shops/stalls etc. As mentioned above, the policies and programmes of the slum wing, have registered change depending upon the ground realities from time to time. There was a stress upto the end of the Sixth Five Year Plan for clearing dangerous buildings and properties and areas becoming unfit for human habitation by providing alternative flats comprising of 23 sq. ft. of plinth area to the evictees under the Slum Areas (Improvement and Clearance) Act, 1956. Since the Seventh Five Year Plan, this approach was abandoned and replaced by the improvement of slum on 'as is where is basis'.

Various Schemes of Slum Wing

(i) *Residential Flats Registration scheme* was launched in 1985 to provide residential flats on cash down or easy terms basis with the recovery period spread over 15 years.
(ii) *Environmental Improvement in Urban Slums scheme* helps provide basic civic amenities such as water supply, sewers, storm water drains, community latrines and bath known as Jan Suvidha Complexes, widening and paving of existing lanes, *dhalao*s, street light, multi-purpose community halls containing provision of baratghars, reading room-libraries, anganwaries, dispensaries, open air theatres, and toilets in notified slums depending upon the need and availability of resources.
(iii) *Environmental Improvement in Jhuggie Clusters scheme* which came into being with the initiation of the Seventh Five Year Plan gives full responsibility to the slum wing, for improving the quality of life of about 12 lakh people living over 700 *jhuggies—jhompries* clusters strewn all over Delhi. Under this programme the DDA provides the following basic amenities: (*i*) pay and use jansuvidha complexes containing toilets and bathrooms at community level, (*ii*) water supply either through water hydrants or deep handpumps depending upon availability of water from municipal mains, street lights on the peripheries for illumination of streets or paths in *jhuggie bastis*, (*iii*) *dhalao*s or dustbins for collection of garbage or rubbish, and (*iv*) paned pathways and drains.

The use of these facilities is available for a nominal charge of 20 paise per use for adult males whereas, women and children are free to use the facilities without any charge. These complexes are maintained by the nominated agencies such as Sulabh International, Indian Institute of Low Cost Sanitation, All India Parivar Kalyan Parishad etc. In some cases, the local community has itself volunteered to maintain the complexes.

A structural Improvement in Slum Katras Scheme is designed to carry out necessary repairs in the slum katras in the walled city of Delhi and its extension for ensuring structural safety of the properties and *katras*. This scheme is applicable only to those katras which are under the management control of Slum Wing, and are economically viable for repairs without heavy investment. For minor repairs and day to day maintenance the slum wing has established nine maintenance stores in various parts of the slum areas, which are capable of carrying out repairs with the building material and technical/non-technical man power available with them.

Re-development of Shahjanabad scheme envisages the urban renewal and the decongestion of the walled city.

(iv) *Private Katras and Their Development*: For re-development of private *katra*s and properties, the slum wing is supposed to issue NOC's under Slum Areas (Improvement and Clearance) Act, 1956. However, this work has now been assigned to Delhi Municipal Corporation.

7. *Vishramgrahs*: As per the 2001 census, there is a population of 6.5 crores in the country and 52,765 in Delhi alone who are considered absolutely shelterless. The fact that they form very much part of the segment of the population, the welfare of which need immediate attention. In Delhi, a scheme of construction of *Vishramgrahs*/*renbaseras* was launched during the Seventh Five Year Plan. The beneficiaries of this scheme are the people who are generally low paid workers, i.e. labourers, coolies, cobblers, load carriers, rag pickers, and others working in minor positions in the informal sector, who in the absence of any house or place of their own sleep on the pavements and open spaces.

Under this scheme, the slum wing has so far constructed such *vishramgrahs* in Basti Nizamudin, Azadpur Subzimandi, Pahar Ganj, Jhandewalan, Mukherjee Market (opposite Red Fort), Shahzada Bagh, and a temporary night shelter at Turkman Gate. For the benefit of Haj pilgrims passing through Delhi, Haj Manzil containing multi-purpose facilities such as night shelter and community facilities complex has also been constructed at Turkman Gate.

In addition, fifteen night shelters or *renbaseras* for the shelterless provide not only space to sleep but also give a feeling of home. The facilities provided at these night shelters comprise the common toilets/baths, water, blankets, jute mattresses, reading material, TV, etc. This facility of using the night shelter is available at a nominal charge ranging from 50 paise to Re 1 for per night stay.

Inadequacies and Deficiencies of Night Shelters

The Comptroller and Auditor General (CAG) had criticized the DDA for its failure to build enough night shelters and for unproductive and excess expenditure. The CAG report said money meant for the construction of night shelters was used for the renovation of old night shelters, purchase of a jeep and purchase of items for the day-to-day business of the night shelters, which were to be met out of the revenues of the DDA.

The Slum Wing of the DDA undertook a survey of night shelters, and it was found that the available accommodation was woefully inadequate.

During the Seventh Five Year Plan, a scheme for the construction of 25 night shelters in different parts of the capital with an outlay of Rs 3 crore was approved. However, the DDA did not make any survey before the implementation of the scheme of the actual number of homeless persons in Delhi. Suitable sites, where the night shelters were actually required, could not be constructed due to the non-availability of land. Thus, the night shelters were constructed at places where the sites were not necessarily the most suitable for fulfilling needs of the shelters. Besides, no effort was made to provide shelters for women and children to fully meet the social objective of providing shelter to the homeless. As for the under utilization of night shelters, the CAG said, of the three shelters constructed at Azadpur Sabzi Mandi in February 1987, one was being used, one was not being utilized and the third was being used for office purposes. Two units constructed in Paharganj in January 1988 were not being used due to resistance from the local public. Thus, the non-utilization of these four units had resulted in an unproductive expenditure of Rs 29.15 lakh.

The survey had envisaged that the maintenance of shelters should be entrusted to non-profit making voluntary organizations. The non-involvement of any voluntary organization in the functioning of the night shelters is an indicator of the lack of perception and proper planning, unless such organizations are full involved in the management and encouraged to participate, the social objectives of the scheme for providing night shelters to the shelterless cannot be achieved.

Apart from providing the comfort of life, programmes for skill upgradation are also taken up. All present in these programmes are being organized by the Sharmik Vidya Peeth, Directorate of Adult Education, Government of India with a focus on improving/increasing the productive capabilities of the inmates. In the slum wing, these programmes have been taken up on experimental basis:

(i) *Conversion of Dry Latrines into Water Borne Latrines* is a socially motivated scheme which has twin objective of improving the sanitation conditions due to the present insanitation in the absence of disposable water borne latrines and to eliminate the inhuman conditions by liberating the scavengers from collecting the excreta manually. Under this scheme as an incentive a subsidy of Rs 500 is provided to the intended beneficiary for converting the dry latrines into water borne latrines.

(ii) *Horticultural Works in Notified Slums* are planned in such a way that their benefits accrue to the target group of slum and *jhuggie* clusters.

(iii) *Developed Plots for Self Housing to Lower Strata of Society and Economically Weaker Sections Including Squatters*: During the Seventh Five Year Plan, a project for the provision of 44,000 low cost developed plots of 26 sq. m. each was approved with an outlay of Rs 52.80 crore. The target group of this scheme is the lower stratas of the society, economically weaker sections including SC and squatters.

(iv) *Income Generating Assets for the Poor Through Commercial Stalls and Tharas Scheme* was operated in the Seventh Five Year Plan.

(v) *Low Cost Units of Work Centres Scheme* is intended for the benefit of economically weaker sections including SCs and entrepreneurs and unemployed youth who are keen in joining manufacturing activities.

Publicity Programme

With a view to removing mental barriers of slum and *jhuggie* dwellers, the slum wing exhibits films on socio-economic and political aspects of life and also on sanitation, child care and health care along with Hindi feature films. Leaflets containing messages for health care, child care, and sanitation are distributed amongst slum dwellers and *jhuggie* dwellers through mobile cinema vans. Regular press notes are issued for opening of various facilities for public use, for giving wide coverage to the activities of the slum wing and also informing the public so that they can make use of the assets created for them.

Research and Innovation

The slum wing is directly related with the execution of projects directly or through the outside agencies. Therefore, it utilizes its past experience for formulating future policies and strategies. It sponsors its employees for various training programmes in the areas concerning the activities of the slum wing to the reputed institutions. Besides, the officers are sponsored for participating in various seminars, workshops organized at the national and international level. Recently, the slum wing has established in-house training infrastructure also with a permanent lecture-cum-conference hall where the lectures are organized by inviting reputed persons from the institutions for the benefit of the staff and officers. It has conducted certain studies on slum upgradation cost recoveries, socio-economic profile of slum and *jhuggie* dwellers and footpath dwellers in consultation with HUDCO and Ministry of Urban Development.

Achievements of DDA: An Overview

The Delhi Development Authority is the sole planning and development authority for the entire metropolis of Delhi. In fulfilment of its objectives and targets, it continues to acquire extensive lands, provide dwelling units for all strata of the society, build more commercial centres, sports complexes, recreational parks, and fitness trails and also develop and preserve vast new green areas. It contributes substantially and significantly to the improvement of dilapidated buildings in the walled city and other sub-standard areas and makes determined efforts to provide minimal civic amenities to the people living in slums. It tries to preserve the city's heritage areas even while releasing building activity and providing for the growth of the infrastructure necessary to meet the relentless march of urbanization. The efforts of the policy makers and administration of Authority are directed towards making the DDA strong, sensitive, and conscious to the needs and aspirations of people and to this end it has simplified and devised many procedures by evolving a system of providing all necessary information across the counter. It has also made efforts to reach and inform people regarding various programmes and policies of DDA through press releases and advertisements. A bird's eye view of its main activities may be given here:

1. **New High in Housing Activities:** The housing programme has crossed the 201,617 mark, thus far exceeding the number of dwelling units constructed by any other development agency in India. Emphasis has been laid on providing houses at reasonable and affordable cost to economically weaker sections.
2. **Development of Land:** Delhi Development Authority being the main executing agency of the Delhi Master Plan has been acquiring and developing land to functionally balance the future growth of Delhi. It has been developing land for residential, industrial, commercial, institutional, and recreational purposes. It has also been developing open spaces and vast green areas to contain pollution and to satisfy the aesthetic needs of the city.
3. **Development of Residential Colonies:** Developing residential colonies and allotting plots or constructed flats has long been one of the important functions of the DDA. Of late, many big housing colonies such as Janakpuri, Vasant Kunj, and Rohini comprising both residential flats and plots have been developed by the DDA and many more such housing colonies in Dwaraka, Jasola, Narela, and Weavers Colony in Ashok Vihar are in progress. Rohini is a multi-purpose township with an area of about 2,500 hectares, which in due course will meet the requirements of a population of 8.5 lakh. Rohini has mostly flats and plots for economically weaker sections numbering about 1,70,000. The planning and development of the Narela Project comprises 380 hectares (in phase-I), Ashok Vihar Weavers Colony comprises 760 plots of 36 sq. m. and Jasola Project covers an area of 164 hectares.
4. **Development and Decentralization of Commercial Activities:** One of the guidelines provided for the development of Delhi under the Master Plan is to decentralize the commercial activities and facilities so as to reduce burden on the public utilities, the DDA has already developed district-cum-office complexes at Nehru Place, Rajendra Place, Bhikaji Cama Place, Laxmi Nagar District Centre and Janakpuri. As many as 25 community centres, 64 local shopping complexes and 346 convenient shopping centres have also been developed. In allotment of shops, special consideration is accorded to the members of Scheduled Castes and Scheduled Tribes, physically handicapped, ex-servicemen, freedom fighters and those whose lands have been acquired by DDA for its urban extension projects.
5. **Horticulture Development:** The Master Plan for Delhi has provided for an integrated and balanced development of the city with a system of linked up residential spaces, recreational centres,

district parks and institutional, industrial, commercial and public and semi-public areas spread all over the metropolis. Special emphasis has been laid on preserving the historical content of the city by preserving and maintaining its monuments, natural greens, river fronts, ridges, lakes, and its sprawling green parks and forests. In the midst of this capital city, humming with all sorts of activity, are the city forests.

6. **Recreational and Sports Activities:** The DDA has made significant contribution towards providing sports and recreational facilities in Delhi. At these sports centres facilities are provided for playing cricket, football, hockey, squash, badminton, table-tennis, and volleyball, and arrangements exist for flood lighting to facilitate playing during late hours. These sports centres are expected to go a long way in promoting the love of sports and games among the citizens of Delhi.
7. **Upgradation of Slums:** The slum wing of the DDA, which is responsible for providing basic amenities to the inhabitants of notified slums, sub-standard areas, and squatter settlements has done a commendable job over the years in all parts of the city.
8. **Quality Control Measures:** The DDA continues its efforts to improve the quality of construction by organizing random checking of material samples and recommending remedial measures for common defects found in the flats.

Future Projects (Master Plan Perspectives 2001)

DDA has many new urban extension projects and other specific schemes for the development of Delhi in order to meet the needs of its fast growing population. The framework for this activity is given in the Master Plan Perspective 2021. The salient features of this plan are: it provides for the growth of the city and the areas to be developed for various urban activities such as housing, transport, employment centres, commercial centres, recreational areas etc. by the year 2021; it seeks to introduce the concept of incremental housing on small residential plots which would benefit the low income groups; it also envisages a rail based mass transport system and development of four directional metropolitan passenger terminals, four freight complexes aid five-state bus terminuses; it introduces the concept of 'Mixed Land Use' and 'Informal Sector'; it provides for the conservation of the natural heritage and environment in the form of the ridge and the river and development of large areas for recreation and sports, at present level; space standards have been extensively modified to suit requirements of the community and also to conserve land as well as to create environment for better quality of life; it identifies 11 rural growth centres for provision of higher level education, health and other facilities; it also provides for (*a*) systematic development code with (*b*) strong monitor unit.

Over the years through its multi-dimensional activities, DDA has not only carved a place of pride for itself in the map of development authorities of the world but has also demonstrated that such an organization, its dedication and hard work, can deliver the goods in almost all spheres of urban activity, making city-building a professional and pragmatic exercise in the art of the possible. It is hoped that other Urban Development Authorities in the country would emulate the example of the DDA in solving the problems of human settlements and meeting the requirements of urban planning and development in providing a clean environment to enable the residents of their respective jurisdictions to lead a healthy life.

Haryana Urban Development Authority (HUDA)

The Haryana Urban Development Authority is a statutory body of the Haryana government constituted in the year 1977, for undertaking urban developments in the state of Haryana and for matters ancillary thereto.

For this purpose, it has the power to acquire by way of purchase, transfer, exchange, hire, management, plan, development, and disposal of land and other property by carving out plots for residential, industrial, institutional, commercial, and other purposes, to carry out engineering, mining, and other operations, and to execute works in connection with supply of water, disposal of sewerage, control of pollution, etc.

Administrative Organization

The Haryana Urban Development Authority has the chief minister as its chairman, chief secretary to the government of Haryana as vice-chairman and a senior IAS officer as its chief administrator and some members including commissioner, Town and Country Planning. It has its headquarters at Panchkula. It is divided into different divisions and wings dealing with land acquisition; engineering; town planning and architecture; electricity; legal and monitoring; technical, vigilance and general administration, and accounts and audits. Administrators are posted at Gurgaon, Faridabad, and Panchkula who exercise supervision and control over estate officers of various urban estates within their respective jurisdictions.

Development Activities of HUDA

1. **Urban Estates:** HUDA has set up urban estates at various places, all over the state at district headquarters, sub-division headquarters and other potential areas, 21 cities in all in the state (these are Ambala, Panchkula, Jagadhri, Shahabad, Kurukshetra, Kaithal, Karnal, Panipat, Sonepat, Rohtak, Bahadurgarh, Bhiwani, Jind, Hisar, Sirsa, Gurgaon, Rewari, Rozkameo, Hathin, Dharuhera, and Faridabad). Thus, Haryana Urban Development Authority has taken up the development activities in almost all parts of the state.
2. **Development of Villages Encircled by Urban Development:** It has been observed that in a number of urban estates, which are being developed, villages are encircled by the urban development and they continue as unplanned settlements devoid of all amenities of urban life. HUDA has therefore undertaken the phased development of such villages, for which the finances and the development cost, could form a part of the over all 'External Development Cost' of the project and 'Internal Development Cost' for the sector or sectors in which they are located.
3. **Development of Mandi Township Areas:** The development of various mandi-townships in the state of Haryana was previously being done by the Colonization Department. On the winding up of this department in 1987, 27 mandi township were divided into two parts, namely (*i*) mandi portion and (*ii*) township portion. The area falling within the mandies at various places were transferred to Haryana State Agriculture Marketing Board with the responsibility for their development and the township areas were transferred to HUDA and made responsible for the development of undeveloped land and vacant plots. In addition, the liability on account of plots which had been sold out had also been transferred to it. The sold out areas were partially developed, i.e. the basic amenities such as water supply, sewerage, electrification and street lighting, etc. were not adequate and now such street services in these areas are to be completed by HUDA.
4. **Development and Sale of Government Surplus Lands:** In 1987–88, the government of Haryana had decided to dispose of the surplus government lands to increase its resources so as to utilize that amount towards the implementation of its various schemes and projects for the welfare of people of the State. HUDA was entrusted with the responsibility to sell such surplus government lands by carving out residential and commercial and industrial plots according to the requirement of particular city or place. Such plots were to be sold to the public through open auction and provided

the required facilities such as water supply, sewerage, storm water drainage, electrification and street lighting, and horticulture works.

5. **Other Development Activities:** As per provision in the HUDA Act, the sectors in urban estates are required to be transferred to the municipal committee, after a period of five years. But it has generally been seen that due to financial constraints, the local bodies are not able to take over the sectors after the expiry of prescribed period. This puts a greater burden on the HUDA with regard to special repair of roads and maintenance of essential services, such as water supply, sewerage, and sewerage disposal. In some urban estates, the roads have been damaged very badly and cannot be repaired with patch work and require special repairs which involve a huge expenditure. The HUDA has, however, decided to repair the roads where 80 per cent of the houses have been constructed. The urban estates also require the construction of community buildings such as community centres in Jhanjghar, asaries, primary schools, police post, etc. and the provision of horticulture works, the development of green areas, such as green belts, parks, and road-side plantation. All these requirements need to be met by the HUDA expeditiously.

Achievements of HUDA

The HUDA proposed to spend Rs 28,357.20 lakhs in 1990–91, which was the highest in the history of HUDA. In spite of all hurdles and financial stringencies, the Authority during a span of 12 years had expanded its business activities and expenditure by about 4.5 times, From a humble expenditure of Rs 645.05 lacs in 1977–78, it has increased to Rs 28,357.20 in 1990–91.[11] While preparing HUDA's budget, maximum consideration is given towards acquisition of new areas, in various urban estates, with the objective of providing developed plots to the public, so as to meet the increasing demand of urban population. Provision up to 60 per cent of the total spending is kept for acquisition of new areas, 20 per cent for completion of development works, and the remaining amount to meet pending liabilities. The minimum (not exceeding 2 per cent) of the total spending is provided for administrative expenditures. Provision of sufficient funds for various development activities shows that the Authority has devoted its full attention towards the speedy and planned development of urban areas and made necessary efforts for providing various facilities to the maximum extent expeditiously thus providing better quality of life to the citizens in various urban estates of Haryana. HUDA has taken up the development activities in almost all parts of the state and has so far floated one lakh residential plots on easy instalments for general public, which is no mean achievement.

In view of the achievement of the HUDA as outlined above, it can be rightly designated as 'A catalyst of urban growth in the service of the masses'. The HUDA and the Town and Country Planning Department, Haryana, bring out a house journal named *Basti* (The Human Settlement) to apprise the public about its various activities.

Despite its creditable achievements, the HUDA is criticized on a number of points. It is contended that it has raised the prices of plots four to five times. HUDA justifies the increase due to the rising cost of land and development on a realistic basis. Second, the possession of plots is not delivered to the allottees for years on end, even when all the instalments of the price of the plots have been paid. This causes frustration which could be avoided by demarcating the plots and delivering these to the allottees as expeditiously as possible. Third, development works of providing roads, water supply, sewerage, electricity etc. are not started, much less completed in the various sectors where plots had been allotted long ago. That might be due to paucity of funds. But the citizens have the right to be provided with the minimum facilities referred to above before they can start the construction of their houses or industrial units. The HUDA should therefore lose no time in fulfilling this obligation. Fourth, the material used in construction is alleged to be of substandard quality.

The vigilance cell of the HUDA needs to be vigilant enough to ensure that material of requisite quality is used by the contractors and the allottees are not fleeced. Fifth, there are complaints of poor maintenance of essential services and environment. The HUDA claims to be doing its best to reduce the grievances of its citizens in this regard. Sixth, allottees of plots carved out of lands, which have become a matter of dispute and litigation, are entitled to allotment of alternate plots and should not be denied this right. Disputes usually take years and years to be finally pronounced which might go against the HUDA, and the helpless allottees should not be made to suffer this agony for no fault of theirs. Lastly, corruption prevails in various establishments of the HUDA, especially estate offices where the building plans are not approved and the occupation certificates are not issued unless the officials concerned are obliged in cash or kind. The HUDA authorities should see to it that the public is not unnecessarily harassed for the favours which should be available to them as a right.

Conclusion

It has been observed that, by and large, the development authorities have shied away from planning the future development of existing built-up areas and have, instead, concentrated on planning and developing green-field areas. This has tended to further accentuate the structural, social, and cultural chasm between the older sections of our cities and the new suburbs. One could safely state that the development authorities, instead of bringing about harmony between the old and the new have contributed to enhancing a duality in our city structures through a faulty planning approach; standing aloof from the municipalities and accessibility to greater resources than the local bodies; the development authorities have thus generally invited the hostility of the municipalities.

The task force set up by the planning commission in 1983 for suggesting strengthening of the municipal bodies had *inter alia* made the suggestion that urban development authority should be merged into the municipal system. By and large, the thinking of all state governments, as also the central government, has been that local bodies need to be supplemented by, not supplanted by, functional agencies and development authorities which are not elected and are directly accountable to government.

The National Commission on Urbanization has suggested the constitution of regional planning authorities with representation on its governing council of the city corporations and town municipalities located within the region, and its chief executive appointed by the state government. Its planning decisions would have an element of participation by the constituent local bodies because of their representation on the governing council. While the regional planning authority should have wide powers of plan preparation and monitoring and evaluation of its implementation, it should not be the implementing agency. This work should be left to the local bodies. The commission has further suggested that in the matter of water supply and sewerage, either a similar arrangement may be made, or the head works, treatment system and the mains and out-falls may be constructed and maintained by the state public health engineering department, with internal distribution being the responsibility of the city corporation or town municipality. Apart from this, there should be no separate development authorities or functional organizations. Those which exist should be merged into the appropriate town municipality or city corporation.

NOTES AND REFERENCES

1. D.S. Chaudhary, *Municipal Administration in Rajasthan* (Jaipur: Romesh Book Depot, 1970), p.135.
2. R.L. Khanna, *Municipal Government and Administration in India* (Chandigarh: Mahindra Capital Publishers, 1967), p. 98.

3. Ashish Bose, *Studies in India's Urbanisation* (Delhi: Tata Mc Graw Hill, 1973), p. 252.
4. S.R. Maheshwari, *Local Government in India* (Agra: Lakshmi Narain Aggarwal, 1984), p. 213.
5. 'Report of the Committee on Budgetary Reforms in Municipal Administration', Government of India, Ministry of Works and Housing, 1974, p. 13.
6. Statement of Dr G. Rao, Chief, Information Audio-Visual Division, and Fund Management, UNCHS, Narobi.
7. S.K. Sharma, Managing Director and Chairman, HUDCO in his speech delivered at 20th Annual General Meeting held at New Delhi on 26 September 1990.
8. Statement of Shri P. Suresh, top executive HUDA after the general meeting are held at New Delhi on 1 October 1999.
9. Message of Smt Sheila Kaul, Minister of Urban Development, Government of India, on the occasion of the award of Habitat Scroll of Honour to HUDCO on 17 September 1991.
10. Master Plan for Delhi, 1962.
11. Basti, House Journal of the Department of Town and Countrv Planning, Haryanna and Haryana Urban Development Authority, Vol. I, No. 2, May 1990.

16

Role of Political Parties in Urban Local Governments

The role of political parties and their participation in the politics of municipal government has been a subject of much controversy. The question has been whether political parties of national and state character should participate in local politics so as to gain control over the local government machinery. In most countries of the world, particularly, the European, national parties actively associate themselves with local politics. In the UK elections to town councils are usually on party lines. The London county council (now known as Greater London Council), the greatest municipal polity in the world has the best organized party system. 'I doubt', says Harbert Morrison, 'Whether the fine reputation of London county council for uprightness and purity of administration would be maintained if the party system in the council were eliminated.'[1] In USA, party politics has been carried to extreme lengths resulting in the evil of bossism, spoils and partisan patronage.[2] The active participation of national political parties in local affairs is almost complete in a communist country like erstwhile Soviet Union and China.

In India, it is interesting to note that while much has been said against party politics in Panchayati Raj bodies, few have argued for party-free municipal politics. In can be attributed to the facts that cities and towns have been centres of origin, growth, and articulation of political parties; that the din and hustle of party activity are merely concentrated in towns and cities; that the literacy and political consciousness in cities and towns being relatively high, the national and state political parties have greater accessibility and sizeable following. But more important is the fact that great leaders like Motilal Nehru, Jawaharlal Nehru, Dadabhai Naoroji, Sardar Vallabhbhai Patel, and Subhash Chander Bose had risen to national eminence after their versatile experience in municipal politics. Again in the cities and towns, the local aspirants have only one channel of climbing to state and national politics and that is through active involvement in the national and state political parties' organizations and activities. Thus, a powerful tradition has come to stay in India for local aspirants to actively participate in national party politics.[3]

The participation of political parties in municipal administration is now almost a settled affair. Political overtones in almost every aspect of the decision of the municipal government are very clearly visible. Politics dominate municipal elections and other municipal affairs. It is a different matter that because of political exigencies, a political party may not contest municipal elections on party basis. But in reality, it would just be a formal stand—if not outright a political camouflage.[4] The case for and against or the merits and demerits of participation of political parties in urban local governments may be discussed as follows:

Merits

1. It is felt that properly organized political parties can do a lot of good by clarifying civic issues, enlightening the electorate, evoking public participation, etc. in the municipal field if they function with a sense of discipline, reality, and clarity in their programmes and with an eye on the good of the community.[5]

2. The protagonists of party system in municipal government further assert that the politics at municipal level forms a piece in the total politics of a developing society and it cannot, therefore, be ignored by any political party except at its own peril.

3. Political parties in municipal institutions will prove to be a powerful solvent of all the traditional business of caste, community, and religion which are strongly entrenched in our society.

4. The party system does not permit things to go unchallenged, proposals are scrutinized, discussed, and debated threadbare and vigilance is exercised over administration.

5. Party discipline eliminates personal ambitions as the members are obliged to work for the interest of the groups or parties to which they owe allegiances; nonpartisanship has not worked, does not work, and will not work in any major city.[6]

6. National political parties tend to control local politics for maintaining their local power base and the local elections serve as useful barometers for measuring the popularity or otherwise of national political parties.[7]

Referring to the significance of the role of political parties in municipal politics, Prof. W.A. Robson observes,

> I do not share the views of the superior persons who look down from Olympian heights with displeasure and contempt at the activities of political parties. Since the electorate are divided on many urgent questions according to their opinions and interests, it is desirable that these divisions of interest and outlook should be canalised and organised in a coherent and clear-cut way. It is only by means of political parties that this can be done.[8]

Demerits

1. On the other hand, the advocates of municipal government being run on partyless basis, mainly because of the influence of Gandhian and Sarvodaya philosophy, plead that local politics is non-ideological in character and therefore should be free from party politics. In the state and national politics, the issues can be advocated on party and ideological basis but they are of no particular consequence to municipal electorate. We cannot think of either communist or capitalist programme of sanitation or water supply. There cannot be any such thing as Akali pavement or Congress sewer pipe.

2. It is difficult for a given political party to have a common programme for all municipalities in a given state as an election manifesto.

3. In the case of a communal party coming into power, it may neglect the localities belonging to minorities.

4. Since most cities are economically and culturally heterogeneous, there is a multiplicity of parties representing various interests. In such a situation, party systems would plague municipal administration; party rivalries could adversely affect the smooth functioning of municipal administration; ruling party would veto

everything that comes from opposition and vice-versa. This would mean the destruction of very assumptions on which civic government as a body rendering primary services is founded.

5. It is further argued that political parties will carry to the local area the evils of corruption, nepotism and favouritism which will poison the democratic fabric at its very roots.

6. The object of local democracy is to provide opportunity of leadership, initiative and responsibility to the local people but the introduction of party politics will deprive the people of such opportunities and concentrate leadership in the hands of political parties.

The overriding consideration for political parties should, therefore, be the broad civic interest and party politics should not be mixed with the civic functions that have to be discharged within the parameters of municipal law.[9] The Late Shri V.V. Giri, former President of India, had rightly observed,

> I firmly believe that there should be no partisan approach to civic matters, the corporators are concerned with the limited objective of improvement of the civic life of the people and in this there is no room for any controversy or conflict of interest. May be the civic elections are fought on party labels but I would urge that once members are elected, they must forget their party labels and work with unity, determination and dedication in solving the municipal problems.'[10]

The Late Giani Zail Singh, former President of India was also of the view that elections to local bodies should be on a non-party basis and the state laws should be amended to this effect if necessary. He had observed in his reply to a civic reception accorded by the Vijayawada Municipal Corporation that the objective of the local bodies is to serve the people and strive for their development. It is not necessary for political parties to participate in the elections to these bodies.[11]

It is obvious from the above discussion that political parties in municipal administration can prove to be beneficial or baneful depending upon such factors as their organization, nature of programmes oriented towards the welfare of the whole community and their constructive approach to the solution of the problems confronted by the concerned local bodies as against their indulging in the pursuit of selfish, sectarian and factional interests and adopting negative, obstructive and destructive attitude in the functioning of municipal polity.

Notwithstanding the criticism and condemnation of the role of political parties in municipal government, it is now an established fact that they do involve themselves overtly or covertly in civic affairs and as such make or mar the smooth functioning of municipal bodies.

Politics in Municipal Governments

The fact that politics operates in municipal government and administration is substantiated by the following observations:

1. Holding of Civic Elections Determined on Political Consideration: Civic elections are not held for years together despite the stipulation that they should be held every three or five years, as the case may be. This very fact reflects that the decision not to hold the elections or postpone them from time to time are based on no other consideration than political, albeit other excuses are put forth by the governments of different political parties occupying the seat of power at different times, like the non-preparation of electoral rolls, non-delimitation or demarcation of electoral wards, non-existence of congenial atmosphere for holding of election as generated by natural calamities like drought, floods and political and communal turmoil and the disturbed conditions due to the activities of the terrorists and so on. The fact, however, is that the political parties in power in the state government have not been sure of capturing power in the municipal bodies at a particular point of time, hence they defer the elections. For example, Akali Dal (L) in Punjab had won a thumping majority in Assembly elections in 1985, but it did not dare to order elections to municipal bodies for the simple reason that it was difficult for it to win in the urban areas where its base was not as strong as it was in the rural areas. On the contrary, in the neighbouring state of Haryana, the Lok Dal and BJP combine, which had been returned with an unprecedented majority in Legislative Assembly, had immediately held elections to the municipal bodies and the alliance had captured power almost everywhere.

2. Supersession of Municipal Bodies: Again, the state governments are vested with the power to supersede the municipal bodies. They have exercised this power invariably on political considerations as is reflected in the supersession by a particular party in power in the state, of a municipal body being ruled by the party opposed to it. The supersession of municipal bodies on partisan and political basis has been confirmed by judicial pronouncements also when the acts of supersession have been challenged in courts. Similarly, the extension of the tenure of municipal bodies enjoying the favour of the ruling party in the state is also determined by political consideration.

3. Contesting of Elections on Party Basis: As a matter of fact, municipal elections are contested entirely on party basis. Candidates are sponsored by various political parties like the Congress, the Bhartiya Janta Party, Lok Dal, the Akalis, and the Communists and independents are supported by them. They are allotted the symbols of their respective parties. Election campaigns are conducted through the employment of usual media. Local as well as state political leaders address public meetings. In most of the wards, candidates fielded by the respective political parties are returned due to the overwhelming support extended to them by the party wielding predominant position in the wards concerned. But some independents constitute the exceptions who are victorious at the hustings on account of their personal qualities of philanthropy, popularity, and humility.

4. Role of Political Parties in Other Decisions: The role of political parties is not limited to election only but is visible in other spheres also. Their participation is conspicuous in elections of the office bearers, president and vice-president of municipal committees, mayor and deputy mayors of municipal corporations, co-option of members, constitution of standing and sub-committees, decision of municipal councils, disciplinary actions against erring employees, grants-in-aid for development and other purposes, and defections. The state governments also act on partisan basis in respect of their decisions and operations affecting the functioning of municipal bodies. The activities of the political parties as also of the state governments in regard to the above mentioned points may be substantiated by the following observations:

(i) *Election of Office Bearers*: In matter of election of president and vice-president of a municipality, and also in the election of mayors and deputy mayors of municipal corporations, political parties play an active role. President is elected by the council from among its own members but his name must be approved by the state government and duly notified in the government gazette. There have been instances when the approval of elections of president belonging to a party other than the party ruling in the state have been unduly delayed or not notified till the president-elect has joined the party in municipal committee enjoying the favour of the state government. Similarly, political parties have been determining the election of the vice-president as well.

(ii) *Removal of President and Vice-President*: Again president of a municipal committee can be removed by state government on the grounds of abuse of power or habitual failure to perform his duties or in pursuance of a resolution passed by a municipal council by two-third majority. Though the charges levelled against the president are brought mainly on the grounds of personal favours and undue advantages extended to their favourites on the party basis may not play any specific role in the motions, yet voting in these cases is done on party lines. Party politics thus plays a vital role in changing the course of careers of presidents and vice-presidents.

(iii) *Removal of Councillors*: In the case of removal of councillors too party politics is very conspicuous. The state government may remove a member for his acts of omission and commission and the municipal council may accept his removal ungrudgingly if the disqualified person belongs to an opposition party. But it may react differently when its own members are involved and his disqualification may be revoked by the government after a resolution for the removal of his disqualification is duly passed by the council. On the contrary, a municipal council may move the state government to disqualify a particular member for serious faults and also condemn his defaults of a very serious nature, but the government may not disqualify him as he belonged to its own party.

(iv) *Co-option of Members*: Municipal councils are empowered to co-opt members. The political party enjoying majority in the council, co-opts its own persons. Co-option is intended to secure the services of persons eminent in the field of municipal public service and or having expertise in municipal administration, but political parties ignore this criterion and co-opt members on political consideration.

(v) *Constitution of Sub-committees*: A municipal council constitutes many statutory standing committees and sub-committees under its by-laws such as building, octroi, vehicle, conservancy, finance and work sub-committees etc. by electing people from among its members. These committees are required to examine different matters, thrash them out in detailed discussions and to make recommendations based on a more careful and prolonged examination than could be made in council meetings. These committees are elected by simple majority vote and not on the principle of proportional representation. The majority party elects its own members to these committees or sub-committees, and as a result the minority groups are denied and deprived of their representation on them. Efforts made by the opposition parties to get proportional representation introduced which secures representation to all the parties on the basis of their numerical strength in the council have been unsuccessful. Consequently, the party in power has managed to get its own members elected to these committees, and its members returned as their chairmen.

(vi) *Decisions on Party Basis*: A municipal council takes decisions on various matters presented to it by the executive, sub-committees, and other items forming the agenda of its meetings. The voting pattern of the council would reveal that items decided through voting are those which affect a particular group or party and are therefore decided on partisan basis. Similarly, the municipal council accepts, rejects or modifies the recommendations of sub-committees or those of the executive officer in pursuance of the interest of their parties.

(vii) *Use of Casting Vote in Parties' Interests*: The presidents of municipal bodies have a casting vote which they exercise to break the tie of equal votes on a particular issue. It has been often observed that the presidents have been using their casting vote to promote the interests of their own party.

(viii) *Evil of Defections*: Defections have also percolated to the municipal level. Defections are indulged in by the members of the council mainly for satisfying their ambition of capturing prestigious offices of president, vice-president, membership of sub-committees, nominations and sponsorship for attending conferences and seminars at state, regional and national levels. Defections are rampant among members of various political parties. This evil practice which does not only cause imbalances in the original strength of political parties and changes in their complexion at various periods of time but is also responsible for the ups and downs in the careers of the office bearers and uncertainties in the smooth functioning of the councils and administrative machinery, leading to the dissolution and supersession of municipal bodies. Some of the councillors change their colours like a chameleon and defect from a party a number of times and join the different parties including their original party, thus losing their credentials and credibility to all the parties. There is hardly any deterrent to the malady of defections. Public opinion matters little, rigid party discipline is not enforced, defectors are not expelled from the party, and they are welcome back at any time. One wonders if anti-defection law should also be made applicable to defections at municipal level to combat this evil.

Conclusion

Analysis of the organization and functioning of municipal governments and administration clearly reveals that elections to the municipal council are contested on party lines, though in some cases independents are also returned on their own personal merits. The candidates are sponsored by the political parties without taking into account their genuine faith in the policies and programmes of the party concerned but with the sole consideration of somehow securing majority in the council. The defections are very frequent and the defectors cross floor for greed of office or profit. The elections of presidents, vice-presidents, standing sub-committees and special sub-committees are manouvered on party-basis. The presidents exercise their casting vote not on the merits of a proposal but to serve their party interests. The recommendations of the sub-committees though made unanimously are turned down by the municipal council or modified as dictated by party interests. The executive officers are obliged to take decisions under political pressure. The actions taken by them against erring officials or the public are undone or altered by the municipal council on party consideration thereby damaging their prestige and causing loss to municipal revenue and impairing the efficiency of administration. The appointments are not made on merit, so much so that even basic qualifications are ignored for certain posts, nor are promotions made according to any principle, certain cases of serious negligence and offences are not proceeded against nor are the penalties imposed on the defaulting officials executed. Favouritism based on political considerations is the determining factor in all these cases. The government also acts in a partisan manner in notifying or withholding the notifications of the president-elect, removing and disqualifying the councillors, postponing elections for indefinite periods, issuing ordinances for co-option of members and associating legislators as members of the council, making appointments and removal of officials subject to their control, accepting or rescinding resolutions of municipal council, sanctioning of grants-in-aid for general and specific purposes and finally superseding the municipal committees and municipal corporations.

All this does not auger well, political intervention in municipal affairs should not be indulged in at the cost of efficiency of administration, sufferings of the public, and denial of democratic right to citizens to elect their municipal council at regular intervals as provided in the statute.

It stands confirmed that political parties definitely play a significant role in municipal administration. The hypocrisy that political parties should remain aloof from local administration has therefore to be given up and the inevitability of their role is unhesitatingly admitted. G.D.H. Cole was precisely for this reason in favour of organized political parties to function on ideological lines. According to him, 'Issues are continually arising which do divide men and women broadly on the same questions as divide them on national policies. If the issues are to be settled democratically, the party system is an indispensable instrument for the purpose.'[12]

What is required of political parties is to take up measures for improving the tone and substance of municipal politics; national/regional political parties should develop comprehensive civic programmes on the basis of enquiries into the needs of urban people, select candidates for municipal elections with adequate care and promote highly successful candidates for higher public offices in order to make municipal offices attractive to persons of ability and integrity. They should exercise overall control over their members in the municipal council, formulate a code of conduct for their guidance and make them continuously conscious of their responsibility to promote civic good and welfare;[13] they should come to a general agreement in regard to making joint efforts to implement non-controversial civic programmes; they should also arrange for leadership training for the elected representatives so that they can develop into responsible, knowledgeable and responsive councillors.[14]

Lastly, the state government should also act with caution. It should decide the municipal issues on their merit and not on party-basis. It is to provide guidance and advice to municipal administration. It is therefore, required to act in an impartial and non-partisan manner. If a municipal administration indulges in some acts of omission or commission, the government should intervene to get these rectified, again unmindful of the fact as to which party is wielding power therein. Only then can the mess created by political intervention, even in the affairs that belong to the domain of statutory functionaries, be cleared and the confidence of public in municipal administration restored.

NOTES AND REFERENCES

1. Harbert Morrison, *How London is Governed* (London, 1949), 68.
2. R.L. Khanna, *Municipal Government and Administration in India* (Chandigarh: Mohindra Capital Publishers, 1967), p. 186.
3. Raghaviah, 'Municipal Government and Political Parties', in M.A. Mutalib and N. Umapathy (eds), *Urban Government and Administration* (Hyderabad: Regional Centre for Urban and Environmental Studies, 1981), p. 83.
4. T.N. Chaturvedi, 'Municipal Administration in India Today', in S.K. Sharma and V.N. Chawla (eds), *Municipal Administration in India: Some Reflections* (Jalandhar: International Book Co., 1975), p. 13.
5. *Ibid.* p. iii.
6. Charles A. Beard, 'Politics and City Government', *National Municipal Review* 6 (1917): 205.
7. Y. Raghavirah, 'Municipal Government and Political Parties', p. 82.
8. W.A. Robson, *The Government and Management of London* (London, 1948), p. 350.
9. T.N. Chaturvedi, 'Municipal Administration in India Today', p. xiii.
10. *Nagarlok,* Vol. II, No. 1, 1970, p. 22.
11. *The Tribune* dated 9 March 1986.
12. G.D.H. Cole, *Local and Regional Government,* (London, 1947), p. 244–45.
13. T.N. Chaturvedi,'Municipal Administration in India Today'. p. xi.
14. Refer to Proceedings of a Seminar on Municipal Government in India, Department of Public Administration, Punjab University, Chandigarh, 4–8 April 1965, pp. 5–6. Also see. S.K. Kaushik, *Leadership in Urban Government in India* (Allahabad: Kitab Mahal, 1986).

Leadership in Urban Local Governments

Every organization, governmental or non-governmental, a political party and a group needs leadership to inspire, motivate and guide its members in their collective efforts to achieve its objectives. Pfiffner and Presthus, accordingly, define leadership as the act of coordinating and motivating individuals and groups to achieve desired ends.[1] Similarly, G.R. Terry is of the view that leadership is the activity of influencing people to strive willingly for mutual objectives.[2] Kontze and O'Dennel observe that leadership is the activity of persuading people to cooperate in the achievement of a common objective.[3] Ordway Tead believes that leadership is the activity of influencing people to cooperate in the achievement of a common objective which they come to find desirable.[4] In the words of Chester L. Bernard, leadership refers to the quality of the behaviour of individuals whereby they guide people of their activities in organized efforts.[5] According to Secklon Henson, leadership in large organizations may be defined as influencing and emerging people to work together in a common effort to achieve the purpose of the enterprises.[6]

Linderman describes the leader as an individual whose rationalizations, judgements and feelings are accepted (responded to) by the group as bases of belief and action.[7] According to Bernard, any person who is more than ordinarily efficient in carrying psychological stimulate to others, and is thus effective in coordinating collective responses may be called a leader.[8] Bogardus is also of the view that a leader is a person, who exerts special influence over a group.[9] Robert Tennebaum and Fred Massarik, define leadership as an interpersonal influence exercised in a situation and directed through the communication process, towards the attainment of a specific goal or goals.[10]

An analysis of the definitions of leadership given above, reveal certain common denominations and characteristics such as; that it is a process of influencing people—a leader is said to have an influence over others when they are willing to carry out his wishes and accept his advice, guidance and directions; that leadership is always related to a particular situation at a given point of time and under a specific set of circumstances; that a successful leader must be able to identify himself very closely with the organization as a whole; that his followers must be able to accept the legitimacy and rationality of its objectives and means; and that a leader sees the importance of individuals and gives them proper recognition.

Cecil Gibb after making a thorough review of the studies on leadership has mentioned that there are three most important principles of leadership, viz. (*a*) leadership is always relative to the situation and flourishes only in a problem situation; (*b*) the nature of role of leaders is determined by the goal of the group; and (*c*) leadership is a process of mutual situation—social interaction phenomenon in which the attitudes, ideals and aspirations of the followers play as an important and determining role as the individuality and personality of the leader.[11]

In India, it was our strong, selfless, sacrificing dynamic leadership in the persons of Mahatma Gandhi, Jawaharlal Nehru, Subhash Chandra Bose, Sardar Vallabh Bhai Patel and others that enabled us to win our war of independence against the British imperialism. Our sovereign democratic republic has adopted parliamentary system of government wherein our political and administrative leaders are expected to play significant role in the task of nation building, socio-economic development of our country and the achievement of the ideals of a welfare state by enlisting the cooperation and support of our people. We elect our political leaders to the Union Parliament and state legislatures through periodical elections who formulate policies and programmes for our well being and get these implemented through bureaucratic or administrative leadership.

Leadership in Urban Local Governments

The leadership at the local level—urban and rural—assumes great significance because it is to serve smaller areas and less number of people as compared to the state and union governments in terms of their territorial jurisdictions and the magnitude of their clients. Moreover, it is closer and nearer to the local people, as it lives among them, comes frequently in contact with them, is easily accessible to them, and is available to them on the spot to register their needs, demands, expectations and aspirations, complaints, and grievances and to help them in realizing and redressing them by formulating necessary policies and getting them implemented through municipal bureaucracy.

The leadership in urban local governments comprises political and administrative leadership, the former consisting of the elected representatives of the local people—the city fathers or the municipal councilors and the elected chairman—the president in municipal committees and mayor in municipal corporations; and the latter representing the bureaucracy at the secretarial and directorate level of the department of urban local government, the deputy directors at the regional level, the deputy commissioner at the district level, the sub-divisional officer at the sub-division level, the administrator and the executive officer in the municipal committees, the municipal commissioner in the municipal corporations and their supporting officials. The political leadership at the state level—the cabinet and specifically the minister holding the portfolio of urban local government also plays a dominant role in contributing to the quality of performance of urban local bodies.

Municipal Leadership: Then and Now

During our struggle for independence many of the national leaders took a great deal of interest in civic affairs and thereby obtained their political and administrative training. For example, Subhash Chandra Bose in Calcutta, Sir Feroze Shah Mehta in Bombay, Jawaharlal Nehru in Allahabad, Sardar Vallabh Bhai Patel in Ahmedabad, Satyamurthi in Madras were some of the illustrious city fathers. In our country, municipal governments have produced many leaders of national eminence and status, who were shining examples of sober and healthy municipal politics and restored to these institutions the authority and dignity they deserved.[12] Municipal governments thus afforded an invaluable training for emerging leaders who after acquiring experience in the art of politics and government at the local level rose as such to the state and national level.[13]

But in free India the cities and towns have failed to send representatives of calibre to the municipal councils. One may come across a handful of able councillors here and there but they are, in general, acutely in short supply. This applies equally well to the administrators. The types of officers that are recruited to work in the municipal authorities do not always match up to the needs of the job. In the face-to-face situation at the local level and in an atmosphere of rising popular expectations, the job of a municipal officer is a very difficult one. But unfortunately, in terms of service, conditions including pay and allowances and career prospect, municipal service have very little to difficult offer to a bright boy, on the top of that, the image of our municipal authorities has been such that municipal service will be opted for as a last resort.[14]

In order to analyse the factors responsible for weak, inefficient and poor quality of municipal leadership, it shall be proper to comprehend the powers and functions of the political and administrative leadership and their role in urban local governments.

Role of Political Leaders at the Central and State Levels

The ministry of urban development, Government of India headed by a minister, a popularly elected political leader provides leadership in planning or policy formulating in the areas of housing, urban development, urban poverty alleviation and urban water supply. But these being essentially state subjects, the Government of India play a coordinating and monitoring role and also support these programmes through central sector schemes, institutional finance and expertise. The leadership of the minister-in-charge of urban development is thus of great significance.

The state level political leaders—the legislators representing the people of state, enact laws covering the urban local governments, specifically their jurisdictions election procedures, powers, functions, sources of finance, nature of state control over them, etc. The cabinet takes policy decisions in regard to urban local bodies and gets these implemented through the minister of urban local government. The urban local bodies look to the minister to act as an effective leader for promoting their interests *inter alia* in the matter of adequate financial allocations for the improvement of civic affairs. They expect the legislators to visit their constituencies as often as possible and to raise their voice on the floor of the legislature for ensuring amelioration and betterment of city life. The leadership provided by the political leaders in the state government especially that of the minister in-charge of local government is, therefore, of vital significance.

Leadership in Municipal Committees

Municipal councillors, elected representatives of the local people constitute the municipal council. They perform a variety of functions in the management of civic affairs in urban governments. They participate in the formulation of municipal policies and programmes. As local legislators, they debate and discuss all vital issues concerning the city government as also the local residents and try to fulfill the promises made at the time of elections. In order to implement municipal programmes speedily, they supervise the programmes of municipal works undertaken in their allotted areas. They also keep an eye on the general standards of performance of the municipal employees. They being local leaders have to keep close contact with their constituents not only for maintaining *status quo* but also to increase further the strength of their party or group. As such they have to work for strengthening the leader-follower relationship. It is in this context that they enquire about the citizens' grievances against the municipal bureaucracy and bring the same to the notice of the appropriate administrative head and/or raise the matter in the council.[15] They encourage public participation in municipal affairs and try to enlist people's cooperation for a bright future of the city government and the people as it is the law of nature that good leadership and enlightened and active cooperation and participation in the affairs by the people cause civic pride and consciousness for building up sound and responsible local bodies administration.[16]

The municipal councillors have generally failed to provide good leadership in the performance of their multi-dimensional responsibilities and to inspire confidence among the citizens in regard to their ability to solve their problems as they are charged with selfishness, apathy and corruption. Lack of dynamic, progressive and unifying leadership at the grassroots level has, thus, affected the vitality of the municipal system. There is no denying the fact that a few municipal councillors possess striking personalities and advocate progressive ideas but their number is very small. It is only the sincere, dedicated and committed councillors that can win the confidence, cooperation and support of the citizens and only such persons should therefore aspire to be the municipal leaders.

The *Municipal President* is elected by the council from amongst its members for a term of five years. He can be removed by the state government even before the expiry of his term on grounds of abuse of power, habitual failure to perform his duties or in pursuance of a resolution passed by two-thirds majority of the members of the council asking for his removal. He is the king-pin of the deliberative and executive wings of the municipality. He convenes and presides over the council meetings. It is his primary duty to see that the meetings are conducted with decorum and dignity. He can take disciplinary action against the offending councillors. On the executive wing he occupies a key position. He executes the decisions of the council and as such supervises the work of the officers of the municipality. He enjoys some emergency or extraordinary powers under which he can order the immediate execution or suspension of any work.

Despite all these powers, he cannot make their best use as he is to depend on majority support, the availability of which is not based on any uniform pattern in the municipal politics. Constant endeavour of groups seeking enlistment of support of members dislodging the persons in authority and the dual position of the President who has to supervise the day-to-day administration and has also to carry the majority with him, makes the municipal administration more susceptible to extraneous influence and this, in turn, sows the seeds of discord and constant party bickerings.[17]

The frequent and often suspicious use of power of no-confidence against the President in municipal committees has further weakened his position. The sword of Damocles constantly hangs on him. This renders him incapable of providing meaningful leadership. But there are examples of presidents not succumbing to the pressure tactics of municipal councillors and steering clear through the rigmarole of party politics and deciding cases on their merit in the interest of the betterment of the city and well-being of its inhabitants. Such presidents have been identified with the progress of the cities concerned and have been elected time and again to this august office. Leadership provided by distinguished presidents needs to be emulated by others.

The *Municipal Executive Officer* is the principal executive authority of the city government. He is appointed by the state government. All the municipal staff is subordinate to him. He is responsible for exercising general control and supervision over the municipal office. He is to see that all guidelines, orders, and instructions given by the state government are properly implemented. He is obliged to lay before the council all important correspondence exchanged between the municipality and the state government. Being the principal officer, he is also responsible for the preparation of the budget and its presentation to the municipal council. The range of his powers being extensive, he exercises them through the heads of various departments and other subordinate municipal employees. In the past, when the executive officers' appointment and removal was vested in the municipal council subject to the approval of the state government, his position was not easy. A supine subservience to the wishes of the councillors made his office ineffective while an uncompromising independence led to such functions as would bring the municipal machinery almost to a standstill. Now with the provincialization of municipal services, he is appointed by the state government and is accountable to it. But if he is a man of vision, imagination and tact, he will prove to be a successful administrative leader enjoying the confidence of the council as also the respect of his colleagues and subordinates.

LEADERSHIP IN MUNICIPAL CORPORATIONS

A municipal corporation is the highest form of urban government with wide administrative and financial powers and autonomy. Its council comprises of elected councillors, co-opted councillors and associated members. The elected councillors owe their allegiance to one or the other political party (with a few exceptions of independents) which supports their candidates in elections, and enjoins upon them to follow their respective policies in decision making and their implementation. The role of political parties in the council, thus, oblige the councillors to act in a partisan manner, indulge in petty squabbles, infighting and impeding the smooth functioning of the corporation. In order to prove themselves as successful leaders, they need to be organized in a manner so as to ensure the fulfilment of the promises they make to the electorate at the time of elections but not to conduct themselves in a style which would mar their image and retard the achievement of the objectives for which the Corporation has been established, viz, the development of the city and the promotion of the interests of the entire civic population.

The *Mayor* is elected by the council and can be removed by a resolution passed by a majority of the council. He is the first citizen of the city, ceremonial head of the city government and represents the city on ceremonial occasions. He presides over the meetings of the council, maintains decorum and can expel or suspend members for their misconduct or disorderly behaviour. He is to ensure proper implementation of the decisions of the council.

The administration of a corporation is based on the principle of separation of powers between the deliberative and executive wings, the former concerned with policy formulation and the latter with its implementation. The mayor is, therefore, not invested with any executive functions. These are exercised by the municipal commissioner and the executive staff. The position of a mayor as a leader is thus very weak, though his office enjoys an enviable status and prestige. It has some legendary charm associated with it. No municipal office is as ostentatious as that of the mayor.

A debate has been going on for some time whether the powers of the mayor should be increased so as to turn him into a strong leader. Calcutta Municipal Corporation has the mayor-in-council scheme (cabinet form of government) whereby the mayor has a strong position, but it is the Bombay Corporation Plan which is in vogue in other municipal corporations in the country. In his position today, the mayor is devoid of any significant statutory authority. He may have to live and thrive more on his extra-statutory influence, and not by the exercise of any specific powers granted to him. The reputation of the mayor may increase in direct proportion to his character, ability, personality, influence and his party's power. A shrewd politician even within the ambit of the non-powerful presiding role can earn goodwill and wide influence by according due recognition to the council members, by being impartial as a presiding officer, by his amicability with the commissioner and by maintaining harmonious relations, with the officers of the Corporation. Maintaining such delicate public relation with various agencies may indeed be difficult but for an intelligent and seasoned politician of talent and tact it should not be beyond his capacity.[18] Such a mayor would prove to be a very successful leader.

The *Municipal Commissioner* is the Chief Executive of the municipal corporation. He is appointed by the state government for a renewable term of three years. He is the king-pin of the municipal administration and as such is at the apex of the municipal administrative hierarchy. Accordingly, he is entrusted with the responsibility of keeping the entire administrative machinery under his control and giving it the necessary guidance and direction. His most important function is to faithfully execute the resolutions of the council and its committees. He is often pressurized by the councillors to grant them one or the other favour. He is expected to deal with them in a tactful manner and keep them in good humour to enlist their support and cooperation in running the administration of the Corporation. The multi-dimensional nature of his activities makes him the pivot of municipal administration. As a full time municipal officer, in charge of municipal administration, he is required to spend most of his time even outside office hours in looking to daily correspondence, planning, designing and reporting for the purpose of improving the welfare of the citizens of the municipal area. His role is hard, the work is heavy and the pressure on him tremendous, yet he can survive and do good work to make the city clean, beautiful and liveable. But all this could be possible if he possesses the qualities of good administrative leadership and brings human approach to bear upon the decisions he makes. It is unfair on the part of the state government not to let him complete his minimum tenure of three years to enable him to prove his worth as a good leader.

Studies on Municipal Leadership

A number of studies on Panchayati Raj institutions including those on emerging leadership in them were made during the 1950s and thereafter, when the ambitious and well-intentioned programme of democratic decentralization was launched in our country but the study of municipal leadership has not been on that scale, because of the lack of interest and attention in urban local governments both on the part of the government and the academicians. Anyhow, in the early 1960s, focus changed a little and some studies relating to the urban governments were undertaken. R. Srinivasan and B.A.V. Sharma made a case study of four corporations and concluded that the political parties play a dysfunctional role in local polities.[19] The pioneering study of Donald R. Rosenthal 'The Limited Elite' shows that local politics is controlled by the ruling party at the state level. Ali Ashraf conducted the study of municipal politics in Calcutta and reached the conclusion that the city government was full of inertia and as such could not perform even the basic functions effectively.[20] He has also made a penetrating analysis of the working of municipal administration and the role performances of the councillors of municipal corporations of Ahmedabad, Calcutta and Kanpur in his latest study *Government and Politics of Big Cities—An Indian Case Study* and came to the conclusion that while the performance of leadership role in Ahmedabad Municipal Corporation has been quite satisfactory, the urban leaders in the other two municipal corporations have not been in a position to give their best to the municipal administration largely due to factionalism and groupism among themselves.[21]

R.W. Jones has examined various aspects of municipal administration and leadership in Indore in his book 'Urban Polities in India'. Besides analysing the extent of state intervention in municipal functioning, he has highlighted the prevalence of faction-ridden politics that has lowered the image of the councillors in the public eye. Vishnoo Bhagwan has vehemently criticized the negative role of political parties in municipal government in his book *Municipal Government and Politics in Haryana—A Case Study of Rohtak*. He has extensively studied municipal leadership and found it wanting in many respects.[22] S.N. Mishra in his *Politics and Leadership in Municipal Government* has concentrated on urban leadership in a medium-sized town of Bihar and examined the socio-economic background of the councillors and its possible impact on the performance of leadership role.[23]

Socio-economic Background of Municipal Leaders: Profile of Municipal Leadership

The behaviour of the political executive is influenced and conditioned by their life experiences, as Bendit and Lipset point out:

> To know who these power wielding individuals are is thought to be sufficient; it is a secondary matter to enquire into how they use their power. That they will do so in their self-interest is self evident, and the nature of interest is inferred from the status they occupy. Hence social and economic status rather than competing strategies of the political struggles are regarded as their sufficient cause of political decisions.[24]

'It is a wide spread assumption of political sociology', says Party, 'that social background and upbringing of a decision-maker will influence his attitudes and policies.'[25] Various studies therefore aim at identifying the social origins, educational levels, and financial position of those who are at the helm of affairs in the urban local bodies.

R.T. Jangam and B.A.V. Sharma had conducted a study of Urban leadership of a medium-size city of Jalna in Aurangabad district of Maharashtra in 1963–64 to find out the educational, socio-economic, political, and organizational background possessed by the city- government leaders and the kind or extent of influence the background had in their ability to function as efficient or successful leaders. The findings of the study were that women councillors stood out as better equipped and more successful than the men councillors. The leadership was relatively young; bulk of the leadership was derived locally, the councillors' level of education appeared to be rather low; leadership represented a fair cross-section of most religious and communal or caste groups in the city; the professional and business backgrounds of the councillors were varied; leaders having wealth in terms of money, land, house, business, vehicles, etc. had a better social and economic standing and could wield a measure of influence with their colleagues and constituents and were better respected by the municipal officials and employees; the leaders had a considerably rich political background and organizational experience, leaders lacked strong motivation and satisfactory public relations; they formed groups and cliques which pulled in different directions, and proceedings in the city council have suffered on account of strains and deadlocks, rowdy scenes, ugly protests and demonstrations and walkouts.[26]

G. Ram Reddy and M. Kishtaiah, in their study 'Urban Political Executive: The social Background of the Chairmen of Municipalities in Andhra Pradesh' in 1980 had tested the hypothesis. The political leadership in urban local bodies is controlled by the upper classes of the society and, therefore, the lower classes do not have a chance of attaining leadership; urban local bodies suffer due to their mostly uneducated leaders; and the unsatisfactory performance of urban local bodies is due to the inadequate experience of their political executives in public office. The findings of the study were that an average city father is from the upper social strata and is the son of the soil; he is middle-aged with impressive educational background; cither agriculture or business is his main occupation; he has a fairly good annual income; majority of them have long experience of municipal politics and they enter politics at a young age.[27]

Professor Zia-uddin Khan and Hoshiar Singh had studied the dynamics of three municipal councils in Rajasthan in 1984 and found that a substantial number of councillors were of 31–40 years of age (higher age group) and a good number were in the age group of 21–30 years (younger age group) and officials were mostly of the age between 31–50 years; the standard of education of the members appeared to be rather low; most of them had studied till middle or lower matriculation. Those who were qualified commanded a certain amount of respect of their colleagues and the citizens as well; and the officers' standard of education was also low. Further, there appeared to be shortage of trained persons to manage municipal administration efficiently. The professional and business background of members was varied—they were advocates, vaidyas and even medical practitioners. However, service personnel and businessman were the dominating elite groups; and among the municipal members, the middle caste group dominated and was followed by the upper caste group, and lower caste persons were the lowest in the rung. Wealth played a very significant role in city politics—leaders having wealth could wield a great influence among their colleagues and citizens.[28]

S.L. Kaushik has examined the role perception and performance of political leaders in urban governments in Punjab,[29] and analysed the socio-economic and political background of the leaders and their interface with the public. He has probed into the relations between the deliberative and executive wings of municipal administration and found that a sort of suspicion and mistrust prevails that leads almost to non-performance of the two wings. General apathy both on the part of the leaders and the municipal employees is on the increase to which general public is also generously contributing by sheer disinterestedness in municipal affairs. The totality of the situation at the local level is largely due to the quality of local leadership. There may be several other factors but the depleting power structure at the local level and the increasing interference by the district and state level leaders have, by and large, been responsible for the deplorable quality of urban leaders.

His other findings were that women councillors stood out as better equipped and more successful than the men councillors and enjoyed a better socio-economic background than men. The majority of the councillors had urban background. The municipal councils appeared to have plenty of young blood. The councillors' level of education appeared to be satisfactory; they possessed a high degree of language proficiency in Punjabi/Hindi, but little in English. They represented a cross-section of all the religions, and or caste groups in the state. Their professional or occupational background varied, leaders having higher income have a better social and economic standing and can wield a measure of influence on their colleagues, municipal officials and constituents. Their formal training was inadequate. Most of the municipalities present collusion of cliques and factions, and irresponsible political behaviour on the part of the councillors. Most of the councillors had a rich political background and had the experience of participating in various socio-economic and political movements and agitations.

Emerging Trends and Traits in Municipal Leadership

Studies conducted on municipal leadership in various states and the facts based on observations and experiences and reports in the press point out some emerging trends, prominent among these may be mentioned as follows:

1. The leadership in the urban government is relatively young, majority of the councillors belong to 31–40 age group. The lowering of the age of franchise from 21–18 years is expected to bring in more young blood to the municipal councils.
2. Women leaders have started showing keen interest in municipal affairs and their number in the municipal councils has shown an upward trend in recent times. Their number is expected to go up considerably with the spread of education among women and their participation in social services of various types such as child welfare, liberation of women, slum clearance and improving the lot of the under-privileged, protection of consumers' interests, conservation of environment etc.
3. More and more of the educated people are emerging as municipal leaders; some of them even possess postgraduate qualifications; illiterate and uneducated people are no longer accepted as leaders, as the citizens realize that uneducated councillors are not in a position to deliver goods.
4. In the absence of formal education at least of high school, the emerging leaders are conscious of their limitations to comprehend the municipal laws, rules and regulations and procedures of work. They, therefore, insist that the relevant records, resolutions and proceedings of the municipal council and its various committees and the communications received from the government should be in their mother tongue, in which they claim proficiency. They are also convinced that the acquisition of proficiency in one or more languages would enhance their comprehension of the working of the municipal bodies and facilitate their communication with their constituents and the municipal officials.
5. Though joint electorate system provides for election of municipal councillors irrespective of their caste and communal affiliations, yet caste and communalism do play a substantial role in the election of leaders as municipal councillors from their respective castes and communities in some places. It will take some time to educate the electorate to vote for the leaders on the basis of their merit and

personal qualifications rather than on extraneous considerations. Most of the emerging municipal leaders are returned on secular considerations but a few of them still make an appeal to the emotions of the voters in the name of religion, caste and group considerations to support them.

6. The emerging leaders have begun to depend more and more on the support of political parties to be elected to municipal councils. They try to get the party ticket, symbol and the resources of their respective political parties in canvassing support in their favour. Some of the political parties compromise to unite to give a fight to their opposite parties and once their candidates are elected, they also agree to distribute the various offices in municipal council among themselves. The party discipline not being very rigid and exacting at the local level, those who are denied party tickets rebel against the party command and contest the municipal elections on their own even at the risk of being thrown out of the party. Municipal councillors of various political parties take decisions in the municipal council on partisan basis and indulge in favouritism and nepotism and other vices inherent in party system, thus vitiating the atmosphere in the conduct of municipal affairs which should be conducive to the well-being of the entire city community and not of a particular group of people.
7. Reservation of seats for scheduled castes/scheduled tribes in proportion of their population in a particular area of municipality has encouraged the emergence of leaders among them who are elected to the municipal council from their respective areas and if the requisite number of them is not returned through the usual election procedure, they are co-opted to the extent they fell short of the requisite number. The scheduled castes/tribes leaders see to it that the interests of their communities in the matter of provision of basic essential services, slum clearance, reservation in employment in municipal services, and other welfare programmes are safeguarded.
8. Municipal leadership is emerging as a result of the provision of co-option made in municipal laws of various states. Though these provisions are made to avail of the services of persons having experience of municipal affairs or expertise in one or the other branch of municipal administration or public service, the system of co-option is used by the party in power in co-opting members of its own party. Such leaders may not be of that much use in decision making as the really deserving people would be. The demand, therefore, is being made that in order to improve the quality of municipal leadership, right type of persons should be co-opted.
9. Municipal leadership comprises representatives from all walks of life, professions, trades and business. But leaders from some profession such as medicine, engineering and teaching are very poorly represented, as they do not want to suffer the tribulations and trials inherent in fighting elections. Municipal leadership has begun to emerge among social workers, as they are able to win over the people with the appreciable work they have been carrying on in their respective fields and are assured of their winning the elections. It is high time that leadership should emerge from the ranks of other professions as well especially those of college and school teaching personnel as they have enough time to devote to comprehending civic problems and offer remedies to solve them.
10. Once municipal leadership was confined to men of wealth but now the leadership is emerging from among middle class and poor people as well because the citizens have come to believe that the representatives from among themselves would be in a better position to understand their problems in the right perspective and strive to solve them to their best advantage.
11. It is unfortunate that in some places emerging municipal leadership believes in the cult of money and muscle power, manipulation and use of malpractices like impersonation, booth capturing and rigging. This tendency needs to be nipped in the bud to enable the really devoted and dedicated leaders to come forward and take part in municipal affairs and administration.

12. It is appreciable that emerging leadership, especially the young leaders appear to have sufficiently strong motivation and direction. They are responsive to the needs and aspirations of the citizens. They visit their constituents and wards frequently, listen to their demands and grievances and do their best to get them satisfied and redressed by approaching the municipal authorities. They set good examples by giving the citizens a lead in organizing various programmes for cleanliness of their localities, initiating various schemes for citizens' welfare on voluntary basis and inspiring them to actively participate in education and health programmes and keeping their environments clean for healthful living and making their cities beautiful.
13. The emerging leaders are also aware of the fact that their role performance would be judged by their constituents by their conduct as exhibited in the meetings of the council, their relations with the municipal bureaucracy and the citizens themselves. The leaders, therefore, have been to appreciate the acquisitions of qualities of patience, reasonableness, resourcefulness and tact to deal with the municipal employees and of courtesy, cooperation and concern to win popularity and support among their colleagues and constituents.

The emerging leadership is, however, reflecting signs of improved quality, yet it leaves much to be desired. It is hoped that the prospective municipal leaders would have clear perception of goals, identification of problems and needs, devise means and measures for implementation of goals, secure cooperation and support of their colleagues, the administration and the constituents in order to prove themselves as effective and efficient leaders. The emerging leadership feels that they require comprehensive training to equip themselves with the knowledge of their rights and obligations and the techniques to comprehend the needs and problems of the citizens and methods to meet them. The state government should, therefore, lose no time in providing the desired training to municipal leaders if we want them to prove themselves as effective leaders.

Factors Responsible for Poor Municipal Leadership

It is evident from the discussion of the roles of leadership of various functionaries of urban local governments that the municipal leadership is weak, unsound, uninspiring, uncreditable, incompetent, incapable, devoid of spirit of service and unaccountable. This state of municipal leadership may be attributed to the following factors/reasons or barriers:

1. Membership of State Legislatures and Union Parliament is More Attractive and Rewarding: Political leaders have greater desire for the membership of the state legislatures and Union Parliament as compared to that of urban local governments for its prestige, dignity, status and the monetary rewards that it carries. Members of the legislature/Parliament represent wider constituencies and larger electorate and therefore, have greater areas of influence and power. They can expect for a ministerial berth or headship of a public corporation or the statutory body. They are provided government residential accommodation, handsome salaries and other perks. The legislators are entitled to payment of substantial daily allowances for the days of the meetings of the legislature, meetings of various committees, free travel by train, security guards and pensions. All these facilities and concessions are conspicuous by their absence in the case of municipal councillors, except that some states like Punjab have started paying a token paltry monthly honorarium to the chairman of municipal bodies.

2. Very Few Powers of Municipal Authorities: The municipal affairs in our country do not seem to evoke as much interest in the citizens as they do in the Western countries. Western countries have historically given a great deal of powers to the municipalities to rule themselves while the municipalities in India are generally anaemic institutions.[30] The powers and functions of our urban local governments are limited by the state governments. It was expected that after the achievement of independence the restrictive approach to municipal functions would give place to augmentation of their functions as visualized in the First Five Year Plan.[31] But on the contrary their powers and functions have been eroded by being taken over by the state government itself or by the creation of multitude of special purpose authorities. This has proved as a disincentive to citizens aspiring for municipal leadership.

3. Negative Role of Political Parties: Despite the desirability of political parties, non-participation in municipal government, as the local issues need to be decided on non-partisan basis, they do take part and interfere in municipal administration with all their evils of factionalism, nepotism and favouritism, infighting and decision making on partisan basis, and the enforcement of rigid party discipline on party candidates in voting on various issues in disregard of their conscience. Citizens, in order to preserve their own individuality and identity, would not like to be tools in the hands of their respective political parties. This has obviously retarded municipal development and stunted the growth of municipal leadership.[32]

4. Excessive State Control over Municipal Bodies: Especially Through Supersession: The state governments exercise excessive controls of negative and restrictive type over the municipal bodies, the most obnoxious of them being that of their supersession mostly on political and partisan consideration, thereby cutting short the tenure of the municipal councillors. Supersessions of municipal bodies all over the country have been rampant. In such a situation, the public leaders would not like to offer themselves for election as people's representatives uncertain of completing their full term of three or five years, the sword of Democles of supersession always hanging on their heads.

5. Poverty and Illiteracy: Poverty and illiteracy are also the factors responsible for poor municipal leadership. There may be well intentioned, honest persons imbued with the spirit of service to their fellowmen but they do not possess the resources to invest in their election campaigns, nor enough education to educate the voters about their problems and to solicit their support. Such deserving persons are thus discouraged to provide the right type of leadership in municipal councils by getting themselves elected as their members.

6. Misuse of System of Co-option: To facilitate the use of talented people, possessing expertise in one or the other aspect of municipal administration and spirit of public service who are otherwise shy and reluctant to fight elections, the state governments have made provision for co-option of such persons by the elected members. But unfortunately this provision is misused by the party commanding majority in the municipal council concerned to co-opt persons showing allegiance to it and ignoring the persons who deserve co-option by virtue of their merit and experience in municipal affairs and the contribution they can make to its purposeful deliberation and decision making processes. This thwarts the objective of strengthening of municipal leadership.

7. Inefficiency of Municipal Administration: The poor performance of municipal authorities in providing even basic civic amenities for civilized living, and municipal administration becoming a byword for corruption and mal-administration have also been responsible for good leaders to keep themselves away from municipal politics. They realize that they need not be party to the notorieties of red tapism, callousness to the legitimate needs and grievances of the people due to infighting among the councillors and apathetic administration, and, therefore, shun to have any association with an inefficient administration unable to deliver goods to the citizens to their satisfaction.

8. Reservation of Seats for Scheduled Castes/Scheduled Tribes: Our constitution provides for reservation of seats for scheduled castes/scheduled tribes in the Union Parliament and state legislatures. The state governments also accordingly, reserve seats for these categories of people, keeping in view the size of the municipal council and percentage of their population in relation to the total population of the municipal area. This reservation is justified to compensate the people of these classes for the injustices they have suffered for long. The reservations were fixed for them initially for 10 years after the inauguration of the Constitution in 1950 but they had since been extended to the end of the present century by necessary amendments in the Constitution and now for another ten years upto 2010. Scheduled Castes/ Tribes, despite elaborate programmes for their uplift still suffer from certain disabilities of lack of education, employment, poverty etc. and therefore are unable to provide leadership of the desired quality in their local municipal councils.

9. Malpractices in Elections: Malpractices such as use of money power, muscle power, rigging, booth capturing impersonation, intimidation of voters, even of candidates, rowdyism, etc. are common at all levels of government including municipal governments. Clashes among supporters of candidates of rival parties including factions of various parties, use of tear gas and firing resulting in loss of lives and property are also usual occurrences in elections. No decent citizen would dare to come forward to seek leadership in such a vicious and dangerous atmosphere charged with corrupt practices and get his election prospects marred by unscrupulous elements, and subject himself to judicial scrutiny when his election is challenged in a court of law.

10. Militant Threats to Boycott Elections: A recent phenomenon of militant threats to boycott elections at all levels of government including the local government and to face liquidation in the event of disregarding the threat, has further deterred the prospective candidates to offer themselves for election and the voters to cast their votes. The low turn-out of the voters at the Parliament, state legislature and municipal elections is attributed to the militants' threats which were not unreal but were actually executed in the gunning down of certain candidates who had filled their nomination papers and the voters who had exercised their right of franchise. This naturally scares away the well meaning citizens to offer themselves as municipal leaders and the voters to cast their votes in favour of the candidates who they feel are really deserving of their support.

11. Evils of Casteism and Communalism: The element of communalism in municipal elections whereby separate communities elected their own representatives from their separate constituencies was introduced by the British to create a cleavage among the different communities inhabiting our country. The separate electorate was substituted by joint electorate in our new Constitution, but communalism still operates in elections at various levels including local government election. Casteism also plays a predominant role in municipal elections as has been established in the various studies made on municipal leadership in different states. A person wedded to secularism and secular approach to local issues would obviously avoid being involved in municipal politics wherein communalism and casteism are deeply rooted.

12. Inadequacy of Knowledge About Municipal Laws: Another factor responsible for poor leadership is the total absence or poor knowledge of the municipal councillors about the various municipal Acts governing the administration of local authorities, their powers and functions, their duties and obligations, procedure of work etc. It is because of illiteracy or low standard of education of the city fathers and the absence or lack of training that they need to be imparted as soon as they are elected and thereafter also through periodic orientation and refresher courses to enable them to keep themselves abreast of the latest amendments of the Acts and the perspective plans and programmes to be undertaken for the development of their cities and towns and the well-being of the citizens.

13. Lack of Proper Qualifications and Qualities of Leadership: Poor leadership in urban local governments can also be attributed to lack of proper qualifications and qualities in the municipal councillors to entitle them as true leaders. The candidates contesting municipal elections are more keen to capture leadership in the council than taking keen interest in the problems of the wards they profess to represent Once elected, they do not bother about their voters; they do not visit their wards to know their problems, they are no longer easily accessible to their supporters; they do not help them in getting their grievances redressed. They connive with bad elements in committing irregularities and violating municipal rules and regulations, in unauthorized occupation and grabbing of municipal lands, and making encroachments on public lands, evading taxes and accepting bribes, and finally getting all illegal acts legalized. Education, youth initiative, dynamism, integrity, and the spirit of service to the people which should be the qualities of a good municipal leader are conspicuous by their absence in a majority of the councillors.

14. Weaknesses of Administrative Leadership: Administrative leadership comprising officers/officials appointed by the government to manage and administer affairs of urban local governments suffers from certain deficiencies and weaknesses. The secretary of the department of urban local government (who is a senior IAS officer) and the director of the Directorate and their joint, deputy secretaries, and joint and deputy directors have the impression and rightly so that the government accords low priority to urban local government and does not give it the consideration that it deserves in view of the rapid rise in urbanization and the colossal problems that it creates for urban local bodies. They are not provided with funds commensurate with their requirements of providing even basic civic amenities to the citizens.

The top men at the administrative hierarchy, therefore, do not take much interest in their respective assignments. They do not have a fixed tenure and are transferred too frequently, the average tenure of a director in Punjab has been of one year.[33] This is detrimental not only to the overall efficiency of the Directorate, but also to its routine functioning as an officer with short tenure cannot be expected to formulate any policy, much less implement it and committed to the objectives of an organization.

Administrative leadership is now seen as a function in which the leader is primarily a coordinator of group effort rather than a man apart using extraordinary powers of insight and dominance to manipulate the groups. Moreover, leadership is a matter of reciprocal social relationships in which the leader acquires recognition and confidence because of his ability to guide group activity toward group objectives.[34] The characteristics of weak and strong leadership as reflected in group relations, have been established.[35] With some exceptions, morale, cooperation, productivity and resourcefulness have been found to increase under responsive democratic leadership. Contrary to what some may presume, quick response and high productivity are best secured by persuasive methods and the use of 'human relations approach'. The leader achieves these ends by a peculiar sensitivity to individual needs and differences.[36] A leader has necessarily to be a coordinator, planner, and spokesman for the group.

It is intriguing that despite the establishment of the Directorate and the regional deputy directors, the deputy commissioner in our country continues to enjoy powers of supervision and control over urban local governments. This arrangement results in overlapping of their jurisdictions, confusion about their respective powers and functions, and absence of coordination leading to deterioration in administration of local bodies.

The state governments have assumed complete authority over the municipal personnel as a result of the provincialization of municipal services in various states. It is now the government who creates the posts, lays down qualifications for different posts and channels of promotion, makes appointments on the recommendations of the selection committees constituted by it, orders transfers from one municipality to another and determines their conditions of service. The government is also vested with the power to take disciplinary action against the personnel who are not accountable to them. This has further eroded the powers of municipal councils and contributed to weak municipal leadership.

15. Leadership of Municipal Employees' Unions: Municipal employees organize themselves into associations and unions to fight for their interests and often resort to strikes, thereby paralyzing the functioning of municipal bodies and causing great hardships to the citizens via the discontinuation of water supply and electricity, letting the heaps of garbage remain on roads and streets causing serious health hazards, and so on. If the confrontation between the municipal authorities and the employees' union remains unresolved and the strikes continue for an indefinite period, frustrates the citizens physically and mentally.

It is clear from the discussion attempted above about the weakness in municipal leadership, both political and administrative, that urgent steps need to be taken to strengthen municipal leadership as it is only a strong and creditable leadership that can win the confidence of the people and help them in meeting their needs and aspirations.

Measures to Invigorate Municipal Leadership

It is rightly said that crisis in administration is the crisis of leadership at all levels but more so at the municipal level as it is closer to the people. The following measures and steps are expected to contribute substantially to the creation of municipal leaders of a desirable quality and nature.

1. Restructuring of Municipal Governments: The municipal governments, as they are constituted at present, are unable to attract or lure capable leaders. They need structural, organizational, procedural and financial reforms as have been recommended by various commissions and committees appointed by central and state governments from time to time. The basic problem with urban local governments in India is that they have become obsolete institutions which have not been restructured to match the modern time changes. These organizations were created by the British to serve their interests. Keeping them in the present form would simply mean that municipal government in India exists to serve the aristocracy and the bureaucracy. The middle class and low income groups have been overlooked and the local services which they deserve, by right, are not provided to them. Our municipal governments need a wholesale reorganization based on the principles of equity, efficiency, and effectiveness. A dynamic local government structure is most needed to begin with. Secondly, we need a creditable political leadership at the local level. Thirdly, innovative methods are needed to deliver local services with the help of private enterprises. Lack of funds is not the only thing which matters for a local government to work efficiently. The finance of local governments should be augmented by allowing them to raise substantial amounts of what they spend. This would contribute to self-reliant and strong but also to a more accountable local government. At present, local government seems to have lost all its status. It has been reduced by the central government as its policy maintaining agency rather than a policy-making elected government.[37] The Nagarpalika Bill (1991) enacted as the Constitution (74th Amendment) Act, 1992, was meant to revitalize the urban local governments to enthuse capable leadership to contribute their best to the urban institutions at the grassroots level.

2. Regular, Free and Fair Elections: Good leaders are not inclined to serve in the local governments as they are uncertain of their tenure. The councillors are removed by the state governments on partisan considerations. Supersessions of municipal governments were rampant and elections to them were not held for indefinite periods. Though the Constitution (74th Amendment) Act, 1992, now provides for election to the superseded municipal councils within six months and regular elections to urban local bodies every five years.

Some public leaders, well meaning and well intentioned, interested in civic affairs, devoted and dedicated are also discouraged to contest municipal elections as these have come to be vitiated with such evils and malpractices as money and muscle power, rowdyism and hooliganism, rigging and booth capturing, violence and killings. Naturally they would not like to involve themselves in politics of this type. If free and fair elections are assured by making stringent election laws and their strict enforcement by awarding exemplary punishments and penalties to the violators of these laws, capable leadership might be available to the urban local governments.

3. Discouragement to Casteism and Communalism: Person possessing a secular perception of the issues and problems facing urban local governments find it hard to participate in municipal policies charged with casteism and communalism. In order to get elected, a candidate needs the support of a caste, a particular community or a communal party which a person imbued with secular and non-partisan spirit cannot muster. It is very rare that an independent is victorious at the hustings on the strength of his own personality and standing among the constituents. Canvassing for votes on the basis of casteism and communalism can be declared by the election commission as a malpractice, competent leadership for municipal government may then emerge.

4. Unimpeachable Character of Leaders: In order to be acceptable to the people and to improve their image as effective leaders, it is absolutely necessary that they should have an unimpeachable character. They should be known for their integrity, selflessness, seriousness of purpose, devotion and dedication to the cause of the whole city community and not of a few persons belonging to their own party or group. They should be easily accessible to their constituents to listen to their genuine grievances and extend their help in redressing them. The exhibition of such qualities will endear them to the people and enable them to serve their constituents to the best of their ability and intention.

5. Maintenance of Decorum and Dignity in the Municipal Council: Prospective municipal leaders are also disgusted with the ugly scenes witnessed in the conduct of the meetings of the municipal councils as reflected in the use of unparliamentary language, disrespect shown to the chair, shouting, and exchange of blows, physical assaults, protest, *dharnas* and walk-outs resulting in pandemonium, disruption of meetings and their adjournments. This total lack of civilized and responsible behaviour on the part of the councillors including the chairpersons is frustrating. If the decorum and dignity in the house can be assured to be maintained by law or moral and ethical values to be practised by the councillors, leaders of eminence and sound character may be attracted to municipal bodies.

6. Minimum Educational Qualifications: Through it is difficult to establish a co-relationship between education and a particular level of efficiency in urban government, it is desirable that the municipal councillors should have education up to the secondary level as this would help them to have a better grasp of the civic affairs and problems than those who fell short of this minimum qualification, and would also contribute to their commanding a certain amount of respect of their colleagues, constituents, and employees.

The prescription of minimum qualifications suggested above would also increase their language efficiency enabling them to communicate among themselves as well as with their constituents and the workable knowledge of English which shall be acquired as a part of this qualification would also help them in making themselves familiar with the municipal records of the councils and committees' proceedings which are usually maintained in English.

7. Greater Induction of Women Councillors in the Municipal Councils: Various studies have established that women councillors are better equipped and more successful than men councillors as they enjoy a better socio-economic background than men and exhibit greater sincerity, devotion, hard work, and straightforward business-like approach to the city's problems. It is, therefore, desirable that more women should be encouraged to be inducted into the municipal council. Their presence in the council would also contribute to city life and politics being much cleaner and better.

8. Proper Use of the Co-option and Reservation Methods: Various municipal acts provided for co-option of members of minority communities and special interests to be elected councillors. It is based on the British system of alderman whom the councillors elect for their rich municipal experience in municipal administration and spirit of public service. It is preferable to nominations as it is not on the government but on the council itself that the onus of nomination falls. But unfortunately co-option system has been misused by the party in power in the municipal council by co-opting members from its own party on consideration other than merit thus depriving the municipal authority of the benefit that it could avail of, if deserving persons were co-opted. It is, therefore, imperative that person of integrity, erudition, and upright character should be co-opted to enhance the quality of municipal leadership.

Similarly, reservations provided for scheduled castes/scheduled tribes, backward classes and women for election to the municipal council should be utilized for the best among these categories of society of the local areas, and not on extraneous considerations but on merit alone to be determined by educational qualifications, spirit of service, interest in citizen's welfare, and dedication.

9. Better Representation of Professionals: It is revealed in various studies in municipal leadership that municipal councillors had varied professional and occupational background, they represented agriculture, industry, business, transport, private service, household, legal practice, medical practices, etc. But the medical practitioners had a disappointingly poor representation presumably for the reason that they have heavy schedule of duties and lack strong motivation to run or improve the city government. It is surprising that college professors and school teachers who form the nucleus of the city's intellectuals or the elite should be conspicuous by their absence in the municipal councils. They have enough time and leisure and knowledge of the city's needs and problems but they are not inclined to involve themselves in the rough and tumble of the city's politics and particularly in the expensive and bothersome business of elections.[38] It is necessary that they should be motivated to associate themselves with the conduct of city's government to add to the quality of municipal leadership.

10. Comprehensive Training of Municipal Councillors: Training with a view to apprise the councillors about their rights and privileges, duties, and obligations and to familiarize them with the municipal laws, rules and regulations, and procedure of work is indispensable to enable them to function effectively and efficiently. Whereas enough concern was expressed regarding making arrangements for the training of Panchayati Raj personnel—official and non-official, in the form of establishments of institutions at particular locations in the country and preparatory training, little attention has been given to the training of municipal councillors. It was on the recommendation of various committees especially Rural–Urban Relationship Committee (1966) and Nuruddin Committee appointed by the Government of India (1963) that Regional Training Institutes for municipal employees have been set up at Bombay, Lucknow, Hyderabad and Delhi but no efforts have been made to provide for the training of municipal councillors. In the absence of training, they cannot be expected to be well-equipped with the knowledge of civic problems and their role in solving them. It is, therefore, urgent that comprehensive programme of leadership training and executive development should be arranged in a phased manner to enable them to develop into responsible, knowledgeable and responsive leaders.

11. Positive Role of Political Parties: Political parties participate in civic affairs by putting up their candidates for election to the municipal council, carry on propaganda in their favour and use all possible means, fair or foul, to get them elected. They also carry with them their vices of factionalism, nepotism, favouritism, and partisanship in the conduct of municipal administration. They are unfortunately not properly organized at the local level, and are unable to impose discipline among the local aspirants for membership of the council as is reflected in the contesting of the elections by those denied party tickets as rebels. In order that political parties should play a positive and effective role in local affairs, it is desirable that political parties should develop comprehensive programmes on the basis of enquiries into the needs of the urban people, evolve areas of general agreements on non-controversial civic programmes, select candidates for municipal elections with care and later on, promote them to higher public offices to make municipal offices attractive, formulate an agreed code of conduct for promoting civic sense and welfare, and for effecting discipline among members.

12. Enlightened Citizenship: The indifference, apathy and disinterestedness in civic affairs on the part of citizens are also responsible for weak municipal leadership. It is rightly observed that people get the rulers they deserve. People on account of their being poor and uneducated and being busy with their bread-earning activities do not pay attention to the various problems of the city governments. They seldom approach the councillors to acquaint them with the needs of the city as a whole except for personal and mundane matters. An enlightened citizenship asserting its right to be served by an efficient administration through its leaders would go a long way in making the leaders behave in a responsible and responsive manner and thus contribute to the ensuring of right type of leadership in municipal governments.

Lack of dynamic, progressive, and unifying leadership at the municipal level has affected the vitality of the municipal system. The measures suggested above especially strong motivation to stimulate leadership functions, satisfactory public relations, and enlightened citizenship would substantially contribute to the emergence of a strong, capable and effective municipal leadership which, in turn, would ensure efficient municipal government in satisfying the expectations and aspirations of the local people.

Conclusion

Political development, democratic growth and administrative capability depend largely on the political system—centre, state and local. Leadership is thus the *sine qua non* of success in all human activities. But in a democratic system, particularly at the lower level, it assumes greater significance and wider proportions. The growing complexity of urban problems and the need to organize the people to help bring community to action make it necessary for individuals and groups to provide leadership.[39] The prime motive of a leader is to organize the activities of his group or party in an effective manner, which should result in achieving maximum goals for the group for its betterment.

Good leadership and meaningful public participation are the necessary pre-requisites for building up a sound and responsive municipal government. The municipal level is considered to be the initial stage for providing education and training not only to the available leadership talent but also to a large variety of town dwellers. Thus, local leadership has to be nurtured well before it is transmitted to the state or national level as experience gained at the local level provides insight into the art of politics and government. In India, urban governments have produced many a leader and statesman like Ferozeshah Mehta, Jawaharlal Nehru, Subhash Chandra Bose, Vallabh Bhai Patel, and G.V. Moolanker. These leaders not only gained valuable experience but also added lustre to the municipal politics. These governments of yore had raised the term 'politics' to the high level of municipal statesmanship.[40] The success or failure of urban governments depends upon leaders who, after having been recruited, are charged not only with setting goals but are also responsible for their efficient and effective achievement.

Political leadership in urban governments is to be provided by elected municipal councillors, chairman of municipal committees, mayors of municipal corporations, and the administrative leadership by the municipal bureaucracy, chief executive officer in municipalities and municipal commissioner in municipal corporations and their supporting official staff. Various studies conducted on municipal leadership in different states have come to the conclusion that political leadership has been poor and weak, inefficient, and ineffective and the administrative leadership unresponsive and unhelpful, and the relations between these two sets of leaders have not been cordial, resulting in the non-performance of municipal institutions.

The factors responsible for poor politic leadership have been: membership of state legislatures and Union Parliament is more attractive and rewarding; municipal authorities have very few powers and even those are being eroded by their being taken over by the state government itself or by constituting special purpose urban institutions for their performance, political parties intervene in municipal affairs with their vices of favouritism, factionalism and take decision on local issues on partisan basis; power of the state to supersede popularly elected municipal councils and not to hold their elections for indefinite periods; poverty and illiteracy of the citizens, preventing them from contesting elections; malpractices in elections especially the use of money and muscle power, rigging and booth capturing etc.; inefficiency of municipal administration, discouraging capable persons to assume leadership; the system of reservation of seats for Scheduled Castes and Tribes and co-option not being used on basis of merit for deserving leaders; evils of casteism and communalism, inadequacy of knowledge about municipal laws and lack of training for municipal leaders; lack of desirable qualifications and qualities of leadership in public men; disinterestedness of the government in building up administrative leadership in municipal bureaucracy by imparting them proper training and making them responsive to public needs and aspirations, and disgusting functioning of the municipal employees' union as reflected in their frequent strikes.

Leadership at the municipal level can, however, be strengthened by taking such steps as revamping the municipal structure, organization and procedure of work; granting more powers to municipal bodies, especially in raising finances commensurate with their responsibilities; creating awareness among the councillors about their rights and obligations through orientation and refresher courses and training programmes both institutional and formal; ensuring free and fair elections; ensuring that political parties play a constructive role and deciding local issues on the basis of general community interests and not those of a particular group or segment of society owing allegiance to them; regular holding of elections and avoidance of the use of power of supersession unless actually required for reasons of proven incompetence of municipal authorities to administer municipal affairs in a satisfactory manner; and strong motivation and commitment of the councillors to work with devotion and dedication to understand the problems of their constituents and to solve them to the best of their capability.

It is encouraging to note that emerging municipal leadership exhibits some favourable trends and traits contributing to the emergence of sound and strong leadership, more young blood is entering municipal councils; number of women councillors is steadily increasing; the councillors represent various professions and occupations, though the representations of intellectuals—college and school teachers is poor but is expected to go up; religion, caste and communalism do play their role in some places but their influence is gradually declining; state governments are showing interest in urban affairs and making efforts to hold elections to the municipal bodies on schedule; middle and low income group people are coming forward to take part in municipal elections and the monopoly of wealthy people is crumbling; educated persons outnumber the illiterate and semi-educated councillors; municipal leaders are becoming conscious of their responsibilities to their clients and the city as a whole and are helpful in understanding their needs and problems and resolving them; the government feels that comprehensive training needs to be given to the leaders to enable them to discharge their obligations in a satisfactory manner. It is expected that Constitution (74th Amendment) Act, 1992, as it would revamp the urban local governments in their structure, organization and powers will contribute to the emergence of municipal leadership of the desired quality.

This emerging scenario of municipal leadership makes one optimistic about the proper performance of its role in making governance and administration of urban local governments effective and efficient and rid them of the ills and deficiencies that have been inherent in their functioning in the past.

NOTES AND REFERENCES

1. Pfiffner John, M. and Robert, V. Peasthus, *Public Administration* (New York: The Ronald Press Company 1960), p. 92.
2. G.R. Terry, *Principles of Management,* p. 18.
3. Koontz and O'Dennel, *General Principles of Management,* p. 69.
4. Tead, Ordway, *The Art of Leadership* (New York: 1935), p. 20.
5. Charles L. Bernard, *Organisation and Management,* p. 83.
6. Hadson Secklon, *Organisation and Management,* p. 239.
7. E.C. Lindeman, *Social Discovery* (New York: 1924), p. 222.
8. L.L. Bernard, *Introduction to Social Psychology* (New York: 1926), p. 520.
9. E.S. Bogardus, *Leaders and Leadership* (New York: 1934), p. 3.
10. Robert Tannenbaem and Fred Massarik (eds), *Leadership and Organisation: A Behaviourial Science Approach* (London: 1961), p. 24.
11. Cecil A. Gibb, *The Principles and Traits of Administrative Leadership in Brown and Cochin,* p. 74.
12. P.R. Dubhashi, in his Foreword to S.L. Kaushik's *Leadership in Urban Governments in India* (Allahabad: Kitab Mahal, 1986).
13. Proceedings of the Seminar held at Lal Bahadur Shastri National Academy of Administration, Mussorie, 1970, p. 47.
14. K. Seshadri, 'The Citizens and the Municipality', in M.A. Mutalib and N. Umapathy (eds.), *Urban Government and Administration* (Hyderabad: Regional Centre for Urban and Environmental Studies, 1981), pp. 90–91.
15. N. Srinivasan, Functions of Municipal Councils, *Nagarlok* 11 (July–September 1970), p. 11.
16. R.K. Bhardwaj, *Municipal Administration in India* (Delhi, 1974), p. 16.
17. Punjab Local Government (Urban) Enquiry Committee Report, 1957, p. 8.
18. P. James and A. Murlidhar Rao, 'Mayoralty in India: Case for More Power', in M.A. Mutalib and N. Umapathy (ed.), *Urban Government and Administration,* p. 67.
19. R. Srinivasan and B.A.V. Sharma, 'Politics in Urban India: A Study of Four Corporations', in S.P. Aiyer and R. Srinivasan (eds.), *Studies in Indian Democracy* (Bombay, 1965).
20. Ali Ashraf, *City Government in Calcutta: A Study of Inertia* (Bombay: Asia Publishing House, 1966).
21. Ali Ashraf, *Government and Politics of Big Cities: An Indian Case Study* (Delhi: Concept Publishing Company, 1977).
22. Vishnoo Bhagwan, *Municipal Government and Politics in Haryana: A Case Study of Rohtak* (New Delhi: S. Chand and Company, 1974).
23. S.N. Mishra, *Politics and Leadership in Municipal Government* (New Delhi: Inter-India Publishers, 1979).
24. Richard Bandit and Seymour Lipset, 'Decision-makers in Contrasting Milieus', in D. Marvick (eds.), *Political Decision Makers* (Free Books, 1961), p. 14.
25. Gerient Parry, *Political Elites* (London: Allen and Unwin, 1979), p. 97.
26. R.T. Jangam and B.A.V. Sharma, *Leadership in Urban Government* (New Delhi: Sterling Publisher Pvt. Ltd., 1932).

27. G. Ram, Reddy and M. Kishtaiah, 'The Urban Political Executive: The Social background of the Chairman of Municipalities in Andhra Pradesh', in M.A. Mutalib and N. Umapathy (eds.), *Urban Government and Administration.*
28. Zia-uddin Khan and Hoshiar Singh, *Leadership in Municipal Government* (Jaipur: RBSA Publications, 1984).
29. S.L. Kaushik, *Leadership in Urban Government in India* (Allahabad: Kitab Mahal, 1986).
30. K. Seshadri, 'The Citizens and the Municipality'.
31. Government of India, Planning Commission, First Five Year Plan, p. 141.
32. Y. Raghavaiah, 'Municipal Government and Political Parties', in M.A. Mutalib and N. Umapathy (eds.), *Urban Government and Administration*, p. 86.
33. Pradeep Sachdeva, *Dynamics of Municipal Government and Politics in India* (Allahabad: Kitab Mahal, 1991).
34. Pfiffner and Presthus, *Public* Administration, p. 95.
35. Kurl Lewin, *Resolving Social Conflicts* (New York: Harpa Bretheus, 1948).
36. James K. Dent, *Managerial Leading Styles, Some Dimensions, Determinants and Behaviourial Correlation* (Ann Arbour: University of Microfilms, June, 1957).
37. Girish, K. Misra, *Nagarlok* 3, no. 4 (October–December, 1991): v.
38. Jangam and B.A.V. Sharma, *Leadership in Urban Government,* p. 99.
39. Warton, W, Krietlow, et al., *Leadership for action in rural communities* (Illinois, 1960), p. 11.
40. National Academy of Administration, Proceedings of a Seminar on Local Governors Mussourie, 1970, p. 37.

People's Participation in Urban Local Governments

Local government is defined by Goulding as the management of their own affairs by the people of a locality.[1] In the words of Harris, it is a government by the people themselves through freely elected representatives.[2] According to Venkatarangia, it is the administration of a locality by a body representing the local inhabitants.[3] Professor W.A. Robson observes that local government presupposes the existence of a local authority as well as the participation of the local community in the administration of its own affairs.[4]

These definitions of local government reflect the crucial significance of participation of people in the management and administration of their local affairs through their periodically elected representatives, municipal councillors, and their own frequent involvement in the formulation and implementation of development plans for their locality and the provision of civic amenities for their better living. Thus, the concept of people's/community/public/citizen participation in local government is of more importance for the successful functioning of a local authority. J.S. Mill and Lord Bryce also stressed the importance of local government because of its most important element *viz.* that it affords the facility for the active participation of people.[5] Local institutions cannot make much headway without the involvement and cooperation of the citizens it seeks to serve. Citizen participation not only enhances the dignity of the individual and sense of community at all levels, but also adds vitality to government programmes.

Citizens' participation makes the programmes more responsive and better adapted to local needs. The importance of local government also lies in the involvement in public affairs not only of those who are elected but also indirectly of the citizens at large who elect them and to whom they are ultimately accountable. People's participation is, thus, the *sine qua non* of the success of local government. Citizens' interest in local administration, unlike the higher levels of government, i.e., central and state government is greater because municipal government is closest to the people, and it is this intimate government-citizen nexus that justifies the existence of local government.

Meaning of People's Participation

What exactly we mean by citizens' participation in local affairs becomes rather enigmatic because everyone interprets this term in his own way. The interpretation ranges from taking passive interest in local affairs as by reading newspapers, listening of radio, viewing TV and discussing matters with others, to taking part in political activities like attending meetings, conferences, etc. and participating in processions and demonstrations. It may even include protest actions like strikes and the like. It is through participation that citizens at large are associated with the decisions taken by the government. Participation can be at various levels and by different sets of people on different issues in each case drawing different segments of community. It may be manifest in different degrees in intensity.[6]

Broadly speaking, the word 'participation' is used to refer to the role of members of general public, as distinguished from that of appointed officials, including civil servants, in influencing the activities of government or in providing directly for community needs. It may occur at any level—from the village to the country as a whole. It may be only advisory, as in the case of an advisory committee to a minister, provincial government or head of a hospital; it may involve decision making, as in the case of governing bodies of local authorities; and it may extend to actual implementation, as it occurs when villagers/town dwellers decide to carry out a community self-help project. The participation may be direct, as in community projects and in the work of private welfare organizations, or it may be indirect, through elected officials or representative bodies responsive to public opinion. Individuals may participate through non-governmental or statutory bodies.

The extent of participation—whether direct or indirect will ultimately depend upon citizens', access to information and opportunity of presenting their views to elected representatives.[7] As local government activities expand, they have more extensive and frequent impact upon people at the local level. The councillors should be prepared to provide more information to the citizens in order to justify their decisions. Yet, as the size and range of government activity has grown, the elected representatives have less opportunity to provide with such information and justification. The need for supplementing means of involving the citizens in local decisions has been precipitated as much by the expanding activities of local authorities as by public pressure. The pressures indicate the inability of the current procedures and institutions to cope with an increasingly articulate public. It is rightly observed. 'It is impossible that people should be able and know what they are able—to exert some influence on local decisions affecting their own lives—(and) if the democratic process is to flourish, there must be ready access to full information about a local authority's activities.'[8]

Factors Responsible for People's Non-participation in Urban Government

Despite the acknowledged and recognized acceptance of the role of people's participation in urban local governments for the achievement of the objectives of their serving as training ground for democracy, the provision of civic amenities and services to the citizen and the development of cities and towns, the people's involvement in urban government has been insufficient and even conspicuous by its absence in some cities, and the people have been indifferent; disinterested, apathetic, and even disgusted and alienated to urban administration. Such a state of affairs can be attributed to the following factors/reasons:

1. Lack of Homogeneity in the Population of the Cities: In India, due to linguistic, religions and community diversities, individuals in big cities tend to move with their narrow community groups. Unless a locality has a culturally homogeneous population, it is doubtful if the people in the city would intermix socially, and own the city community belonging to them as one.

2. Lack of Attachment with City Governments: It is a common feature of city life that quite a substantial part of its population tends to look at the city merely as a place for earning money and they would likely go back to the distant villages or towns to which they originally belong. Loyalty to the cities grows out of continual urban living, but many of our urbanites have still their firm roots in remote villages or small towns. The citizens have, therefore, little attachment with the municipal government. The citizens, in general, exhibit an attitude of aloofness, even hostility at times, which is a peculiar personality trait possibly reared by the primary social groups such as family and communal groups.

3. Lack of Able Leadership and Its Poor Image: In the past our urban local governments had leaders of national eminence and stature like Ferozeshah Mehta, Moti Lal Nehru, Jawahar Lal Nehru, Subash Chandra Bose, Vallabh Bhai Patel, Lala Lajpat Rai, etc., who were shining examples of sober and healthy municipal politics and restored to these institutes the authority and the dignity they deserved.[9] But our urban governments now suffer from dearth of able leadership. The municipal councillors of today are unqualified—some of them illiterate, semi-educated, and devoid of a spirit of dedication and service. Various researches made in respect of municipal leadership confirm that the councillors belong to particular social strata and many qualified persons, professionals etc. do not seek elections to local bodies. As such the standing of the people's representatives in local bodies is not high in the eyes of the people. Further the councillors are not reticent while they exercise their power or claim their privileges. They also do not hesitate to throw their weight around. They thus fail to endear themselves to the people. They also do not even find it necessary to report to the electorate on their performance as their representatives. This results in the creation of a negative image of the local bodies which needs to be converted into a positive one, if we seriously and sincerely mean to make grass-roots democracy a success in India.[10]

4. Absence of Continuous Contact of the Councillors with the Public: It is unfortunate that people are approached by the prospective candidates for election to municipal bodies at the time of elections only. People are considered as only vote banks by them. Once the councillors are elected they do not bother about the electorate. They seldom visit their wards to know about their needs and grievances. They do not create awareness in them about their responsibilities in paying for the benefits of the city living through appropriate taxes and other charges and observing discipline and helping in the management of services such as better solid waste management or traffic management.[11]

5. Bureaucrats' Attitude to People: One main factor responsible for alienation of people is the attitude of the bureaucrats at all levels of government including the local government. The municipal bureaucracy acts in a bureaucratic and autocratic manner and under-rates the intelligence and capability of the people to offer any suggestions for improvement of city administration, development programmes, and betterment of services and does not hold them fit enough to participate in decision making. They do not extend the normal courtesies to the people to which they are legitimately entitled. The officials forget that they are public servants. This attitude frustrates the people and results in the loss of their interest in municipal affairs.

6. Rampant Corruption: Our municipal governments have become synonyms of corruption, favouritism, nepotism, and inefficiency. The common people have to experience a lot of inconvenience, disappointment and frustration when they have to get their building plans sanctioned, water and electric meters and connections installed, inflated water, sewerage and electricity bills corrected, and to procure licences and are obliged to run from pillar to post to get their legitimate demands enquired into and accepted by the municipal authorities, and to realize in the end that they cannot get justice without bribing the municipal officials and the councillors. They learn, to their shock, that it is only the well-to-do, influential, and elite sections of the society who are favoured with better quality of services of paved streets, metalled roads, abundant uninterrupted water supply and other benefits for better living. All this tends the people to lose faith in the municipal agencies.

7. Misconception About Government's Obligations: People generally have the misconception that the government has the responsibility to perform every possible function for their welfare and better living. The modern tendency is to expect the government to do everything for the people and they must get maximum benefits at almost no cost. This wrong thinking on their part also renders the people indifferent and callous towards local bodies.

8. Lack of Consciousness and Awareness Among People About Their Role in Municipal Affairs: The people because of their illiteracy and ignorance are not aware and conscious about their rights and obligations and the role they are expected to play in the administration of local bodies, nor does the government or the elected representatives make any serious efforts to create such an awareness among the people through various means. The government does not take the public into confidence while making plans for their well-being. It just meets the legal requirement of publishing notices in the government gazette or newspapers or by some other means of making it known that a certain plan is under preparation or some changes are in the offing, etc. and it does not involve the people in decision making in respect of the plans, projects or schemes. The people are, thus, denied the opportunities for participation in the proposals affecting their lives.

9. Poor Public Relations in Municipal Administration: Public relations is defined by J.D. Millet as knowing what the public expects and explaining how administration is meeting their desires. This activity on the part of local governments assumes great significance as the people being in close touch with the administration would be eager to know what it has achieved in satisfying their needs and what are the constraints if any, which hinder the government in meeting their aspirations. Most of the municipal bodies are deficient in this important aspect of their organization. They do not possess a machinery or agency to cultivate relation with the public and to inform them about their activities through the various media of publicity. In the absence of such a much needed activity, the people fail to appreciate the achievements or failures of their local bodies and, therefore, do not evince any interest in their affairs.

10. Absence of Machinery for Redressal of Grievances: People have numerous grievances against the local authorities for their acts of omissions and commission, denial of their rights, perpetuation of injustices, never-ending delays, non-provision of civic services, non-grant of building plans, licences, water sewerage connections, overcharging in the bills and their rectification, etc. but they have no specific agency/authority in the local bodies to listen to their grievances, entertain their representations and petitions and to give them expeditious justice. All this results in the aggravation of their frustration and disenchantment with the local bodies.

11. Inadequacy of People's Associations and Organizations: The inadequacy of people's associations and organizations is another major factor for lack of people's participation in local governments. The citizens grumble and groan against the mal-administration of local bodies individually when they are made to suffer at the hands of local authorities but they do not organize themselves into associations and well-knit organizations to fight for their common interests, for adequate provision of civic services or development of their particular localities. If the citizens form associations for safeguarding their civic interests under public leaders known for their honesty and integrity, they can win their battle against the high-ups. The absence of such associations and organizations, thus, contributes to the lack of people's participation in local governments.

12. Appalling Poverty: One of the major impediments to civic consciousness and people's participation in local government is the appalling poverty and living conditions in all our big cities. With the exception of a small minority of affluent class, the public in general have been used to facing almost a perennial scarcity of essential civic amenities like water, roads, schools, even burial grounds. On top of it, slums are an endemic phenomenon where urban poverty assumes the ugliest scene. Goods, citizenship and people's participation cannot be expected to emerge from bad living environment.

13. Inefficiency of Municipal Administration: The alienation of citizens is also, to a large extent, a direct result of municipal administration inefficiency. Several studies made on municipal administration have come to the conclusion that our municipal governments are in bad shape. Rural–Urban Relationship Committee (1966) noted sense of despair and lack of confidence in the capacity of the local bodies to tackle the problems that face towns and cities. The image of a local body in the public mind is that of inefficiency, maladministration, delay and corruption. Such an image and poor performance of functions by the local bodies have further accentuated the indifference of citizens towards the affairs of the local government.[12]

14. Existence of Multitude of Local Authorities: The government has the tendency to set up more and more urban authorities like Improvement Trusts, Housing Boards, Water Supply and Sewerage Boards, Pollution Control Boards, etc., to provide the services to the people which primarily belong to the municipal governments themselves. This fragmentation of administration does not only cause problems of coordination, but also confuses citizens who have to approach a number of authorities to get their needs fulfilled. This arrangement erodes the authority of elected municipal bodies and discourages the citizens for participation in the sphere of activity of local government.

15. Deficiencies in Structures of Local Government: The present structure of our urban local governments also does not facilitate people's participation in their administration based as it is on centralization of power in the city hall located at a place not easily accessible to the public due to the long distances to be traversed by various means of transport entailing expenses and time consumption, absence of federal principle of distribution of power between the Centre and its constituent units and the decentralization of powers to facilitate people's participation. The zonal committees in Delhi, Borough Committees in Calcutta and the 'Ward' Administration in Mumbai are half-hearted attempts to bring administration closer to localities. A system of two-tier municipal government as provided in the Constitution (74th Amendment) Act 1992 is intended to ensure better people's participation.

16. Vicious Role of Political Parties: The people are fed up with the vicious role of political parties in the administration of local bodies, as is manifested in the decisions being taken on partisan and political consideration as against on merits of individual cases, favours being shown to the residents of the wards belonging to the councillors of the party commanding power in the municipal body at a particular time, persons indulging in evasion of taxes and corrupt persons going scot free, infighting among the councillors and supersession of elected municipal bodies exclusively on partisan considerations. It is desirable that political parties if they are, at all, to participate in the elections and management of the affairs of local bodies should play a positive and constructive role and not interfere in municipal affairs to promote their partisan interests. They should work for the interests of the entire local community. Once the people are convinced of the role of political parties contributing to the overall development of the town and well-being of the whole community, they are bound to evince interest in municipal bodies and actively participate in their activities.

The cumulative effect of the factors mentioned above has resulted in the alienation of people by local administration and the dilution of their interest to participation in local affairs.

The Potentials of People's Participation in Local Government

The lack of interest and participation of people in local government and administration as discussed above, however, should not lead us to conclude that the people do not possess the capability, potential and will to participate in local affairs. These qualities they possess in abundance and have exhibited these in participating in the affairs of local bodies in various forms, such as constituting citizens councils for the ventilation of their needs, expectations and aspirations to the local authorities, taking up certain activities for keeping their localities clean, owning various roundabouts and road crossings for their beautification, improving environments, through planning projects and programmes and taking follow-up actions by the environmental societies, dumping of garbage and solid wastes at fixed places, cleaning of holy tanks through *kar sewa*, desilting of public pools and lakes (Sukhna Lake in Chandigarh), and forming voluntary organization to help the people in distress afflicted by epidemics and natural calamities like floods, fires, droughts, earthquakes, and migrants' activities and observing health and sanitation days and weeks to create awareness among the people about their obligations to keep their surroundings, streets and roads, clean and so on. The potentials of the people for participation in local affairs need to be exploited to the maximum.

Our urban local governments, faced as they are with the daunting task of providing physical and social services and gainful income opportunities to about 700 million urban poor estimated to be living by 2000, financially bankrupt and organizationally almost stagnant, unable to raise the resources required to extend and maintain services to the deprived sections and areas, saddled with other formal institutions unwilling and or/unable to reach out support in appropriate forms due to legal, structural, attitudinal and procedural constraints; and most of them unable and ill-equipped to draw upon people's internal resources, creativity and initiative, confronted with general resource constraints in a situation of competing priorities in other sectors and fields, recognizing the limitations of voluntary effect in effectively reaching out to large numbers in sustained manner, in diverse roles and services, the urban community development projects appear to be useful instruments to reach out, to organize, deliver services to and finally integrate low income communities with the mainstream of city life. Community participation in urban community development projects may, therefore, be discussed in some details.

Community Participation in Urban Community Development Projects

The most significant effort on the part of the government to achieve community participation on a sustainable basis in the urban sector is through the urban community development programme, started in 1952. The United Nations has conducted a number of studies of various aspects of community development programmes, i.e., programmes to stimulate self-effort, to provide technical and material help to make such efforts effective and to associate people generally with government activities.[13]

Urban community development is designed to function as part of the local body and is viewed as a link between the people and the municipal body.

The staff is given scope to develop activities according to the felt needs of the people and to cover activities normally not covered by the local body. The aim is to create in problematic urban areas stronger communities with their own leaders who would plan, finance and carry out self-help projects. To achieve this, local voluntary organizations are strengthened and bustee-level agencies/committees are set up. The project activities are guided by the assumption that neighborhood, no matter how poor, can do something to improve itself by its own efforts, and that any approach for outside help should be resorted to only after it has exhausted its own resources fully.

The Third Five Year Plan had mentioned the need for each city to mobilize its own resources to help create better conditions for its citizens and placed emphasis on the need for and the potentialities of urban community development. The Rural–Urban Relationship Committee had reported that there was a lack of awareness among people that the municipality was there to serve their needs. It had stressed the need for constant discussion of local problems and need, so as to help people verbalize their felt needs, to motivate, change and encourage people to exercise their own initiative in planning and carrying out important projects. The then Ministry of Health, Family Planning and Urban Development had formulated a scheme based on these recommendations which was viewed as a continuation and expansion of the experimental work that had already commenced. During the last years of the plan, the Government of India proposed to start 50 pilot UCD projects in selected cities with a population of above one lakh. Initially, it was decided to start 20 pilot projects but only 13 projects could be started by 1976 due to lukewarm response from the states.[14]

The country's two most successful UCD projects have been in Hyderabad and Vishakhapatnam. The former attempts to cover the entire slum population and other low income home dwellers (about a million people in the city) and tries to deliver multiple services, such as housing, slum improvement, education, health, nutrition, child care, family welfare, income supports, community organization, etc. by channelizing resources of various government and non-government organizations and also be mobilizing the community's internal resources through participatory work practices. In view of its success, planners and policy makers are recommending the Hyderabad UCD programme as a model for replication in other Indian cities.

Measures to Promote People's Participation in Civic Affairs

Despite the desirability, advisability and rationality for people's participation in urban local governments, barring a few exceptions like the urban community development (UCD) projects and the activities of some non-governmental voluntary agencies, not much planned effort is visible, either to involve people in urban development processes, projects and schemes, or even to offer them incentives to find their own solutions for local problems. The following measures can go a long way in encouraging, motivating and ensuring people's participation in urban local government to the desired extent:

1. Constant Contact of the Councillors with the People: The councillors should maintain regular and frequent contacts with the people of their respective constituencies/wards by visiting them as often as possible to acquaint themselves with their needs, expectations and aspirations and to report to them about the interest they are taking in the development of their area, and providing better living facilities and explaining to them the constraints they are facing in implementing the programmes and executing the projects for achieving the objectives of a good local government.

2. Change in the Attitude of the Bureaucracy: Municipal bureaucracy has alienated the public due to their inaccessibility, rigid adherence to rules, regulations and procedures and arrogant attitude due to their misconception of being 'big bosses' and '*mai-baap*' the legacy inherited from the alien British rulers which is out of place in a democratic and free country. The bureaucrats, therefore, need to change their attitudes to the people, so as to reflect that they are public servants and friends, philosophers and guides of the people, easily accessible, helpful and sympathetic to them. This will stimulate the interest and involvement of people in civic affairs.

3. Role of Educational Institutions: Educational institutions, schools and colleges can play a significant role in inculcating the spirit of contributing fully to the fulfilment of the essentials of civic life and the cultivation of habit of a good citizen in one's self as to create them in others. Students form the core citizenship and happen to be at the critical stage of habit formation. The school can, therefore, play an important role in cultivating virtues of good citizenry including the sense of participation in civic affairs. The teachers and the local leaders can mobilize students in cleanliness drives and adult education. They can adopt certain localities for their activities and enlist public support as well in their endeavours to keep the environments of the neighbourhood clean and fit for healthful living. The high school and college students are rendering appreciable services in providing civic amenities and educating the public about their obligations to local bodies under the National Service Scheme by organizing campaigns for removal of illiteracy, imparting information about various development and welfare programmes of civic bodies and enlisting public support.

4. **Role of Voluntary Agencies:** Citizens imbued with the spirit of service and civic sense form non-governmental organizations/voluntary agencies to formulate and implement various plans, projects and programmes for the development of urban areas and welfare of citizens on their own and/or with the support of the local governments. These programmes include development and improvement of slum areas, running institutions for removal of illiteracy, welfare of women and children, the deprived and disadvantaged sections of society, the disabled and the aged living in various territorial areas of local bodies. Voluntary organizations spring up spontaneously when we are threatened by a great emergency like external aggression or natural calamities. There is need to strengthen the existing voluntary organization and to establish them in the areas where they do not exist at present to promote citizen's participation in civic affairs.

5. **Role of Public Relations Agencies of Municipal Governments:** The role of Public Relations is to inform the public about the programmes and activities of the government undertaken for their welfare and to feed the government about the expectations and aspirations of the people. Unfortunately, proper attention has not been given to this important aspect of municipal administration. Unless the citizens are imparted proper information, they cannot be expected to evince any interest in the affairs of municipal government. It is, therefore, imperative that a regular system of communication between the citizens and municipal administration is set up, and citizens are informed about the civic problems, plans and development by the Public Relations Department/agency of municipal governments through communication media like radio, television, leaflets, brochures, journals, meetings, seminars, and group discussions. This will facilitate the communication of information to the citizens, arouse their interest and generate their participation in local affairs.

6. **Restructuring of Local Governments:** The structure and organization of our urban local governments is more than one hundred years old. It needs to be restructured and remodelled, in order to facilitate citizen's participation in municipal affairs. Instead of keeping a range of allied civic services in the hands of a single, compendious municipal government, the general tendency in our country is to create a number of competitive local authorities, mostly without any popular base, each having control over specific functions. Concentrating all the civic functions in one single municipal authority, a system of two tier municipal government on the federal principle of distribution of power between the centre and its constituent units and elective group at the local level and the city level, are sure to widen the scope for popular participation. These suggestions for the revamping and reforming of municipal governments have been given due consideration and incorporated in the Constitution (74th Amendment) Act 1992. This will help citizens to take adequate interest in the municipal affairs.

7. **Redressal of People's Grievances:** Local inhabitants have multitude of grievances against local government such as unhygenic and unsanitary conditions, water scarcity, upkeep and maintenance of

roads with particular reference to the maintenance of pot-holes, street lights, cattle nuisance, lack of transport and communication facilities, lack of medical facilities, lack of educational facilities, lack of recreational facilities, delay in sanctioning building plans, over-charging of electric, water and sewerage services bills, etc. The municipal authorities are callous in matter of entertaining even genuine grievances and redressing them adequately, promptly and properly. The citizens have to bribe the councillor and officials to get their rightful demands accepted and grievances redressed. This causes frustration and disgust among the citizens and alienates them against the administration. It is desirable that a proper machinery to look into citizen's grievances and redress them speedily and effectively should be set up to create confidence and goodwill of the citizens in local authorities and to promote their participation in the local affairs.

8. Creation of the Institution of Municipal Ombudsman: The institution of ombudsman to receive complaints about injustice and mal-administration from aggrieved persons against the administration was set up in Sweden in 1809 and has, since then, been established in numerous countries. Since the citizen's dealings with the local government are closer and more frequent, public administration at the local level becomes of crucial importance, and since the institution of ombudsman has been found useful by many countries at different levels of government, there has been a feeling that this institution may be of great help to the citizens at the local level also.[15] Ombudsman surveillance of local government activities was introduced in Sweden in 1957 and in Britain in 1974.[16] The creation of an ombudsman for local government in our country would substantially contribute to the speedy redressal of grievances of citizens and promote their participation in local government.[17]

9. Competent Leadership: Municipal administration suffers from weak and incompetent leadership. Municipal councillors who are expected to provide strong and capable leadership are lacking in the qualities of good leadership, *viz.,* integrity and honesty, selflessness and responsiveness to public. They are not only deficient in intelligence, intellect and integrity, but also instrumental in encouraging corrupt practices. Many of them have been found to be corrupt and removed from the membership of the council. They are party to unauthorized constructions, encroachments, leakages of taxes and violation of municipal rules and regulations. Mayors and Chairmen also do not inspire confidence among the citizens as they work on partisan basis. The municipal bureaucracy consisting of Municipal Commissioner/executive officers and other officials who are to act as leaders and seek the cooperation of the public, also fail to win over the people because of their bureaucratic attitude and lack of sympathy with the citizens. A strong and competent leadership is, therefore, necessary to inspire people's confidence and participation in local governments.

10. Healthy Role of Political Parties: The interference of political parties in municipal government and administration has damaged its image and has been responsible for the alienation of citizens to local bodies. It is rightly complained that the management of municipal affairs is very much dominated by group and party politics. It is also alleged that the sanction of various development work is delayed because of the anxiety of the councillors to benefit sectional interests. People's participation in municipal affairs can be ensured if the political parties refrain from promoting the interests of their respective constituencies and work for the well-being of the entire local community. The party in power in the state government also needs to decide local issues on their merits and not on partisan basis as has been in evidence in the matter of supersession of local bodies being governed by the opposition parties. The confidence of the people can be won if they are convinced that political parties are immune from the vices of groupism, favouritism, and nepotism which are generally associated with them.

11. **Creation of Consciousness of Citizens' Rights and Responsibilities:** A citizen conscious of its rights as well as responsibilities is essential for the proper functioning of an administration. This is all the more important for the success of local government which is founded on the principle of people's participation in local administration. But, unfortunately, the citizens are not conscious of their rights and responsibilities *vis-a-vis* local government. It is, therefore, essential that necessary measures should be taken to create awareness among the citizens about their rights and duties in order to make local government a success. The relationship between the citizens and local bodies should be based on mutual understanding, responsiveness and cooperation and that is possible only when citizens are conscious of their rights as well as duties.

12. **Efficient Delivery of Essential Civic Services:** The alienated citizen is, to a large extent, a direct result of municipal administrative inefficiency. There is no denying the fact that the municipal administration works under many constraints. Yet, the average citizen can be won through the efficient delivery of essential civic services. A good park, a good road, adequate water supply, a timely sanction of building plan—all these are direct routes to the citizen's heart. The best way of winning the confidence of citizens is to make municipal administration service-oriented. Red tapism and rigid bureaucratism are, in a way, incompatible with local government administration. Promptness and a greater degree of informality are expected of municipal administration because of its location at the local community level.

Recommendation of the National Commission on Urbanization for People's Participation in Urban Local Government

The National Commission or Urbanization has made the following recommendations[18] for people's participation to ensure and facilitate people's participation in the formulation and implementation of programmes and projects to meet their needs, to improve the civic services and for development for their cities and town:

1. Strengthening the urban local bodies by holding popular elections wherever those are superseded; improving the financial positions of local bodies; and making necessary changes in laws governing the working of the municipal bodies, systems and procedures to enable them to utilize the skills and resources of individuals, groups, agencies and institutions in planning, execution and monitoring of development activities.
2. Initiating urban community development projects through the municipal bodies in cities with a population above 5,000, with necessary changes in their organizational structure, mandate, financing arrangements and institutional linkages.
3. Designing UCD projects as effective vehicles to reach out to, motivate, service and organize the urban poor, and as agencies for coordination and convergence of service delivery and poverty alleviation schemes, and projects and programmes of different government and semi-government agencies.
4. Ensuring adherence to participatory and consultative procedures prescribed in the law but neglected or circumvented in practice by cultivating attitudes and evolving tools and methodologies within responsible/concerned planning and implementing agencies.
5. Ensuring that the mandatory public hearing before finalization of city development plan is effectively gone through, without anyone in any way benefiting from the process.

6. Providing proper methods of communication and information sharing and appropriately designed consultation platforms for useful feedback for planners and education for the people.
7. Recognizing the existing role and work of non-government voluntary agencies in the urban areas and creating facility/support arrangements of the CAPART model for urban projects and works of non-government agencies. This facility should finance study, research, advocate action, demonstration projects and other innovative, relevant effort of urban-based, non-government voluntary agencies.
8. Encouraging, assisting and facilitating networking among NGOs working in various sectors at regional and city level for information and experience sharing.
9. Facilitating entry and encouraging role by the NGOs at the macro-policy formulation and programme design levels. The Planning Commission, the Urban Affairs Ministry and many other agencies of the government have started inducting into their service senior and experienced workers from the NGOs. This arrangement needs to be further strengthened at the city level. The interaction, dialogue and outcome will be mutually beneficial.
10. Establishing the National Urban Council for Citizen Action at the national level (NUCCA), the State Urban Council for Citizen Action at the state level (SUCCA) and the Forum for Citizen Action (FOCIA) at the city level to enable nongovernmental voluntary agencies to play watch-dog, facilitator, promotional, educational, advocacy and innovative roles and to activate citizen participation in the urban development field in general and in city development, in particular.

The Nagarpalika Bill for constitutional amendment introduced in the Parliament in 1989 incorporated some of the recommendations of the National Commission on Urbanization aimed at strengthening the urban local bodies by providing regular elections to be conducted by the State Election Commission, Finance Commission for augmenting the local finance, audit by the Comptroller and Auditor General of India and Ward level committees in two and three tier municipal structure for larger municipal bodies. This innovation was intended to bring in more participating of the people at local level. The bill was passed by the Lok Sabha but it could not muster the requisite majority in Rajya Sabha and could not, therefore, be placed on the statute book. The Bill was again introduced and passed as the Constitution (74th Amendment) Act in 1992, incorporating the administrative measures to promote people's participation in urban governments.

Conclusion

Local government is conceived as an instrument for the creation of the widest possible participation of the people in grass-roots government. As Dorald C. Stone puts it 'An enlightened citizenry, ready and capable of participating in political action and community decision making, is the foundation of democratic self-government.'[19] The local institutions depend for their successful working, not on the formal arrangements but on the degree of participation and cooperation of citizens.

Local government is founded with an ostensible objective of ensuring people's participation in its programmes. Unlike other higher level of government, the local governments, being closer to the people have maximum contact and a strong communication with the citizens which help them in devising ways and means of serving the needs and aspirations of local community living within their jurisdictions. The local government thus provides an important forum for serving the needs of the local population according to their wishes. An enlightened citizenry and an articulate civic consciousness, therefore, prove to be a valuable asset for the local authorities.[20] However, in spite of relatively larger history of their existence, the local authorities have not been able to receive people's participation adequately.

Numerous factors are responsible for the lack of civic consciousness and people's involvement in local affairs. Some of these are:

Lack of homogeneity in the population of the cities, and consequent lack of their attachment with city government, poor leadership, absence of continuous contacts of the councillors with the public, bureaucratic attitude, inefficiency of municipal administration, rampant corruption, lack of awareness among people about their role in municipal affairs, poor public relation, absence of machinery of redressal of citizen's grievances, inadequacy of the people's associations and organizations, appalling poverty, erosion of the authority of municipal bodies by the creation of multitude of urban authorities, deficiencies in the structure of municipal governments and their organization, and the vicious role of political parties as manifested in their interference in municipal administration on partisan considerations.

Despite these factors/reasons/causes responsible for the indifference and alienation of people to municipal administration, they have been participating in local administration by electing their representatives periodically, organizing themselves to help the local authorities in emergencies like external aggression, and natural calamities, and rendering assistance to municipal bodies in improving city life by carrying out cleanliness campaigns, adopting certain areas for improvement of civic services, removing illiteracy, and assisting the destitute, the deprived sections of society, women and children, the aged and the addicts.

But the people's participation in municipal government and administration leaves much to be desired. Various measures need to be initiated to exploit their potential to the maximum. These may include: constant contact of the councillors with their constituents, change in the attitude of bureaucrats, utilizing educational institutions for inculcating spirit of service and civic sense among the students, strengthening voluntary agencies to perform their roles as catalysts for people's participation, instituting Public Relations agencies to serve as a bridge between administration and the people, providing mechanism for speedy redressal of citizen's grievances and institutions of Ombudsmen at local government level, competent leadership, efficient delivery of essential civic services, constructive role of political parties in the interests of the whole urban community and not of a particular section of society, and finally restructuring of the local governments so as to make it more democratic and responsive.

It is only with the active involvement and participation of people in urban governments that the latter can justify their existence and serve as instruments for the provision of essential basic services to the people.

NOTES AND REFERENCES

1. L. Goulding, *Local Government* (London, 1955), p. 19.
2. Harris, G.M., *Comparative Local Government*, London, p. 9.
3. Venkatarangia, K. (ed.) *Local Self Government in India* (Bombay: Allied Publishers), p. 1.
4. Robson, W.A. *Encyclopaedia of Social Sciences,* Vol. 9 (New York, The Macmillan Co.), p. 574.
5. Harold, J. Laski, *Grammar of Politics* (London: George Allen and Unwin Ltd., 1941), pp. 411–29.
6. K. Seshadri, *Rural Linkage and Rural Development* (Delhi: National, 1976), p. 178.
7. Roy Darke and Ray Walker, *Local Government and the Public* (London: Leonard Hill, 1977), p. 89.
8. Department of Environment, Publicity for the Work of Local Authorities Circular, 45/75.
9. Refer to S.L. Kaushik's *Leadership in Urban Governments in India* (Allahabad: Kitab Mahal, 1986) and Ziauddin Khan and Hoshiar Singh, *Leadership in Municipal Government* (Jaipur: RBSA Publications, 1984).
10. V.S. Murti Government at the grassroots and the 21st century Foundation Lecture, Regional Centre for Urban Environmental Studies, Osmania University, Hyderabad, 18 May 1986.
11. H.D. Kopardekar, 'People's Participation in Metropolitan Management', *Quarterly Journal of the All India Institute of Local Self-government.* Bombay, 71, no 2 (April–June, 1991): 67–75.

12. 'Report of the National Commission on Urbanization', Ministry of Urban Development, Government of India, 1988, p. 311.
13. 'Report of the Rural Urban Relationship Committee', Vol. 1. Ministry of Health and Family Welfare, Government of India, 1966, p. 109.
14. Public Administration Aspect of Community Development Programmes (Sales No. 59, 112) Approaches to Community Development in Urban Areas. Notes on recent experience in twenty-four countries and territories. Documents ST/SOA/SER, O/32 and ST/TAO/SER.D/32.
15. Justice T.V.R. Tatchari, Lok Ayukta, Himachal Pradesh. Proceedings of First All India Conference of Lok Ayuktas, Shimla, 26–30 May, 1986.
16. Norman Lewis and Bernard Gateslull, *The Commission for Local Administration: A Preliminary Appraisal* (London: Royal Institute of Public Administration, 1978).
17. Pradeep Sachdeva, 'Indian Ombudsman: Some Perspectives', *Administrative Change* 15, no. 1 (July–December, 1987): 71–81.
18. 'Report of the National Commission on Urbanization', pp. 313–14.
19. David C. Stone, The Future of Cities, cited by Walter Bor, in the *Making of Cities,* 1972, p. 51.
20. T.N. Chaturvedi, *Civic Consciousness* (New Delhi, I.I.P.A., 1979), p. 1.

Performance of Urban Governments

The significance and role of urban local governments, as an integral part of local self-government has substantially increased with the advent of independence. Consequently they could not remain only field agencies for the development and maintenance of civic services and for the execution of national programmes in their respective areas but they were also called upon to act as primary units of democratic governments. There is, however, a common feeling, that they have failed to achieve the twin objectives referred to above. The expected role of the urban local governments to act as a forum of political education has not been realized at all. Democracy rests on the assumption that a government is basically an affair of the people and that all the problems are to be solved with fuller participation and consent of the people. The municipal committees and corporations have unfortunately failed to perform such a role since their supersessions have been rampant and they have not been resuscitated for years on end and elections to some of them have not been held for decades ever since their inception.

The people all over the country feel that the urban local governments have failed to meet their aspirations. The general level of administrative efficiency has been deplorably low; the standards of civic amenities have been disgusting, factionalism, and groupism have been vicious; corruption and graft have been endemic; a healthy civic ethos has not evolved; right type of civic leadership has not developed and morale has been, by and large, at a very low ebb.

Causes for Poor Performance of Urban Local Governments and Its Remedies

Some of the factors responsible for and the causes contributing to the poor performance of urban local governments may be enumerated as follows:

Explosion of Population and Urbanization

Our country is becoming urbanized at an alarming rate. There are at present 285 million people living in 3,301 urban settlements all over the country and by 2001 when the total population of the country is projected to exceed one thousand million, urban population is likely to swell to 350 million, representing

35 per cent of the total population. The rising number have accentuated the problem of urban squalor and placed heavy strains on basic civic services.

Century Old Structure of Municipal Bodies

Our urban local bodies are hampered in providing even the minimum basic needs by a structure that is 117 years old and their system of functioning which is equally ancient. While Article 40 of the Constitution casts a mandate on the state to ensure the working of village panchayats, there is no specific corresponding mandate regarding urban local bodies. These are, however, specified in Entry 5 of the State List. The Central Council of Local Self Government and Urban Development has passed several resolutions about the need for the constitutional recognition of local bodies and for statutory delineation of their powers, functions and resources. The All India Council of Mayors, as also the National Commission on Urbanization, has stressed the grant of constitutional status to urban local governments. The absence of adequate constitutional provision for urban self-government had landed municipal administration in a mess in most parts of the country. The urban local bodies, therefore, need to be granted a constitutional safeguard for their revitalization.

Absence of Any Criterion for Constituting Urban Governments

There is no generally accepted set of criteria regarding even what constitutes an urban agglomeration, let alone the manner in which it should be run. The colonial categorization of India with separate rural and urban India and devising separate sets of structure for them does not suit our country any longer. In the colonial system of municipal administration, there was no place for development planning and no role for development activity. The development of India is not possible without planning for development in our urban settlements, as much as in our rural settlement. Indeed, planning as the crucial interface between the rural hinterland and the urban settlement will be the chief progenitor of accelerated growth. There is, therefore, the need for a linking structure between the rural hinterland and the urban growth centre and to achieve this, the existing structure needs to be recast with 'nagar panchayats' representing transitional structure, establishment of two tier system for the medium size towns—the lower tier comprising the small elected unit for each locality, ward or *mohalla* to whom the municipality will devolve local powers, local responsibilities and such finances as are required to carry out their assigned tasks; and a three tier system with intermediate tier corresponding to the Borough Council in corporation areas, which could have functions similar to the administered zones which exist in cities like Bombay and Delhi. This measure would facilitate democratic decentralization, more effective participation and more responsible municipal administration.

Postponing of Elections for Indefinite Periods

Elections to municipal bodies as mentioned earlier are not held for decades after their coming into being or at regular intervals thereafter, and to the superseded municipal institutions for an indefinite period. The state government's well developed allergy for local elections stems from the reasons that they become the barometer of the political parties' standing with the masses; the state governments feel safer and more secure to deal with bureaucracy placed at the helm of civic administration than with the popularly elected councillors and corporators and municipal bodies run on a system of graft and patronage cannot stand scrutiny by elected bodies. The state government has thus been able to insulate civic administration from the people and run it by edicts from the state capitals. In order to ensure the functioning of democracy at grass-roots level, it should be obligatory for the state government to hold elections to local bodies at the expiry of the term of the council and no extension should be granted to their tenure and they should not be superseded without judicial scrutiny and elections should be held within a period of six months of supersession.

Misuse of Co-option

The device of co-option is intended to avail of the services of public spirited and seasoned persons who refrain from fighting elections due to the inconveniences involved. But, unfortunately, this device is exercised to get berths to their supporters by the political parties commanding majority in the councils. It would be desirable to make use of this provision by co-opting the right type of people irrespective of their party affiliations to serve best the interests of the inhabitants of the town/city.

Indirect Election of Chiefs of Municipal Councils

Direct elections of the president/mayors would be more democratic as compared to indirect elections and, therefore, should be preferred.

Absence of Proportional Representation System for Sub-Committees

The election of sub-committees on the basis of proportional representation system and devolution of powers on them will further improve the functioning of civic bodies.

Erosion of Municipal Functions

Municipal committees and municipal corporations are assigned by the state government a large number of functions of almost identical nature, with the only difference that the municipal corporations have been endowed with greater powers and finances. The functions are classified into obligatory and optional, the former are concerned with the minimum basic needs of the city people such as paved streets, metalled roads, drainage, sewerage, lighting and water supply, while the latter aim at improving quality of their life by providing such facilities as gardens, parks, swimming pools, play-grounds, stadia and other recreational facilities, institutions of higher educations, libraries, reading rooms, cultural and art galleries, tourist resorts and other programmes for the beautification of the city. After Independence their functions should have increased to tackle the problems of tremendous increase in urbanization and population and to achieve the objectives of a socialist and welfare state to which our polity is committed. On the contrary, the municipal bodies have suffered a great setback in the steady diminution of their functions which have either been taken over by the state governments themselves or transferred to special purpose agencies on the pretext of their inefficiency and inadequacy to perform them.

Failure of Municipal Bodies to Perform Their Functions in a Satisfactory Manner

It is regrettable that the performance of municipal committees has been disappointing in carrying out even their obligatory functions, and more so in regard to their discretionary functions. They have not been able to provide basic civic amenities to their population generally and especially in the suburbs which comprise of unauthorized and unplanned colonies accommodating 50 per cent of their population, piped water supply and sewerage facilities have covered only a minority of population, roads are in deplorable conditions, encroachments are galore, unsafe buildings continue to constitute a constant threat to the lives of the inhabitants, stray cattle are on the increase, traffic hazards are unabating, insanitation and unhygienic conditions in the form of heaps of garbage are a nuisance even in posh localities, and slums have emerged in almost all parts of the cities.

The cities can be restored their pristine glory and made liveable if the state governments make a judicious selection of functions to be assigned to them and do not impose upon them such functions as transport which have proved a great liability for every city; and make adequate provisions for finance, the lack of which has rendered many municipal bodies unable to take up any development work in their respective areas. It has been rightly observed that devolution of powers and functions necessarily involves devolution of finances also. The state governments, therefore, should observe this principle if they want the urban bodies to discharge their functions effectively.

Deficiencies in Personnel Management

Municipal services were provincialized in various states with a view to eliminate the evils of nepotism, favouritism and political patronage of separate personnel system and to ensure their efficient performance. But unfortunately this innovation seems to have failed to realize the desired objectives of recruitment on merit by centralized selection committee, better avenues of promotions, more favourable conditions of service including transferability, etc., due to the reasons that municipal services selection committees, dominated as they are by *ex-officio* bureaucrats and experts nominated by the government to the exclusion of any public men, fail to inspire confidence of fair recruitment. The importance of training for the municipal staff has not been realized as no training facilities have been made available in most of the states through the establishment of training institutes. The promotion avenues though provided to an extent of 50 per cent from within are seldom available in practice owing to the lack of finalization of seniority lists for decades and the complicated and dilatory procedures. The pay scales are not comparable with those of state services. The transfers are done at the whims of the bureaucrats sometimes en masse which not only result in avoidable inconvenience to the transferees but also smack of money changing hands. Corruption is rampant so much that the Executive Officers are suspended and the Vigilance Bureaus are obliged to look into alleged irregularities in the functioning of Municipal bodies including charges of corruption levelled against high-ups in the administrative hierarchy. Several vacancies existing in the sanitation, octroi, water supply and fire brigade departments of the corporations and the committees are not filled for years on end. Municipal councillors are sore that their authority has been eroded and whereas the municipal personnel are paid by their respective municipal bodies, they are not amenable to their control and so on.

The remedy lies in exploring the desirability of revamping the municipal services selection committees by inducting in them men of integrity or setting up of Municipal Civil Service and the establishment of Municipal Civil Service Commission on the pattern of State Public Service Commission as such an autonomous and statutory body will not only ensure selection on merit but also contribute to depoliticizing the administrative process and help dilute occasional tensions between the officers and councillors, making arrangements for the training of municipal councillors and personnel, simplifying promotion procedures and granting promotions expeditiously when due; improving conditions of service by equating these with those of state government employees in matters of pay-scales, allowances, gratuity and pension. (Haryana Government has accepted the demands of Haryana Nagarpalika Karamchari Mahasangh to grant parity in pay scales to municipal employees on a par with government employees as the per announcement of Dr Mangal Sel, the then deputy chief minister of Haryana made on 31 July 1989 while addressing the state level convention of the Mahasangh), formulating a sound policy of transfers and particularly ensuring that the heads of the Directorate of Local Government complete their full term of three years to ensure continuity of policy and holding them responsible for their proper implementation; and taking strong disciplinary action against those found guilty of committing irregularities and indulging in graft.

Financial Scarcity

Municipal finances are in an unmitigated mess, due to the failure of the municipal councillors to impose and revise different kinds of levies and taxes owing to the fear of incurring the displeasure of their constituents, evasion of municipal revenues, calculation of octroi, one of the main sources of income, on weight and not on their value basis, exemption on octroi given to certain industrial units, accumulation of arrears into crores of rupees, meagre amount of grants, their non-utilisation or diversion to purposes other than those for which they were sanctioned, rigid stipulation for raising of loans with the prior approval of the state government and Reserve Bank of India and the non-seriousness on the part of the state governments to either determine or siphon off to the municipal bodies their share, despite the statutory provisions, which the state governments are violating with impunity.

Financial stringency has become the biggest hurdle for almost all municipal bodies on account of ever increasing expenditure on establishment which has gone up to about 60 per cent of the income, virtually no money is available for development work; municipal committees of many small towns even find it difficult to disburse salaries to their employees in time; many civic bodies have not been able to provide even the basic civic amenities in the areas which have been included in their jurisdiction during the last couple of decades, these suburbs, in many cases, have no arrangement even for scavenging of streets, much less the facility of piped water supply and sewerage systems; municipal committees have defaulted the payment of their share of the cost of water supply and sewerage works carried out in their areas. Some municipal institutions are facing great financial crisis and a few of them are virtually on the brink of bankruptcy.

Municipal bodies can overcome their financial crisis if the municipal councillors exploit, to the maximum possible extent, the resources which they are empowered to determine and raise, if evasion of municipal revenues is checked and leakage is plugged by raising flying squads, and by deploying municipal police and municipal magistracy for expeditious decisions of cases as these have been found to be quite effective in some municipal bodies; the exemption on octroi given to industrial units is withdrawn, grants-in-aid are liberalized, system of special matching grants is introduced and loans procedures are simplified and municipal bodies are allowed access to commercial banks; they are assured of their share in revenues accruing to them under the statute by the state government; are encouraged to take up remunerative enterprises, exercise economy in expenditure; a Revolving fund, a Municipal Finance Corporation, an Urban Development Finance Corporation, similar to the National Bank for Agriculture and Rural Development (NABARD) which has functioned with great success in rural India, are set up to help them in meeting their financial needs as also Municipal Finance Commission is constituted on the lines of National Finance Commission to review municipal finances and recommend principles on the basis of which sound finances of the municipal bodies can be secured.

Excessive State Government Control

It has been a continuous curse on our urban local bodies that they have been under the control of state governments and their bureaucracy. The state governments have always treated them as appendages to the departments. Despite the constitution of Directorate of Local Government and the establishment of its field agencies, the Deputy Commissioners continue to exercise their erstwhile powers with the same vigour. It is because there is no clear cut demarcation of powers of the Regional Deputy Directors and the Deputy Commissioners, and sometimes their jurisdictions and functions overlap resulting in confusion and inefficiency. There is, therefore, simmering demand that the Directorate should be wound up as it has proved to be very costly to the municipal bodies who are since required to contribute substantially for its maintenance.

Supersessions, the most obnoxious type of control, have been rampant, arbitrary and prolonged. Some municipal bodies have remained superseded for decades. Elections to some of them have not been held even since their inception. The local self-government institutions have thus become defunct, moribund and non-existent. The urban local bodies are at the mercy of the state government for their finances, inhibited as they are in matter of imposing are raising taxes, etc. without government approval, and depend as they do, on the state government for sanction of loans and allocation of uncertain and meagre grants and faced as they are with similar rigidities in matters of expenditure. The state control over civic bodies has thus been restrictive, negative and oppressive. It is high time to grant them democratic freedom to function independently and to provide them guidance and cooperation in managing their own affairs. Resort to supersession should be made very sparingly subject to the approval of the state legislature and dissolved bodies should be reconstituted within six months.

In order to ensure healthy relationship between the state government and urban bodies, the Directorate of Local Government which is a bureaucratic organization and has failed to deliver goods may be replaced by a Board which should be headed by a minister of local government and reflect a sufficiently large democratic element.

Finally, the judiciary, which plays an important role in securing justice to the aggrieved parties against the arbitrary and unlawful actions of municipal bodies and state government, should *inter alia* ensure expeditious justice. Establishment of municipal courts could be one of the means to achieve this objective.

In short, the government control should not be so meticulous or minute as to destroy the autonomy or self-reliance of urban local bodies; rather the purpose of state control should be to develop the local self-government institutions as efficient institutions of administration capable alike to formulating policies and executing them.

Partisan Role of Political Parties

However, forcefully with logical, cogent and canvassing arguments we may deny and decry the participation of political parties in municipal governments, *inter alia,* for the reason that civic affairs being non-ideological and concerned with improvement of civic life of the people should not be conducted on partisan basis, yet we cannot afford to be oblivious of the fact that political parties do involve themselves overtly or covertly in civic affairs. They operate at two levels. First, the political party wielding power at the state level acts as the arbiter of the fate of Municipal bodies by their partisan decisions in determining whether election for them should be held or not, notifying or withholding the notification of the elected President, removing or disqualifying the councillors, making appointments, effecting transfers and removing Executive Officers and other municipal staff, accepting or rescinding the resolutions of municipal councils and finally superseding them and postponing their election for indefinite periods.

Secondly, political parties operate within the municipal bodies themselves. Political parties contest elections by putting up their own candidates or extending support to independents, elect the president and vice-president on party lines, co-opt the members from their own parties, constitute sub-committees on party basis, and take decisions on various issues on party considerations. The Presidents exercise their casting votes to promote their party interest and political considerations are the determining factor in recruitment and promotion of municipal employees and for taking disciplinary action against them. Above all, political parties indulge in the pernicious game of defections resulting in the erosion of ethical values, changing the complexion and character of political set-up in the council and leading to rise and fall of office bearers and deterioration in administration.

In view of the fact that political parties play a significant role in municipal administration, their participation in civic affairs should be given due recognition; and they should play a constructive and healthy role by laying down proper norms and rules for nominating their candidates for election, actively campaigning for them on relevant issues, educating them for faithful execution of their responsibilities for the welfare of the citizens, exercising control over them and taking action against them if they default. Similarly, the party in power in the state government should consider the interests of the city people to be supreme and they should decide the civic issues on their merit and not on party lines. Such an approach on the part of the political parties would go a long way in mitigating the vices of political intervention in municipal administration and in ensuring the promotion of healthy civic life.

In order to remove the defects and deficiencies in the construction, composition, functions and powers of the municipal bodies and to revamp and rejuvenate them so as to enable them to work as efficient and effective democratic institutions, the Constitution (74th Amendment) Act, 1992, relating to municipalities (known as the Nagarpalika Act) was passed by Parliament in the winter session of the Parliament of 1992 and it received the assent of the President on 20th April 1993. The act seeks to provide a common framework of the structure as effective democratic units of local self-government. It is expected that the faithful implementation of the various provisions of the Act will absolve the urban local governments of their infirmities and shortcomings highlighted in the foregoing discussion of their unsatisfactory performance.

Index

D

E

F

G

H

I

J

L

M

N

O

P

Q

R

S

V

W

Z